Contents

The Short Works of Mark Twain

A Critical Study

Peter Messent

PENN

University of Pennsylvania Press

Philadelphia

10 9 8 7 6 5 4 3 2 1

Published by
University of Pennsylvania Press
Philadelphia, Pennsylvania 19104-4011

Library of Congress Cataloging-in-Publication Data
Messent, Peter B.
    The short works of Mark Twain : a critical study / Peter Messent.
        p.   cm.
    ISBN 0-8122-3622-X (alk. paper)   1 00 273599 X
    Includes bibliographical references (p.) and index.
    1. Twain, Mark, 1835–1910 — Criticism and interpretation. 2. Humorous stories,
American — History and criticism.
PS1338 .M48 2001
818'.409 — dc21   2001027428

Note on Texts and Abbreviations

Unless otherwise stated, all references to Twain's short works and novels in this book are to the Oxford Mark Twain, ed. Shelley Fisher Fishkin (New York: Oxford University Press, 1996). The introductions and afterwords to this edition are abbreviated as IN and AF.

AZ R. Kent Rasmussen, *Mark Twain A to Z: The Essential Reference to His Life and Writings* (New York: Oxford University Press, 1996).

CHHR *Mark Twain's Correspondence with Henry Huttleston Rogers, 1893–1909*, ed. Lewis Leary (Berkeley: University of California Press, 1969).

CR *Mark Twain: The Contemporary Reviews*, ed. Louis J. Budd (Cambridge: Cambridge University Press, 1999).

CU-MARK California University: The Mark Twain Papers (Berkeley).

ETS1 *Early Tales & Sketches*, vol. 1, *1861–1864*, ed. Edgar Marquess Branch and Robert H. Hirst (Berkeley: University of California Press, 1979).

ETS2 *Early Tales & Sketches*, vol. 2, *1864–1865*, ed. Edgar Marquess Branch and Robert H. Hirst (Berkeley: University of California Press, 1981).

LM Marcel Gutwirth, *Laughing Matter: An Essay on the Comic* (Ithaca: Cornell University Press, 1993).

MTEB Hamlin Hill, *Mark Twain and Elisha Bliss* (Columbia: University of Missouri Press, 1964).

MTHL1 *Mark Twain-Howells Letters: The Correspondence of Samuel L. Clemens and William D. Howells, 1872–1910*, vol. 1, ed. Henry Nash Smith and William M. Gibson (Cambridge, Mass.: Belknap Press, 1960).

MTHL2   *Mark Twain-Howells Letters: The Correspondence of Samuel L. Clemens and William D. Howells, 1872–1910*, vol. 2, ed. Henry Nash Smith and William M. Gibson (Cambridge, Mass.: Belknap Press, 1960).

MTL1   *Mark Twain's Letters*, vol. 1, *1853–1866*, ed. Edgar Marquess Branch, Michael B. Frank, and Kenneth M. Sanderson (Berkeley: University of California Press, 1988).

MTL2   *Mark Twain's Letters*, vol. 2, *1867–1868*, ed. Harriet Elinor Smith and Richard Bucci (Berkeley: University of California Press, 1990).

MTLP   *Mark Twain's Letters to His Publishers, 1867–1894*, ed. Hamlin Hill (Berkeley: University of California Press, 1967).

MTNJ3   *Mark Twain's Notebooks & Journals*, vol. 3, *1883–1891*, ed. Robert Pack Browning, Michael B. Frank, and Lin Salamo (Berkeley: University of California Press, 1979).

RG   James D. Wilson, *A Reader's Guide to the Short Stories of Mark Twain* (Boston: G. K. Hall, 1987).

SSF   Tom Quirk, *Mark Twain: A Study of the Short Fiction* (New York: Twayne, 1997).

TSSE1   *Collected Tales, Sketches, Speeches, & Essays*, vol. 1, *1852–1890*, ed. Louis J. Budd (New York: Library of America, 1992).

TSSE2   *Collected Tales, Sketches, Speeches, & Essays*, vol. 2, *1891–1910*, ed. Louis J. Budd (New York: Library of America, 1992).

Introduction

> I never go prowling after a short story; it has to come prowling after *me*. For I am dam wise in my generation, & very very thoughtful.
>
> — Mark Twain, letter to Henry Loomis Nelson, 12 January 1897.

There is surprisingly little written on Twain's short works. There are only two books that attempt a career-long survey of them: James D. Wilson's *A Reader's Guide to the Short Stories of Mark Twain* (1987), and Tom Quirk's more recent *Mark Twain: A Study of the Short Fiction* (1997). And neither of these pays any more than cursory attention to my own critical target, the collections of short writings that Twain issued during his own lifetime. Both base their approach on the analysis of individual short narratives. Both, too, include within this category stories like "Jim Blaine and His Grandfather's Ram," published in Twain's lifetime only as part of his second "travel book," *Roughing It* (1872), and thus just one comic sequence among the many that compose that text. Quirk's explanation can be taken as paradigmatic here (and I have much sympathy with it): "As with many of his tales included in longer works, there is a self-sufficiency to this piece that makes its appearance in *Roughing It* almost incidental, and this fact is corroborated by Twain's frequent use of the tale on the lecture circuit" (10).

Such decisions taken by these two critics, the difference in their book titles, and the quotation marks I place around the words "travel book" above, suggest the problem with generic definition that confronts any critic writing on Twain's work, particularly on his shorter pieces.[1] William Dean Howells, writing to Twain concerning the review he had written of *Sketches, New and Old* (1875), said: "You can imagine the difficulty of noticing a book of short sketches; it's like noticing a library" (MTHL1: 106). It is the very number and variety of Twain's sketches to which Howells primarily refers here. But his words provide fitting commentary on Twain's books of short writings as a whole. This work shifts, in terms of length, from the one-page squib to the sketch and from the short story to the novella.[2] And it extends, in terms of generic difference, from the use of a startlingly wide range of fictional forms to his moves beyond the limits of fiction altogether.

In his review of *Sketches, New and Old*, Howells referred to Twain's use of satire, the grotesque, the romance, "pure drolling," and the ghost story. This just touches the surface of the various types of fiction Twain employed in his short writings.[3] His collections of short works are assemblages that contain not just fiction, but plays and speeches, literary criticism and poems, political tracts and biographical sketches, historical, philosophical, and scientific essays, and even an introduction to a language guide. So *The £1,000,000 Bank-Note and Other New Stories* (1893), for example, actually contains only two pieces that remotely deserve the label ("stories") given in its title.[4] It may be that the variety of this generic mix has led critics generally to avoid these collections, for apart from the Introductions and Afterwords in the Oxford Mark Twain series (1996), no sustained critical studies of them have been written. It is this variety, too, that explains the rather flat-footed nature of my present book's title, for anything more specific would only mislead.

Twain himself saw no problems in the movement between fiction and non-fiction (and indeed in blurring the boundaries between the two) or between different genres generally. James D. Wilson, while still working within the parameters of the title of his own book, puts it rather well:

Never a formalist, Mark Twain wrote relatively few short stories that would satisfy strict application of genre requirements. Lines of demarcation between invention and reminiscence, fact and fiction, sketch or anecdote and story, are indistinctly drawn, and the author himself showed little disposition either to classify his work according to standardly accepted genres or to confine his comic genius within the rigid structural patterns those genres impose. (RG, xi)

It is such ignoring of conventional lines of demarcation, taken to even further degree, that marks the contents of Twain's collections of short writings.

It is not my intention in this present book to address the question of genre definition. Modernist paradigms, for example, that define the short story as a distinct genre measured in terms of individuality (its "lonely voice") and epiphany are particularly inappropriate to Twain's case.[5] Twain always had a tendency to judge his work on its financial rewards as well as its aesthetic merits. And in the January 1897 letter to Henry Loomis Nelson quoted at the beginning of this introduction, he expresses dissatisfaction with his short stories in terms of the payment he received for them. He also suggests, however, that he sees the distinction between the short story and the novel form as a flexible one, with the latter as (apparently) the logical development of the former:

When a sudden impulse kicks me into attempting a short story, & the attempt succeeds to my satisfaction (which is unspeakably seldom) I'm perfectly ready & willing to part with it at customary rates. But I have to have the kick. Without it I shouldn't ever care to make the attempt. For it usually takes 2 weeks & 3 false starts to get such a thing planned out in what you recognize to be the right way, & then half or all of another week to flutter it from the pen. Then it makes 5,000 to 10,000 words, & *those* are what you are paid for; $100 to $150 per 1,000 words. The short story is the worst paid of all forms of literature.

N.B.1. A poor short story isn't worth printing.

N.B.2. A good short story is a novel in the cradle.

Often when I take it out of the cradle to play with it, I take a liking to it & *raise* it. That is what happened with a number of my books.

N.B.3. In the cradle it is . . . worth a few hundred dollars — maybe a thousand. Raised, it can be worth (Huck Finn is a case in point) forty-eight thousand.[6]

Critics have generally tended to see Twain's collections of short writings in terms of the type of financial considerations here foregrounded, often composed of previously published newspaper and magazine materials later thrown together to make a quick buck. This, too, may help account for the general critical silence on these texts. But Twain did take his short pieces seriously and was not quite so cavalier about the collections made from them as has commonly been suggested. One part of my own critical intention is to trace as far as I am able, and to reappraise, the part Twain played in the selection and making of these books. In my discussion of the first two collections considered here, *The Celebrated Jumping Frog of Calaveras County, and Other Sketches* (1867) and *Sketches, New and Old*, I necessarily rely heavily on the previous work of Robert H. Hirst. As I then proceed, I cover less well tracked critical ground.

In many ways the publication of the twenty-nine volume Oxford Mark Twain in 1996, edited by Shelley Fisher Fishkin, provides the impetus for my own work. Both for the writers and critics involved and for its readers, this project gave an unusual opportunity for an overview and reassessment of the work Twain published during his lifetime, especially in the case of his collections of short writings. I use the seven collections republished there as the basis for my book, partly at least because of their newly remade general availability. This is to omit the essay collection, *How to Tell a Story and Other Essays* (1897), to focus specifically on the books described as containing tales, sketches, and stories. I recognize the contentious nature of this decision, but I do see *How to Tell a Story* as different in kind (however slight that difference might finally be) from the texts I consider, all of which have an explicit grounding — at least in terms of title and presumably audience appeal — in their fictional contents.[7] My

decision to concentrate on the seven collections is necessarily contentious in other ways, too: in terms of the (original) editorial standards of
the books themselves and the fact that the representation of Twain's
short works they contain is far from complete. I address these latter
questions as I proceed.

Though my book is not entirely rigid in its patterning, it is generally
structured as follows. Taking each collection in chronological order, I do
three things. First, I look to trace the part, smaller or greater, that Twain
himself played in the selection and production of each collection. This
ties in with the second item on my critical agenda. The very fact that
Twain's short pieces have previously been approached from the individual point of view means that no critics, prior to those writing for the
Oxford edition, have looked to see if there is any thematic coherence or
other logic (for example, in the type of humor employed) to the collections as a whole. My contention is that these collections make up a significant amount of Twain's literary output and should accordingly play an
important part both in our tracing of the general outlines of his literary
career and in determining the nature of his main techniques, concerns,
and even state of mind at any point within it. Whether the author played a
large or small part in the making of the books does not necessarily matter
greatly in the accomplishing of such critical work. In these first two areas
(though with the previously noted exception in the case of *The Celebrated
Jumping Frog* and *Sketches, New and Old*), I see my book as providing a new
and vital direction and contribution to Twain studies. At times I have
been unable to go as far as I would have liked in uncovering the publication history of a particular book and have been constrained by space in
my examination of the chains of connection within it. But I will be more
than content if this preliminary groundwork stimulates later and more
detailed critical work in such cases.

My third and final intention here, once I have given such a general
overview of a particular collection, is to use a separate chapter then to
give a close critical analysis of one (or sometimes two) of the stories or
essays within it. Sometimes my choice is predictable, as in the case of the
title story in *The Celebrated Jumping Frog*. Sometimes it is less so. I use these
chapters as types of case studies where I can examine Twain's thematic
concerns, literary techniques, and forms of humor, and the relation of
his texts to their surrounding cultural context, in greater depth, and thus
counteract any tendency to the broad-scale and overly general that might
appear elsewhere. My choice of key texts is to some degree arbitrary.
These are the stories and essays that, for me, stood out from the collections, having some special significance and resonance. But there were
other texts I might alternatively have chosen. My hope is that, as my
critical work continues, so certain significant patterns in Twain's work,

and in the forms of humor he uses, become apparent. Such patterning can then be connected back in turn to his better-known and longer fictional and nonfictional works.

Some of my work in this book, then, will be on Twain's humor. A constant danger in writing about such a subject is to take something we associate with the playful, the spontaneous, and the unexpected and weigh it down with critical analysis. The language and intention of the latter will always make an uneasy match with the comic text on which it focuses. E. B. White said, "Humor can be dissected, as a frog can, but the thing dies in the process and the innards are discouraging to any but the pure scientific mind."[8] His metaphor is a particularly appropriate one, given the content of Twain's most celebrated — or should it be notorious? — short story: that which starts, and gives its title to, his first book of sketches.[9]

In his introduction to the Oxford edition of the *Celebrated Jumping Frog* collection, Roy Blount Jr. echoes White's warning. "There is nothing less useful," he writes, "certainly nothing less funny, than explaining why something is funny" (xxxviii). In this book I choose to disregard the first part of that pronouncement. As I analyze some of Twain's comic effects, I am aware of the traps that lie in my critical path (of which over seriousness is just one) and suspect I am likely to fall into some of them. But, to modify White's metaphor in the direction of Twain's story, I hope that the life, the spring, in Twain's humor is not killed but complemented by such critical work, and that my analysis does not act like so much lead shot holding the figurative frog to the ground. Comparing Twain's comedy with that of his nineteenth-century contemporaries, Blount celebrates the fact that "Mark Twain's humor still jumps" (xxxiii). I trust it will still jump for my reader both as he or she tackles this book and afterward. The very best I can hope for is that occasionally my analysis might even give Twain's comic energy an extra little critical punch behind.

1

The Celebrated Jumping Frog of Calaveras County, and Other Sketches

TO

JOHN SMITH

WHOM I HAVE KNOWN IN DIVERS AND SUNDRY PLACES ABOUT THE
WORLD, AND WHOSE MANY AND MANIFOLD VIRTUES DID ALWAYS
COMMAND MY ESTEEM, I

Dedicate this Book.

It is said that the man to whom a volume is dedicated, always buys a copy. If this proves true in the present instance, a princely affluence is about to burst upon

THE AUTHOR

— Dedication to *The Celebrated Jumping Frog of Calaveras County, and Other Sketches.*

Twain's first book of short writings, *The Celebrated Jumping Frog of Calaveras County, and Other Sketches* (1867), starts, as one might expect, with a joke, in the dedication reproduced above. One might gloss its words to suggest several prompts lying behind its humor, interconnecting relays between author and the textual material he is presenting. First, there is some evidence of Twain's knowledge of the audience to which he is likely to appeal: the common male denominator that the name "John Smith" suggests.[1] Second, we might identify an implicit anxiety on the part of the author with the economics of this first book-length publishing venture, his own financial stake in the matter, and the nature of the market into which he might be tapping. The fact that he puts a universal rather than merely national emphasis on the John Smith reference ("in divers and sundry places about the world") and the allusion to his own potential monetary rewards ("a princely affluence") support such a reading.

Already the danger of reading far too much into what is just a squib becomes apparent, but Twain's joke does have, to pursue the marketing issue, a prophetic quality. Twain wrote to the San Francisco *Alta California* on publication of the *Jumping Frog* collection:

I hope my friends will all buy a few copies each, and more especially am I anxious to see the book in all the Sunday School Libraries in the land. I don't know that it would instruct youth much, but it would make them laugh anyway, and therefore no Sunday School Library can be complete without the "Jumping Frog."

Robert H. Hirst claims that "the uneasy, almost apologetic tone of this newspaper letter suggests that Mark Twain was not wholly sanguine about the prospective sale of his first book."[2] Profits and potential sales figures were very much on the mind of a writer whose economic status was still far from secure. It was only some eighteen months earlier that he had written from California to his brother Orion that he was "in trouble, & in debt. . . . If I do not get out of debt in 3 months, — pistol or poison for one — exit *me*."[3] The *Jumping Frog* book did not in fact sell well in America, but it would do so in England, with some 42,000 copies sold by July 1873.[4] And the prediction Twain apparently made to pocket miner Jimmy Gillis, when he first tried to write down the story told by Ben Coon at Angels Camp in Calaveras County, was an accurate one: "He used to say: 'If I can write that story the way Ben Coon told it, that frog will jump its way around the world' " (MTL1, 321). The "Jumping Frog" sketch and the book in which it was consequently reprinted do then serve as some indicator both of the affluence and reputation which Twain's career as a comic writer would eventually bring.[5]

The money Twain made from his work stemmed largely from the breadth of his popular and comic appeal. If the John Smith joke has relevance in this respect, there is a further dimension to its use in this text, for Twain keeps coming back to that name and its humorous potential in the collection (77, 122–24, 150, 162). John Smith's name is one that both confers and blurs identity. In "Among the Spirits," the first-person narrator:

Got tremblingly up and said with a low and trembling voice:
  "Is the spirit of John Smith present?"
  (You can never depend on these Smiths; you call for one and the whole tribe will come clattering out of hell to answer you.)
  "Whack! whack! whack! whack!"
  Bless me! I believe all the dead and damned John Smiths between San Francisco and perdition boarded that poor little table at once! (122)

Twain has skeptical fun at the expense of spiritualism here. His distinctive comic voice, though, is already clearly evident in this early sketch, particularly in the punning deflationary move that comes as the narrator asks one of the Smiths, "What do lost spirits call their dread abode?" and gets the answer, "They call it the Smithsonian Institute" (124). One can, however, also see here an early indication of that concern for the problematics of identity (What separates one individual from another? What distinguishes personality from anonymity?) that would come to trouble Twain's writing increasingly as time went on.

The most obvious reading of Twain's dedication, however, is in terms of the democratic nature of his audience. Twain's decision to write for the John Smiths of this world (those he would later call "the Belly & the Members" as opposed to "the cultivated classes")[6] is the corollary of his choice of vocation as a humorist. Twain's ambiguous attitude as he decided on this career choice is well known and was one that would never entirely be resolved. Thus he wrote to his brother Orion, on 19 October 1865, saying that an ambition to be a "preacher of the gospel" had failed, partly because he had never "had a 'call' in that direction." But, he continued, "I *have* had a 'call' to literature, of a low order — *i.e.* humorous. It is nothing to be proud of, but it is my strongest suit." Twain went on to describe that vocation in terms of "turn[ing] my attention to seriously scribbling to excite the **laughter** of God's creatures. Poor, pitiful business!" and concluded that section of the letter by saying, "I will drop all trifling . . . & strive for a fame — unworthy & evanescent though it must of necessity be" (MTL1, 322–24).

This is a frequently quoted passage, though, as so often with Twain, we must be careful not to take what he writes too much at face value. It is possible to detect both an exaggerated note of self-abasement here and an emphasis on the spiritual realm that may speak more of his brother's attitudes than his own. But the timing of the letter is important. Twain had finished writing his "Jumping Frog" sketch only the day earlier. On that day, he had also seen, reprinted in the *San Francisco Dramatic Chronicle*, the praise given his comic talents in a New York newspaper. This described him as "the foremost among the merry gentlemen of the California Press, as far as we have been able to judge," adding that "he may one day take rank among the brightest of our wits."[7] Twain's statement of vocational commitment, then, can be directly connected to the writing of what remains his best-known short work and to an emerging reputation in the Eastern metropolis. This added to his success at the Western regional level, where his work for newspapers and literary weeklies had already brought him celebrity status.

Twain's commitment to a career as a humorist was, and would remain, remarkably ambivalent. The note of rhetorical inflation in the phrase "excite the laughter of God's creatures" is bracketed on one side by the paradoxical "seriously scribbling" and on the other by the denigratory "poor, pitiful business!"[8] The words "fame" and "unworthy," too, are twinned. When the "Jumping Frog" sketch proved a success both at a New York and national level, Twain wrote to his mother and sister (on 20 January 1866) about the irony of his new reputation resting on his writing of "a villainous backwoods sketch." But he then pasted a review in the letter which praised the sketch as having "set all New York in a roar . . . the papers are copying it far and near. It is voted the best thing of the day" (MTL1, 327–28). Fifteen months later, again writing to his mother, there is no note of self-disparagement present, only pride, when he reports (probably incorrectly as it happens) that "James Russell Lowell . . . says the Jumping Frog is the finest piece of humorous writing ever produced in America."[9]

If Twain dedicated both his book and his talent to the entertainment of the common man (John Smith), he held a divided attitude toward such an implied reader and the exercise of his own talent. His reference to the "stupid people and the *canaille*" who read the *New York Weekly Review*, a journal which had previously reprinted five of his letters from the Sandwich Islands, is suggestive not only of a search for "larger audiences" but also of a certain self-distancing from, and even contempt for, the democratic mass.[10] It certainly raises questions about the "manifold virtues" associated with the ordinary reader in his book's dedication.

A series of paradoxes and ambivalences begin to emerge here about Twain, his attitude to his audience and to his art, and further aspects of this will emerge as my book progresses. Twain is a writer marked by extraordinary shifts in tack and tone, and his work contains a number of seemingly incompatible elements. Louis J. Budd has spoken of Twain's status as an American icon and the way that "under tight focus" his image "blurs, shifts, and splits."[11] The same might be said of his writing in terms of its form and content. So, for instance, the *Jumping Frog* book starts with a joke, then moves into its opening title sketch, a brilliant comic tale. But the collection ends with "Short and Singular Rations," a short, nonfictional, account of the loss of the clipper *Hornet* and "the courage and brave endurance" of its men, who succeeded in reaching Hawaii after "forty-three days adrift . . . in open boats" (194). The main emphasis of this sketch is on the shortage of food suffered on this journey and the crew's survival on such substitutes as "cutting their old boots into small pieces and eating them" (195). The story does end with a joke, but it is a very grim one, told by one of the survivors:

Speaking of the leather diet, one of the men told me he was obliged to eat a pair of boots which were so old and rotten that they were full of holes; and then he smiled gently and said he didn't know, though, but what the holes tasted about as good as the balance of the boot. This man was very feeble, and after saying this he went to bed. (197–98)

The gentle smile and the suggestion of the following of one's own thought processes in a somewhat distracted way sound a typical Twain comic note. And the joke about the difference between boot and hole, presence and absence, is a good one. But the predominant tone of the sketch is serious, even horrific, with its references to the real possibility of cannibalism.[12] And the ending of both the sketch and the book is anticlimactic and abrupt. In this first collection we already see, then, something of that sense of diversity and even of strain (as different kinds of material collide) that would always be a feature of Twain's work, whatever genre he was to use.[13]

Twain's involvement in the production of his first published book of sketches was sporadic and inconsistent, and to some degree, in consequence, his attitude toward it was ambivalent. There was undoubtedly a rushed and piecemeal quality to this collection, as Budd suggests when he writes that "following up on the wildfire success of his yarn, pirated by newspapers across the country, [Twain] cobbled together *The Celebrated Jumping Frog of Calaveras County, and Other Sketches*."[14] The book may have been "cobbled together." But, as Budd indicates, Twain played rather more of a part in the making of this book than he would ever admit.

Just before publication, Twain commented on the role of Charles Henry Webb, the book's editor, in its production. Webb was founder of the *Californian*, the literary weekly and "Twain's chief literary outlet" in late 1864 and the spring and summer of 1865 (when he was living and working in San Francisco).[15] Webb, by now a friend, had made the move to New York some months before Twain himself, who arrived on 12 January 1867. And when Twain had difficulty getting a publisher to accept a book of his sketches, Webb agreed to take on the role (see MTL2, 12–14). Twain reported back on Webb's part in this process in a letter of 19 April 1867 to the *Alta California*, saying that:

Webb . . . has fixed up a volume of my sketches . . . and the American News Company will publish it. . . . He has gotten it up in excellent style, and has done everything to suit his own taste, which is excellent. I have made no suggestions. He calls it "THE CELEBRATED JUMPING FROG, AND OTHER SKETCHES, by 'Mark Twain.' Edited by C. H. Webb."

Robert H. Hirst also quotes Twain's later 1906 recall of this event, to conclude that both "privately and publicly, in 1867 and 1906, Mark Twain said that his first book was edited and produced by Charles Henry Webb" (ETS1, 504–6).

Twain, for most of his life, would be both a businessman and an artist. The difficulty of reconciling both these roles and the different traits and skills on which they depended was to be a recurrent feature of, and point of tension in, the developing shape of his career. His disavowal of agency in the production of the *Jumping Frog* book serves, perhaps, as an early sign of the problems he was always to have in moving from one role to the other, in juggling all the different balls that made up his professional and financial life and taking responsibility for the way they fell. There is a telling line in Twain's earliest published letter following his move from California to New York, to British lecture agent Edward Hingston asking for his managerial help in launching a career as a comic lecturer in the East, where he says: "I want you to come and engineer me" (MTL2, 8). This metaphor, a highly resonant one in the fast-modernizing world of post Civil War America, provides an early hint of Twain's later work exploring the conjunction between the mechanical and the human, especially in *A Connecticut Yankee in King Arthur's Court* (1889). His own self-positioning as passive material to be managed and effectively applied by his prospective agent suggests that some part of him wished to keep his role as artist and performer separate from the business side of things. But such feelings were intermittent at best. For someone who could write to his sister-in-law Mollie in February 1867 that "I abhor everything in the nature of business" (MTL2, 10), he was to spend an awful lot of his life figuring and scheming to achieve success in that field.

A similar tension occurred in the case of the *Jumping Frog* book, though here with particular regard to Twain's part in preparing the book for publication. Twain seems to have positioned himself from the first as uninvolved in the final making of the book, the supplier of original material now "fixed up" and published by somebody else. Only on one known occasion did he admit to taking a role in its production, as having "compiled a volume of his sketches for publication" (see MTL2, 12–13). And his comments and behavior concerning the collection were soon to lose the enthusiasm of the *Alta California* ("gotten . . . up in excellent style") letter. Thus, when the book came out, he wrote to Bret Harte of his absence from New York at the time and his consequent inability to check its proofs, saying that he found "the Frog sketch . . . full of damnable errors of grammar & deadly inconsistencies of spelling."[16] Part of what became an ongoing dissatisfaction with the book may well have been due to poor American sales, but it also stemmed from his sense (and here we see the start of what would be another repeated pattern) that Webb had "swindled" him financially on it.[17] Twain's dislike of the book is seen at its clearest in a letter to Olivia, his wife-to-be, on December 31, 1868, where he writes: "*Don't* read a word in that Jumping Frog book, Livy— *don't*. I hate to hear that infamous volume mentioned. I would be glad to know that every copy of it was burned, & gone forever. I'll never write another like it."[18]

By January 1870, indeed, Twain was talking of suing Webb to get him to "yield up the copyright and plates of the Jumping Frog, if I let him off from paying me money. Then I shall break up those plates, and prepare a new vol. of Sketches, but on a different and more 'taking' model" (MTLP, 30). In mid-December of the same year, he did buy the copyright back from Webb and destroy the plates. This, though, was by no means to be the end of these versions of Twain's texts. In his invaluable "Textual Introduction" to volume one of Twain's *Early Tales & Sketches*, Robert H. Hirst charts in full the "extraordinary situation" that resulted as Twain's later authorized collections of sketches were drawn from earlier unauthorized British copies ("pirated" by the publisher John Camden Hotten), taken in their turn from Webb's original collection (ETS1, 607). So material from this first book continued to be reproduced elsewhere despite the author's earlier intentions to the contrary.

But Twain's part in the *Jumping Frog* book, despite all his dissatisfactions with it, was rather larger than he would generally imply. This whole story is recounted in scrupulous detail in Hirst's essay, and I repeat the gist of his findings. Hirst proves that in fact, and despite his disclaimers, Twain "played a large and important role in shaping [the collection] for the press" (ETS1, 506). Twain's scrapbook, put together in San Francisco before he came to New York, is the clear "major source of printer's copy" for the book. His selections, revisions (sometimes carried over into the published text, sometimes "further altered," sometimes "quietly ignored"), and explanatory notes all played their part in the production of the book (509). And there is clear evidence that Twain modified his texts with an Eastern audience in mind: for instance, he "deleted or softened allusions to sex, damnation, and drink" (507). But the final selection, and version, of the sketches seem to have been left to Webb, and it was he who "saw [it] through the press" (541), with the author absent in St. Louis at the time. Hirst sums up:

[The *Jumping Frog* book] presents an unusual situation in Mark Twain's works, for all of the sketches that it reproduces are in some degree the product of an intermingling of authorial and editorial decision about what sketches to reprint, which portions to select, and even what words to use. The editorial process was carried out in such a way that confident distinctions between the literary contributions of Webb and Mark Twain are now no longer possible. (542)

Twain both trusted and (at least initially) accepted Webb's editorial work. It was only later that he started to regret the amount of textual control he had given him. His letter to Elisha Bliss, the publisher of *The Innocents Abroad*, is significant in this respect, where he writes, "I don't much like to entrust even slight alterations to other hands. It is n't a judicious thing to do, exactly."[19]

Budd talks of Twain's first book as "cobbled together." Twain himself wrote to his family about an earlier plan, following on the back of the success of the "Jumping Frog" story, to collaborate with Bret Harte on a book of their previously published newspaper and magazine sketches. He said that Harte wanted him "to club a lot of old sketches together with a lot of his, & publish a book together. . . . My labor will not occupy more than 24 hours, because I will only have to take the scissors & slash my old sketches out of the Enterprise & the Californian" (see ETS1, 502).

Hirst uses this letter to comment more generally on the book publications of his short writings: "This early emphasis on easy money[20] — the "scissors & slash" method — came to dominate Mark Twain's attitude toward republishing his short works and to influence the way in which he collected and reprinted them long after he had achieved a measure of renown" (502). However, we have to be a little careful about taking Twain's self-constructions as slapdash and lazy too seriously.[21] The editing work he did put in on the *Jumping Frog* book and Edgar Branch's comments on "the energy" which Twain put into his early book projects — and "especially sketch books" (ETS1, 38) — suggest another point of view. One of my aims in this book is to see, on the evidence available, just how far Twain's short works are cobbled together, what signs there are of a more considered approach, and the nature of the relationship between author and publisher in such a process. Hirst's "scissors & slash" verdict — and this looks forward to what will follow — is only one part of a more complicated truth.

The immediately most distinctive feature of *The Celebrated Jumping Frog of Calaveras County, and Other Sketches* was its cover, with the "gorgeous gold-stamped frog" that was featured there. The frog, what is more, jumped: it appeared at different places depending on the copy of the book bought. This was a nice idea, and one Twain himself appreciated fully, writing in April 1867 that "it would be well to publish the frog and leave the book out." As Beverley David and Ray Sapirstein note: "The famous jumping frog became a personal trademark and helped to spark in Twain what would become a sustained interest in book design and illustration."[22]

The book itself was relatively short and had, in turn, a number of very short pieces in it. It contained twenty-seven sketches in just under two hundred wide-margined pages, and these ranged from just over a page ("Among the Fenians") to twenty-four pages in length ("Answers to Correspondents" — itself composed of a number of much shorter sequences). The book was published on 30 April 1867 (ETS1, 542), some eight weeks after the death of Artemus Ward on March 6. There is symbolic significance here as Twain was to take over the mantle of Ward as the foremost American humorist of the age, but writing in a style that was much more accessible than his and, indeed, than the majority of the well-known American comic writers of the time. It is noticeable in this respect that Webb, in the "Advertisement" that prefaced the *Jumping Frog* book, implicitly drew particular attention to the difference between Ward and Twain, commenting that "Mark Twain never resorts to tricks of spelling nor rhetorical buffoonery for the purpose of provoking a laugh; the vein of his humor runs too rich and deep to make surface-gilding necessary."

It is common knowledge that Twain's technique as a humorous lecturer owed much to Ward and his "deadpan style."[23] John Camden Hotten's description of Ward's methods in terms of their mix of "rollicking fun" and "considerable valuable information" also fits Twain's own platform performance. But Twain's comic writing was quite different from Ward's, particularly in its usual disavowal of "tricks of spelling." Hotten warns Ward's readers to "be careful to distinguish betwixt what is dialect and what mere incorrect orthography . . . simply burlesque or cacographic."[24] Twain generally steered clear of the latter mode of representation. So both Ward in *Artemus Ward, His Book* and Twain in *Jumping Frog* write sketches called "Among the Spirits." Ward's reliance on orthographic distortion is obvious, though, from the start of his piece: "My naburs is mourn harf crazy on the new fangled idear about Sperrets. Sperretooul Sircles is held nitely & 4 or 5 long hared fellers has settled here and gone into the sperret biznis excloosively." Twain uses other narrative tactics. His first-person voice speaks in standard English, though with a colloquial edge, and even when dialect is introduced, it is "contained" within quote marks:

There was a *séance* in town a few nights since. As I was making for it, in company with the reporter of an evening paper, he said he had seen a gambler named Gus Graham shot down in a town in Illinois years ago by a mob, and as he was probably the only person in San Francisco who knew of the circumstance, he thought he would "give the spirits Graham to chaw on awhile." (116)

The tone of both writers is, as one would expect, skeptical: Ward's entry to the séance he attends is met with the words, "Hear cums the skoffer at trooth."[25] Twain's sketch, however, ends on the more indeterminate note. If the two writers share a predictable joke about the warmth of the climate in the spirit world, for the most part the sketches go their different comic ways. And in his move away from Ward's reliance on the comedy of orthographic effect, Twain was taking American humor in new and less limiting directions.

In his "Advertisement," Webb also pointed to a tension and potential contradiction already present in Twain's work, one that would (in modified forms) get increasingly problematic as his career continued. He repeated the two descriptive titles given to Twain in California: "The

Moralist of the Main" and "The Wild Humorist of the Pacific Slope." It is the latter side of Twain that is more evident in this collection, for the humour in the book is generally unrestrained and more strongly antagonistic to domesticity, femininity, sentimentality, and other bourgeois values than in Twain's later work. Roy Blount argues that it is the very quality of "mischief, riffraff and foolery" in this book, its unaffected status as "quicksilver" comic text, that makes it so successful. The frog of the title story becomes (for him) metaphoric for the "bounce" of the collection as a whole (IN, xxxv and xxxii).

This selection of sketches, drawn from Twain's early newspaper and journal work in California, is not random. Twain played a significant part in the selection of material for the book. Even while he was still in California, but thinking of book-length publication (the project with Harte), he was making decisions about which of his works he wanted to see reprinted. He wrote to his family concerning his sketches in the Virginia City *Territorial Enterprise* and the *Californian*, saying, "I burned up a small cart-load of them lately—so *they* are forever ruled out of any book—but they were not worth republishing" (MTL1, 328). Edgar Branch stresses the "staggering" nature of the "sheer number of words" Twain turned out as an apprentice writer ("easily three or four thousand . . . separate pieces").[26] *Jumping Frog* begins the process of sorting out this apprentice work (for so we might call it) into book-length material. This process, updated to include the Eastern work done since, would be completed in *Sketches, New and Old* (1875).

Given the variety, number, and divergent lengths of the sketches in the *Jumping Frog* edition, it is difficult to make critical generalizations about it. However, there are a number of concerns and techniques that thread their way through the collection and act as a marker from which further continuities, developments, and contrasts in Twain's short works can be identified. This chapter serves in particular to preface the analysis of *Sketches, New and Old*, as an initial sketching out of the defining features of Twain's early short work discussed more fully there.[27]

What is perhaps most significant and striking about this first collection is its distinctive use of voice. Samuel Clemens had been using the pen name "Mark Twain" as a constructed comic persona since 1863. This voice worked, according to Edgar Branch, by means of "a relaxed, informal kind of humor—personal narrative, the genre that became Mark Twain's chief literary form" (ETS1, 22). Twain's voice and the very form of his humor, then, are identified in symbiotic relationship. And it is the multifaceted nature of this voice/persona that is especially evident. So, for instance, in "A Complaint About Correspondents," Twain is the irritable victim of his thoughtless Eastern correspondents, railing against the "poor, bald, uninteresting trash" they send him: "Yet how *do* you write? — how do the most of you write? Why, you drivel and drivel and drivel along in your wooden-headed way about people one never heard of before, and things which one knows nothing at all about and cares less. There is no sense in that" (26–27). The mixture of powerlessness (reliant as he is on family and friends for news of home) and abusive spleen operates to drive the humor.

In "A Touching Story of George Washington's Boyhood," however, the first-person narrator takes on a quite different role to become a type of half-innocent, half-malicious obsessive.[28] He falls "victim to the instrument they call the accordeon" (135). The disruptive effect he then has on the lives of those around him is presented in a typically hyperbolic manner:

For three nights in succession I gave my new neighbors "Auld Lang Syne," plain and unadulterated. . . . But the very first time I tried the variations the boarders mutinied. . . . I was very well satisfied with my efforts in that house, however, and I left it without any regrets; I drove one boarder as mad as a March hare, and another one tried to scalp his mother. I reflected, though, that if I could only have been allowed to give this latter just one more touch of the variations, he would have finished the old woman. (137)

The wild exaggeration that renders this voice so obviously unreliable, the focus on violent extremes, the antidomestic animus, and the afterthought that metaphorically trumps the previous joke all are typical of the early Twain and the frontier tradition that had helped to mold him.

There is another point of interest to this last sketch, though, in that Twain only returns to his title, and to his "admirable story about Little George Washington, who could Not Lie," at its very end. He then wraps up the sketch in a rapid and deflationary manner by saying that "writing such a long and elaborate introductory has caused me to forget the story itself; but it was very touching" (139–40). A similar narrative tactic is used in "The Launch of the Steamer Capital." Here Twain introduces himself in the guise of the reliable reporter of a significant historical event, the first words of the sketch's subtitle reading: "I get Mr. Muff Nickerson to go with me and assist in reporting the Great Steamboat Launch" (153). In fact, the narrator and his companion retreat inside the steamboat to drink at its bar ("We took pure, cold, health-giving water, with some other things in it," 154). The meat of the narrative then consists of Nickerson's story, "The Entertaining History of the Scriptural Panoramist," and of the "wooden-headed old slab" the panoramist hires to play the piano for him. The story hangs on the incompatible relation between the lecturer's rhetorical effects and their inappropriate interruption by the music played by "the old mud-dobber" (156–57):

"Ladies and gentleman, this exquisite painting illustrates the raising of Lazarus from the dead by our Saviour. The subject has been handled with rare ability by the artist, and such touching sweetness and tenderness of expression has he thrown into it, that I have known peculiarly sensitive persons to be even affected to tears by looking at it. . . ."
Before any body could get off an opinion in the case, the innocent old ass at the piano struck up:
   "Come, rise up, William Ri-i-ley
And go along with me!" (160)

This narrative within a narrative makes humorous use of the divide between the spiritual and the secular and between their clashing kinds of performance and discourse (with Twain unafraid to satirize an overblown and overly pious religious sensitivity). It also gains comic effect from the loss of linguistic and emotional control on the panoramist's part as he finally loses all patience with his helper: "That lets you out . . . you chowder-headed old clam! Go to the door-keeper and get your money, and cut your stick! vamose the ranche!" (161). But the sketch's final (anti-)climax comes as we learn that no report of the steamer launch of the title is to be included, as "they launched the boat with such indecent haste, that we never got a chance to see it" (161). In both this and the "George Washington" piece, the Twain persona leads the reader up the garden path, part of the comedy lying in the poker-faced undermining of the supposed main focus of interest and expectation, combined with the reader's gradual awareness of such narrative indirection and digression. Twain would rely on versions of such a technique in many of his best comic short works (with "The Jumping Frog" itself as most obvious example).

The first-person voice ("Mark Twain") in the early Twain, then, shifts from one textual moment to another. The irresponsible reporter and poker-faced hoaxer of "The Launch of the Steamer Capital" becomes, in "Aurelia's Unfortunate Young Man," a burlesque version of the male agony aunt.[29] In "Honored as a Curiosity in Honolulu," the persona adopted is that of hypocrite and small-time thief. When a "solemn stranger" faints in Honolulu on learning that he is neither missionary, whaler captain, nor government minister (apparently, the exclusive occupations of Americans there), the narrator says, "I was deeply moved. I shed a few tears on him, and kissed him for his mother. I then took what small change he had and 'shoved' " (177–78). These are just some of the various poses identified with "Mark Twain" in the collection.[30] Their

highly playful and flexible quality is one of the most noticeable and vital
features of the author's early work.

What is equally significant in this book, however, is Twain's use of the
clash of voices within sketches, the way different registers of discourse
both meet and contrast, and the focus on language itself as a theme.
These are all highly significant for his future development as a writer.
Nickerson's voice takes over from the narrator in "The Launch of the
Steamer Capital." The described contrast between the panoramist and
the pianist's ways of representing the same material then gives way to the
discordant registers of the former's speech, as his description of the
"touching sweetness and tenderness" of an "exquisite" religious scene is
replaced by his abuse of his "chowder-headed old clam" of an accompa-
nist. In "A Complaint Against Correspondents," the author shows a similar concern with the way different voices, and the values with which they
are associated, interact. So, for instance, "Twain" makes comic play out of
the scattershot method of his Aunt Nancy's letters and the lack of common ground between author and recipient:

> "O Mark! why *don't* you try to lead a better life? Read II. Kings, from chap. 2 to
> chap. 24 inclusive. . . . Poor Mrs. Gabrick is dead. You did not know her. She had
> fits, poor soul. On the 14ᵗʰ the entire army took up the line of march from — ". . . .
> "Read twenty-two chapters of II. Kings" is a nice shell to fall in the camp of a
> man who is not studying for the ministry. The intelligence that "poor Mrs.Ga-
> brick" was dead, aroused no enthusiasm — mostly because of the circumstance
> that I had never heard of her before, I presume. But I was glad she had fits —
> although a stranger. (28–29)

Twain positions himself outside the pale of genteel moral respectability
here, and his secular outlook and resistance to moral tuition are nicely
caught in the military metaphor he introduces to describe that part of
the letter's effect. The sense of flailing in the dark as he and we attempt to
follow the mental and verbal processes of his correspondent links this
story, too, to the title sketch of the collection. It further connects it to the
larger theme of epistemological uncertainty (implied here in the lack of
shared knowledge and understanding between letter writer and reader)
that runs through so much of Twain's work.

Twain's humor, then, strongly depends on the use of contrasting voices
to create comic effect. In "A Complaint Against Correspondents," we
even get an early hint of *Huckleberry Finn* as Twain praises the letters he
receives from children on the grounds that "they write simply and naturally, and without straining for effect." The writing of an eight-year-old
girl provides illustration of this: "Uncle Mark, if you was here, I could tell
you about Moses in the Bulrushers again, I know it better now. . . . Sissy

McElroy's mother has got another little baby. She has them all the time. It has got little blue eyes, like Mr. Swimley that boards there, and looks just like him" (31–2). The specific mention of "Moses in the Bulrushers" clearly looks forward to the later novel, though the transparent reference to sexual transgression is more typical of this earlier stage in Twain's career. The use of a naive voice for unwitting comic effect would be one of the author's most effective comic weapons, not just in his most famous novel but in a large number of his sketches and other full-length works besides.

In "A Page from a Californian Almanac," Twain says at one point: "Beware of all light discourse — a joke uttered at this time would produce a popular outbreak" (143). A surreal form of humor initially arises in the disjunction between different conceptual categories (jokes and the weather) here. But the further implied reference to the existence of different levels of discourse is indicative of one of Twain's great comic talents, for he moves from one language level to another with consummate ease and skill. In "Answers to Correspondents," he addresses "Socrates Murphy," who has "given offense to a gentleman at the opera by *unconsciously* humming an air which the tenor was singing at the time":

I can tell you Arizona opera-sharps, any time; you prowl around beer cellars and listen to some howling-dervish of a Dutchman exterminating an Italian air, and then you come into the Academy and prop yourself up against the wall . . . and go to droning along about half an octave below the tenor, and disgusting every body in your neighborhood with your beery strains. [N.B. — If this rough-shod eloquence of mine touches you on a raw spot occasionally, recollect that I am talking for your good, Murphy, and that I am simplifying my language so as to bring it clearly within the margin of your comprehension; it might be gratifying to you to be addressed as if you were an Oxford graduate, but then you wouldn't understand it, you know]. (55–56)

Twain here self-reflexively foregrounds the comic moves he makes between different modes of language and comprehension.

So, throughout the *Jumping Frog* collection, we see such interactions at work. One moment he parodies legal discourse ("Answers to Correspondents," 46). At another, he uses the tone and language of the society columnist to draw attention to the gap between the pretensions and the performance of the San Francisco society world he satirizes (" 'After' Jenkins," 85–88). In "Answers to Correspondents" (again) he quotes Byron's poetry with no apparent recognition of its author, and invents a critical vocabulary to brilliantly match the assumed superiority but actual naivete — both aesthetic and linguistic — of the persona he adopts:

That ["The Assyrians came down, like a wolf on the fold"] may be very good Dutch Flat poetry, but it won't do in the metropolis. It is too smooth and blubbery; it reads like buttermilk gurgling from a jug. What the people ought to have is something spirited—something like "Johnny Comes Marching Home." However, keep on practicing, and you may succeed yet. There is genius in you, but too much blubber. (41)

Twain skillfully handles the Western vernacular, too, not just in the title sketch but in a second (short) "Simon Wheeler" extract in "Answers to Correspondents" (37).[31]

Twain's skillful layering of different registers of language in the *Jumping Frog* book is complemented in his recurring concern with language itself as a theme. There is an inspired piece in "Answers to Correspondents" on the difference between geometry and conchology which plays on the multiple possibilities and punning slippages in the relation between signifier and signified:

Conchology is a science which has nothing to do with mathematics; it relates only to shells. At the same time, however, a man who opens oysters for a hotel, or shells a fortified town, or sucks eggs, is not, strictly speaking, a conchologist—a fine stroke of sarcasm, that, but it will be lost on such an intellectual clam as you. (54)

"Literature in the Dry Diggings" is related to "The Jumping Frog" in its subject matter (Ben Coon and Angel's Camp) and its heavy reliance on the vernacular voice. But it also anticipates *Roughing It* [1872] in its thematic use of *Webster's Unabridged Dictionary* and the way it starts "sloshing around" (in this case) a mining camp. The colloquial style and the paratactic flow of Coon's language is comically poised here against the orderly categorizations and official linguistic authority of the dictionary. And the metaphorical weight of the language the miners meet between the book's covers dooms them to defeat in their attempts to make much sense of it. It is the twin subject of language and meaning that becomes the very subject of the sketch as Twain describes the miners' trials:

Now Coddington had her for a week and she was too many for *him*—he couldn't spell the words; he tackled some of them regular busters, tow'rd the middle, you know, and they throwed him; next Dyer, *he* tried her a jolt, but he couldn't *pronounce*'em . . . ; he used to worry along well enough, though, till he'd flush one of them rattlers with a clatter of syllables as long as a string of sluice-boxes, and then he'd lose his grip and throw up his hand. (83)

This concern for language as a theme again would prove a consistently important element in Twain's work. It is one he would still be exploring even in his last collection, *The $30,000 Bequest and Other Stories* (1906).

The *Jumping Frog* collection of sketches shoots off in any number of thematic directions, loosely held in check by Twain's use of the first-person narrative voice and a general concern for the interaction of different voices and values.[32] A number of other recurrent motifs can be briefly identified. It may be an odd way to begin such a process, but it is difficult to talk about this book without at least mentioning the Civil War (which ended in 1865, just two years prior to publication). The war scarcely figures in the book, and usually then by indirection: the mention of the arrival of "war news" in San Francisco and Nevada (28, 149); a cat called General Grant (32); and the occasional use of military metaphors in the sketches (29, 42). There is just one sketch that directly concerns the war, "Lucretia Smith's Soldier," first published in the *Californian* on 3 December 1864. Both a "burlesque condensed novel" and a satire of self-indulgent sentimentalism, this short piece was Twain's response to "those nice, sickly war stories which have lately been so popular" (89), and it achieved immediate success in both the West and the East.[33] As in "Aurelia's Unfortunate Young Man," the tale works as black humor. Grocery clerk Reginald de Whittaker enlists in the war but is foolishly spurned by his love, Lucretia, before she realizes that he has done so. Reginald becomes "a morose, unsmiling, desperate man, always in the thickest of the fight, begrimed with powder" (96), while Lucretia weeps, knowing that "no soldier in all the vast armies would breathe her name as he breasted the crimson tide of war! . . . 'Drat it!' " (95). Reginald is eventually wounded, "a ball had shattered his lower jaw, and he could not utter a syllable" (97). Lucretia rushes to his side to nurse him, only to find that she has been "slobbering over the wrong soldier" when, eventually, his many bandages are removed to expose "the face of a stranger!" (98) This is one of the many burlesques of sentimental and romantic fiction in the early Twain. It serves partly as signal of his own commitment to a realist agenda, partly too as an expression of an early interest in the matter of doubling and the problems of identity. But there is surely something surprising about the use of a Civil War setting in a comic tale, even while that war was in progress, and about the story's widespread success.[34]

Any comment here about the relationship between historical event, fictional text, and reader response will be tentative and purely speculative. We might see, though, both in this particular story and in the book as a whole, signs of Twain's ability to move beyond the barriers of sectional difference and to use his comedy to appeal to, and even help in the construction of, a new mass national audience and sense of identity in the years following the Civil War. Part of my analysis of "The Jumping Frog of Calaveras County" in the next chapter returns to this subject. Certainly, this notion of Twain as a writer who could both represent and bridge sectional difference might be reinforced by the use of Western materials in this book. Twain and Webb's confidence in reprinting sketches, many of which make use of regional references and dialect, for a wider audience, again points to the potential mass appeal of Twain's humor, whatever its contextual base.

The *Jumping Frog* collection is less restrained, more aggressive and anti-social in its forms of humor than any that would follow. There is clear evidence in the book of Twain's early membership in what Randall Knoper calls "a bachelor subculture,"[35] an element in his work that would gradually fade as his career progressed. The prejudices of the Western single male persona can be seen on full display in the complaints that go to make up "Concerning Chambermaids." These commence with the launching "against all chambermaids, of whatsoever age or nationality . . . the curse of bachelordom." A series of details, including the moving of his pillows away from the wrong end of the bed where they are most conducive to the narrator's reading and smoking, illustrate how easygoing habits and routines that operate according to "the ancient and honored custom of bachelors" are upset by the "tyranny" (167) of this group of women. In "A Touching Story of George Washington's Boyhood," as we have seen, Twain recounts his experiences as an accordion-playing boarder, disturbing a succession of landladies and fellow lodgers. In "Curing a Cold," too, his self-projection has an antidomestic edge. Describing the loss of home and happiness in a fire, he continues:

The loss of [these] was a matter of no great consequence, since a home without a mother or a sister, or a distant young female relative in it, to remind you, by putting your soiled linen out of sight and taking your boots down off the mantle-piece, that there are those who think about you and care for you, is easily obtained. (68)

Twain would not quickly discard this persona, although the misogynistic tinge that sometimes accompanied it — as in " 'After' Jenkins," for example — did fade. Indeed, *Roughing It* depends upon it.[36] But his own new status as a family man (he married Olivia Louise Langdon on 2 February 1870) as well as the changing nature of his audience, once he had moved east, would eventually affect and alter this aspect of his early work.

Finally, a recurring concern in Twain's work, and one which evidences itself here, is that of epistemological uncertainty: the difficulty in finding, in terms of a knowledge of reality, any firm and solid ground on which to stand. "An Item Which the Editor Himself Could Not Understand" is symptomatic of the anxieties brought about by such uncertainty, and it closely anticipates the sequence concerning the Horace Greeley letter in *Roughing It*.[37] Like that letter, it also connects back up with Twain's interest in the nature of language previously noted.[38] The narrator of the sketch, a subeditor of the *Californian*, inserts a late item in the paper. This is brought in by a Mr. John William Skae and concerns a "distressing accident" that has happened to his friend William Schuyler. The item is then reprinted in the sketch, the meandering string of subclauses in its first twenty-two-line sentence completely obscuring the sense of the piece. The narrator, checking the article after a complaint for his "boss-editor" (111), finds that he totally fails to gain purchase on this textual ground as he tries to make grammatical and literal sense of it:

I have read his absurd item over and over again, with all its insinuating plausibility, until my head swims; but I can make neither head nor tail of it. There certainly seems to have been an accident of some kind or other, but it is impossible to determine what the nature of it was, or who was the sufferer by it. (115)

This is just a squib, like so many of the sketches in this collection. But the moves it contains between apparent meaningfulness ("insinuating plausibility") and interpretive bewilderment, between textual ground and the complete loss of bearings that comes with the failure to figure it out, are indicative of a theme that will reverberate through Twain's fiction as a whole.

2

Indeterminacy and
"The Celebrated Jumping Frog"

> And Simon Wheeler said, "That has been a lesson to me." And I say to you, let that be a lesson to you. Don't put too much faith in the passing stranger. This life is full of uncertainties, and every episode in life, figuratively speaking, is just a frog.
>
> — "Morals Lecture"

It seems particularly appropriate that Twain's career as a writer of books of short pieces should commence with a collection named after the comic short fiction for which he was then, and is now, best known. Twain's literary career would take him in any number of formal and thematic directions, and the tone and type of humor that he used would vary widely. But this early very short story is marked by a set of narrative tactics, concerns, and comic techniques that (whatever their literary sources)[1] blend in a particularly effective combination. "The Celebrated Jumping Frog" showed Twain, right from the start, to be a powerful and distinctive voice in the American comic tradition.

This story has been subject to an enormous amount of critical attention but remains worth discussing, due to the complexity that its length and subject matter would seem to belie and the adept way it yokes together content and technique. My analysis here serves as a prelude to that of later Twain stories which share similar qualities, particularly "The Stolen White Elephant."

The textual version of the narrative referred to here requires some comment. Twain himself saw the particular version of "The Jumping Frog" sketch that Webb published as corrupt, a verdict with which Robert H. Hirst, the authoritative source on the early publications, agrees. In consequence, contemporary commentators generally use the Branch and Hirst version of the story (based on its original New York *Saturday*

Press publication) as the text from which to work.[2] However, and follow-ing on from the decision to examine Twain's published collections of short writings sequentially, I use the text as it was originally printed in the *Jumping Frog* book. The same is true of the other sketches from the collec-tion and for a number of related reasons. "The Jumping Frog" story was something of a work in continual progress for Twain, subject to authorial change and revision at any stage of its (many) reprintings. It is clear, for instance, that Twain had no particular commitment to the opening ad-dress to Artemus Ward that appeared in the *Saturday Press* version:

MR. A. WARD,
    DEAR SIR: — Well, I called on good-natured, garrulous old Simon Wheeler, and I enquired after your friend Leonidas W. Smiley, as you requested me to do, and I hereunto append the result.[3]

When the story was reprinted, in *Sketches, New and Old* (1875),[4] contained within " 'The Jumping Frog.' In English. Then in French. Then Clawed Back into a Civilized Language Once More by Patient, Unremunerated Toil," it was the 1867 (Webb) book opening that continued to stand. And as the story continued to be reprinted — ten times in its first ten years — so the text was further edited and "tinker[ed] with," sometimes by Twain himself, and sometimes by his various publishers (both English and American).[5] Twain did thoroughly revise the sketch, almost certainly in 1869 (see Robert Hirst on "The Doheny Jumping Frog"). But this was "never used as a printer's copy" for any published edition of it.[6]

In other words, there was no "authentic" version of the text generally available to those who actually read Twain at this time, just a story that tended to change its shape at each reappearance. To give a brief instance, the closing line of the *Saturday Press* version of the story (prior to the "Yours, truly, MARK TWAIN" that also appears there) runs: " 'O, curse Smiley and his afflicted cow!' I muttered, good-naturedly, and bidding the old gentleman good-day, I departed." This remains — though without the "Yours, truly. . ." addition — almost the same in the *Jumping Frog* book, with the exception that "Oh! hang" replaces "O, curse" (19).[7] With *Sketches, Old and New*, the line has been revised to read: "However, lacking both time and inclination, I did not wait to hear about the afflicted cow, but took my leave."[8] Anyone who wants a detailed account of such changes (up to 1875) should consult the scrupulous editorial work con-tained in Branch and Hirst's two-volume *Early Tales & Sketches* (and espe-cially vol. 2, *1864–1865*, 666–82).

This book, then, employs versions of Twain's texts as they appeared in the various collections of short writings issued during his lifetime, despite the editorial problems thus raised, especially in the case of the *Jumping Frog* book. But these were the versions available to Twain's nineteenth-century (book) readers and available again in the Oxford Mark Twain. Such versions were also, in many cases, at least partly the result of Twain intentionally altering and adjusting his work as he republished it. However, to rebut (in the case of "The Jumping Frog" story) the inevitable charge that I thus merely repeat Webb's "damnable errors," where changes have been made to the original *Saturday Press* text (as published in ETS2), they are noted in square brackets within my text. This would seem to be the most pragmatic way to proceed.[9]

The first thing to note about "The Celebrated Jumping Frog of Calaveras County" is its structural complexity. The tale starts off with a first-person narrator who can be identified with the fictional persona "Mark Twain."[10] Following the request made by "a friend . . . who wrote me from the East," this narrator calls on "good-natured, garrulous old Simon Wheeler" in the "ancient mining camp of Angel's" in Calaveras County, California. He then asks after "my friend's friend, *Leonidas W. Smiley*" (7–8, no emphasis in the *Saturday Press* version), a gospel minister. Wheeler responds by telling a "monotonous" and "interminable narrative" about a *Jim* Smiley who had been at the camp "in the winter of '49 — or maybe . . . the spring of '50" (8–9). The first narrator finally interrupts this story, but only by moving out of the range of Wheeler's words as he makes his own exit:

> "Well, this-yer Smiley had a yaller one-eyed cow that didn't have no tail, only jest [just] a short stump like a bannanner, and — "
> "Oh! hang Smiley and his afflicted cow!" I muttered, good-naturedly, and bidding the old gentleman good-day, I departed. (19)[11]

From an early stage in the narrative we are then, as readers, juggling five characters whose relationships stretch in a particularly disjunctive manner. Moreover, after the introductory paragraphs of the sketch, a quick shift in narrative gear pulls us, together with the first narrator, into what seems an entirely different story from that originally engaged. This happens as Wheeler starts to tell his recollections of Jim Smiley and the various gambling incidents that characterize him as a man who would bet on "any thing that turned up you ever see" (9). It may help illustrate the story's density and technical adeptness to lay out its various moves and narrative levels in abbreviated form.[12]

"The Celebrated Jumping Frog of Calaveras County"
Tale written by Mark Twain (first published 18 November 1865)
Setting: Angel's Camp, California.
First narrator — unnamed, but assumed to be "Mark Twain" as fictional persona — commences with a retrospective frame. This is the time of retelling ("I hereunto append the result") of a previous event when the speaker "called on . . .

Simon Wheeler," as requested by a friend from the East, to ask about Leonidas W. Smiley.

The narrator looks back from the present — presumably in, or close to, 1865 — on a (presumably) recent incident. He retrospectively speculates on both Smiley (the "lurking suspicion that [he] is a myth") and his friend's intentions in getting him to ask his question.

Narrative moves/returns to the time of the previous events described (the calling on Wheeler that has already been mentioned). It (re)commences at the time immediately prior to the narrator's (already noted) enquiry: "I found Simon Wheeler dozing." Narrator describes, more fully this time, the asking of his question about Leonidas W. Smiley, now identified as "a young minister of the gospel."

Coming change of narrator signaled as first narrator describes Simon Wheeler's commencing his "queer yarn." Before this yarn is told, though, the first narrator describes the manner of Wheeler's telling ("a vein of impressive earnestness and sincerity") and the general nature of its content (about "two heroes . . . men of transcendent genius").

Move to third narrative level.[13] Wheeler's story commences ("There was a feller . . ."), now told in his own voice. A further chronologically retrospective move to Angel's Camp in 1849 or 1850 is made as Wheeler tells his rambling tale.

Initially, the narrative focus is on the first "hero"
Jim Smiley as central protagonist
in stories of his willingness to bet on anything: horse-race, dog-fight, cat-fight, chicken-fight, two birds on fence and "which one would fly first," Parson Walker and the success of his camp-meeting exhortations, a straddle-bug and "how long it would take him to get wherever he was going to," the health of Parson Walker's wife and her chances of survival (a series of examples, all in the one paragraph, with the gradual adding of detail as the paragraph proceeds).

Narrative focus then shifts from Smiley to the behavior and actions of
Smiley's mare (on which he bets) — a single short paragraph
And then to Smiley's bull-pup, *Andrew Jackson* (another animal on which he bets) and the bull-pup's behavior and actions — one long paragraph giving Andrew Jackson's usual routine in fight: winning by grabbing the other dog "jest [just] by the j'int of his hind leg[s]"
And his consequent defeat by a dog with no hind legs.

A brief narrative reference is then made back to Smiley himself and his betting on rat-terriers, tom-cats, etc., prior to his catching and training of the frog, *Dan'l Webster*.

The narrative then focuses, in some length, on the behavior and actions of Dan'l Webster and Smiley's betting on him.

Introduction, next, of second "hero": "a stranger in the camp."
Narrative of Smiley vs. the stranger
[This section is the longest in terms of the story's text time, taking up approximately a quarter of the printed space used]
Description of the bet made: *Dan'l Webster vs. stranger's frog*
The stranger's trickery vs. Smiley as dupe

Stranger's repeated (punch) line: *"I don't see no p'ints [points] about that frog that's any better'n any other frog"* (16,18)
Smiley's discovery of fraud, failed attempt to catch stranger.

"And —." Move back to the time of Wheeler's narrative telling as his continued story is broken off by the calling of his name from outside the "dilapidated tavern" where his story is told.

Move back to first narrator — who starts to depart.
Swift return (as the first narrator reaches the tavern door) to Wheeler — recommences narrative (Smiley and his "yaller one-eyed cow").
Equally swift move back to the first narrator — who departs.

What is immediately apparent here, given the story's brevity, is just how much narrative movement, incident, and development of different types of relationship it contains. Our readerly attention is directed (to pick out the more significant stages of the process) from the first narrator to Smiley to Wheeler, to Wheeler's mare, bull-pup (Andrew Jackson), and frog (Dan'l Webster), to the stranger. And we are taken back from there to Wheeler and the first narrator again. We might reduce the story structure charted above to more compressed form:

Mark Twain as (silent) author
First narrator "Mark Twain" (friend from East / Leonidas W. Smiley)
>>   Simon Wheeler (second narrator)
>>   Jim Smiley — and his mare / bull-pup, Andrew Jackson / frog, Dan'l
       Webster
       [Smiley vs. the stranger]
       [Dan'l Webster vs. stranger's frog]
>>   Wheeler >> first narrator
>>   Wheeler >> first narrator (exits).
Twain ends story.

As readers we are being asked to focus on a number of thematic and narrative chains here. The description of Smiley's jumping frog and his (and its) defeat by the smart but dishonest stranger is the structural center of the story, as both Twain's title and the text time given to its recounting confirm. To call it the center, however, seems inappropriate given the (apparent) meandering progression of the overall narrative and the inconclusive nature of its ending. To concentrate just on that one sequence is, moreover, to risk a reductive reading of the text and to leave other questions unanswered. Why are we led through so many levels of narration before we reach the frog story? And how are we intended to respond to the first narrator ("Mark Twain") and his exasperated response to Wheeler's tale-telling? In a story whose central incident is one of trickery, who — more generally — is fooling whom, and to what thematic end? Why is there the concern with broken-off and unfinished narratives here (Wheeler is interrupted at the point when the story of Smiley and the stranger may or may not be completely over; his cycle of stories remain unfinished), and analogously, with sequences of frustrated relationships? What comic techniques does Twain use in the story, and where exactly do its main humorous effects lie? And why was it so successful with his national audience? How important are time and place to the narrative, and what are the regional and national implications of the story? Why are human names and attributes given to two of the animals? Previous critics have, in one way or another, addressed such questions, without fully resolving the puzzles of Twain's story and the connections between its structural levels, the creation of its comic effects, and its thematic intentions.[14] I explore aspects of these concerns below.

Themes of uncertainty and of (potential or actual) reversal run through the several levels of "The Jumping Frog," themes skillfully complemented by the techniques used to portray them. Twain presents different voices and value schemes in his narrative but leaves his reader unable to choose between them. Right from the start of his writing career, in other words, Twain is using his comedy to raise a set of problems that would obsess him throughout his (literary) life. How do we decide between one way of seeing and speaking about the world and another? And how, and with what certainty, do we know whether our *own* assumptions and frames of knowledge and judgment are correct?

The difficulty of interpretive choice in "The Jumping Frog" starts with the two internal narrators of the story, and the question of how as readers we are meant to respond to the clash of voice and value they represent. One of the distinguishing features of Twain's humor generally is the use of a deadpan narrator. A particular influence on Twain here was Artemus Ward and the technique he used to release the "nub" of a joke:[15]

by dropping it in a carefully casual and indifferent way. . . . Artemus Ward used that trick a good deal; then, when the belated audience presently caught the joke, he would look up with innocent surprise, as if wondering what they had found to laugh at. . . . To string incongruities and absurdities together in a wandering and sometimes purposeless way, and seem innocently unaware that they are absurdities, is the basis of the American art.[16]

A double effect (not uncommon in Twain) applies in "The Jumping Frog," for it is both the controlling author and Simon Wheeler the character who spin their (overlapping) rambling, disjointed, and gravely told set of stories. I remain with Wheeler for the present.

Critics such as Kenneth Lynn have seen Simon Wheeler as a deadpan westerner deceiving the "indulgently superior" narrator with his tall tales. Wheeler's "innocence of . . . expression" in such a reading becomes "in fact a mask, cunningly assumed to deceive the outsider [and one apparently convinced of his own cultural superiority] by seeming to fulfil all his pre-conceived notions of Western simple-mindedness."[17] Wheeler may, therefore, be deliberately conning the stranger (for so "Mark Twain," the first narrator, is called, 18–19), showing him up as a greenhorn and thus cultural inferior. This greenhorn is marked as an outsider by his inability to relax and enjoy the tall stories being told or even to realize that he is being fooled. He never acknowledges that these *are* tall tales and that Wheeler will apparently never get to any final point as he strings one after the other, nor ever inform him about the Leonidas W. Smiley after whom he first enquired.[18] If this is so, then Wheeler reverses the thrust of the central frog story where it is the other "stranger" who comically tricks Smiley, a member of the Angel's Camp community. But if Wheeler *is* deceiving his auditor, there is no hard evidence of it. The author, Mark Twain,[19] remains silent throughout the tale, and there are no other members of the Angel's Camp community represented who might give evidence — as "privileged members" of Wheeler's audience — of a deliberate joke being played on the stranger.[20]

Indeed, another and equally tenable interpretation of the story is that Wheeler never sees the funny side of the tales he tells and that, correspondingly, he cannot represent any sense of Western communal or collective value, as would occur in the traditional tall tale. James M. Cox refers to "the impossibility of being sure of Wheeler's deadpan."[21] The garrulous old man may indeed be the earnest, simple, and sincere figure of the first narrator's report: an eccentric who fashions a world of stories, with whatever relation they may or may not bear to some original reality, and tells them not for the benefit of any audience (single or communal) but mainly to satisfy a subjective need.[22] Certainly there is no proof of anything other than this. Wheeler may, literally and figuratively, lose himself in his own stories. He may be absolutely unaware of the response, whether appropriate or not, of the audience of one who listens to him. We might justifiably assume that any question remotely pertaining to the subject of Wheeler's anecdotes is enough to start him off telling them and that, as long as he has an audience, its attention or interest is quite beside the point.

If this is so — and that is the critical position advanced here — then what Twain's story represents is the relativity of voices and the indeterminacy of values. For neither of the story's two narrators can be said to act as the locating point for readerly identification. The implied presence of the authorial figure, moreover, does absolutely nothing to help in the search for interpretive meaning in the tale.

There is an obvious difference, however, between the voice of the first narrator, "Mark Twain," and that of Wheeler. This does suggest that a choice of communities (and values) may be at stake here. Quite what that choice might consist of, though, is open to some dispute. The first narrator's language is both grammatically and orthographically correct, and it only departs from standard American English in its somewhat elaborate formality ("hereunto append" and "conjectured," 7). Though associated with the East (through the mentioned friend), we do not know for sure that he is an easterner.[23] Nor do we know the exact regional background of the other "stranger" in the story, Smiley's antagonist. Although this second stranger uses the vernacular (an't [ain't], I'd bet you, p'ints [points], 16), this may possibly be only "the affectation of Western speech."[24] After all, his first words are elaborate in their syntactical punctilliousness, barring the casual use of the apostrophe for elision's sake: "What might it be that you've got in the box?" (15).

Wheeler himself, though, is firmly associated with vernacular language. The contrast with the speech patterns of the first narrator does accordingly point to some regional dimension to the story (western vernacular versus eastern genteel), however relatively undeveloped and even blurred the boundaries between the various voices might be.[25] The first narrator clearly belongs to a different world than Wheeler and has, as his response to the latter's stories suggests, a different value scheme. But we are kept as readers from any substantial form of identification with him. He is not, and does not particularly try to be, what Wonham calls a "competent listener" in the particular rhetorical, social, and regional context of Angel's Camp.[26] He seems largely incapable of enjoying the comic effects of Wheeler's stories as they move from plateau to "plateau of more systematic irrelevance."[27] He shows no immediate evidence of enjoying the anthropomorphism and other figurative play that helps to move these stories beyond the level of conventional realism. Indeed, one of the elements in the humor of "The Jumping Frog" comes, paradoxically, in the first narrator's failure to respond (at least, initially) to the possibility of comedy in the tales Wheeler tells. That western humor which strains the bounds of literal plausibility — in the attribution of human emotions to dogs and frogs (Andrew Jackson giving his owner "a look, as much as to say his heart was broke") and in the absurdist touch of the fighting dog whose legs have been "sawed off by [in] a circular saw" (13) — is, if not completely lost on him, then judged pointless.[28] He cannot wait to get away from what to him is meaningless and dull drivel.

Twain, in other words, shuttles us between readerly positions and perspectives here. Stuart Hutchinson puts the relativism that results nicely when he suggests that "where Twain finally stands in this story is impossible to say. No perspective governs; all are kept equally in play."[29] As readers we shift from one limited way of saying and seeing things (that of the first narrator, "Mark Twain") to another (that of Wheeler). We shift, too, from an awareness that Wheeler may be a boring old fool (a fact which does not stop us from enjoying his stories and their unconscious humor) to an alternative: that Wheeler is both conscious of his stories' comedy and is engaged in the further level of humor that lies in duping his frustrated and serious listener.[30]

Twain skillfully manipulates conventional generic expectations in this tale. A major part of his comic effect—one that relates to the play of interpretive uncertainty in the text as a whole—lies in destabilizing his readers as he moves them between one genre (the tall tale) and another (the hoax). The difference between the two forms can be briefly summed up in terms of the enjoyment and appreciation of the majority audience: the tall tale is used to entertain, whereas the hoax is used to dupe.[31] "The Jumping Frog" actually builds something of the movement between the two genres into the reading experience itself.

Twain raises the possibility of the hoax in the first paragraph of the story through the first narrator: the "Mark Twain" who "represents himself . . . as a trapped audience and a clueless storyteller at the same time."[32] The latter's retrospective sense of having been the butt of a joke, however, only helps to confirm his general incompetence as a listener and the lack of awareness that characterizes him. He has no sense of being hoaxed by Wheeler; instead, he suspects the friend who wrote him from the East.[33] Wheeler is mostly judged an old bore, with his "tedious" and "infernal" reminiscences. But the first narrator does have "a lurking suspicion that *Leonidas W.* Smiley is a myth." He suspects that his friend, knowing Wheeler will embark on his series of stories if the name Smiley is mentioned, has set him up as fall guy, made to suffer silently while Wheeler tells his long-winded tales, and that "if that was the design, it certainly succeeded" (7–8).[34] Several things can be noted here. First, the speaker never considers the possibility that Jim Smiley might be a myth, too, the stories about him perhaps comic invention and not fact.[35] This failure confirms his narrowness of perception, his single, and even closed, mindedness. Second, it raises the question of trust. The possible untrustworthiness of the friend in the East and the possible untrustworthiness of the tales Wheeler tells (as he wanders around the limits of the plausible) suggest a narrative world of considerable uncertainty, of expectations constantly subject to reversal. This returns us to the central frog story itself, as Twain's message prefacing this chapter, "don't put too much faith in the passing stranger," extends to become "don't put too much faith in the passing friend" as well. Third, the first narrator's words foreground the question of exactly when he suspects a joke has been played on him. Is it when he makes his escape from Wheeler? Or is it long before that, when he is unable to make that escape because he is pinned in a corner by him? Or is it only sometime later, when he realises the repetitive nature of the routine to which Wheeler had subjected him (assuming it is a routine): sees himself from the outside, as it were, as the victim of his eastern friend's amusement?

What Twain (cleverly) does here is continually move his reader between story levels (the relation of inside story to outside, of one joke's victim to the next) to disorienting effect. Our interpretive bearings are constantly disconcerted, redirected, and even frustrated, as the various strands of the story both reflexively inform one other and yet resist any totalizing critical impulse. Disorientation operates to both central stylistic and thematic effect in the story, the upsetting of expectations which its various narratives repetitively trace formally reproduced in its problematization of interpretive stability and certainty.

This problematization, crucially, takes in reader as well as the first narrator, for part of his predicament is in a way ours, too. For when, we might ask, do we realize that *we* are being hoaxed: that the sketch is leading nowhere in terms of the initial set of readerly expectations raised? Do we, like the narrator, patiently work our way through Wheeler's stories, waiting for the final narrative "snapper" to come, only to find ourselves finally left up in the air as the framing narrator walks off with Wheeler still in mid-flow? If so, we may consequently find ourselves left with an anticlimactic sense of nothing really having happened in the story. There is a "nub" to the central frog narrative. The stranger's own deadpan one-upmanship, his ability to take Smiley on at his own (betting) game and unfairly but deliberately stack the odds in his own favor, and his mock-innocent exploitation of Smiley's own innocence (as Smiley fetches the stranger a frog and trusts his own in the latter's hands), leads up to his particular snapper, the repetition of his earlier phase: "*I* don't see no p'ints about that frog that's any better'n any other frog" (18). Here the stranger's triumph is signaled: his duping, as outsider, of his naive host.[36] For the reader, though, the frog story may appear, even despite the story's title, to be just an incident in a chain of other incidents. There is no comic climax, in terms of a clear sense of an ending, to either Smiley's or the first narrator's story: indeed, exactly the opposite. For as the one is brusquely interrupted, and the other is swiftly and disgruntledly closed, the reader may find her or himself, too, left formally dissatisfied, searching for the story's "point."

Twain, in his telling of the story, destabilizes our own sense of readerly certainty about both the direction of the narrative and its intent. The boundary is insecure between our sense of ourselves as "insiders" reading along with the author and enjoying both the tall tales that Wheeler tells and the first narrator's discomfiture, and "outsiders" unsure of, and even fooled by, the author's writerly intentions.[37] Arguably, this is exactly Twain's point as a comic writer who continually, in this story, wrong-foots, or partially wrong-foots, his reader.[38] The interpretive naivete of the first narrator, "Mark Twain," which has everything to do with his set of conceptual boundaries and expectations, may be the same quality Twain as author plays on in his readers, too. The first and third paragraphs give out the information that Wheeler will not fulfill the expectations of his auditor. But it still takes some time for the penny to drop that Wheeler's comic ramblings (and the frustrated response of that auditor) *are* the point of Twain's story. Wheeler's apparently irrelevant stories contain all the narrative climaxes and resolutions, in the conventional sense of these terms, that we can expect.

It is obvious that readers will respond to "The Jumping Frog" variously. Nonetheless, *all* readers, as they work their way through the story, have to come to the realization that the story is going nowhere — in terms either of the first narrator's expectations or of an inside narrative (Wheeler's) that leads up to a clearly defined conclusion. We are having the wool pulled over our readerly eyes if we think that the story is structured toward any other kind of final snapper or nub than lies in the first narrator's failure to see the nub: the entertaining quality of Wheeler's gloriously comic tales and of the quality (however intentional) of his performance.[39] Most readers do see the point of Twain's story, somewhere along the line.[40] I would suggest, however, it is when we realize what this point is that we also realize that we have (until that readerly stage) been the victim rather than the sharer of the joke, outsider rather than insider, the subject of a hoax rather than the connoisseur of the tall tale. For we, too, have been caught, as it were, on the hop. We are not sure how to respond to the first narrator's expectations, to Wheeler's tales, or to their mutual interaction, to where exactly the comic intention of the text lies. The continuing appeal of this story may well lie in its self-reflexive tactics.[41] This is a comic tale where the creation of comic effect and the problems of interpretation become major issues in their own right.[42]

To recapitulate, we cannot be sure whether Wheeler's deadpan is intentional and whether he deliberately frustrates the first narrator by telling his long-winded stories about Jim Smiley. Whatever Wheeler's intentions, he appears to become completely immersed in the stories that he narrates. As in so many tall tales, these stories teeter on the edge of absurdity without ever quite leaving the plausible behind.[43] The human characteristics, emotions, even names, attributed to Smiley's animals make them central protagonists in the stories told and also locate Wheeler's own yarns "somewhere between the extremes of metaphysical wit and naive error."[44]

Wheeler tells three main stories, which in turn take on increasing detail, about Smiley and the animals he bets on. First there is his mare, which despite its slowness and succession of illnesses:

always at the fag-end of the race she'd get excited and desperate-like, and come cavorting and straddling [spraddling] up, and scattering her legs around limber, sometimes in the air, and sometimes out to one side amongst the fences, and kicking up m-o-r-e dust, and raising m-o-r-e racket with her coughing and sneezing and blowing her nose — and always fetch up at the stand just about a neck ahead, as near as you could cipher it down. (11–12)

Then there is the bull-pup, Andrew Jackson, who "wan't [warn't] worth a cent, but to set around and look ornery," but who becomes "a different dog" once money is put on him: "his under-jaw'd begin to stick out like the fo'castle [for'castle] of a steamboat, and his teeth would uncover, and shine savage like the furnaces." Jackson meets his match, though, when his favorite fighting ploy (grabbing his adversary's back leg) is blocked by a dog with front legs only. Accordingly, when he makes:

a snatch for his pet holt, he saw in a minute how he'd been imposed on . . . and he 'peared surprised, and then he looked sorter discouraged-like, and didn't try no more to win the fight. . . . He give [gave] Smiley a look, as much as to say his heart was broke, and it was *his* fault, for putting up a dog that hadn't no hind legs for him to take holt of . . . and then he limped off a piece and laid down and died. (13)

Finally there is Dan'l Webster, the frog Smiley trains up both to jump and to catch flies:

I've seen him . . . sing out, "Flies, Dan'l, flies!" and quicker'n you could wink, he'd spring straight up, and snake a fly off'n the counter there, and flop down on the floor again as solid as a gob of mud, and fall to scratching the side of his head with his hind foot as indifferent as if he hadn't no idea he'd been doin' any more'n any [done any more'n any] frog might do. (14–15)

Smiley's frog is beaten, too, filled with quail-shot by the stranger just before a jumping contest. So, when the competition starts, Dan'l gives "a heave, and hysted up his shoulders — so — like a Frenchman, but it wan't [wasn't] no use — he couldn't budge; he was planted as solid as an [a] anvil" (17).[45]

A number of points can be made concerning the thematic content of these stories, the relation between them, and Wheeler's narrative voice in recounting them. All three stories feature comic reversals and the upsetting of expectation. In the case of Smiley's mare, she who seems least likely to win in fact "cavorts" her way to victory. Twain uses a wonderfully expressive word here. The "heedless and purposeless manner" associated with cavorting links the mare's running technique to Wheeler's yarn-spinnings and potentially transfers a sense of indirect purposefulness from the former to the latter. Moreover, the fact that this term can be used of both horse and rider prepares the reader for the attribution of human characteristics to animal protagonists that shortly follows: first to the mare herself, as she coughs, sneezes, and (the comic clincher) blows her nose; then, more strongly, to the bull-pup and the frog in the two stories that come after.[46]

Dan'l Webster would seem, in direct contrast to the mare, to be a hot favorite, well trained and "gifted," in the contest in which he is entered.[47] A stranger's trickery and his owner's misplaced trust (in that stranger), however, defeat him. The fictional world we enter here is one where the concept of the dead certainty turns out to be meaningless, where things are never quite what they seem (unchanged on the outside, Webster is weighed down with shot within), and where unexpected reversal is the order of the day. Both the stories of the bull-pup and the frog draw attention, moreover, to the frames of knowledge that organise the owner and the animal's conception of the sporting world, and on which they mutually predicate their behaviour. The breech of these boundaries—in the one case, physically, by the dog with no hind legs; in the other, morally, where the expected rules of the gambling encounter are broken by deliberate cheating—directly relates both to the larger meanings of the sketch and to our own position as readers. The story's larger epistemological meanings are engaged too by Wheeler's own refusal—or so the first narrator claims, and so Wheeler's own story would seem to confirm—to make relative judgment on his two "heroes." Thus both Smiley, the man who, in Edgar M. Branch's words, "makes risk the condition of his existence," and the stranger who pragmatically and cynically fleeces him are both judged equally.[48] "The Jumping Frog," then, represents radical uncertainty as a basic condition of existence. The comic reversals of these micro-narratives, the collapse of individual frames of organization and understanding and of the shared standards of behavior that they presume, and the indeterminacy of perspective they represent, all imply an unstable relationship between values and viewpoints. A similar indeterminacy is, as we have seen, also suggested in the various interfaces between the narrators and auditors/readers in (and of) the text and in the competing levels of discourse that compose it.

One of the remaining topics yet to be discussed is the historical dimension to "The Jumping Frog." Written in 1865 but dealing with events (concerning Smiley) that occurred fifteen or sixteen years earlier, the story takes us from boom to bust, from the gold rush to its bypassed remains, the "dilapidated tavern" in Angel's Camp.[49] The story of "betting on any thing that turned up" (9) and of seizing the main chance wherever one found it (in the shape here of mare, bull-pup, or frog) seems particularly relevant to its regional and historical setting. So, too, does its use of confidence men (for Smiley, "enterprising" and "uncommon lucky," is a confidence man, too) and its motifs of reversal and bitter and sudden disillusion, most especially that of the bull-pup, Andrew Jackson. However, the fact that the narrative resists any fully developed allegorical reading along such lines is symptomatic of an interpretive indeterminacy about the story, as it relates to its larger historical context too.

Stuart Hutchinson says that "West and East in Twain elude theory" in the story.[50] The narrative may be read in terms of "Green Easterner imposed upon by the Old Westerner," a putting down of the "indulgently superior" first narrator in favor of the "radical democracy" and vernacular values of the frontier.[51] The West, according to a similarly slanted analysis, can be "shown to have a capacity to be complete unto itself." Thus Wheeler's performance and its oral mode, his non-teleological narrative approach, his seeming lack of concern for his auditor, and his existence on the margins of a dominant competitive and capitalist ethos, might allow us to see him as representing a West which has its own styles and values; one which is "liberated from the East and unconscious of [it]." But it is possible, too, quite to reverse this approach and see the East (as represented by the first narrator's friend, if not the first narrator) as "taking possession" of the West, converting its regional materials to its own ends as entertainment. Twain colludes, after all, in such an incorporative act in producing a sketch focusing on social decay and the comic and eccentric regional voice which is its by-product (to posit one possible reading of the text) for an eastern literary market. As Hutchinson — who projects both these possibilities — again says, "Only the interest of the East, it seems, rescues [Wheeler] from oblivion . . . only on the East's terms does he have significance."[52] These interpretive jumps are encouraged by a text that cannot ever quite be neatly pinned down in a single reading. Twain appears both to encourage an allegorical response, in terms of regional identity, and to frustrate it, leaving his readers caught between a series of conflicting interpretations, just as he strands them between Wheeler's and the first narrator's entirely different voices and values.

We might say the same, too, about Twain's temptingly provocative references to past national political figures in the sketch. His use of the names of Andrew Jackson and Dan'l Webster for Smiley's bull-pup and his frog has received comprehensive critical comment, nowhere more so than in S. J. Krause's "The Art and Satire of Twain's 'Jumping Frog' Story." Here the ways in which "the bull-pup evokes the ironies of Jackson's reputation as a frontiersman, while the frog evokes the various flip-flops that characterised Webster's career" are traced in some detail.[53] Broadly speaking, Krause develops his reading along lines of East-West regional and historical difference, whereas Kenneth S. Lynn shifts the parameters to those of North, South, and West. Thus Krause says that in "the pairing of the two animals, we get a western name [Jackson] pitted against an eastern one [Webster], a frontier democrat (supposedly) and National Republican against a Whig and spokesman for eastern capital." He argues, not altogether convincingly, that in his sketch Twain modifies both "eastern and western attitudes" to suggest an "ideal [which] . . . seems to require a blending of the Whiggish paragon of the self-made man with the realization of it achieved by an Andrew Jackson in the unfettered conditions of the frontier."[54] Lynn, however, interprets the use of the names differently, contextualizing them with reference to the recently ended Civil War. He sees the comic reference to the two (Republican and Whig) politicians as "not playing political favorites in the old way at all, but . . . in fact saying a plague on both houses of a tragic era." Thus, "Simon Wheeler's tall tale does not take sides on past history, it rejects the past altogether, and turns toward the West and the future. . . . Catching the upturn of the national mood at the close of the Civil War, the 'Jumping Frog' was an instantaneous success."[55]

But there are other ways of interpreting Twain's use of these names. Lynn may be correct in identifying the use of the two names with changes in the national political culture and a rejection of the past. The collapse and death of the bull-pup (Jackson) and the immobilization of the frog (Webster) certainly fit such a reading. Webster was a man who dominated national politics in the first half of the century: in Henry James's words he "filled the sky of public life from pole to pole."[56] But his association with northeastern manufacturing interests, the part he had played in the 1850 Compromise (which failed to prohibit the spread of slavery to the West), and his death in 1852 may well have meant that, to Twain and his audience, he symbolized a now-irrelevant political tradition. And Neil Schmitz refers to the postbellum demise of Jacksonian values — "the Jacksonian style" and the "credit" and "confidence" on which it was based — in his discussion of Twain's first novel, *The Gilded Age* (1873).[57] This may provide a prompt for seeing the use of Jackson's name in Twain's earlier sketch in a similar light. That part of Lynn's reading which speaks of a postbellum historical turn toward the West is problematic to say the least, for Jackson was always closely associated with the West (with a "Young America and Manifest Destiny . . . bright with purpose").[58]

What becomes clear in all this is just how tentative any such reading must be. In giving his readers the names of the two politicians, Twain undoubtedly has fun at their expense. The association of Jackson with a bull-pup and Webster (the distinguished lawyer and orator) with the weighted-down frog works well in terms of a straightforward anthropo-morphic joke. At any deeper level, Twain, in his use of the two names, tempts, but only to frustrate, the making of any single and convincing allegorical reading. That Krause and Lynn read the story both in terms of North-South and East-West coordinates suggests a denial of "definitive interpretive choice" that operates at every level of this very tricksy story. It may be that this is what gave "The Jumping Frog" part of its undoubtedly wide audience appeal. The very fact that Twain provokes a regional or political reading of his story but leaves his final meanings opaque may have given the story a sense of national significance while denying any clear single sectional or political identification. Henry B. Wonham claims that what Twain affirmed in his writing "was an unending process of dialogue and interpretation, of performance and response."[59] That is exactly what we see occurring in "The Jumping Frog." And if Twain was later to go on to allegorize his frog as life (my epigraph), then the inter-pretation of life, as he saw it, was and remained a very indeterminate business indeed.

3
Sketches, New and Old

"Jim, he b'iled his baby, and he took the old 'oman's skelp. Cuss'd if *I* want any breakfast!"
And he laid his lingering potato reverently down, and he and his friend departed from the restaurant empty but satisfied.
— "My Bloody Massacre"

. . . that frequently neglected treasure trove *Sketches New and Old.*
— Clark Griffith, *Achilles and the Tortoise: Mark Twain's Fictions*

Robert Hirst describes *Sketches, New and Old* (1875) as "Mark Twain's most ambitious, most thoroughly sifted, and most fully revised collection of his apprentice work. It was also his final one."[1] As this suggests, the book can be seen as a benchmark in Twain's literary career. It provides a selection of his best work to this point and illustrates, in both its variety and its general comic exuberance, exactly the qualities that made the author such an enormous success. At the same time, the book stands as a culmination. It marks a general turn on Twain's part from the very short sketch to a rather fuller, and more artistically developed, use of short forms. His delight in the ludicrous, too, would be increasingly modified by other competing (and more serious) elements in his work. If such transitions (and tensions) are already present here, they would become ever more apparent as Twain continued writing.

All Twain's earliest work was short and aimed at newspaper or journal publication. Before 1871, he had already written for the Virginia City *Territorial Enterprise,* the San Francisco *Dramatic Chronicle* and *Alta California,* the Sacramento *Union,* the New York *Tribune* and *Herald,* the Buffalo *Express,* and the New York *Galaxy,* among others.[2] By 1875, however, Twain had turned to the extended literary genres of travel narrative and novel. With *Sketches, New and Old*, he was to put the brief journalistic sketches written during his early literary life more or less behind him.

Sherwood Cummings talks of the sixty-three pieces in the book as taking us through "what might be called Mark Twain's alternate writing career" (AF, 1). He is referring here to the insight they give us into Twain during the thirteen-year span of their composition (1863–75). We should not, however, make too much of the contrast between the sketches and what Cummings calls the "mainstream career": *The Innocents Abroad* (1869), *Roughing It* (1872), *The Gilded Age* (1874), and "Old Times on the Mississippi" (1875). Any boundary between independent sketches and sustained long work tended for Twain to be permeable. Thus some of the former were reworked and republished in *Roughing It*.[3] And when Twain wrote his early full-length travel narratives, he was fully aware of the debt they owed to his skill and ease with short journalistic forms. As he told Dan De Quille:

the winning card is to nail a man's interest with *Chapter 1*, & never let up on him for an instant. . . . That can't be done with detached sketches; but I'll show you how to make a man read every one of those sketches, under the stupid impression that they are mere accidental incidents that have dropped in on you unawares in the course of the *narrative*.[4]

But certainly, by the time he published *Sketches, New and Old*, Twain's energies were no longer focused on the production and publication of short pieces. His career — never single-faceted — had moved on considerably. He was now married (on 2 February 1870) to Olivia Langdon. He had gained an international reputation as the author of "a phenomenal best seller," *The Innocents Abroad*.[5] By August 1869 he was writing to Elisha Bliss that he had more "irons . . . in the fire (marriage, editing a newspaper [the Buffalo *Express*], and lecturing,)" than he could easily cope with: "it was most too many, for the subscriber" (MTLP, 27). In the year that *Sketches, New and Old* was being prepared, he also had his hands full with other projects, of which two were particularly noteworthy. He was writing the series of seven articles, "Old Times on the Mississippi," which would appear in the *Atlantic* magazine (edited by his friend William Dean Howells) from January to August 1875. He was also working on *The Adventures of Tom Sawyer* [1876] which he had been writing on and off since 1873 but finished in that same summer of 1875 (see MTHL1, 91). Domestically, too, life was full, with the new child, Clara (born 8 June 1874).

Moreover, by this stage in his career, Twain was busy rejecting more of the sketches he had produced in earlier years. Robert Hirst describes how, as he revised the 1873 collection *The Choice Humorous Works of Mark Twain* (of which more later), he deleted a number of pieces, writing comments like "literary vomit" (against "Origin of Illustrious Men") and "puling imbecility" ("Earthquake Almanac") as he did so (ETS1, 604–5). But he was still concerned enough over his short writings to be accumulating "more or less deliberate[ly]" those that were "not readily adapted to a longer narrative" for separate publication. And *Sketches, New and Old*, when it appeared, was given an "official" status not accorded the other short works published before this date: "It stood, in the author's lifetime, as the only authorized and widely available edition of sketches written before the author was forty years old." It contained a significant amount of new material (mostly written between 1872 and early 1875) never collected in book form before.[6] It constituted a sifting and sorting of his short work to that point in his career—though even at the time Twain would seem to regret that the pruning process had not been still more severe: "I think [my volume of *Sketches*] is an exceedingly handsome book. I destroyed a mass of sketches, & now heartily wish I had destroyed some more of them—but it is too late to grieve now" (MTHL1, 99). This, then, is an important collection in all sorts of ways.

To suggest that *Sketches, New and Old* follows directly from the *Jumping Frog* in the sequence of Twain's collections of short works is inaccurate. But the move (almost) straight to this book can be justified in a number of ways. Twain himself endorsed the importance of this particular text, both in the work he did on it and the official status he gave it. The book contained many, though by no means all, of the sketches published by Twain in the intervening period. Finally, and most important, this was the first substantial book of sketches since the *Jumping Frog* that Twain had published in America and for his native audience.

The story of Twain's short works and their publication, between the *Jumping Frog* and *Sketches, New and Old*, is a complicated one and must be repeated in its bare outlines to give a proper knowledge of the latter's history. But I necessarily depend, as in the first chapter, on the skillful literary detective work of Robert H. Hirst and his "Textual Introduction" to *Early Tales and Sketches, Volume 1*. Those who wish to find out more can read that essay. For those who are satisfied with a précis, then that is what follows, with full acknowledgments to my source and apologies for any oversimplifications. Both the books and pamphlets of sketches published by Twain in this period are selectively listed, with the relevant dates of publication and brief explanatory commentary.

1867–72. Four editions of *The Celebrated Jumping Frog* were issued in England, initially in pirated versions, by George Routledge (3) and by John Camden Hotten (1).[7] The 1870 (second) Routledge edition also included "Cannibalism in the Cars" as a "New Copyright Chapter" (ETS1,

552)[8] as Routledge moved toward becoming, if on a temporary basis only, Twain's authorized British publisher. The 1872 Routledge edition further included the two main pieces from the 1871 pamphlet below.

1871. Mark Twain's (Burlesque) Autobiography and First Romance. A fifty-page booklet produced by Sheldon and Company (publishers of the New York *Galaxy*). Hirst calls this "an experimental interlude in the evolution of Mark Twain's plans to issue an American edition of his sketches" (561). Twain signed a contract with Elisha Bliss of the American Publishing Company—publisher of *The Innocents Abroad*—for such a collection of sketches, probably early in January 1871. He did considerable planning and preparatory work, but Bliss temporarily reined in the project for the effect it would have on the sales of Twain's other books (571–86).[9]

The "Burlesque Autobiography" pamphlet included the title sketch (a new work), the revised "An Awful—Terrible Medieval Romance," and cartoons and captions ("The House That Jack Built") based on the Erie Railroad scandal. Hirst calls the pamphlet, and particularly its relatively high price, "an instructive mistake" for Twain, who was nonetheless fascinated "by the prospect of fast, easy money" (560–61) from such schemes.

1871. Eye Openers and *Screamers* (for full titles see Hirst, 586). These were both Hotten British piracies, "small volumes" (586), but including material, some of it recent, taken from the New York *Galaxy* (1870–71), the Buffalo *Express*, and like sources. *Screamers* contained six sketches attributed to Twain but written by "Carl Byng" (taken by Hotten for a Twain pseudonym). Twain was considerably irritated by this mistake.

1872. A Curious Dream; and Other Sketches and *Mark Twain's Sketches.* Both authorized British editions with Routledge, initially planned as one larger volume. Twain played a significant part in the preparation of these books. Extraordinarily, though, he used *Eye Openers* and *Screamers* (along with many of the editorial revisions Hotten had made, and the books' typographical errors) as he prepared *Mark Twain's Sketches.* Thus he was effectively "pirating his own pirate" (593).

Mark Twain's Sketches was composed of much of the Hotten material, but with many of the sketches revised; the 1870 Routledge edition of *Jumping Frog*, with revisions and twelve of its twenty-eight sketches removed; and fifteen sketches, most from the *Galaxy* and the Buffalo *Express*, not previously published in England. Most of this new material probably came from the edition of Sketches he had previously been preparing for Bliss (see above: the January 1871 contract). This was a bulky volume of some 360 pages, with sixty-six sketches written between 1863 and 1871. *A Curious Dream*, a much slimmer book, just contained the fifteen new sketches. These latter, then, appeared in both books.

1873–74. The Choice Humorous Works of Mark Twain. In 1873, Hotten published this "immense volume" (601) consisting of a biographical sketch, the whole of *Innocents Abroad*, and 107 sketches. Mainly these were drawn from the volumes of short works he had previously published, but seven of the new sketches from the 1872 Routledge books were also included. This collection became the basis, following Hotten's death (also in 1873), for a reissue by Chatto & Windus in the following year. This 1874 edition was, however, revised and corrected by Twain himself, following negotiations first with Hotten and then with Chatto.[10] Hirst details the cuts (seventeen sketches) and revisions Twain made, which sometimes duplicated "with uncanny precision" (605) those made for the Routledge *Mark Twain's Sketches*. He describes the "extraordinary situation" that resulted from the use and reuse of largely the same material by the two English publishing firms. Thus, for instance, many of the versions of the sketches that now appeared "had been heavily edited by Webb or Hotten, as well as by the author himself" (607).

1874. Mark Twain's Sketches. Number One. Authorised American Edition. In early 1873, plans were still on hold for Bliss to produce an American volume of sketches. For Twain now was hard at work, with Charles Dudley Warner, on *The Gilded Age* (1874). But Twain again got interested in what Hirst calls "his old flame, the project of a cheap pamphlet of sketches" (609) and wrote to Bliss (on 7 July 1873) about producing "*a good fat 25 cent pamphlet*" (MTLP, 79). This plan went through a number of permutations, but the pamphlet was published by the American News Company in the late spring/early summer of 1874. Including "The Jumping Frog" and nine other items from *Mark Twain's Sketches*, it also contained three new pieces, "A Memorable Midnight Experience," "Rogers," and "Property in Opulent London," written in 1872 or 1873 and taken from Twain's projected but abandoned book about England. If this cheap pamphlet was seen by Twain as potentially the first in a successful series (as its title would suggest), it seems not to have made much money, and the unsold copies ended up being sold in 1877 to a Life Insurance Company for advertising purposes. All the sketches, bar one, were used in the next year's *Sketches, New and Old*.

1875. Sketches, New and Old. Despite the "authorized" status of this text, and in line with what we have previously seen of Twain's short work, the final version of the sketches in this volume had been through a number of reprintings, authorial changes, and unauthorized editorial "improvements." The bulk of the printer's copy for the book, indeed, was taken straight from *Mark Twain's Sketches* and the 1874 version of *The Choice Humorous Works of Mark Twain*, with the various editing and tampering to which they had previously been subject (ETS1, 607).

Despite all this, it is difficult to entirely join Hirst in dismissing these versions of Twain's texts as "completely corrupted by the hands of Charles Henry Webb, John Camden Hotten, and even Elisha Bliss" (656). In their editions of the *Early Tales and Sketches*, Branch and Hirst do (admirably and invaluably) "recover [Twain's sketches] . . . in their original form" (655).[11] But, to pursue my earlier argument, most of Twain's contemporary audience read his texts in one of their succeeding versions. And Twain himself, for whatever reasons, was happy to continue tinkering with his sketches and stories and often to accept the tinkering of others when it met his own authorial ends. Thus Hirst himself refers to the kind of "compulsive revision" (620) that the putting together of a book of sketches encouraged in him.

What, too, is noticeable over this whole period is "an overall pattern of cleansing" (613) of the sketches. Generally, the earlier the sketches the more work they required on Twain's part as he tidied them up, deleting slang and extreme or vulgar language, for a wider (and presumably more respectable) audience. Previously, as he revised the 1874 *Choice Humorous Works of Mark Twain*, the author "furthered Hotten's attempts to modify his strong or vulgar language for more fastidious audiences" (606).[12] So now a similar process took place: "perdition" became "destruction," and "the phrase 'it had soured on my stomach' was too vivid, and so it was removed" (636–37).

It is true that Twain could show an 'exasperating indifference' (655) to the books made up from his sketches and short writings. It is also true that many of the errata and unauthorized changes introduced over these years could not now be effectively corrected, given that Twain did not return to the original version of his sketches as he made his revisions. But *Sketches, New and Old* is an important collection, and it is difficult to rule it out of critical court on the grounds of authenticity, particularly since Twain showed a real willingness to take an active (if erratic) part in the process of reworking these pieces for publication. And Hirst's own words encourage taking this sequence of published volumes of sketches (including *Sketches, New and Old*) as an index to Twain's artistic development, even while recognizing the problems involved. For he writes:

[Twain] did hold to a remarkably steady purpose throughout nine years of revision and republication [to 1875]. He consistently tried to sift his material for

sketches "worth republishing," and he was quite merciless in ruling some material "forever . . . out of any book." . . . [D]own through his final destruction of a
"mass of sketches" for [*Sketches, New and Old*], Mark Twain reprinted only what he
thought would endure, rejected what he came to regard as too topical or too
juvenile, and revised what he did reprint to meet the standards of his eastern and
eventually his English audiences. (655)[13]

I now briefly turn to the content of *Sketches, New and Old*, and Twain's
part, as Hirst details it, in the composition and revision of the volume.
Twain first prepared a version of the book for James R. Osgood, the Boston publisher, as he looked to move away from Elisha Bliss and the cheap
production methods of the subscription book business.[14] He seems at this
stage, however, to have forgotten, or ignored, the contract he had signed
(in 1871) with Bliss for such a book. The matter was sorted out, inevitably
in Bliss's favor, and Twain then seems to have done further preparatory
work for the volume. His initial handwritten list of contents for the proposed collection (almost certainly prepared for Osgood) is reproduced
in Hirst (ETS1, 624–32).

Hirst describes, in some detail, the "complex mingling of authorial
and non-authorial choices, both in the selections [finally] chosen and in
the revisions" made to the sketches (644–45).[15] Twain had carefully orga-
nized his initial list of contents to balance older and newer, shorter and
longer, stronger and weaker material (641). But the number of sketches
to be used in the book was cut down (from eighty-one to sixty-four), with
Bliss making "immediate decisions about which of the listed sketches to
set in type, and in what order . . . sometimes independently, sometimes in
cooperation with the author" (642). As he prepared the new book, Twain
sifted through, and selectively revised, older pieces from *Mark Twain's
Sketches*, the 1874 *Choice Humorous Works*, and *Mark Twain's Sketches. Number One*. But the compositors of *Sketches, New and Old* evidently had no
access to the marked copy of the latter pamphlet, and thus set its textual
material from unrevised printings elsewhere. As a result of some carelessness in Bliss's instructions, they also were sometimes left to choose between different versions of a text that appeared in both *Mark Twain's
Sketches* and the *Humorous Works*, where Twain himself had clearly signaled which one should be used.[16]

In addition to the selection and revision of material from earlier collections, Twain had gathered fifteen "new" (unpublished or uncollected)
items, mostly written between 1872 and 1875 (640). These, not least
because of their comparative length, were considerably to influence the
collection's overall tone and shape. He read proofs for the book too,
though not in a sustained or systematic way. One short sketch that he had
not written, "From 'Hospital Days,' " crept in as a result of a mistake on
Bliss's part as he looked to fill up empty space.[17] Despite all such editorial

intrusions and adjustments, however, Twain's part in the making and shaping of *Sketches, New and Old* was still a significant one.

Any commentary on the short writings produced throughout Twain's career has necessarily to be selective. This is particularly true in the case of *Sketches, New and Old*, which is exceptional both in its number of pieces and its range. The book contains speeches, short stories, poems, first- and third-person narratives, hoaxes, satires, burlesques, autobiographical and biographical sketches, fables, travelogues, sociopolitical critiques, and much more besides. In length, these vary between the half-page squib such as "Johnny Greer" — included, perhaps surprisingly, in Twain's original list of contents for the proposed collection — and his recently written twenty-two-page story "Some Learned Fables, for Good Old Boys and Girls."[18] Indeed, this move from the brief squib to the longer sketch or short story indicates a significant change in Twain's writing practice, presumably motivated by his move away from newspaper work and increasingly toward journal and book publication.

The very range and variety of the sixty-three sketches (omitting "From 'Hospital Days'") in the book can be seen as a positive attribute. In *Persona and Humor in Mark Twain's Early Writings* (1995), Don Florence places great stress on the "kaleidoscopic" quality of Twain's early work and the "play of language and attitudes" to be found there.[19] Florence stresses the fluidity and playful relativism, the resistance to stable meanings and fixed patterns, of this early humor and "the hidden formlessness of life" thus revealed (that "there are no sure standards of knowledge by which to determine what is false . . . and what is true").[20] This gives only half of a more complicated story.[21] When Howells reviewed *Sketches, New and Old*, he wrote of a "growing seriousness of meaning in [its] apparently unmoralized drolling."[22] I would argue that such seriousness had been part of Twain's artistic armory from the first. Nonetheless, Howells does identify here a tension, even a sense of paradox (depending on how one reads that "in"), that complicates any one-dimensional reading of this book. Indeed, his words resonate in their application to Twain's writing career as a whole.

Much of my commentary on *Sketches, New and Old* necessarily develops and complements my discussion of the *Jumping Frog* collection. The later book, though, has greater range and variety and is cumulative: it repeats some material from the earlier text but gives a fuller and more rounded representation of the early Twain. More particularly, it introduces a substantial amount of recently written material. These factors, then, lead me to embroider and extend that earlier reading at the present point.

Again, the use of the protean-first person voice of "Mark Twain" is the most crucial element in Twain's early work. As in his earlier book, Twain takes on, and lays aside, a whole series of identities in *Sketches, New and Old*. Florence sees this as one of the methods Twain used in "exploring different ways of looking at the world and playing with possible forms of self-expression." Exploring the textual relationship between the author (Mark Twain, the "literary personality that is both in and behind a given work") and his fictional persona (the "Mark Twain" who appears "as narrator and character" within it), he rightly points out the overlapping quality of these categories.[23] Sometimes author and narrator appear identical, thus "The 'Jumping Frog.' In English. Then in French" starts: "My attention has just been called to an article . . . in a French magazine. . . . I am one of these humorists Americans dissected" (28–29).[24] At others, there is a clear gap between the two. So in "The Facts Concerning the Recent Resignation," the protagonist/narrator "Mark Twain," "clerk of the Senate Committee on Conchology," is clearly a fictional version of the authorial subject. A comic fool, he naively assumes his own self-importance in turning up, for instance, to attend a cabinet meeting. He constantly proffers his ill-conceived opinions, thus advising the secretary of war on the Indian problem: "Sir . . . the time has come when blood-curdling cruelty has become necessary. Inflict soap and a spelling-book on every Indian that ravages the Plains, and let them die!" (265).

Twain's comedy often depends on such an awareness of the disjunction between author and narrator/character. And as this narrator speaks and acts, the reader's attention is also drawn to the veiled authorial stance: in this case, on existing U.S. policy decisions concerning Indian affairs.[25] "Mark Twain" goes on in this sketch to engage sympathetically with the hard lot of government clerks: "there are clerks that have no clerkships, and are waiting, and waiting . . . for a vacancy—waiting patiently for a chance to help their country out—and while they are waiting, they only get barely 2000 dollars a year for it" (269–70). Again, a productive discord exists between this (naive) narrative voice and the satiric critique of the inefficiency of those on the federal payroll implied by the author. In this example, though, the authorial stance is more clearly evident.

Multiple versions of "Mark Twain" are projected in this book: the successful but boastfully ignorant author of "A Mysterious Visit," the aspiring political candidate of "Running for Governor," the accomplished chicken thief and thus "poultry-raising" expert (81) of "To Raise Poultry."[26] These personae can overlap. So the observer of "John Chinaman in New York" shares a naive romantic racialism with the vacationist of "Niagara," who tells how "I came upon a gentle daughter of the aborigines. . . . I hesitated a moment and then addressed her: 'Is the heart of the forest maiden heavy? Is the Laughing Tadpole lonely? Does she mourn over the extinguished council-fires of her race?' " (68–69).[27] But more often it is the shifts and changes of persona that we notice: changes that can occur within sketches as well as between them. Conventional notions of the unified subject are disturbed in such moves. To focus too strongly on these various versions of "Mark Twain" may, however, be to underplay the authorial figure who stands behind all the sketches, and figures transparently in some of them, speaking what we can take to be his own thoughts and feelings. I return to this subject at a later point.

The multiple use of the "Mark Twain" persona in *Sketches, New and Old* does, however, create a sense of fluid identity. And the book's many generic shifts and crossovers endorse such a sense of playful instability. Twain's sketches are often difficult to categorise. He constantly throws his reader off balance as s/he attempts to determine genre and meaning. "The Siamese Twins" is a comic narrative about the impossibility of categorization: of distinguishing individuality from joint identity, one twin from the two.[28] Generically, too, the piece evades firm definitional boundaries. What starts off as an intimate biographical memoir of the real Siamese twins, Chang and Eng, soon turns to burlesque, as the sentimental narrative of true and unswerving friendship ("bosom companionship") is ridiculed: "The Siamese Twins . . . have clung to each other with singular fidelity throughout a long and eventful life. Even as children they were inseparable companions" (208). The play between the metaphoric and the literal here helps prepare for the mind-jolting comic move that follows: "The Twins always go to bed at the same time; but Chang usually gets up about an hour before His brother" (209).

This comic play, however, contains within it a number of concerns that Twain would take very seriously elsewhere. Indeed, this relation between a playful comedy and such "seriousness" becomes an ongoing motif of my book. Here, for instance, after noting that "it is believed that [the Twins] have never failed to . . . sleep together on any night since they were born," the narrator comments, "How surely do the habits of a lifetime become second-nature to us!" (209). This is comic pseudo-philosophizing but nonetheless the allusion to the problematic relation between the natural self and a "second-nature" conditioned by environment and by training does remind us of the obsessive concern over that subject in so much of Twain's work: "The Facts Concerning the Recent Carnival of Crime in Connecticut" (1876), *Huckleberry Finn* (1885) and *Pudd'nhead Wilson* (1894) are only the most obvious examples. Similarly, what emerge in other texts as deep anxieties about interconnected questions of identity, agency, social stability, and the law are also present here, but in (almost entirely) humorous form.

For Twain, the comic properties of Siamese twinship were automatically linked to speculation about identity and agency. Here that concern is apparent throughout: Chang and Eng's taking of "each other prisoners" in the Civil War, for example, raising the "vexed question . . . [of] which one was properly the captor, and which the captive" (209). The issue of agency—how one can decide who acted first—gets inevitably and irretrievably confused here with that of the relative identities of captor and prisoner.[29]

We are soon back, however, to more straightforward comic territory as Twain takes some delight in describing the problems that romance raises in the brothers' lives. Talking of their love affairs and marriages, he parodies the language of sentimental piety while nonetheless raising the transgressive specter of sexual scandal in his description of the two couples "all liv[ing] together, night and day, in an exceeding sociability which is touching and beautiful to behold" (211). And the story reaches its illogical and anticlimactic end with the type of absurd non sequitur of which Twain was particularly fond: "Having forgotten to mention it sooner, I will remark in conclusion, that the ages of the Siamese Twins are respectively fifty-one and fifty-three years" (212).

Twain twists and turns us in a number of comic and generic directions here. We are metaphorically left, with that ending, up in the air in any attempt to impose a single coherent meaning to, or intention behind, a sketch that mocks the attempts at serious "interpretation." Indeed, in many of these sketches, and in the movement between them, we struggle to pin Twain down. Many things add to this effect: the book's generic variety; its shifts between the realistic and the surreal or absurd; the use of multiple and unreliable narrative voices; the occasional disruption of the very mechanics of narrative; the stress on language, its differences and its confusions; and an overall thematic focus on untrustworthiness, indecipherability, and relativistic uncertainty.

Twain's moves between the fact and fiction borderline further illustrate the type of indeterminacy produced on the book's reader. Other formal and thematic effects he uses (as detailed above) suggest a landscape of interpretive confusion: the creation of what Florence calls "an epistemological void."[30] But to read these sketches only by way of their sense of fluidity and instability is one-sided, for as I show—following Howells—a rather different and more firmly grounded literary consciousness is also at work here. In the chapter that then follows, I give a more extended reading of two of the most important narratives in this collection, "A True Story. Repeated Word for Word as I Heard It" and "Some Learned Fables, for Good Old Boys and Girls," once more to indicate and examine such a contrast (and to reveal, in the latter case, its somewhat unstable quality).

As Twain projects his multiple versions of the self in this early work, so he shifts back and forth between fact and fiction to sometimes disconcerting effect.[31] Thus the naive author of "A Mysterious Visit," clearly a projected fictional persona, is also (autobiographically) a successful lecturer and the writer of *The Innocents Abroad* (318). Similarly, the fictional "Experience of the McWilliamses with Membranous Croup," with its gentle satire of domestic relations, is clearly modeled on the factual details of Twain's own domestic life.[32] Such category confusions are introduced in the opening sketch, "My Watch. An Instructive Little Tale." This starts as an apparently biographical and nonfictional account of the first-person narrator/author — identified as "Mark Twain" by the accompanying illustrations — and his problems with "his beautiful new watch" (17).[33] It soon drifts into the fictional territory of the absurd, as Twain disrupts expectations of an appropriate fit between language and the reality it describes. The watch's mechanical faults are described in the comically inappropriate terms of human illness, with a hyperbolic twist then added: "My watch began to gain . . . faster and faster day by day. Within the week it sickened to a raging fever, and its pulse went up to a hundred and fifty in the shade" (18). The sketch draws to a close with comic violence as the narrator consults the last of several inept watchmakers, "a steamboat engineer of other days," to solve his problem. The latter responds, using a form of discourse that is equally incongruous. His nonsensical words are, in turn, met by the narrator/protagonist's even more inappropriate reaction — that is, as judged by any "realistic" or rational standard:

[The watchmaker] said –
"She makes too much steam — you want to hang the monkey-wrench on the safety-valve!"
I brained him on the spot, and had him buried at my own expense. (20)[34]

As we move from autobiographical realism (Twain and his watch) to the fiction of the absurd, we remain aware of the comic hyperbole involved, that an actual event quite possibly stands behind the exaggerated retelling. This is a typical Twain tactic with the boundary lines between truth and fiction, and between expected and excessive response, placed recurrently at issue. The reader is left, to a degree, ungrounded, caught between fact and fiction, author and projected persona, as this occurs.

Such moves between fiction and nonfiction, and the frequent taking of an indeterminate middle ground, occur throughout the book. "My Late Senatorial Secretaryship" is, for instance, loosely based on actual experience: the two-week stint Twain served in Washington in late 1867 as private secretary to Senator William J. Stewart of Nevada. Twain slightly distorts the factual base, using Senator James W. N**'s name to replace Stewart's in the sketch.[35] Other details, such as the allusion to a dispute over the "right to . . . water-lots" (150) in San Francisco, further lock the narrative to actual current events (see TSSE1, 1041). But we quickly move (again) to the comedy of exaggeration and non sequitur in the gap that opens up between the letters sent by the Senator's constituents and his secretary's increasingly insensitive, but highly inventive, replies. Thus to a request for "the establishment of a post-office at Baldwin's ranch," "Mark Twain" replies: "No, don't bother about a post-office in your camp . . . it would only be an ornamental folly. What you want is a nice jail, you know—a nice, substantial jail and a free school. . . . These will make you really . . . happy. I will move in the matter at once" (149). The imaginative energies that these letters reveal may say something about the author's feelings at that previous time while he was weighing the attractions and limitations of a political sinecure against the launching of a career as comic lecturer and/or writer. But it is clear that the autobiographical realism of the framing situation serves mainly as excuse and launching pad for the fictional play that Twain then enjoys. In such moves we see again something of the instability and playfulness that permeate this textual world.

Twain's interest in language and representation, and contrasting voice and language register, feature strongly in the *Jumping Frog* book. The same motifs recur in the 1875 collection. The instability and untrustworthiness of language and point of view serve as an immediate source of humor and as an underlying theme in a number of its sketches. As the move between world and word takes place, all kinds of confusion and breakdowns occur. One of the funniest sketches in this book,[36] "How I Edited an Agricultural Paper," sets "Mark Twain's" faulty knowledge of agricultural matters against the known reality shared by his immediate audience—the subscribers to his newspaper—and by the readers of the sketch. The comedy lies both in the gap between the responses of these two audiences and in the complete failure of the narrator's words to match the world he would describe. Instead, he inventively combines the names of vegetables, animals, and so on, their attributes and actions, to produce an effect of comic rupture as, for instance, one inappropriate word renders what would otherwise be a logical sentence dramatically askew: "Now, as the warm weather approaches, and the ganders begin to spawn" (235).

At one level, this sketch works quite simply. Verbal mismatches ("gander" and "spawn") produce immediate humor, with the narrator's linguistic/conceptual "mistakes" set against the shared norms of both sets of readers. As the full-time newspaper editor lists the narrator's ignorance, further humorous release occurs both in this category confusion and in the play between the irritability of the internal audience at that ignorance (and the form that irritability takes) and the appreciation of the readers of Twain's sketch for the comic effects produced. Thus the editor rails:

you talk of the moulting season for cows; and you recommend the domestication of the pole-cat on account of its playfulness and its excellence as a ratter! Your remark that clams will lie quiet if music be played to them was superfluous — entirely superfluous. Nothing disturbs clams. Clams *always* lie quiet. Clams care nothing whatever about music. (237)

There is, however, another level to the piece. The editor's (irrelevant) insistence on the superiority of his own knowledge of clams raises certain questions about who knows what (about clams) and how we can measure the accuracy of that knowledge. The allusion to the gap between the natural world that surrounds us and our (often feeble) attempts to make intellectual and verbal sense of it introduces a note of relativistic uncertainty to the comedy of the text. This is confirmed when the narrator speaks back, with a snorting riposte on the general ignorance of newspaper editors and reporters:

it is the first time I ever heard of a man's having to know anything in order to edit a newspaper. You turnip! Who write the dramatic critiques for the second-rate papers? Why, a parcel of promoted shoemakers and apprentice apothecaries, who know just as much about good acting as I do about good farming and no more. Who reviews the books? People who never wrote one. . . . Who criticise the Indian campaigns? Gentlemen who do not know a war-whoop from a wigwam. (238)

Despite that qualifying adjective ("second-rate") there is nonetheless a suggestion of a more general ungrounding of certainty here. For if the question "How do we know what we know?" is partly answered by reference to the authorities that we trust and the information that we read, the further question is then implicitly introduced: "How, then, do we know for sure that this is reliable knowledge?"

Such questions concerning the uncertainty and unreliability of knowledge and the relative nature of our views of the world we inhabit are consistently sounded in the collection. In "The Petrified Man" and "My Bloody Massacre," Twain self-reflexively returns to two of his early (1862 and 1863) Virginia City *Territorial Enterprise* hoaxes.[37] These sketches, perhaps significantly, follow immediately on from "How I Edited An Agricultural Paper," planned in that order by Twain himself (ETS1, 629). Rather than merely reusing these hoaxes, however, the author now comments on their earlier effect. He describes how convincing "the 'Petrified Man' squib" was, claiming that the "unfair pretence of truth" accompanying its "string of roaring absurdities" almost fooled even him, the author: "I was in some danger of believing my own fraud." He tells of

the give-away clues in the original narrative: the "suggestive position of
the petrified man's hands" (241) literally thumbing his nose at his audience. Despite this, he says, the story was both generally believed and
much reprinted, until his comic fabrication "swept the great globe and
culminated in sublime and unimpeached legitimacy in the august London *Lancet*" (242).[38] "My Bloody Massacre," too, tells how readers' interest in the "bloody details" (245) and "thrilling particulars" of Twain's
fabricated "gorgeous massacre" (246) prevented them from picking up
the clear signs of its fraudulence. His tale of the hay-man from Truckee
who reads the account with ever-widening eyes over his breakfast (see the
quote at the chapter's start) becomes a paradigm for the uncritical naivete of a larger readership:

I found out then, and never have forgotten since, that we never *read* the dull
explanatory surroundings of marvellously exciting things when we have no occasion to suppose that some irresponsible scribbler is trying to defraud us; we skip
all that, and hasten to revel in the blood-curdling particulars and be happy. (246)

A hoax blurs the dividing line between truth and falsehood.[39] Our
"culturally founded faith that ink and newsprint are the stuff of fact and
truth"[40] is betrayed both by the manipulations of an "irresponsible scribbler" (though Twain here undersells his serious intentions in writing
these sketches)[41] and by our own credulity as readers/believers. When
Twain tells how he as author was almost taken in by his own fictional
creation, he is clearly joking.[42] The joke, however, points in the same
direction as the hoax itself: toward the problematic status of "sure [stan-
dards of] reliable knowledge." The hoax raises the question of how we
find out what *is* true and on what we base this belief. Indeed, the original
"Petrified Man" sketch goes one step further, for the unreadable stone
figure thumbing its nose at its center suggests a difficulty in figuring out
what *anything* really means.[43] Imposture and the (im?)possibility of dis-
covering it is an ongoing area of inquiry and concern in all Twain's
writings. The hoax, and the burlesque, too,[44] temporarily unravel any
sense of a fixed and firm center, of firm and foundational knowledge
and truth.

A powerful sense of comic disorientation and relativism (focused
around issues of language, genre, and meaning) figures in this collection. In "The 'Jumping Frog.' In English. Then in French. Then Clawed
Back into a Civilised Language Once More by Patient, Unremunerated
Toil," Twain returns to his most famous early story to focus on language
diversity and its implications. Translating the published French version
of his sketch back into English, "Mark Twain" naively makes foreign
words and phrases subject to the straitjacket of exact and literal transposi-

tion of meaning. The controlling author creates considerable comic effect in so doing. Thus, "Why blame my cats if he don't weigh five pound!" (34) becomes in French "Le loup me croque, s'il ne pèse pas cinq livres" (38), and — on retranslation — "The wolf me bite if he no weigh not five pounds" (43). "I don't see no p'ints about that frog that's any better'n any other frog" (34) becomes, on similar retranslation: "Eh bien! I no saw not that that frog had nothing of better than each frog." The narrator then comments in a bracketed note: "If that isn't grammar gone to seed, then I count myself no judge. — M. T." (42). And of course, that is the comic point. "Mark Twain" *is* no judge of this alien language.[45] Exact and literal translation is an impossibility given the different structures of expression, syntax, metaphor, and thought which (always) operate when two languages engage with each other on intersecting planes. Twain's humor here, as in so many similar cases in his work, results from his narrator's denial of the relativization of discourse at the core of translation and his own (and the reader's) awareness of its inevitable presence.

The undermining of authoritative voice, stable subject position, and fixed form and meaning is then a common and repeated element of *Sketches, New and Old*. But there is also a clear countermovement to the sense of playful fluidity and multiplicity to be found here. For, remembering Howells's comment in his review of *Sketches* concerning the author's "growing seriousness of meaning," we can identify quite another element in evidence: a "serious" side to Twain that stands alongside his use of absurdist humor and comic extravagance. Where Florence tends to see mainly relativistic play in Twain's early work, I would identify a sense of paradox and tension that will, in various ways, influence the shape of his whole literary career.[46] Comic instability and a delight in the ludicrous lie in (an increasingly uneasy) conjunction with a set of (more sober) moral, social, and historical concerns. Something of this tension is at work even within Twain's earliest works.

Much of the success of this collection lies in its use of the flexible first-person persona, "Mark Twain," and the variation in voice consequently introduced. But, as we have seen, the figure and the values of the author himself are also recognizably present here. And this definable *authorial* identity and value scheme — the Mark Twain who stands behind, and sometimes speaks in, these short works — cannot be downplayed. While I would not underestimate the difficulties of separating out author from comic persona or of easily identifying the authorial stance, I nonetheless do see a clearly defined series of often compatible social and political stances adopted in some of these sketches.[47] Such activity cuts against and contradicts the relativistic play elsewhere.

Thus, to take a fairly unproblematic example, in "Disgraceful Persecution of a Boy," Twain critiques the mistreatment of the Chinese immigrant population in the West. The sketch, following the title's lead, works in an ironic mode, siding with a " 'well-dressed' boy, and a Sunday-school scholar" who has been arrested for "stoning Chinamen" (117). Twain shows that this act cannot be separated from a general social conditioning that allowed the Chinese "no rights that any man was bound to respect." He charts the double standards and inconsistent laws of that place and time, and thoroughly condemns the institutional racial abuse aimed at this particular section of the community. The biting quality of his words leaves little room for misinterpretation. One example will suffice:

It was in this way that the boy found out that the Legislature, being aware that the Constitution has made America an asylum for the poor and the oppressed of all nations, and that, therefore, the poor and oppressed who fly to our shelter must not be charged a disabling admission fee, made a law that every Chinman [sic], upon landing, must be *vaccinated* upon the wharf, and pay to the State's appointed officer *ten dollars* for the service, when there are plenty of doctors in San Francisco who would be glad enough to do it for him for fifty cents. (118–19)

Indeed, throughout this collection, Twain's authorial voice satirizes social hypocrisies and political corruption of various types. There may be elements of inconsistency here, but there can be no doubt of his serious intent. The book ends with such a passage, as the voice of the naive narrator and protagonist of "A Mysterious Visit" is informed by the more knowing and critical presence of the author. Advised by a wealthy acquaintance on the intricacies of tax avoidance, the narrator identifies widespread fraud and moral shabbiness among the supposedly most respectable of American citizenry:

This gentleman [his advisor] stands away up among the very best of the solid men of the city — the men of moral weight, of commercial integrity, of unimpeachable social spotlessness — and so I bowed to his example. I went down to the revenue office, and . . . stood up and swore to lie after lie, fraud after fraud . . . till . . . my self-respect [was] gone for ever and ever.
But what of it? It is nothing more than thousands of the richest . . . and most respected . . . men in America do every year. And so I don't care. I am not ashamed. I shall simply, for the present, talk little, and eschew fire-proof gloves, lest I fall into certain dreadful habits irrevocably. (320)

The voice that speaks here critically exposes such behavior and comically accepts its own complicity with it. We are aware that the narrative does not end accidentally: that the (silent) author structures the text to this specific satiric end and distances himself from the final insouciance of his narrative persona.[48] We get a clear reminder of Twain's Western soubriquet, "The Moralist of the Main," in such sketches.

On a number of occasions in this book, then, we can identify an authorial presence both addressing existing social problems and suggesting — in varying degrees of explicitness — his own attitude toward them. Critical observations about an American justice system and particularly its use of "an insanity plea that would have saved Cain" (180 –81) are made in "After-Dinner Speech" and the more substantial "A New Crime. Legislation Needed." And Twain's lifelong campaign for reform of the copyright law, to protect authorial interests more fully, motivates "Petition Concerning Copyright." He turns a sharply satiric eye on the difficulties of negotiating the bureaucratic machinery of American government and on the potential for fraudulent financial profit to be made there in the twinned sketches "The Facts in the Case of the Great Beef Contract" and "The Case of George Fisher."

In these cases, then, we can "recover" a satiric and moralistic authorial intent. In all Twain's sketches and stories, though, that same authorial presence stands behind the text. And one of the distinguishing features of his work, relating to his use of first-person personae, is just how often the authorial point of view is hidden from us or where any commentary on that point of view has to be extremely tentative. Thus the prior discussion of "The 'Jumping Frog.' In English. Then in French" focused on the author's awareness of linguistic relativity. This is a reasonable interpretation, one that accords both with other Twain writings and with the available contextual evidence. But if we take the sketch on its own self-sufficient terms, the questions necessarily hang unanswered of how we can know the authorial position for sure, and whether (and to what degree) the author shares any of his narrator's annoyance for the effect the process of translation has on his original sketch and his impatience for the linguistic conventions of others. Similarly, in "The Experience of the McWilliamses with Membranous Croup" (though here the Twain persona is not used) we might ask how much anxiety about actual family illness lies behind the story. We remember that on 2 June 1872 — some two and a half years prior to the events alluded to in the fiction — Twain and Olivia's first child, Langdon, had died of what seemed to start as a cold but then became diphtheria.[49] Seen in this light, the story then may be read as symptomatic of the author's tendency to respond to emotional pain and stress with expressions of comic nonsense.[50] We might also ask to what extent we can read the story as a gentle satire of Twain's own home life, with its henpecked and domestically inept husband submitting in a mildly ironic way to the wishes and whims of an overanxious and irrational wife. Or whether something more aggressive is implied in the stress on the wife's dismissive authority over her husband ("She *shall* chew it, too. So there, now!" 86) and the violent and destructive nature of his actions (kicking a chair, burning the rug) when he meets with domestic mishaps. It is, of course, possible to identify the authorial figure with all these positions. My point remains the frequent difficulty—but particularly in the sketches that feature the "Mark Twain" persona—of conclusively identifying authorial intentions and values.

These sketches and stories in *Sketches, New and Old*, then, pull in a number of directions. Sometimes an authorial value scheme can be convincingly discovered. At others it remains ambiguous, opaque, or just plain irrelevant. Some sketches build on a playful relativity and a strong awareness of the ludicrous. In others, a more serious and moralistic intent can be discovered. Sometimes we can place a sketch or story on one or the other side of this divide, but sometimes both elements will be contained within the fabric of a single work. And when the latter is the case, some element of internal strain and tension is always likely to show. The *Hartford Times* review summed up *Sketches, New and Old* with the words: "Here we have fun alive" (CR, 149). If this is a partial reading of a collection of considerable range and variety, it does suggest that the present critical disregard of the book is unfortunate, for it represents some of the very best of Twain's early short work.

4

"A True Story" and "Some Learned Fables, for Good Old Boys and Girls"

"Oh, no, Misto C——, *I* hain't had no trouble. An' no *joy!*"

— "A True Story. Repeated Word for Word As I Heard It"

Erect, and in a row, were a sort of rigid great figures . . . belonging to the long extinct species of reptile called MAN, described in our ancient records. . . . When it was stirred with happiness, it leaked water from its eyes; and when it suffered or was sad, it manifested it with a horrible hellish cackling clamor that was exceedingly dreadful to hear and made one long that it might rend itself and perish, and so end its troubles. Two Mans being together, they uttered noises at each other like to this: "Haw-haw-haw — dam good, dam good," together with other sounds of more or less likeness to these, wherefore ye poets conceived that they talked, but poets be always ready to catch at any frantic folly, God he knows.

— "Some Learned Fables, for Good Old Boys and Girls"

I

Sketches, New and Old illustrates, particularly in its most recently written pieces, signs of the changes and developments that were taking place in Twain's work. Thus Sherwood Cummings, in his afterword to the Oxford edition comments on four of the newest items in the book: "we can . . . observe a reaching out, a willingness to experiment, and a dramatic breakthrough" (12).[1] Twain shows an increasing tendency to modify and to discard the use of the "Mark Twain" persona — adopted initially as a journalistic device. He tries out other voices and extends the formal limits of his short works. In "The Jumping Frog" story, Twain had shown an early skill in ventriloquism in the interplay between the first-person voices of "Mark Twain" and Simon Wheeler. "The Undertaker's Chat" (written in 1870) again uses the Twain persona but to more minimal effect.[2] And as that persona starts to drop away, so signs can be seen of an important shift in the author's artistic directions.

"The Undertaker's Chat" tells of the title figure's appreciation of the "accommodating" nature of one of his recently deceased clients. It commences: " 'Now, that corpse,' said the undertaker, patting the folded hands of deceased approvingly, 'was a brick' " (247). The interjection by the narrator given here is the only interruption to the undertaker's own first-person flow of speech until the last brief paragraph of the sketch, when we return once more to his framing voice. We can read this sketch then — together with "A True Story" — as preliminary moves toward *Huckleberry Finn* and its reliance on a first-person vernacular voice completely to carry an extended narrative. Sherwood Cummings notes the connection in saying that the main voice in "The Undertaker's Chat" "speaks in a vernacular uncannily like Huck's" (11). Indeed, both Huck's words and his pragmatic sensibility are foreshadowed in such passages as this: "Corpse said never mind, shake him up some kind of box he could stretch out in comfortable, *he* warn't particular 'bout the general style of it. Said he went more on room than style, any way in a last final container" (247).[3] Twain also makes extensive use of a vernacular voice in "A True Story. Repeated Word for Word as I Heard It." And this latter narrative has further connections with Twain's best-known book. For as Neil Schmitz notes, "All [the] discourse shifting and story breaching in *Huckleberry Finn* is remarkably foretold in 'A True Story,' which warns us about reading Jim as Uncle Remus, seeing in him what Misto C [first] sees in Aunt Rachel."[4]

Twain first sent "A True Story," somewhat tentatively, to Howells for consideration for the *Atlantic Monthly*. The relevant section of his letter reads: "I enclose . . . a 'True Story' which has no humor in it. You can pay as lightly as you choose for that, if you want it, for it is rather out of my line. I have not altered the old colored woman's story except to begin it at the beginning, instead of the middle, as she did — & . . . traveled both ways." Howells, though, responded enthusiastically to the piece: "I've kept the True Story which I think extremely good and touching with the best and reallest kind of black talk in it. . . . This little story delights me more and more." He later remembered paying Twain "twenty dollars a page" for the story, "a rate unexampled in our [the *Atlantic's*] modest history," in "the highest recognition of his writing as literature."[5] Howells here appears to privilege the social and moral seriousness of "A True Story" over the normal comic run of Twain's writings.[6] A similar privileging occurs in his review of *Sketches, New and Old* where he ends by focusing on this piece:

by far the most perfect piece of work in the book is "A True Story." . . . It is simply the story an old black cook tells of how her children were all sold away from her, and how after twenty years she found her youngest boy again. . . . Evidently the critical mind feared a lurking joke. Not above two or three notices . . . recognized [it] for what it was, namely, a study of character as true as life itself, strong, tender, and most movingly pathetic in its perfect fidelity to the tragic fact. . . . The rugged truth of the sketch leaves all other stories of slave life infinitely far behind, and reveals a gift in the author for the simple dramatic report of reality which we have seen equaled in no other American writer. (CR, 152)

There are several things worth noting here. First is the stress on the representational transparency of the narrative — "simply," "true as life itself," "perfect fidelity to . . . fact," and "simple . . . report of reality." For Howells, "literature" and "authenticity" become one and the same. There is also an awareness here of one of Twain's most pressing artistic anxieties: how to reconcile his status as a humorist with his serious artistic intentions. Twain's audience (of critics) knew Twain's past work (and not, like Howells, his present aims), and was consequently primed for the put-on, the hidden joke. This meant that even "rugged truth" could be judged suspiciously, as possibly merely a comic trick. Twain found partial ways of dealing with this problem as he varied forms, voice, tone, and humorous mode. But it would never be entirely resolved.

If some of Twain's contemporaries may not have known how to respond to "A True Story," however, there has been little doubt of its seriousness since. Recent critics have followed Howells in praising its high literary quality. Henry Nash Smith and William Gibson describe it as "one of the best short pieces [Twain] ever wrote" (MTHL1, 25), while Sherwood Cummings calls it a "shining jewel . . . handled with consummate delicacy" (AF, 13). There may still be some tendency to equate moral intent and literary value here, for the elements of sentimentality, melodrama, and generic predictability (the separation and emotional reunion of mother and son) in the narrative are rather too close for comfort to those Twain would mercilessly burlesque elsewhere.[7] But undoubtedly in terms of his control of the vernacular voice, his changing attitude toward race, and the very nature of his subject matter, this story marks an important stage in Twain's literary development.

Once Twain's serious intentions are accepted, the social and moral meanings of "A True Story" are clear. But this is not the transparent version of reality ("repeated word for word as I heard it") that Twain would claim and that Howells accordingly valued so strongly. The story is certainly based on autobiographical fact.[8] It was evidently told to Twain by Mary Ann Cord, a former slave and now the cook at Quarry Farm, Elmira (his summer retreat). Twain recounts her tale of family separation on the auction block, the escape of her youngest son, Henry, to the North, and the dramatic recognition scene that later reunited them. But his narrative is not an entirely unmediated transcription of actual events.[9] The story is framed by the presence of the narrator, Misto C, whom Tom Quirk calls "an only slightly disguised version of Mr. Clemens."[10] It is this presence, and the shaping of the story round it, that gives the piece much of its success. The information we are given about Mary Ann Cord and her family is also slightly inaccurate.[11] And material is omitted that could complicate the reading of the tale, particularly the fact that Henry was evidently the son of Mary Ann Cord by the owner of the plantation on which she had worked.[12] Twain may not have known this detail. Given his later interest in miscegenation and its implications, however, and particularly in *Pudd'nhead Wilson*, it does seem potentially significant.

Twain brought his own authorial skills to his "transcription" of Mary Ann Cord's tale. His rendering of African American dialect is skillfully managed: "impeccably nuanced but never obscure."[13] Quirk, indeed, calls the story "a vernacular tour de force" (SSF, 60). But it is not just in the move from oral to written form that we see Twain's interventions. The manuscript version of the story shows that while Twain apparently "wrote the whole at one stretch" he nonetheless made nearly one hundred additions and deletions to his text.[14] For instance, he revised the catch-phrase that particularly identifies his heroine, Rachel (her fictional name).[15] Rachel here, and ironically, assumes the hegemonic attitudes of social superiority that in her own (racial) situation are responsible for her enslaved condition and treatment. In this case, however, they operate in the direction of her fellow slaves, for she repeats the words of her Maryland-born mother: "I want you niggers to understan' dat I wa'nt bawn in de mash to be fool' by trash! I's one o' de ole Blue Hen's Chickens, *I* is!" (206). Twain, the textual evidence shows, changed the first part of this catch-phrase throughout his story from the original, "I ain't [jes] houn'-dog mash to be trod on by common trash."[16] Considerable reworking then took place on the oral tale he had originally been told.

It is in the introduction and dramatic use of the first-person narrative presence, however, that Twain most effectively structures and controls this narrative. Quirk, despite his association of Twain with Misto C, notes that we are left with only a version of the author, for the "persona in the story" has been "clearly altered to enhance Rachel's dignity and to emphasize his own unfeeling stupidity."[17] And, without making any such authorial identification, it is very clear that the narrator is socially and emotionally blinkered. Misto C's naive starting assumption is that "Aunt Rachel's" joyful laughter signifies a happy life: "Aunt Rachel, how is it that you've lived sixty years and never had any trouble?" (202).[18] This is then soberly corrected by her narrative of slavery, of geographical displacement, and of family torn apart: "dah was my ole man gone, an' all my chil'en, all my seven chil'en — an' six of 'em I hain't set eyes on ag'in to dis day, an' dat's twenty-two year ago las' Easter. De man dat bought me b'long' in Newbern, an' he took me dah" (204). Neil Schmitz's comment is powerfully apt here: "Liberated, enabled, [Twain's] Southern writing already occupies in 1874 the fictive space Toni Morrison has come to define in . . . *Beloved* (1987), African American family history at the critical juncture of emancipation."[19]

As in "The Jumping Frog," the voice of a socially superior, though misguided, first-person narrator introduces that of the ill-educated vernacular figure (and see SSF, 59). This whole narrative, however, plays round notions of superiority and inferiority on a number of levels to achieve an integrated and powerful effect. In *The Incorporation of America*, Alan Trachtenberg discusses Howells and the democratic politics behind his realist aesthetic. In theory, that aesthetic encouraged the free play of all types and classes of American voices in its literature. In practice, however, it proved difficult to break away from the "discourse of respectability" and the assumptions of cultural superiority associated with a predominantly middle-class world. Thus the ungrammatical discourse of the "low" would, as in Howells's own *The Rise of Silas Lapham* (1885), usually be contained by a controlling, and grammatical, narrative voice that represented just such a socially superior perspective.[20]

"A True Story" is only a very short story but, nonetheless, Twain does turn such literary practices and the assumptions that informed them quite around. A satiric impulse, gradually realized, underpins the story and affects our reading of the socially superior and unconsciously racist voice of the first narrator. The respective spatial positioning of the protagonists is crucial throughout the narrative. The story starts with the setting of the scene: "We were sitting on the porch of the farm-house, on the summit of the hill, and 'Aunt Rachel' was sitting respectfully below our level, on the steps." Here inequalities of class and race are naturalized as the narrator (associated with porch-time leisure and the owning of servants) links the words "respectfully below" to an assumed set of social and racial hierarchies: "*for* [my emphasis] she was our servant, and colored." Further racial stereotyping then occurs in his description of Rachel, with its connotations of a natural gaiety and carelessness: "She was a cheerful, hearty soul, and it was no more trouble for her to laugh than it is a bird to sing . . . she was being chaffed without mercy, and was enjoying it" (202).

The first narrator is then silenced as Rachel tells her own "true story." His own facile assumptions are critiqued as the African American voice is given powerful and central status and as Rachel recounts her deeply serious testimony of slave experience.[21] Exceptionally, in terms of standard narrative forms, no final return is made to the voice of the first narrator, though his presence is signaled throughout. Indeed, he is addressed directly and ironically in the story's last line, when Rachel returns to his original question with the words, "Oh, no, Misto C——, I hain't had no trouble. An' no *joy!*" (207). As Schmitz astutely comments: "This sentence is like a freeze-frame, Misto C's term in a wreckage of negatives."[22] Moreover, Twain does not use his "respectable" narrator to frame the African American vernacular voice. Rather, after the opening passage, he allows "Aunt Rachel's" voice and story alone full authority and impact. This is a formally radical move and one that, as is generally recognized, points toward the use of that other marginalized and socially powerless voice in *Huckleberry Finn*.

Conventional narrative hierarchies (with a final return to the voice of "respectability") are disrupted here. So, too, Twain skillfully maneuvers spaces and bodies, and their relationship, to emphasize the reversals of narrative and moral authority that occur. The spatial moves are obvious and have received widespread critical attention, so I can be brief. There are two literal "platforms" in the narrative: one positioned, so to speak, "inside" Rachel's story; the other the place from which that story is told. These platforms are explicitly linked, as Rachel informs her audience in telling her story, that the auction block is "a stan' as high as dis po'ch." On that "inside" platform, Rachel and her family are seen (socially) purely as objects of commerce, to be separated and sold at their owner's will and whim. Despite her absolute social powerlessness, and however futilely, Rachel uses what physical resources she has to resist the human outrage (focused now on the loss of her "little Henry") that takes place. So she reports, "dey got him, de men did; but I took and tear de clo'es mos' off of 'em an' beat 'em over de head wid my chain; an' *dey* give it to *me*, too, but I didn't mine dat" (204).

Rachel's words ("I'll kill de man dat tetches him!") and violent actions are equally ineffectual in this past situation. But as she tells her story, on the porch (the other platform) and in the changed circumstances of postbellum America, her words get the full attention and respect of the white audience.[23] Her narrative power and the moral authority which that narrative reveals — her suffering, her deep love for and commitment to her child — are set against the silence of the first narrator and the facile judgment with which he is initially associated. In the only intervention made by Misto C once her story is under way, we are told that "Aunt Rachel had gradually risen, while she warmed to her subject, and now she towered above us, black against the stars" (204). The spatial shift that occurs (from "below our level") metaphorically renders conventional social and racial hierarchies irrelevant. Rachel's physical and moral presence dominates both her immediate audience and the more distanced one: the readers of "A True Story."

Rachel's other gestures add to such an effect.[24] These become particularly significant at the end of the narrative as she recalls the climactic moment when she recognized Henry following their long separation. As we learn in a skillful proleptic narrative insertion,[25] he has escaped slavery, joined the Union army, "ransacked the whole Souf" (205) looking for his mother, and has just recognized her by the catch-phrase he remembers from his childhood. As Rachel tells it:

I was a-stoopin' down by de stove, — jist so, same as if yo' foot was de stove, — an' I'd opened de stove do' wid my right han', — so, pushin' it back, jist as I pushes yo' foot, — an' I'd jist got de pan o' hot biscuits in my han' an' was 'bout to raise up, when I see a black face come aroun' under mine, an' de eyes a-lookin' up into mine, jist as I's a-lookin' up clost under yo' face now; an' I jist stopped *right dah*, an' never budged! jist gazed, an' gazed, so: an' de pan begin to tremble, an' all of a sudden I *knowed!* De pan drop' on de flo' an' I grab his lef' han' an' shove back his sleeve, — jist so, as I's doin' to you, — an' den I goes for his forehead [there are old and recognizable scars in both places] an' push de hair back, so, an' "Boy!" I says, ". . . De Lord God ob heaven be praise', I got my own ag'in!" (207)

This is an extraordinary passage. Rachel presses the narrator into immediate involvement in the acting out of her story as she makes increasingly intimate physical contact: from the pushing of his foot to the pushing back of the hair.[26] In doing so, she disturbs any sense of insulation that he might feel as a mere listener. In the space of a few gestures, she then directs and transforms his own role in her story from an irrelevant object (the stove) to the most deeply involved of subjects (her son). As she does so, a crossing of symbolic boundaries occurs between black and white, master and servant, nonfamily and family member. Both parties in the exchange are consequently (and again symbolically) constituted as social and racial equals and, indeed, as something more: now joined in a mother and son relationship (see AF, 13).

The same disruption of expected conventions occurs in the long and close gaze with which Rachel fixes the narrator. To avoid, or to meet, the eye of the master has considerable significance in the history of slavery. The slave was not expected to look the master in the eye, for this was a sign of equality and thus a challenge to the status quo. The recognition scene between mother and child here personally implicates the white first narrator. But another (racial) recognition scene overlays it, as he is forced to look this black female servant full in the eyes and to recognize her value, her full humanity, and the real equality that the social and racial barriers of the time (both ante- and postbellum) would deny.

In "A True Story" Twain renegotiates his attitude to African Americans, questioning commonly assumed stereotypes and the forms of humor based on them.[27] This is what Cummings means when he speaks of Twain's "dramatic breakthrough" in this sketch. If we look at Twain's other references to African Americans in this collection, in "Johnny Greer" (100), "Riley—Newspaper Correspondent" (157), and "Curing a Cold" (304), we can still see the dehumanizing racial caricatures that disfigure his early work. If we might not want to criticize Twain's treatment of his racial subject matter too strongly (for such representations were standard contemporary comic practice), "A True Story" nonetheless acts as a benchmark in Twain's work, indicating a "sea-change in the author's racial attitude" (AF, 13).[28]

If Twain is critiquing something of his own racial blindness in his depiction of Misto C, he is also critiquing that of his white fellow countrymen and women. Twain wrote the story in the summer of 1874, at a time of considerable racial tension in America, and not long before the collapse of Reconstruction (in 1876). If some of Twain's contemporaries did not quite know how to read this story, its meaning is clear, once his ability to move beyond an expected comic mode is acknowledged. Twain addresses one of the most urgent and serious of current American social issues in "A True Story" and makes his own attitude toward it transparent.

Twain wrote "Some Learned Fables, for Good Old Boys and Girls" and "A True Story" in 1874, and submitted them to the *Atlantic Monthly* at the same time. "Some Learned Fables," though, shows a very different side of the author, with the relativistic forms of humor it engages. The story does, however, have a satiric target, too, as Howells revealed when he turned it—but not "A True Story"—down for publication. I focus here particularly on the moves *between* satire and comic relativism and the consequent affinities this narrative shares with work produced much later in Twain's career.

A three-part fable, Twain's story describes how "the creatures of the forest" (small animals, insects, and reptiles) send a great expedition, led by their most learned scientists, to go "out into the unknown and unexplored world . . . to verify the truth of matters already taught in their schools and colleges and also to make discoveries" (126). What they find are traces of a nineteenth-century human culture now thought to be extinct. Part of the satire in "Some Learned Fables" is directed at conventional religious pieties and the language in which they are expressed. It was this element of the story that led Howells to reject it. He told Twain:

I am going to . . . sen[d] back . . . your contributio[n]. Not . . . that I don't think [it is] very good. But The Atlantic, as regards matters of religion, is just in that . . . condition when a little fable like yours wouldn't leave it a single Presbyterian,

Baptist, Unitarian, Episcopalian, Methodist or Millerite *paying* subscriber — all the dead-heads would stick to it, and abuse it in the denominational newspapers. Send your fable to some truly pious concern like Scribner or Harper, and they'll extract it into all the hymn-books. But it would ruin *us*. . . . There are parts of the Fable that I think wonderfully good even for you — that touch about Sisyphus and Atlas being ancestors of the tumble-bug did tickle me.[29]

Henry Nash Smith and William M. Gibson usefully explain just what it was that raised Howells's anxieties:

Howells as editor must have been wary of *Atlantic* readers' potential objections to the comment, "Thus inscrutable be the ways of God, whose will be done!" when the "stinking" Tumble-Bug and the "illustrious" Duke of Longlegs lie down together, drunk, after the animals chance upon a jug of whiskey; to the havoc wrought within a single week by a detachment of missionaries, among a "timid, gentle" race of "heathenish" spiders, "not three families being by that time at peace with each other or having a settled belief in any system of religion whatsoever"; to the animal archeologists' belief that the inscriptions "For Sale Cheap," "Billiards," "S. T. — 1860 — X," "Keno," and "Ale on Draught" must be "religious maxims"; and to the conclusion of Professor Wood-louse that Man "imagined he had a soul, and pleased himself with the fancy that it was immortal." Howells may also have feared the effect of Mark Twain's hoax, when the animals mistake a mass of manure for a monument, and carry it home in triumph.[30]

Twain's satire, though, also shoots off in another direction in the general mockery of science and its discourse which forms a consistent strand to the narrative.[31] For the certainties of scientific knowledge are comically undermined. The forest scientists, "the very greatest among the learned" (127), consistently misinterpret and mistranslate the objects of their inquiry. Thus when the expedition comes across some railway tracks — "two endless parallel bars of some kind of hard black substance, raised . . . above the general level" (128) — the geographer, Professor Mud Turtle, describes them as "indeed . . . a discovery. . . . We have found . . . what the wisest of our fathers always regarded as a mere thing of the imagination. . . . [W]e stand in a majestic presence. These are parallels of latitude!" When "a demoniacal shriek" and "clattering and rumbling noise" are heard, followed by "a vast terrific eye" shooting by "with a long tail attached" (129), the Professor deliberates "long and profoundly" before saying, "Give thanks for this stupendous thing which we have been permitted to witness. — It is the Vernal Equinox!" When a second train then passes, Lord Longlegs pronounces, to general jubilation, that it is "nothing less than the transit of Venus!" (129–31).[32]

Twain takes particular delight in satirizing the (faulty) scholarship of the philologist, Professor Wood-louse. Throughout his writing career, Twain showed a deep (and for his time precocious) interest in the process of naming and translating, the slippage between linguistic systems, and the nature of the relationship between signifier (word) and signified (object). Thus the forest creatures discover a series of advertising signs with words and pictures set in complementary relation to one another. The two words "dentists office" (sic), for example, are placed with a single half of a set of false teeth placed between them (Twain's own original illustrations are reproduced here, as polished up by True Williams).[33] Wood-louse uses such findings to decide that the human language was one "which conveyed itself partly by letters, and partly by signs or hieroglyphics," and proceeds to translate, though "not to the perfect satisfaction of all the scholars" (140). The general level of his skills is illustrated in his translation of a memorial marking a flood disaster: "In 1847, in the spring, the river overflowed its banks and covered the whole township." This comes out in his version as telling of the destruction of a city: "One thousand eight hundred and forty-seven years ago, the (fires?) descended and consumed the whole city" (144–45).[34]

The scientists involved on this journey of discovery are called Manologists. Their "speciality is the deciphering of the ancient records of the extinct bird termed Man. [For it is now decided that Man was a bird and not a reptile]" (145). As they make their exploration, they come across what is a thinly disguised version of the waxworks section of Barnum's ("Varnum's") American Museum, though Wood-louse mistranslates that final word as "Burial-Place."[35] Here, in one of the best comic sequences in the story, the "long extinct species" of man is proved definitively to exist (rather than being merely "a myth and a superstition") by the presence of certain "tall fossils." These "rigid great figures" have inscriptions on their breasts: "One read, 'CAPTAIN KIDD, THE PIRATE;' another 'QUEEN VICTORIA;' another, 'ABE LINCOLN;' . . . etc." (141). After checking with other scientific records describing what is known of man, his appearance and habits, these fossils are confirmed as human. They are, moreover, seen further to "la[y] bare the secrets of dead ages." Thus, "The specimen marked 'Captain Kidd' was examined in detail. . . . With great labor its loose skin was removed, whereupon its body was discovered to be of a polished white texture, thoroughly petrified. The straw it had eaten, so many ages gone by, was still in its body, undigested — and even in its legs" (142).

We see here the delight Twain takes in transgressing the boundaries of any single form of humor, as satire gives way to comically absurd category mistake. The final conclusions of the forest scientists then make Twain's use of what is at base a comedy of playful relativism more explicit:

To sum up. — We believe that man had a written language. We *know* that he indeed existed at one time . . . also, that he was the companion of the cave bear, the mastodon, and other extinct species; that he cooked and ate them and likewise the young of his own kind [this last set of certainties stem from the expedition's discovery of a fake exhibit of primeval man in Varnum's museum] . . . that he imagined he had a soul, and pleased himself with the fancy that it was immortal. But let us not laugh; there may be creatures in existence to whom we and our vanities and profundities may seem as ludicrous. (143)

Another strand of the story's humor is aimed at Darwinian assumptions, especially at evolutionary theory.[36] And here, too, satire and relativistic forms of humor coexist. To the worms, spiders, and mud turtles (and so on) that make up the expedition, man's presence "in the earliest ages of creation" marks him out as an inferior species, "the companion of the other low orders of life that belonged to that forgotten time" (142). The creature scientists find a human house and mistake it for a natural rock formation. The many layers of mortar (or "decomposed limestone") between the bricks ("Old Red Sandstone") are consequently perceived as separate rock strata. Thus "all received geology" concerning the world's age and development is refuted. The "presence of fossil ants and tumble-bugs" in the lower strata of this formation is taken as convincing proof that "these vulgar laborers belonged to the first and lower orders of created beings." There is, however, seen to be "something repulsive in the reflection that the perfect and exquisite creature of the modern uppermost order owed its origin to such ignominious beings through the mysterious law of Development of Species" (138). And when a human book is later found, a sentence is translated which reads: "*In truth it is believed by many that the lower animals reason and talk together.*" The expedition's official report gives the astonished response: "Then there are lower animals than Man! . . . Man himself is extinct, but *they* may still exist. What can they be? Where do they inhabit?" (148). Twain satirizes both the limited horizons of the scientific mind and the assumptions that lie behind the evolutionary theories they propose. But at the same time, the nature of his comedy undermines the very possibility of firm knowledge (or "truth") and leaves his reader in a spiraling world of scientific and metaphysical uncertainty.

In *Mark Twain and Science*, Sherwood Cummings sees this story as countering Twain's general enthusiasm for science. He offers a useful summary of some of its satiric effects:

This story treats satirically . . . the methods and conclusions of archeologists, paleontologists, and geologists. Throughout, the point of view is staunchly obscurantist. . . . Never seeing a man, [these scientists] are nevertheless willing to theorize on his physical appearance and culture. The hero of the fable is the Tumble-Bug, whose humble vocation and earthy common sense lead him closer to the truth than the scientists' speculations.[37]

Cummings's final reference to the Tumble-Bug introduces a further component of the story. Twain strongly valued the qualities given to this insect and would recall them in creating his human "hero" in *Huckleberry Finn*. The Tumble-Bug is only a "vulgar labore[r]" (138) in the expedition but this "vulgar ignorant carpe[r]" consistently deflates the grandiose theories and speculations of his social and intellectual betters. This doubly vulgar and "obscene" (148) insect generally speaks in a different register than his apparent betters, though he is not given Huck's insistently vernacular voice. On the bottom of the social pile like Huck, he says what he sees and in doing so pierces the pretensions of others. When the expedition meets "a long and lofty barrier" outlined against the sky (a cliff face?), Professor Bull Frog judges it "the wall that enclosed the earth." He solemnly pontificates: "Our fathers have left us much learning, but they had not traveled far, and so we may count this a noble new discovery." The Tumble-Bug, though, "said he believed it was simply land tilted up on its edge, because he knew he could see trees on it." But he is immediately silenced. "You are hired to dig, sir — that is all. We need your muscle, not your brains" (127–28). Later, a Mound is discovered and judged to be "a Monument" established by a "mysterious and forgotten race of Mound Builders."[38] But the Tumble-Bug spots it for the old pile of shit it is: "to an ignorant poor devil who has never seen a college, it is not a Monument, strictly speaking, but is yet a most rich and noble property; and with your worships' good permission I will proceed to manufacture it into spheres of exceeding grace." (146).

The Tumble-Bug also brings an element of the carnivalesque to the narrative in the part he plays in upsetting established hierarchies. Twain's use of a carnival motif is of considerable importance in his work.[39] Here, the moment of carnival occurs in the first part of the story. A jug of liquor has dropped from one of the passing trains, and the Tumble-Bug, who gets intoxicated as a result, familiarly slaps his superiors (the scholars) one after the other on the shoulder, saying "Nice ('ic!) nice old boy!" He literally falls about due to his lack of bodily control: "the force of [an] unchecked impulse . . . projected him, limber and sprawling, into the lap of the Lord Longlegs." When asked about his reported "find" (the liquor jug), he advises the company to "Mosey out 'n' see. It'll pay." They discover the Norway Rat busy delivering alcohol "to the mob" via his tail (dipped into the jug and then removed). Carnivalesque disruption of the normal social order, rules, and restraints then occurs, as the "uncontrolled mob . . . [goes] mad . . . by reason of the drink": "All that partook of [this liquor] were immediately exalted with great and pleasurable emotions, and went staggering about singing ribald songs, embracing, fighting, dancing, discharging irruptions of profanity, and defying all authority."

The leaders of the expedition then, as a logbook entry reveals,[40] are "seized upon" by the "reckless" mob:

and within the hour we, even we, were undistinguishable from the rest — the demoralization was complete and universal. In time the camp wore itself out with its orgies and sank into a stolid and pitiable stupor, in whose mysterious bonds rank was forgotten and strange bed-fellows made, our eyes, at the resurrection, being blasted . . . with the incredible spectacle of that intolerable stinking scavenger, the Tumble-Bug, and the illustrious patrician my lord Grand Daddy, Duke of Longlegs, lying soundly steeped in sleep, and clasped lovingly in each other's arms. (132–34)

All hierarchies are turned topsy-turvy here in the ribaldry and drunkenness that occurs, and the Tumble-Bug is the prime mover and actor in this event. Even when the normal order is restored, he continues to act as a thorn in the side of his social superiors, with his clear-sighted undermining of their pretensions. And it is significant that both the first and final parts of the story end with the Tumble-Bug and his sardonic point of view.

"Some Learned Fables, for Good Old Boys and Girls," then, operates as a satire reinforced by the Tumble-Bug's presence and perspective. But the disruption of the social order described in the carnivalesque scene above does not accord with satire's traditional end (the remedy or correction of a faulty value scheme). Rather the general collapse of boundaries and the loss of discipline described reveals a social and moral world in complete flux, with all conventional ordering points removed.[41] And the (temporary) loss of stability in the carnival scene points toward a similar but more fundamental loss of firm value judgments in the text as a whole, as satire tends to take something of a backseat to forms of playful relativism.

We see this happening at almost every point in the story. Fraudulent forms of scientific deduction and science's claims to authoritative knowledge are satirized. But any notion of firm bearings (what *would* form a sound basis for scientific knowledge?) is also questioned by the narrative's stress on indeterminacy. Knowledge itself is shown as an entirely relative thing.[42] The Duke of Longlegs confirms the passing of the train as the transit of Venus across the earth's face, "*for we have SEEN it!*" (131) The forest scientists see railway lines as parallels of latitude because of a similarly limited set of preconceptions and expectations. For Twain, all truths are partial and necessarily incomplete. Our condition, as scientists or as seekers after knowledge in any sphere, is like that of the prisoner in Morgan le Fay's dungeon in *A Connecticut Yankee*. Seeing through a "crack," an "arrow-slit" cut in a "vast wall of native rock," he watches his own home from a distance for a period of twenty-two years. With a wife and five children left in the outside world, the five funerals he sees leave him "tortured" as to which "unspeakably precious" family member remains alive. In fact, however, these all have been fake funerals, stage-managed by le Fay out of her hatred for the prisoner. And her "sublimest stroke of genius," we are told, is to leave the family one funeral short, "so as to let [her victim] wear his poor old soul out guessing" who might still be left.[43] This stands as an allegory of the limitation of the human viewpoint. What we see may be entirely "true" from where we stand. But we are in fact in the dark (the dungeon) and, looking through a thin crack in a very thick wall, are given only a partial view of a much fuller picture. That picture, moreover, usually turns out to be quite different from the way we thought it looked.[44]

As the insect and animal scientists look out at the world, they read everything in terms of the importance of their own species and from the limited perspectives available to them. Man is not (as they think) extinct — as the train and liquor jug confirm — but operates on the fringes of their vision and beyond the narrow parameters of their knowledge. The absurd category mistake that confuses waxwork and fossilized human body (with straw in the legs) comes about similarly. A relativist perspective and the comic play that accompanies it cut against satire here and its corrective sense of a knowable "right order."

The same is true of the Darwinian references. Satire operates here in the interrogation of human assumptions of superiority in the evolutionary scale. But it is the impossibility of constructing such a scale with any certainty that drives the destabilizing humor. The very idea of relative highs and lows is mocked by the forest creatures' assumption of superiority over man. The view of the world and of its evolutionary cycle shifts according to the particular perspective taken. Throughout his career, Twain would query an evolutionary narrative that rested on man's sense of his self-importance and centrality in the cosmic scheme of things, and this is what is at final issue in "Some Learned Fables." In "Letters from the Earth," for instance, he plays with perspective in just the way he does here but to more sardonic effect, when he refers to Noah and the Flood:

Noah and his family were saved . . . yes, but they were not comfortable, for they were full of microbes. Full to the eyebrows; fat with them. . . . The microbes were by far the most important part of the Ark's cargo, and the part the Creator was most anxious about and most infatuated with. . . specially precious creations.[45]

And in "Was the World Made for Man?" Twain writes an account of the evolutionary process, where the role of mankind in the grand scheme of things is held up to half-ironic, half-anxiously indeterminate examination. He starts off with the gradual evolution of the oyster:

An oyster has hardly any more reasoning power than a scientist has; and so it is reasonably certain that this one jumped to the conclusion that the nineteen million years [leading up to his appearance] was a preparation for *him*; but that would be just like an oyster, which is the most conceited animal there is, except man.

He then moves on (?) from there, ending up with man:

And at last came the monkey, and anybody could see that man wasn't far off, now. And in truth that was so. The monkey went on developing for close upon five million years, and then turned into a man — to all appearances.

Such is the history of it. Man has been here 32,000 years. That it took a hundred million years to prepare the world for him is proof that that is what it was done for. I suppose it is. I dunno. If the Eiffel Tower were now representing the world's age, the skin of paint on the pinnacle-knob at its summit would represent man's share of that age; and anybody would perceive that that skin was what the tower was built for. I reckon they would, I dunno.[46]

The double "I dunno" in the last paragraph suggests the deep uncertainties underlying Twain's attitudes toward teleology and anthropocentrism. It is his comic relativism that predominates in "Some Learned Fables," however, and links the story, and other early pieces like it, to a significant strand in the later work. The moves between languages and worlds (that of the forest creatures and of the human) that take place in the 1874 story foreshadow, for instance, the destabilizing properties of a narrative like "Three Thousand Years among the Microbes" where the microbic world is represented as a microscopic version of the human one. A vision of a limitless and relative chain of being consequently develops with vertiginous moves occurring between the human and microbe worlds (and beyond), and with conventional human assumptions ("*all* of God's creatures are included in his Merciful scheme of salvation") relocated to a microbic context.[47] The comic impulse here recalls the moment in "Some Learned Fables" when the forest creatures tell of man's (absurd) belief in the soul and immortality, then refer to the possibility of other "creatures in existence to whom we and our vanities . . . may seem as ludicrous" (143). The sense of spiraling relativity released is remarkably similar.

There is then a type of comic double-effect operating in this story and one that finally cannot quite hold together. This effect is repeated throughout Twain's work and is evidence of a deep internal strain and tension that cannot be resolved. His satiric effects always necessarily suggest the possibility of human change and improvement. His comic relativism, though, speaks of indeterminacy and the spiraling ungrounding of certainty: seeing the joke in the human situation rather than attempting to remedy it.[48] The two modes sit uneasily beside one another. His humor spans a spectrum between the entirely serious social and moral intent underlying "A True Story" and work that moves — but with a shifting balance — between satire and a comic and cosmic relativism.[49] "Some Learned Fables" belongs to the latter category. If these forms of humor (and the worldviews they represent) cannot ultimately be finally reconciled, it is not difficult to understand their copresence in Twain's work. To see human life finally as absurdist joke does not necessarily mean that one should not still work to improve the practices and institutions that form the immediate circumstances of one's daily life. This, I would suggest, is exactly Twain's position.[50]

5

The Stolen White Elephant, Etc.

So he took his carpet sack and a portable telephone, and shook the snow of his native city from his arctics, and went forth into the world. He wandered far and wide and in many States. Time and again, strangers were astounded to see a wasted, pale, and woe-worn man laboriously climb a telegraph pole in wintry and lonely places, perch sadly there an hour, with his ear at a little box, then come sighing down, and wander wearily away. Sometimes they shot at him, as peasants do at aeronauts, thinking him mad and dangerous. Thus his clothes were much shredded by bullets and his person grievously lacerated. But he bore it all patiently.

— "The Loves of Alonzo Fitz Clarence and Rosannah Ethelton"

The Stolen White Elephant, Etc., published in 1882, is generally seen as one of Twain's weakest collections. Everett Emerson calls it the "least distinguished" of all his books.[1] Even Twain himself was to refer to it later as "a collection of rubbishy sketches, mainly."[2] A note by J. L. (probably Twain's nephew, the second Jervis Langdon) dated April 1933 both confirms Twain's low opinion of the book and offers an account of its genesis:

Mr. Clemens said one day that the "Stolen White Elephant" was not an important book; it was just the result of another publisher, (the delightful Osgood this time,) pushing him to satisfy a public, clamorous for a new book by Mark Twain. More Sketches, for he was finding it difficult just then to carry on sustained writing. (CU-MARK)

While the idea of satisfying a clamorous public may be something of an exaggeration, there are two important details given here: the hiatus in Twain's literary productivity at this point in his career, and the use of a new publisher for this work.

The years from 1876 (after *Tom Sawyer* was written) to 1882 are generally considered something of a low point in Twain's writing life. James D.

Wilson sees it as "a period of considerable aesthetic decline and frustration": "Committed to becoming a genuine man-of-letters, Mark Twain seems to have lost control of his career and enthusiasm for his art; attempts to break clear of patterns established in his successful early fiction produce uncertainty and disastrous attempts at new genres."[3] The introduction to the *Notebooks & Journals* for 1877–83 refers to Twain's "flagging interest and energy" during the extended European tour (April 1878 to September 1879) that he made to collect material for *A Tramp Abroad* (1880). It notes, too, how on his return to America Twain:

found himself confronted with the business affairs that had helped drive him to Europe. His investments in the Kaolatype engraving process and his scrapbook enterprise consumed more and more of his time and money. He also found himself embroiled in the extensive redecoration of the Hartford house.[4]

Hamlin Hill adds: "By 1881, Mark Twain was virtually a full-time investor and entrepreneur" (MTLP, 128).

It is true that Twain did modify, and move away from, the techniques that had brought him his early acclaim at this time. Everett Emerson, most particularly, dates "the strange disappearance of Mark Twain" — the created literary persona of the early sketches, stories, and travel books — from exactly this period.[5] And the problem he had faced in "A True Story" as to how to move from predominantly "comic" materials to more serious subject matter was one that continued to occur.[6] But Twain produced a relatively steady stream of short stories and sketches and longer works (including *The Prince and the Pauper* in 1882). He also expanded his formal and thematic range. I would not therefore dismiss the *Stolen White Elephant* collection as quickly as some previous critics have done, or as Twain himself did. I see him trying out ideas here that are expanded and developed in some of his most important work. These focus around questions of race, the opposition between individual agency and expression and social conformity, and the conditions of American modernity. Given that this book was being prepared just before Twain researched *Life on the Mississippi* (1883), and that the completion of *Huckleberry Finn* (1885) was not too distant, it would perhaps be a mistake to overemphasize any aesthetic lull or collapse at this time.

Twain published a number of collections of short writings between *Sketches, New and Old* and *The Stolen White Elephant*. In 1877, James R. Osgood published the thin book — ninety-six pages including advertisements — *A True Story, and The Recent Carnival of Crime*. In 1878, *Punch, Brothers, Punch! and Other Sketches* was issued. This was a "little collection of reprinted sketches . . . designed primarily to promote his scrapbook [the self-pasting scrapbook Twain had invented], a book with no writing in it at all."[7] Sold at twenty-five cents and published by Slote, Woodman and Company (a firm run by Dan Slote, Twain's friend from the *Quaker City* days, and now his business colleague),[8] it included nine sketches, seven of which were reprinted in *The Stolen White Elephant*.[9] Chatto and Windus published an English edition of the *Punch, Brothers, Punch!* pamphlet but heavily extended it to a 310 page book. This came out, also in 1878, under the title *An Idle Excursion*.[10] Indeed, the British firm paid Twain a relatively low royalty when they then published *The Stolen White Elephant* owing to "the considerable portion of the contents of the volume already included in . . . 'Idle Excursion.' . . . [W]e shall have to make larger abatements to the 'trade' to keep it in stock."[11] In line with earlier practice, I omit further comment on these various collections to focus on the cumulative American collection that then followed.

Twain changed his American publisher at this time. Elisha Bliss, who ran the subscription house, the American Publishing Company, was Twain's publisher from *The Innocents Abroad* through to *A Tramp Abroad*.[12] Their often difficult relationship, which helped to shape both Twain's career and his writing methods, is described in some detail in Hamlin Hill's *Mark Twain and Elisha Bliss*. Hill shows how, despite Twain's increasing suspicion that Bliss was swindling him of profits accruing from his books, he nonetheless stayed with the company until Bliss's death in September 1880. Twain, though, had "flirted with other publishers in the mid-1870s" and was particularly attracted to James R. Osgood, whom he called (in 1877) "the best publisher who ever breathed."[13] Osgood was a friend of Twain, and the prestigious Boston publishing house he ran stood in the author's mind both for high-quality books and for literary respectability. It was his firm that published *The Prince and the Pauper* and *Life on the Mississippi*, as well as *The Stolen White Elephant*. But Osgood's move, with Twain's strong encouragement, into the subscription publishing field was one of the factors that caused his bankruptcy and business failure (not for the first time, it has to be said) in 1885.[14]

Twain's role in the making of *The Stolen White Elephant, Etc.* was greater than has generally been recognized. Henry Nash Smith and William M. Gibson speak of Twain's "remarkable . . . nonchalance in turning over to Osgood and Howells the responsibility for deciding what to include in the book" (MTHL1, 400). James D. Wilson says that Twain asked Osgood "to consult with . . . Howells and put together a volume of short stories garnered from the files of the *Atlantic Monthly* and the stock of unpublished pieces [he] had assembled. Mark Twain had no role in the selection or ordering of contents of the resulting book" (RG, 75). Both these accounts seem partly endorsed by Twain's letter to Osgood of 4 March 1882, written playfully in African American dialect form:

Dear Osgood —

I's gwyne to sen' you de stuff jis' as she stan', now; an' you an' Misto Howls kin weed out enuff o' dem 93,000 words fer to crowd de book down to *one* book; or you kin shove in enuff er dat ole Contrib-Club truck fer to swell her up en bust her in two an' make *two* books outen her.

Dey ain't no use to . . . plan out no 'rangement er de stuff ontwel you is decided what you gwyne to do.

I don't want none er dat rot what is in de small onvolups to go in, 'cepp'n jis' what Misto Howls *say* shel go in.

I don' see how I come to git sich a goddam sight er truck on han', nohow.[15]

These words, though, do indicate that Twain played some part in the initial selection process for the book. And the "resumé" he apparently included with the letter confirms this. I quote it in full as previously unpublished material:

RESUMÉ.	words
Original matter —————	30,000
In Punch, Bros, Punch —————	30,000
In small envelops numbered	
1, 2, 3, 4, 5, & 6. —————	7,500
A Curious Experience —————	9,200
Carnival of Crime —————	7,000
Magnanimous-Incident Literar —————	2,400
Great Revolution in Pitcairn —————	4,300
McWilliamses & the Lightning —————	3,000
	93,400

Uncle Remus contains, ostensibly, 56,000, but really scarcely more than 50,000. Adventures of American Consul Abroad contains 54,000.
Prudence Palfrey, 62,000

Consequently we must weed out the above mess in a pretty wholesale way, or add a lot of stuff from Contributors' Club [a section of the *Atlantic Monthly*] & make *two* books.

	No. of MS. pages
White Elephant —————	116
Concerning the American Language.	14
The Shakespeare Mulberry —————	12
The Legend of Sagenfeld —————	32
On the Decay of the Art of Lying ——	30
Adam's Expulsion —————	11
Paris Notes —————	10
Love Song —————	4
Heidelberg Notes —————	10
A Boy's Adventure —————	30
Invalid's Story —————	22
	291

With average blanks before & after chapters, this new matter makes 30,000 words.
Punch Bros — 30,000 words. — 25,000, *any* way.[16]

Twain's use of the first-person plural here suggests his engagement in what is seen as the mutual task of preparing the book. The kind of detail involved suggests that we should not put too much stress solely on the roles played by Osgood and Howells. Twain does designate among this list of material every one of the sketches and stories that would appear in the final volume, except for "Speech on the Babies."[17]

This is not to underestimate Howells and Osgood's part in the final editing of the book. On 7 April Howells, having presumably seen Twain's resumé and the accompanying material, wrote to Osgood as follows:

I think [Twain's] book ought to be made up as follows:
4. The Stolen White Elephant.
1. Rambling Notes of Idle Excursion.
2. Carnival of Crime.
3. Magnanimous Incident Literature.
6. A Curious Experience.
5. Punch, Brothers.
7. Great Revolution in Pitcairn.
8. Mrs. McWilliams and Lightning.
9. Decay of Lying.
11. Legend of Sagenfeld.
13. Rosanna [*sic*] Ethelton, etc.
10. The Canvasser's Tale.
17. Paris Notes
    Speech on the Babies. [crossed out]
16. The American Language.
12. The Canvasser's Tale. [crossed out]
16. Rogers.
18. Encounter with Interviewer.
15. New England Weather.
14. Speech on Babies.
  The numbers in pencil show *order of preference.* I would omit Heidelberg Notes, Love-Song, Adam's Expulsion, Shakespear [sic] Mulberry, Bull and Bees, Montreal [speech], Philadelphia, Welcome to Grant, and Military Speeches, and the Tale for Struggling Young Poets. Yours ever.[18]

Osgood's letter to Twain, the following day, passed on Howells's advice about the omissions and told Twain: "This leaves 18 pieces, making in all about 80,000 words. If this is too much [Howells] has indicated 8 more which might be omitted, viz Encounter with Interviewer.[19] The putting together of this collection, then, appears to have been very much of a three-way process, with Twain, Howells, and Osgood all involved.
  There is some evidence, too, that Twain may have had a hand in the

final editing process, following Osgood's receipt of Howells's 7 April letter. The inclusion of "The Invalid's Story" in the book as part of "Some Rambling Notes of an Idle Excursion" suggests such a finding. "Some Rambling Notes" had first appeared in the *Atlantic* in four parts, commencing October 1877. Tom Quirk notes:

> Howells had advised that Twain exclude "The Invalid's Story" from this contribution because it was indelicate. Later Howells recommended that he remove it from *A Tramp Abroad*. Twain continued to like the piece, however, and he included it in his collection *The Stolen White Elephant, Etc.* (SSF, 75)

If Osgood was working, where appropriate, from the *Atlantic* files as he collated material for the collection, the reappearance of "The Invalid's Story" within this text is unexpected. Its insertion carries all the signs of Twain's own involvement, if only in the form of instruction or advice to Osgood. Though it is possible that the latter made this decision alone, it seems unlikely. The change of order of the stories and sketches from that Howells had originally advised may, however, have been down to Osgood, though any conclusions here must remain speculative.

Four of the stories and sketches that appear in *The Stolen White Elephant* are, as Twain's textual footnotes reveal, leftover materials from *A Tramp Abroad*. The title story, plus the much shorter "Paris Notes," "Legend of Sagenfeld, in Germany," and "Concerning the American Language," were either "crowded out" (242, 265) of the book or, as Twain jokingly puts it in the case of the "Sagenfeld" piece, "left out . . . because its authenticity seemed doubtful" (246, and see also 7).[20] The other pieces in the collection date (in terms of their first appearance) from 1874, when "Rogers" and "An Encounter with an Interviewer" were published, onward. "Punch, Brothers, Punch" (previously titled "A Literary Nightmare"), "The Facts Concerning the Recent Carnival of Crime in Connecticut," and "The Canvasser's Tale" all first appeared in the *Atlantic* in 1876.[21] "Speech on the Weather" was given to the New England Society of New York in December 1876. "Some Rambling Notes of an Idle Excursion" commenced in the *Atlantic* in October 1877. "About Magnanimous-Incident Literature" and "The Loves of Alonzo Fitz Clarence and Rosannah Ethelton" were published in the same journal the next spring. In March 1879, "The Great Revolution in Pitcairn" also appeared in the *Atlantic*, while "Speech on the Babies" was given at a reunion banquet of the Army of the Tennessee in Chicago that November. Twain presented "On the Decay of the Art of Lying" to the Hartford Monday Evening Club in April 1880. "Mrs. McWilliams and the Lightning" appeared in the *Atlantic* the following September. "A Curious Experience" was published in *Century* in November 1881. Everything else — the leftover material from *A Tramp Abroad* and "The Invalid's Story" part of "Some Rambling Notes" — first appeared with *The Stolen White Elephant*.[22]

This then was comparatively recent work. All but two of the pieces in the book had been published since *Sketches, New and Old*, and the majority of its contents first appear during the period of the supposed "aesthetic decline." Eight of its stories or sketches had first appeared in the *Atlantic*. The collection can be said to represent the period when Twain had attained a certain recognized literary respectability and, perhaps as a result of that fact, felt further able to extend the range of his writing.

If *The Stolen White Elephant* is of variable quality, it has plenty of strong material and the title piece is one of the comic highlights of Twain's career. A full analysis of that story follows in my next chapter. More generally, and despite the inclusion of a few very short (three- and four-page) pieces, a continuing move can be identified on Twain's part toward a more carefully structured and developed use of short forms. This can be at least partly explained by the turn to magazine rather than newspaper publication. One of the notable things about Twain, as Hamlin Hill points out in the context of subscription publishing, was his adeptness at writing to fit the formal requirements of whatever his targeted market.

The longest piece in the book is "Some Rambling Notes of an Idle Excursion," an account of Twain's trip to Bermuda in May 1877 with his friend, the Hartford clergyman Joseph Twichell. This takes up just under a quarter (sixty-nine pages) of its whole textual space. Howells, his *Atlantic* editor and usually a very sympathetic reader, responded positively to this travel narrative, as Twain first submitted its four episodes to him:

I've just been reading aloud to my wife your Bermuda papers. That they're delightfully entertaining goes without saying; but we also found that you gave us the only realizing sense of Bermuda that we've ever had. I know that they will be a great success. . . . That joke you put in Twichell's mouth advising you to make the most of a place that was *like* Heaven, about killed us. . . . No. 4 of your Notes . . . is glorious. I nearly killed Mrs. Howells with it.[23]

Twain himself seems to have been less sure about "Some Rambling Notes." He wrote to Howells of being "still plagued with doubts about Parts I & II." And when he received the proofs of the latter he responded: "Dern that article, it made me cry when I read it . . . it was so oppressively & ostentatiously poor" (MTHL1, 186, 199). If the finished narrative is patchy in quality, there is also plenty that is good in it. Moreover, in its engagement with American modernity, it establishes a contrast between a sense of anxiety and constraint and of premodernist leisure and relaxation that recurs both within this collection and in Twain's full-length works. It may accordingly be relevant that Twain took on an assumed name in making the original Bermuda trip on which he based his narrative. This escape from the pressures associated with his public persona seems to have contributed considerably to his pleasure: "Lord, what a perfectly bewitching excursion it was! I traveled under an assumed name & was never molested with a polite attention from *any* body."[24]

"Some Rambling Notes," despite its comparative brevity, bears structural resemblance to Twain's earlier travel narratives, *The Innocents Abroad* and *Roughing It*. Hamlin Hill describes a subscription publishing readership as expecting a mix of entertainment and information ("the statistics and descriptive materials in the travel volumes satisfied their curiosity"), of sensationalism and piety or didacticism (MTEB, 160, 165). Twain's best work does considerably more than bridge these extremes, but there is good cause for seeing his writing through such a lens. "Some Rambling Notes" follows such a pattern as it recounts factual details about Bermudan life and scenes but balances a sentimental and lyric tendency with sharp notes of comic deflation:

The early twilight of a Sunday evening in Hamilton, Bermuda, is an alluring time. There is just enough of whispering breeze, fragrance of flowers . . . to raise one's thoughts heavenward; and just enough amateur piano music to keep him reminded of the other place. (79)

Twain introduces a more grotesque and extravagant form of comic entertainment in "The Invalid's Story," one of those self-sufficient and often very funny anecdotes and stories that he would typically insert into his travel narratives. Here, a box of guns (but with Limburger cheese placed on top of it) is taken into a locomotive express car and consequently mistaken for a coffin. The chief comic effect arises from the vernacular language and sensibility of the conductor as he responds to the apparent outrage of the stinking corpse that shares his space. The first-person narrator (the deceased's friend) filters his words:

After a few moments Thompson [the conductor] said, —
    "Pfew! I reckon it ain't no cinnamon 't I've loaded this-yer stove with!"
He gasped once or twice, then . . . sat down near me, looking a great deal impressed. . . . After a contemplative pause, he said, indicating the box with a gesture, —
    "Friend of yourn?"
    "Yes," I said with a sigh.
    "He's pretty ripe, *ain't* he!" (98)[25]

Again Twain moves rapidly between modes, for his broad humor here contrasts strongly with the standard reverential piety engaged in another story (on "the chronometer of God," 44–48) inserted earlier in the same text.

The approach Twain uses, then, in "Some Rambling Notes" structurally follows his previous full-length works in the genre. The travel narrative particularly suited him. It has a shape imposed on it but one that is extremely flexible, for the linear description of the journey could be alternated with pauses where a dramatic scene, a description (of people, scenery, or an event), a joke or story, a thought or associative digression, could be inserted.[26] However, there is also a clear and significant difference between this and his earlier full-length travel texts (and sketches and stories, too). For Twain is nowhere near as dependent here on the use of the first-person persona "Mark Twain" and the comic effects thereby created. Everett Emerson in fact claims that he is replaced in this narrative by a much more transparent authorial figure: "Samuel Clemens, an observant, curious, rather dignified man of forty-two."[27] I would contend, rather, that the constructed comic persona is still evident, although its range, force, and shape shiftings are much diminished.

"Some Rambling Notes" relates intertextually to some of Twain's most important writings in its main concerns. Recently, critics have shown a particular interest in the ways in which his work provides an often oblique commentary on the post Civil War modernization process and the changing America it produced. Thus, for instance, *Tom Sawyer*— the novel written shortly before the Bermuda trip — has been read in terms of the author's deep ambivalence as he both resists and accepts the logic of American capitalist developments. So, on the one hand, Tom is associated with "boyhood's free spirit" at play in an earlier (pre-Civil War) and simpler small-town America.[28] On the other, he can be seen as a protocapitalist and emergent businessman, one well attuned to the entrepreneurial and materialistic Gilded Age setting of Twain's own time.[29]

"Some Rambling Notes" can be read in a similar contextual frame. Here, however, the ambivalence and complexity that make *Tom Sawyer* such a stimulating novel are absent. Bermuda is seen from the very start of the narrative as a type of antimodernist haven. Indeed, the very thought of the voyage serves the narrator as a release from the demands of an American business world. For "pure recreation," idleness and freedom are immediately contrasted with "bread-and-butter . . . business," and the pressures that "the mails and telegraphs" bring (36). Similarly, once New York is left behind, the idea of an escape from telegrams, letters, and news proves "an uplifting thought": "It was still more uplifting to reflect that the millions of harassed people on shore behind us were suffering just as usual" (40). Once Bermuda is reached, its tidiness and charm — "snowy houses . . . gleaming out from flowers and foliage" — are contrasted with conditions in "black London" or "nearly any American city": "Nowhere [in Bermuda] is there dirt or stench . . . neglect, disorder, or lack of . . . neatness" (70–71).

When Twain then writes, "We felt the lack of something in this community," this "elusive something" turns out to be tramps, a significant problem in America during the economic depression of the mid-1870s. Twain
ironically suggests that Bermuda become the new virgin land where such
people might find a home:[30] "Let them go there, right now. It is utterly
virgin soil. Passage is cheap. Every true patriot in America will help buy
tickets. Whole armies of these excellent beings can be spared from our
midst and our polls" (90). Twain shows his more reactionary side here.
But the polarity he often implicitly constructs between an American
urban and business/industrial order (and its problems) and the allure
and variety of the physical geography of the island (73), its agrarian
economy, and its social harmony is highly significant for any consideration of the developing concerns of his work. Twain describes how, on
Bermuda:

We saw scores of colored farmers digging their crops of potatoes and onions, their
wives and children helping, — entirely contented and comfortable, if looks go for
anything. We never met a man, or woman, or child anywhere in this sunny island
who seemed to be unprosperous, or discontented, or sorry about anything. (89)

Clearly a romantic and nostalgic sensibility is at work in such passages.
And generally "Some Rambling Notes" lacks the ambivalent and often
anxious note that marks so many of Twain's other texts. But the author is
engaging here the same tensions that underlie so much of his best-known
writing: those between the rural and agrarian pre-Civil War society of
his boyhood (of which Bermuda provides an unconscious reminder)
and the "Yankee enterprise and technology,"[31] urban-industrial developments, and changing social relations of his own time. It covers the same
thematic ground of some of Twain's richest creative writings, particularly
A Connecticut Yankee (1889).

Another of Twain's major themes — that of race — also surfaces in this
text, though again in undeveloped form. The description of neat little
white Bermudan cottages with "masses of bright-colored flowers about
them" (70) offers just a hint of the start of Pudd'nhead Wilson (1894).
There would, however, be no "colored farmers" digging their crops in
the pre-Civil War southern context of Twain's later book. Throughout the
Bermuda sequences of "Some Rambling Notes" the topic of race (and
whiteness) noticeably intrudes. Whiteness, indeed, is everywhere in Bermuda. Hamilton is a "wonderfully white town; white as snow itself. White
as marble; white as flour" (64). The whitewash on Bermudan houses is
"the whitest white you can conceive of, and the blindingest" (69). White
here, though, carries none of the social significance it would in Twain's
own American South, where a "white town" would have very different

connotations. Race relations in Bermuda, as Twain sees them, are entirely different than in America (North or South), for here nationality and not race comes first. At his first close sight of the island Twain describes, gathered on the pier, "one or two hundred Bermudians, half of them black, half of them white, and all of them nobbily dressed, as the poet says" (63). Color is not the issue that it is back home. Black and white citizens appear to have equal social status and to mix easily and without any sign of tension. Evening service at Hamilton's Episcopal church brings out "five or six hundred people, half of them white and the other half black, according to the usual Bermudian proportions; and all well-dressed" (79).

On one of the walks Twain takes, he finds "soothing . . . twilight" replacing the sun's "bewildering glare." Looking up, he finds that "it proceeded from an intensely black negro who was going by." The two men pass, saluting each other as they go (71). Later, fearing "thugs and garotters" on a lonely road, Twain and his companion are confronted by "a vague shape" and hear a voice demanding money. The voice, though, turns out to belong to one of a group of "Sunday-school scholars . . . little black pious children" collecting for a new Methodist church (80–81). "Black" here does not signify threat or feared "other" but rather piety, innocence, good citizenship, and social grace. Twain does almost nothing with this material (in terms of explicit social or political comment) except to introduce it somewhat inertly into his text. Its presence is nonetheless significant. One can almost see Twain's ideas on race and sociality bubbling away behind the descriptive surface of the sketch, ready to develop more provocatively in his novels. Indeed, he had already begun to write the most famous of these (*Huckleberry Finn*) the year prior to the trip that "Some Rambling Notes" describes.

"Some Rambling Notes of an Idle Excursion" falls away rather, and it has a particularly weak ending. Nonetheless, the nature of its concerns suggests increasing and important connections between Twain's short and book-length works. There are also a series of connections between this narrative and others in the *Stolen White Elephant* volume. The more one examines Twain's collections of short writings, the more one notices the ties that (sometimes loosely) bind them.

In "Some Rambling Notes" Twain describes Bermuda as "the right country for a jaded man to 'loaf' in. There are no harassments; the deep peace and quiet of the country sink into one's body and bones and give his conscience a rest, and chloroform the legion of invisible small devils that are trying to whitewash his hair" (93). On the following page, he again draws an implicit contrast between Bermudan life and America and its modern technologies:

The Bermudians are hoping soon to have telegraphic communication with the world. But even after they shall have acquired this curse it will still be a good country to go for a vacation, for there are charming little islets scattered about . . . where one could live secure from interruption. The telegraph boy would have to come in a boat, and one could easily kill him while he was making his landing. (94)

In these two passages, both modern technology and individual conscience are (separately) associated with the "harassments" of Twain's contemporary American life. This suggests a scenario where the individual subject is cursed and bedeviled from within and without, able to escape such pressures only by physical flight (to a simpler world) or through violent means (chloroforming and killing).[32]

As Twain represents his American world in these narratives, however, we see a third source of individual pressure in the apparatus of middle-class domesticity. In "Mrs. McWilliams and the Lightning" it is not conscience but the wife that harasses the male protagonist. A cursory glance at Twain's work suggests two things. First, social pressure and conformity are particularly associated with the female figure. Second, the boundaries between correct social behavior and virtuous moral action (prompted by the sting of conscience) are extremely porous.

In "Mrs. McWilliams and the Lightning" we return to the domestic setting of the earlier "Membranous Croup" story. Once more, here, the satire of domestic life is gently done. However, the final picture of Mr. McWilliams, who again responds patiently and with mild irony to his wife's demands, is of the male adult and authority figure, the supposed head of the family, as complete comic fool.[33] He follows Mrs. McWilliams's irrational instructions on how to avoid lightning only to become the subject of his neighbors' mockery: standing on a chair (insulated by glass tumblers on its legs), wearing a nightdress, fireman's helmet, sabre, and spurs and ringing a large dinner bell. To add insult to injury, the supposed lightning he is avoiding turns out to be the flash of a cannon announcing a political event (Garfield's nomination for the presidency). If Twain celebrates "loafing" in his work, one of its aspects is composed of a male escape from social and community pressures. The correlative of this is found in this story in the undoubted frustration expressed at the limitations and boundaries of that (female-coded) conventional bourgeois life.

"Mrs. McWilliams and the Lightning" connects in turn with one of Twain's best-known short pieces, "The Facts Concerning the Recent Carnival of Crime in Connecticut." But while the former represents the male protagonist as a foolish but self-aware victim, bound within genteel domestic limits by consideration and an assumed love for his wife, the latter celebrates the violent escape both from conformity and conscience. In the "literary extravaganza" that is "The Recent Carnival of Crime,"[34] house and home are primarily places where violent murder occurs, not — as in the "Membranous Croup" story, for example — where a family is lovingly raised. The first-person narrator does not just chloroform, but kills, his harassing conscience, represented here not as a "legion of invisible small devils" but rather in the figure of a single and visible "shrivelled, shabby dwarf" (106):

After so many years of waiting and longing, he was mine at last. I tore him to shreds and fragments. I rent the fragments to bits. I cast the bleeding rubbish into the fire, and drew into my nostrils the grateful incense of my burnt-offering. At last, and forever, my Conscience was dead! (128–29)[35]

There has been much critical work on "The Recent Carnival of Crime." This has centered particularly on its philosophical nature (and Twain's "growing sense of moral 'seriousness' ") and on its definition of "conscience."[36] The relationship between this story and Huck's debate with his conscience in chapter 31 of *Huckleberry Finn* has also been extensively discussed.[37] I focus only on its links with the McWilliams story. The extreme violence of the narrator's attack on his conscience forms the other side of McWilliams's passivity and henpecked submission to his wife's instructions. Despite the very different narrative worlds of the two texts, the one a domestic comedy, the other a kind of metaphysical allegory, they share some common ground. "Carnival of Crime" also contains a female figure (Aunt Mary) associated with respect for the normative Victorian order of things. And her status is similar to Mrs. McWilliams in the respect and authority accorded her: "she was the person I loved and honored most in all the world, outside of my own household. She had been my boyhood's idol; maturity . . . had not been able to dislodge her from her pedestal" (106).

In both narratives, too, the central protagonist is a loosely disguised version of the author. In "Carnival of Crime," the conscience, called into visible life by the narrator's own wish that his "most pitiless enemy" might appear (107), mocks the appearance, manners, and habits of his host. And there is one unmistakable reference to the authorial figure in the dwarf's burlesque version of the "exasperating drawl" (108) that was Twain's most identifiable lecture platform feature.

Moral rectitude (the workings of conscience) is closely linked to social conformity in this story. Indeed, the lines between the two are blurred. We learn at the start that Aunt Mary's moral influence over the narrator is already faded, with the matter of his smoking — the "hateful slavery of tobacco" (128) — seen as the proof of the matter.[38] But whether smoking is a sign of moral weakness or behavior that is socially and/or medically unacceptable but *cast in the terms of* a moral failing is undecidable. Other issues raised — the feeding or not feeding of tramps, and the support or non support of the poor and distressed — are matters as much of social responsibility as moral integrity. In other words, the line between external social influence and inner moral agent ("harassment" from within or without) cannot be drawn in any absolute or clear-cut way.

The narrator joyfully destroys his conscience, both for its perversity and for having "*dogged* me, all the days of my life" (117).[39] The carnival of crime, on which he then embarks, concludes the story. Once his conscience is dead, the narrator reports himself to be:

a free man . . . a man WITHOUT A CONSCIENCE! . . . I settled all my old outstanding scores, and began the world anew. I killed thirty-eight persons during the first two weeks. . . . I swindled a widow and some orphans out of their last cow, which is a very good one, though not thoroughbred. . . . [M]edical colleges desiring assorted tramps for scientific purposes, either by the gross, by cord measurement, or per ton, will do well to examine the lot in my cellar before purchasing elsewhere. (129–30)

Freedom and relief from harassment in "Some Rambling Notes" is a matter of finding the right country to loaf in. In "Mrs. McWilliams and the Lightning," loafing is not an option in the American domestic setting that defines the harassed male protagonist. In "Carnival of Crime," freedom is a matter of throwing off "conscience" and, with it, all sense of social and communal responsibility. The social pressures and expectations of genteel American life *and* the inner drives that tend to reinforce those pressures are both violently discarded. Between them, the three narratives tend to suggest that only outside nineteenth-century America and its various realms — both public (its new urban-industrial landscape and its business culture) and private (the domestic province) — can proper breathing space be found. And a complete escape from harassment appears, in Twain's fable about conscience, to be a matter of the violent destruction of every given moral/social norm: those that apply both within the domestic circle (smoking) and outside it (killing tramps).

But we must at this point remind ourselves that "Carnival of Crime" *is* a type of fable rather than a realistic narrative endorsing aberrant social behavior. The word "carnival" used in its title connotes both comedy and laughter as well as social upset and reversal. Tom Quirk says that "the story might . . . be described as an apologia for the humorist as citizen and moralist." His view, that Twain in his role as humorist is "like the dwarf, a disinterested agent who merely [comically] exaggerates existing transgressions and absurdities in order to make us see them more clearly," offers a useful critical angle on the story (SSF, 68–69). But there is another possible and perhaps riskier way of tying the story to Twain's identity as a humorist. For we might suggest that the misrule and loosing of boisterous energy that ends the tale, and the radical upsetting of social norms that occurs, figuratively relates to the function of comedy and of carnival itself. Marcel Gutwirth describes carnival as the time when "chaos [could be] celebrated in relief from the oppressiveness of order. As a release of (demonic?) energies pent up under rule, folly . . . could do boisterous justice to all the culture perforce repressed" (LM, 50–51). Twain's humor in other words may look symbolically and aggressively to burst out of (rather than to endorse) the social policing that affects every area of our lives. I leave this idea undeveloped at this point, but will return to it in the different context of "The Stolen White Elephant."

Bermuda, in "Some Rambling Notes," is constructed as a type of pre-lapsarian alternative to America. Although it has its towns, conditions there are similar to those in the country (70–71). Race relations are harmonious. The climate is "delicious," the people are "kind-hearted," and there is food enough for all (90). Although specie exists, most transactions are carried out in onions, one of the main island crops (77). Twain is, of course, making a hyperbolic joke here, but the reference to a system of exchange that does not depend on money connects this narrative to "The Great Revolution in Pitcairn." Both narratives depend on the contrast between earlier, easy going, and simple forms of society and a present-day America and the supposed "improvements" with which it is associated. And the antimodernist emphasis of both texts fits into the general patternings of the collection as a whole.

"The Great Revolution in Pitcairn" focuses on an (other) island state, whose first patriarch's name, John Adams, hints at the original first father. That the island was first settled by the mutineers of the *Bounty* and existed as a British protectorate helps to undermine such connotations. But the use of the name nonetheless suggests the primitivist impulse that drives the story. Twain shared common ground, in this respect, with many of his Victorian contemporaries as they faced, or rather reacted against, the impact of rapid modernization.[40] Here the term *primitive* is used to describe the people of Pitcairn, whose lives Twain portrays as taking place in a "deep Sabbath tranquillity, far from the world and its ambitions and vexations": "The sole occupations of the people were farming and fishing; their sole recreation, religious services. There has never been a shop in the island, *nor any money*. . . . No alcoholic liquors . . . are used" (190–91, my emphasis).

This narrative (again a type of fable) has a clear intertextual relationship with *A Connecticut Yankee*.[41] "One stranger, an American," named Butterworth Stavely, settles on the island and turns out to be "a doubtful acquisition" (193). The same words would serve precisely for Hank Morgan and his colonialist impact on the primitive culture he so drastically affects.[42] Twain's attraction for simpler forms of community is clearly evident here. Staveley's impact results in the establishment of an independent nation of ninety people (the island population). He himself becomes the emperor Butterworth I: like Hank Morgan, he is "The Boss." Class hierarchies proliferate and "great offices" (200) are handed out broad-scale, with the consequent resentments that follow. Taxes are levied to support a standing army. Bonds and paper money are introduced to fund the newly created national debt. Eventually Staveley causes so much havoc that he is put out of office:

The next day the nation . . . rehoisted the British flag, . . . reduced the nobility to the condition of commoners again, and then straightway turned their diligent attention to the weeding of the ruined and neglected yam patches, and the rehabilitation of the old useful industries and the old healing and solacing pieties. (204–5)

This is a slight sketch and one again that contains few of the ambiguities and resonances of Twain's best fiction. But it reveals both his ironic awareness of the flimsy nature of his own country's supposedly democratic political system and the attraction he felt for the apparent simplicities of earlier and more primitive societies.

Staveley, however, is different from Hank Morgan in that he is not identified with modern technology and *its* dubious benefits. But a clear anti-technological impulse is at work at various points in the collection. In "Some Rambling Notes" for instance, the telegraph is judged a "curse." George Beard, author of *A Practical Treatise on Nervous Exhaustion (Neurasthenia)* (1869) and *American Nervousness: Its Causes and Consequences* (1881), identified the telegraph as one of the main causes of neurasthenia (the debility of the nervous system).[43] Neurasthenia, in turn, he saw as a specifically "*American disease*" and a product of modernization.[44] For Beard, the disease and the "electrical technologies" with which it was associated had adversely affected the very "character of American society."[45]

Beard conceived of the relationship between the human body and technological energies in symbiotic terms. Thus the body was itself seen as a type of motor or machine, associated on the one hand with energy and productivity, and on the other with the (machine's) tendency to overload, to break down under stress. So he would write:

when new functions are interposed in the circuit [man's central nervous system], as modern civilisation is constantly requiring us to do, there comes a period . . .

when the amount of force is insufficient to keep all the lamps actively burning; those that are weakest go out entirely.[46]

Though there is no evidence that Twain read Beard, there is an intriguing connection between such ideas and "Punch, Brothers, Punch," published seven years after *American Nervousness*. The narrator of this story — and here the "Mark Twain" persona is once more assumed — is harassed and eventually reduced to "a tottering wreck" by a set of "jingling rhymes" that take "entire possession" of him (141–42). He first reads these lines in a newspaper (Beard, we should note, identified "the periodical press" as another prime cause of neurasthenia).[47] Their compulsive effect is produced by the rhythmic imitation of the repetitive and mechanical actions performed by the conductor on a streetcar:

Conductor, when you receive a fare,
Punch in the presence of the passenjare!
A blue trip slip for an eight-cent fare,
A buff trip slip for a six-cent fare,
A pink trip slip for a three-cent fare,
Punch in the presence of the passenjare!

     CHORUS.
Punch, brothers! Punch with care!
Punch in the presence of the passenjare! (141)

The narrator passes on the burden of this obsessively "captivating jingle" (144) to his friend, "the Rev. Mr. –."[48] Significantly, it is while the latter travels to a funeral service *by train* that the jingle then takes full hold of him:

the car wheels began their clack, clack — clack-clack-clack! . . . and right away those odious rhymes fitted themselves to that accompaniment. . . . Why, I was . . . fagged out, then. . . . My skull was splitting with headache. It seemed to me that I must go mad. . . . I was almost a lunatic when I got to Boston. (145–46)[49]

Even while engaged on his own kind of conducting (that of the funeral service), the Reverend cannot forget the jingle. And when an "aged maiden aunt of the deceased" asks him about her relative's last moments, his response is comically predictable.

"I was there — *I* was there!" [he replies]
"Oh, what a privilege! What a precious privilege! And his last words — oh, tell me, tell me his last words! What did he say?"
"He said — he said — oh, my head, my head, my head! He said — he said — he never said *anything* but Punch, punch, *punch* in the presence of the passenjare!" (146–47)

This is a fine comic sketch that was extremely popular on its publication (see AZ, 380). The connection between nervous exhaustion, mechanical repetition, and modern technology (the clacking of the train wheels) allows us, however, to place it within the wider discourse of modernization and its effects: the "intolerable demands [they place] upon the human motor."[50] An antimodernist subtext underlies the humor that predominates.

I alluded in my last chapter to the ambivalence of Twain's attitude to science. And, despite the analyses above, the same is true of technology. In the *Stolen White Elephant* collection, and indeed throughout his writing career, he wavers between a championing of modernization and a penetrating critique of its effects. If it is the latter that predominates in this book, it is not all a one-way movement. There is evidence of ambivalence here, too, an ambivalence that would become more thoroughgoing in later books (and especially *A Connecticut Yankee*).

Thus we see a more complicated attitude to technology in the book's final tale, "The Loves of Alonzo Fitz Clarence and Rosannah Ethelton." Critics have generally had little time for this piece, mainly put off by the broad-scale nature of its burlesque romance and by the repetitious nature of its one basic joke: a love affair carried out completely by telephone. So Frank Baldanza, for instance, says Twain handles his subject here about "as gently as a steer in a slaughterhouse."[51] But it is Twain's use of new technology in the story that makes it (to my mind) of more than passing interest.

The telephone that serves as the plot vehicle in this story is modeled on the first commercial telephone, introduced in 1877 (the year the story was written).[52] Twain, we know, was a very early owner of a domestic telephone (in his Hartford house) and would indeed express considerable irritation at its shortcomings. Later, in the June 1880 *Atlantic Monthly* he would publish "A Telephonic Conversation," a short sketch reporting "that queerest of all the queer things in this world": the overhearing of one side of a telephone conversation (see TSSE1, 738). At an early point in the invention's commercial development, then, Twain was showing a precocious literary interest in the interface between the human agent and this form of electrical technology and the startlingly new and curious effects thereby produced.

"The Loves of Alonzo Fitz Clarence" opens with a description of the Maine snow, its "dead-white emptiness, with silence to match" (272). This metaphorically foreshadows the air space between Maine and San Francisco, New York and Honolulu, which the telephones in the story bridge. Technology at this time was busily altering "every aspect of [human] consciousness and activity."[53] One particular example of such dramatic change was the telephone's "severing [of] speech from human presence."[54] Twain uses the possibilities inherent in that fact in his plot when Burley, a rival in love, imitates Alonzo's voice over the telephone to "diabolically" (295) sabotage his relationship with Rosannah. An even more crucial effect of the telephone (and the telegraph) as a key instrument of modernity was its part in what Marx's powerful phrase would call "the annihilation of space by time."[55] So Alonzo crosses three thousand miles almost instantaneously in the telephone conversations he makes to his beloved.

The telephone and its modernist properties are central to Twain's story. However, he conceals the instrument's existence at the narrative start. The early telephone was an oblong box bolted to a table, with no separate ear or mouth-piece.[56] So one of Alonzo's first actions is to lean his chin on his desk and speak "as if to the floor" (280), the fact that he is engaged in a phone conversation going unexplained. Only in the third part of the story is the existence of a "private telephone" (293) first mentioned. Twain thus both confuses the responses of his readers and suggests the apparently magical properties of the new invention, with the questions the narrative raises of what is happening and how, and with the unexplained allusion to the simultaneous presence of different places and times.[57]

In the story's focus on the two main human agents and the information network they use, the latter becomes as important as the former. The relays and signals between the human voice and the telephonic system are paradigmatically suggestive of the larger interpenetration of bodies and machines in a modern technological culture.[58] And the use of the telephone carries its own significance, not just in the huge expansion of communication it suggests (one can talk to anyone, anywhere) but also in the possibilities of identity confusion and entropic verbal breakdown it brings with it. So here the absence of visible physical presence means that Burley can replace Alonzo on the line without his correspondent Rosannah being any the wiser.[59] While in *A Connecticut Yankee*, when a telephone clerk mishears "hellishness" for "holiness," Hank Morgan reacts by saying: "Confound a telephone, anyway. It is the very demon for conveying similarities of sound that are miracles of divergence from similarity of sense" (304).

Here we see Twain intrigued by modern technology and exploring its implications. He does not overlook its negative potential. Alonzo does have a mental breakdown — caused by extensive travel, "carpet sack and portable telephone" in hand, as he listens in at the wires to find his temporarily lost love (see the inspired quote that prefaces this chapter, yoking the spectacle of visual absurdity to motifs of alienation and — fittingly — disconnection). But neurasthenia is just one narrative concern. The possibilities and transformations associated with the telephone obviously stimulate and excite the author. He is also clearly fascinated by modern technology and the impact of its modernizing effects.

Coverage of *The Stolen White Elephant* has been necessarily partial, and there are other pieces here (and especially "A Curious Experience" and "An Encounter with an Interviewer") that deserve consideration.[60] But if Twain's writing was going through a difficult period, this book is far from being the artistic disaster that some have judged it. Whatever the "nonchalance" Twain showed toward this book, it still forms a significant marker in the development of his artistic identity and concerns. Indeed, two of its short stories, "The Stolen White Elephant" and "The Recent Carnival of Crime in Connecticut," remain among the best known and most popular of his short works.

6
Seeing the Elephant?
"The Stolen White Elephant"

The Elephant is the most largest Annymile in the whole world. He eats hay and kakes. You must not giv the Elephant Tobacker, becoz if you do he will stamp his grate big feet upon to you and kill you fatally Ded. Some folks thinks the Elephant is the most noblest Annymile in the world; but as for Me, giv Me the American Egil and the Stars & Stripes.

— Artemus Ward, "A Juvenile Composition. On the Elephant"

When detectives called for a drink, the would-be facetious bar-keeper resurrected an obsolete form of expression and said, "Will you have an eye-opener?" All the air was thick with sarcasms.

— Mark Twain, "The Stolen White Elephant"

In this chapter, I look closely at one of Twain's most puzzling short stories, "The Stolen White Elephant," to identify how, in this specific case, the narrative works and where its comic effects lie. In considering these questions, I circle back to the wider issue of how we read Twain's humor, and the intentions behind it. The discussion of *Sketches, New and Old* traced the moves in Twain's work between an absurdist comedy and his use of different, and more serious, forms of humor working to clear social and moral ends. Even as I made that distinction, however, the problematic nature of such boundary lines was evident. But I am also interested in the way that Twain, a little like the elephant in this story, stands as a very large authorial (and cultural) presence who is often very difficult to "catch," or pin down. His comedy tends to move *between* levels, frustrating any single or one-dimensional reading of its effects.

It is quite possible to read "The Stolen White Elephant" as straightforward burlesque, one of Twain's "farcical pieces that expose the absurdity of detectives and their methods."[1] But it is also possible to read deeper "meanings" into the story: to see it, for instance, as a type of self-reflexive allegory about the role of comedy and its relationship to a hegemonic (and repressive) social order. I will trace such variant possibilities. My more general argument though is twofold. First, I would argue that many of Twain's texts are marked by undecidability. It is often difficult to know quite how, or on what level, to read them, or how to indicate the authorial intentions with any certainty.[2] Second, I would suggest that attempts to categorize Twain's humor also often break down. His comedy moves between the antic and the serious, but it is also quite capable of engaging both responses within the limits of the same story or sketch, and *even at one and the same time*. I show something of what I mean as I discuss this story. But I will return to this subject, especially in chapter 12 when I discuss another burlesque of the detective genre, "A Double-Barreled Detective Story."[3] In both these chapters, and exceptionally in this book, I rely heavily on comic theory (in this first case, that of Marcel Gutwirth) to support my arguments. I do so because of its particular appropriateness to the cases in hand.

Critics have tended to dismiss "The Stolen White Elephant" as minor work. In her afterword to the Oxford Mark Twain edition, Lillian S. Robinson calls it an "admittedly slight story" (9). Tom Quirk is more sympathetic, calling the narrative a "rollicking treatment of the incompetence of detectives" though one that "seems somewhat dated now."[4] At the time of publication, the London *Literary World* summed up what perhaps still remains a typical response to the story. Describing the plot, it said: "Of course all this is nonsense . . . but a man must be morose and stolid in the extreme who does not . . . feel constrained to laugh heartily over nonsense which reaches such a pitch of cleverness and absurdity."[5] And the story has had a continuing public appeal. So when Louis J. Budd examined the record of foreign translations of Twain's work between 1932 and 1986, he was struck by its "continuing, very wide popularity."[6] "The Stolen White Elephant" is a puzzling story, and it may be this that has led to its lukewarm critical reception. Nothing quite adds up in it. The sheer size of the elephant and its incongruity in an American setting make it unmissable. Yet, in Twain's narrative, it has been stolen and has supposedly disappeared from view. The detective looks for clues to find the vanished elephant, but it is in fact visible and obvious, barging chaotically around the landscape as he performs his detailed work. There are, however, ways of seeing such a stress on instability, incongruity, and shifting perspective, as crucial both to the effect of the text and its importance.

"The Stolen White Elephant" is a narrative that appears to be "pointedly pointless."[7] The reader is left with a peculiar sense of not having got the joke. This sense of puzzlement, the struggle to interpret satisfactorily a problematic text, is (self-reflexively) signaled as a subject of narrative concern when Inspector Blunt, the chief of the detectives employed to recover the stolen goods, places an advertisement in the morning papers to open negotiations with the thieves. His message remains a form of gibberish for both the narrator and the reader (though their response to it implicitly differs). Shared codes break down as both are left on the outside, as it were, the point of the communication completely blunted. The detective's cryptogram is impenetrable:

"A. — xwblv. 242 N. Tjnd — fz328wmlg. Ozpo, —; 2 m ! ogw. Mum." (32)

The reader has a similar feeling of being left stranded at the end of Twain's story. But the enigmatic nature of the text as a whole takes a different form than that of Blunt's brief message. The language of "The Stolen White Elephant" is straightforward enough. Its cryptic element does not lie in any inability to understand the individual phrase or sentence. Rather, it is the overall humorous intent that remains obscure and causes the sense of frustrated expectation.[8]

I would suggest, however, that it is in this very sense of readerly frustration and disorientation that the comic ends of the tale (uncomfortably) lie. A type of double effect operates here, for it is only as our initial sense of puzzlement is explored, or so I would contend, that another level of humor becomes apparent.[9] We then discover a comedy of estrangement that speaks to the very condition of the modern — a form of humor that operates both at an epistemological and (to more limited degree) a historical level. The story finally operates as a form of anti-narrative "programmed to go nowhere," and it is here that its deeper "joke" is to be found.[10]

It is at this point that I repeat the note of hesitation and qualification made in my introduction concerning the nature of my own critical activity. An indication of Twain's mastery of the comic form is that to try to interpret or explain his humor is to risk falling, figuratively, flat on one's face. When I advance such "explanations," I always have the sinking feeling I may be missing the point entirely, ending up as the victim of Twain's joke. The gap, in "The Stolen White Elephant," between the myopic logic of the detectives and the elephant's random force is the main incongruity round which the story pivots. The former are burlesqued for "their pompous assumption of infallibility and ridiculous inappropriate procedures" (RG, 248). As I do my own critical detective work, here and in the rest of the book, trying to pin down and explain the incongruities and shifting effects in Twain's work, I hope to avoid a similar fate.

On first reading "The Stolen White Elephant," clear parallels emerge with Twain's other humorous sketches, particularly in the use of narrative frames and a central deadpan narrator. The title of the story is followed by a footnote attributed to the author (M. T.). This note both gives the provenance of the sketch and immediately comically destabilizes the relation between the real and the fictive: "Left out of 'A Tramp Abroad,' because it was feared that some of the particulars had been exaggerated, and that others were not true. Before these suspicions had been proven groundless, the book had gone to press."[11] A first narrator (presumably the same M. T.) then briefly introduces the teller of the main tale as "a chance railway acquaintance . . . a gentleman more than seventy years of age . . . [whose] good and gentle face and earnest and sincere manner imprinted the unmistakable stamp of truth upon every statement which fell from his lips" (7).[12] The latter's tale is then told, in the first-person voice, with no return made to the initial narrator. The move from suspected exaggeration to the deep earnestness of the central narrative voice strongly indicates to any seasoned Twain reader that the story may well be some kind of hoax.[13]

Susan Gillman sees Twain's fondness for this comic mode as "responding to an insatiable appetite, both on popular and literary levels of culture, for the hoax and the stunt, often in the form of the sensational . . . 'true crime' report." She links Twain to the showman figure of P. T. Barnum, whose career "exploited the national appetite for fraud."[14] Barnum himself figures in Twain's tale, cutting a deal with Blunt, as a telegram reports, for "exclusive privilege of using elephant as travelling advertising medium from now till detectives find him. Wants to paste circus-posters on him" (25). Barnum's presence, and the comic rupture in narrative expectation and logic which has the elephant then "plastered over with circus-bills" within hours of the original despatch, while large numbers of detectives continue unsuccessfully in its pursuit, all confirm — if it needs to be confirmed — the nature of Twain's literary form.

Moreover, any of Twain's contemporaries reading with even one metaphorical eye open would probably have made the connection between the subject of Twain's story and the frontier expression "seeing the Elephant." Forrest G. Robinson speaks of Twain's own predisposition during his years in the Far West (described in *Roughing It*) to "fall lock, stock and barrel for the practical joke that the mining frontier amounted to." "To see the Elephant," in this mining context, was to be aware of this joke, to see through the hoax, for behind western illusions of wealth and success lay mainly "the Elephant of gross self-deception and inevitable failure." Robinson comments further on the relation between the hoax that the frontier turned out to be and Twain's art, when he writes that "having seen the Elephant, [Twain] would plant a whole herd."[15] In the title and subject matter of this sketch is clear acknowledgment of one such literary planting.

When Marcel Gutwirth describes comic surprise in terms of "the good laugh at [one's] own expense" that follows "the joyous sense of having been had — in no very material sense, however — and having gotten over it" (LM, 91), he might have had the hoax in mind. Twain was a master of the deadpan. I have shown in chapter 2 the difficulty of penetrating narrative imposture in "The Jumping Frog" story: how Simon Wheeler's representation leaves us uncertain about who precisely is duping whom. The question of the identity of the hoaxer is also central to "The Stolen White Elephant." Its main narrator, the aged gentleman, is unflinchingly straight-faced throughout the story, but there is little evidence of any hoax being played on his part. His deadpan appears not to conceal anything but rather only to represent both his naiveté and gullibility. So the narrative ends with an affirmation of his "undimmed . . . admiration" for Inspector Blunt as "the greatest detective the world has ever produced" (35), despite all the evidence both of the detective's ineptitude and of the speaker's own duping.

It is, then, the first narrator (M. T.?) whose deadpan in this story seems to conceal the hoax.[16] He is the one who vouches for the truth of a story that contains so many patent absurdities, and who speaks of the possibility of exaggeration only to deny it. If the hoax is being perpetrated on the reader as s/he follows the plot of a detective story to its generically unsatisfactory ending, it is nonetheless of an odd kind. Two different aspects of the narrative work against each other here, and any attempt to foreground either one at the expense of the overlooked other cannot succeed.

The comic incongruities in "The Stolen White Elephant" make it clear that the detective story genre is being burlesqued and undermined. They also alert us to the fact that a "swindle" is occurring: that the whole story is a comic fabrication. Indeed, such incongruities put us in the position of detector rather than victim of this swindle. At the same time though, we are caught up as readers in the detective plot and *cannot help* but follow it to its strange and elliptic conclusion. Blunt places his coded advertisement, the meaning of which remains obscure. He then leaves his client (the main narrator) supposedly to meet with the criminals at midnight. Both client and reader are kept ignorant of what then occurs and are left to puzzle over a series of unanswered questions. *Are* there any criminals actually involved? Does a meeting take place? Is the detective duping his client? Finally Blunt literally stumbles over the rotting corpse of the stolen elephant — if it ever *was* stolen — with no further detail given of the clues or information that led him there. The detective is then celebrated as a hero for recovering the elephant, whose death renders that act of recovery pointless. The narrative ending, then, operates in completely antithetical relationship to the logical clarity with which detective stories, and their closures, are conventionally associated.

Twain's comedy might accordingly be explained as operating precisely in the gap between the story's two narrative strands. The reader is aware of the incongruities that render its status as a detective story absurd. S/he is nonetheless involuntarily caught within the fictional system and, once engaged, is made to follow that detective story through to its frustrating — as far as the conventions of the genre are concerned — conclusion. This may be where at least one element of the hoax lies: on a reader who has been caught between variant ways of reading and responding to a text; who is led to read a story in two ways and ends up stalled between them. "That is what a joke is," Max Eastman says, "getting somebody going and then leaving him up in the air" (quoted in LM, 105). Here, Twain's hoax works in catching us (briefly) mentally off guard. Having placed ourselves in a superior position to the main narrator, and aware (unlike him) that everything in this story tells us not to take it seriously, we nonetheless fall into the trap of puzzlement or frustration at the detective story's unsatisfactory end. We end up looking for readerly satisfaction in a form of narrative that has already been burlesqued, which we have been thus warned not to take seriously.[17] These two responses cannot be squared. Recognizing that we have been left up in the air, all we can do is acknowledge our awareness that we have been taken in by the narrative joke.

I retrace my steps at this point to explore the ways in which we come to know that this narrative is a comic fabrication as we read it and not a detective story to be taken seriously. If humor can be associated with "the playful character of contradictory signals that come at [consciousness] . . . simultaneously" (LM, 80), then "The Stolen White Elephant" complies with comic expectation from the first. A gift from the king of Siam to the queen of England, the white elephant of the title is stolen from the main narrator, a member of the Indian civil service and responsible for conveying the present from one country to the other. The theft occurs in Jersey City. Although an explanation is given for the presence of the elephant in that last location — the journey has been broken in New York and the animal is in need of recuperation — some sense of (potentially playful) disconnection and of the anomalous has already entered the narrative. This occurs in different ways: in the range of geographical locations introduced, and in the presence of this exotic beast, a "transcendently royal . . . token of gratitude" of specifically "Oriental" nature

(8), in a modernized and urban, western and republican setting. It comes, most of all, in the mental and visual play that is released with the idea of an elephant, the epitome of loud enormity, now become the pro-verbial needle in the haystack, the invisible object that must be found.[18] From the first, the problematic quality of the relationship between pres-ence and absence is placed right at the center of the text.[19]

The process of detection itself is parodied as Blunt proceeds to ascer-tain the facts of the case. He first asks a set of routine questions that apply to missing persons, and then responds to the elephant's disappearance in the manner common to burglary cases. Something of the overt sense of comic contradiction which now plays through the text comes from the mutually inconsistent nature of the two responses and the fact that nei-ther is appropriate to the stolen beast:

> "Now — name of the elephant?"
> "Hassan Ben Ali Ben Selim Abdallah Mohammed Moisé Alhammal Jamsetje-jeebhoy Dhuleep Sultan Ebu Bhudpoor."
> "Very Well. Given Name?"
> "Jumbo." . . .[20]
> "Parents living?"
> "No, — dead." . . .
> "Very well. . . . Now please describe the elephant, and leave out no particular, however insignificant." . . .
> [Blunt takes down the description and reads it back to the narrator]
> "Height, 19 feet . . . length of trunk, 16 feet . . . footprint resembles the mark left when one up-ends a barrel in the snow . . . limps slightly with his right hind leg, and has a small scar in his left armpit caused by a former boil." (10–11)

The comic effect stems from the obtuseness of the detective as he applies his "strict and minute method" (10) to the case in hand and as he keeps making the category mistakes on which humor, and Twain's humor in particular, thrives. Thus he has, for example, fifty thousand copies of the elephant's description "mailed to every . . . pawnbroker's shop on the continent" (11). This is the humor of incongruity, "a derogation . . . from that which holds together in the mind as fitting" (LM, 85), though to put it that way is to diminish Twain's individual comic incident in pursuit of (Gutwirth's) general rule.

The further description of such humor in terms of the "clash of levels" that occurs as the playful and logical sides of the self collide, though, offers a much more stimulating point of critical entry into the story. Gutwirth analyzes the comic moves that take place as one such side of the self meets the other, and notes the rupture caused by our awareness of the resulting incongruity. He sees such effects in terms of a type of "joke played by our irresponsible, our ebullient selves upon our sober-sides logical selves trudging glumly in the inescapable tracks of purposive existence" (LM, 97–98). These words can be reapplied to the comedy of "The Stolen White Elephant," which stems from the gap between the figure of the detective as Twain constructs him, with his logical and myopic approach to existence (both eyes open but seeing in a very limited manner), and the ebullient and random force of the white elephant on the loose. This is to suggest a widening of Gutwirth's frame of reference from internal to external reality, from the grounds of self to that of the represented world. A similar comic effect is then produced in the move between the high seriousness of the attempt to order and control reality and the alternative acceptance of its unwieldy and dislocating nature, mocking any human urge to exercise control over it. The detective here, to use an amended version of the earlier quotation, purposefully trudges along, applying his set procedures to the letter, but the tracks he follows are those of an eruptive and uncontainable presence. He sticks to his grounds and to his conventional way of operating, while the elephant, a paradigm of irresponsible ebullience, moves on leaving complete havoc in its wake.

In discussing the theft of the elephant, I earlier compared the consequent search to that for a needle in a haystack. Such a comparison is, of course, metaphorically inept. It does, however, fit a version of the world where the sober-sides Blunt methodically searches for the "good clews" (15) that will eventually enable him and his fellow "experts" (16) to find the vanished object.[21] As Inspector Blunt persists with his fixed routines, comedy continues to emerge both in the wholly inappropriate nature of his measures to the case at hand and in the disparity between cause and effect, between the obviousness of the "evidence" and the assumed difficulty of detection. Among the measures Blunt takes is the "search [of] all suspicious persons" in the railway and ferry depots and at other exit points from Jersey City. Once such measures are put into effect, he turns to the narrator confidently (and comically) to state: "I am not given to boasting, it is not my habit; but—we shall find the elephant" (15–16). The elephant does turn out initially to be as elusive as that needle, but it is nothing like as invisible. It crashes through the local environment causing mayhem. It is reported "dispersing a funeral . . . and diminishing the mourners by two" (25) in Bolivia, New York, and breaking up a revival at Baxter Centre, "striking down and damaging many who were on the point of entering upon a better life" (26). The elephant, momentarily captured, also brains Detective Brown ("that is, head crushed and destroyed, though nothing issued from debris," 27) when the latter tries to identify it by looking for the boil scar under its armpit. It then escapes once more.

Gutwirth associates laughter with "the threat of uncontained disorder" and refers to "the anarchic potential of an outburst that is apt to occur in any context." He speaks of comedy as "a field of force-on-the-loose" (LM, 55, 107). Language like this prompts me, given the way Twain represents his elephant, toward a (very tentative) figurative reading of it. Certainly this elephant comes to signify disruption and disorder in the text, as the "glaring head-lines" of newspaper reports clearly indicate. The narrator illustrates their general tone:

THE WHITE ELEPHANT AT LARGE! HE MOVES UPON HIS FATAL MARCH! WHOLE VIL-LAGES DESERTED BY THEIR FRIGHT-STRICKEN OCCUPANTS! PALE TERROR GOES BE-FORE HIM, DEATH AND DEVASTATION FOLLOW AFTER! AFTER THESE, THE DETEC-TIVES. BARNS DESTROYED, FACTORIES GUTTED, HARVESTS DEVOURED, PUBLIC ASSEMBLAGES DISPERSED, ACCOMPANIED BY SCENES OF CARNAGE IMPOSSIBLE TO DESCRIBE! (27)

Rituals of religion and their accessories (the elephant eats Bibles), forms of community, means of sustenance, and patterns of work — all these are disrupted by the elephant. The close fit between Gutwirth's theorizing language and Twain's description suggests an allegorical relation between the elephant and the comic principle itself. Comedy would here be represented as a potentially anarchic force, a threat to the established social order and all the codes and conventions on which it depends.[22]

I am aware of treading on thin ground, but it does seem that such an allegorical reading, once made, can then bear further development. A common analysis of the way humor works is to identify it with the misrule and lawless energy that oppose oppressive authority systems. But the other side to the same definitional coin is that humor is also subject to containment, a force which functions only briefly while these normal authorities are temporarily disrupted, challenged, and even overthrown. Gutwirth, offering one of several definitions of humor, claims that "laughter preserves the equilibrium of a culture as it does that of a group, by timely release of an outburst that dissipates animosities." If this is so, however, that disorder or outburst must soon be brought under control. Laughter, in such a view, is an "aid in maintaining whole our allegiance to an orderly existence." Or, to put it another way, comedy is subject to a peculiar form of social policing. Seen like this, the "disorder" of laughter is accepted in the "well-regulated state" as a healthy part of the social process. It contributes to "the creation and maintenance of a living order."[23] If humor threatens and disrupts authority, the challenge it presents to the established system is always temporary (which is not to say it cannot effect changes in that system), for it is to the accepted forms and norms that a return is soon made.

My heavy use of Marcel Gutwirth at this point suggests how closely I follow his analysis of what he defines as the "socio-integrative approach" to humor (LM, 29). However, we might wonder, as we return to Twain, if his view of comedy accepts the pattern of lawless release and hegemonic incorporation suggested by such an approach. To continue with my (tentative) allegorical reading, the disruptive force of the elephant, once it gets out of control and commits its "red crimes" (28), is not allowed free (or even limited) run, but is subject to immediate challenge by the dominant society. It is shot at with small cannon balls by the citizens of Bolivia, New York. And it is pursued by the detectives — the next best thing to the police — until it is dead, its rotting corpse found in the recesses of the very room in which these men sleep. The detectives regain their authority at the cost of the elephant's life. The central narrator uses a rather odd and unexpected phrase and speaks of the elephant as "my irresponsible agent" (28) at exactly the point at which its anarchic power is most evident. Might we shift the referent and read this (and thus the story as a whole) in terms of Twain's ambivalent response to his own comic art? To do so is, from one point of view, to see the white elephant as "transcendently royal" and signifying great value: a positive agency acting as a powerful subversive and anarchic force, only held in check by the representatives of a repressive society which constitute it as a type of feared other ("the dread creature," 28). From a different perspective, the value of the elephant is cancelled once it runs unchecked, for its force is now identified only with negative forms of destruction, and it has to be contained by the social body if that body is to continue to function properly.

If there is a veiled allegory at work in this narrative, then it is this last reading which might seem initially the more convincing: that humor and the humorist, unchecked, act as dangerously irresponsible opponents of a conventional social existence. The violence done by the elephant and the people killed and maimed appear to endorse such a view. However, it is at this point we step back to remind ourselves that this is a comic sketch and *not* a direct representation of reality. Humor may have the power to fundamentally disrupt social convention, so Twain will write in *The Chronicle of Young Satan* that "against the assault of Laughter nothing can stand."[24] But humor is essentially a form of "nonviolent dissent." The comic treatment of both death and violence in "The Stolen White Elephant" can only endorse our knowledge of their essentially *unreal* qualities. Detective Hawes reports, "Elephant . . . killed a horse; have secured a piece of it for a clew. Killed it with his trunk; from style of blow, think he struck it left-handed" (22). This is an absurdist and cartoon violence, any aggressive quality modified by the "consciousness of inconsequentiality" (LM, 57, 66), our knowledge that real pain is not at issue here.

In short, there is no simple reading available here concerning the relationship between the elephant (the comic?) and social convention. Those who represent the social in the tale are themselves associated with violence, as the maiming of the elephant with cannon balls shows. The justice and the health of the order being maintained are also open to question, for the chief detective uses the elephant on the loose mainly to buttress his own prestige and financial position. Moreover, the violence of the elephant, contained within the comic frame of the story, can be contrasted with the *actual* violence associated with the figure of the detective in the period when Twain is writing. To move from Twain's text to its framing historical context is to be made aware of the detective's role (and especially that of the Pinkertons) as a forcefully repressive social agent.

There are clear allusions to Allan Pinkerton's National Detective Agency in Twain's story. The "wide-staring eye" and the "WE NEVER SLEEP" legend of the detective badge "printed in gold on the back of detective novels" (30) are the motifs that "grace[d] the spines — and covers — of Pinkerton's books."[25] And the Pinkertons were clearly allied after the Civil War with the hegemonic order. Agent James McParland, for instance, was accused of playing the part of "agent provocateur" in the Molly Maguires case of the late 1870s and acting on behalf of powerful business interests. These interests, in turn, were sustained by means of legalized violence, for following McParland's testimony, twenty Irish coal miners were hanged.[26] The Pinkertons played a similar role throughout the later years of the century, used as spies and strike-breakers under the authority of the large employers. Their part in the 1892 Homestead Steel Strike — where "strikers fought it out with an army of rifle-bearing Pinkerton detectives imported by the Carnegie Steel Company" — would confirm the nature of such a reactionary social function in trumps.[27]

If "The Stolen White Elephant" can be read as an allegory about the comic, the relationship between the power of humor and its hegemonic containment is presented in ambivalent and unresolved terms. The anarchic potential of comedy can be interpreted in two contrasting ways. On the one hand, it can be viewed as a beneficial and potentially revolutionary counter to a dull, authoritarian, and repressive social order. Alternatively, and unless properly harnessed within strict boundaries of acceptability, it can be seen as a negative and destructive force that disrupts necessary social routines, systems, and beliefs. The story can also be read in terms of its juxtaposition of two contrasting types of violence: the one symbolic and associated with comedy in its aggressive mode; the other literal and physical, wielded by the sociopolitical establishment in the exercise of its power. But if a one-to-one allegorical frame can be identified in the relationship between the elephant and the comic, the allegory only develops so far. Its point and purpose, the clarity which underlies the allegorical form, finally gets lost, to borrow metaphorically from the text, in a type of foggy indeterminacy. This *may* just suggest Twain's own ambivalence about his own comic art.

Whether or not it was his conscious intention, Twain's use of the white elephant at the center of this story does encourage a figurative reading. Indeed the elephant starts off, in the text's own terms, as the ground on which one such reading is constructed: its physical presence a sign or token of gratitude and propitiation. A straightforward account of the value of the white elephant is given at the start of the sketch: "You know in what reverence the royal white elephant of Siam is held by the people of that country. You know it is sacred to kings . . . even superior to kings" (7). Such an account, though, does raise problems concerning figurative or representational value, for though such a creature might signify the "transcendently royal" and the holy in Siam, that is not to say it signifies equally in the American context of the narrative. More, the question of whether we can trust our narrator's interpretive account is also at stake here. He is, after all, to be depicted in the story that follows as both naive and uncritical in his reading of events.

A white elephant is not only a "rarity in nature . . . considered sacred and precious" but also (and this is the more common meaning today) something you cannot get rid of, "an unwanted possession [now] up for sale." The latter meaning, indeed, evidently derives from the tale of a Siamese king who "used to make a present of a white elephant to courtiers he wished to ruin."[28] This might lead us to think again as to the exact nature of those "Oriental ideas" (8) motivating the king of Siam as he sends his gift to the queen of England.[29] And we should remember that Twain's comic fictions repeatedly play around the relativistic shift in value centers, especially regarding assumptions of cultural superiority.[30] The question of what the white elephant might figuratively connote runs right through Twain's text as the reader puzzles over precisely what it is doing there: whether it is just a literal presence (a very unusual animal); what relevance, if any, the first-given figurative meaning has (the sign of the transcendentally royal); or whether the elephant signifies some other concept(s) or term(s). I would suggest that we cannot help but speculate on this last possibility. We know anyway that this is a phrase that carries a heavy figurative charge; indeed, that normally we would *only* use it in a figurative sense.[31]

Marcel Gutwirth claims that it is the changing relationship between figure and ground which constitutes humor itself. He quotes Gregory Bateson: "The joke may be thought of as involving a shift between the figure and the ground, where the figure is altered or the ground is reconstituted or a reversal of the figure-ground is taking place." This sounds complicated, but the example that follows helps to clarify. Referring (via E. H. Gombrich) to those trick figures that can be read, depending on the angle or way of looking, as either (for instance) a duck or a rabbit, Gutwirth continues:

> The mystery of illusion resides in the impossibility of capturing both views simultaneously. . . . Is laughter then the apprehension of that inability? Do we not in the art of raising a laugh voluntarily expose the single-track character of a mental apparatus incapable of focusing at once on the figure and the ground? (LM, 98–99)

This becomes doubly interesting when applied to Twain's story. If the elephant in its animal literalness is the ground, what then is the figure we can read onto it? Is that elephant a metaphor for the sacred and the valuable? For the principle of the unexpected and the alien (a type of mysterious stranger figure but taking animal form) which disrupts everyday logic and routine and which may suggest unknown determining influences (the intentionally malevolent gift)? For the comic spirit itself? And does the humor of the narrative arise from our confusion as readers as we try to fit a "straightforward" narrative of an elephant on the loose with a variety of clashing figurative possibilities, and from our awareness that that confusion is being cleverly manipulated by Twain?

What makes for the doubling of the interest is that there appears to be a self-reflexive play on the relationship between figure and ground as Twain's narrative develops. His elephant, now taking the part of the moving figure at the center of the narrative, literally disappears into its given (back)ground toward the story's end.[32] For the dense fog which closes the second part of the narrative means that "all trace of the elephant [is] lost." The sighting of a "dim vast mass" at "the most absurdly distant points" (29) confirms the confusion that now reigns as the white elephant disappears into the fog, as figure and ground become more or less indistinguishable.

This takes me circuitously back to the relationship between figure and ground in comic theory. Gutwirth states that "laughter [of what he calls 'frank amusement'], to come into being, has to be sure of its ground" and has to be based on a sense of the self that is "utterly secure." If— to use again the duck/rabbit example as an analogy of the way the comic perception might be seen to function—it is the awareness of our "single-track" mental apparatus that produces laughter, then this laughter comes from a position of mental strength. We are sure of ourselves, of our sanity and normality, and know that the mental confusion that has occurred is merely momentary. The "pleasurable helplessness" we briefly feel as our minds are taken in by that "shift between the figure and the ground" depends on a more fundamental sense of being absolutely sure of our (larger) ground: the sense of our own firm mental grounding and stable relationship to the reality that surrounds us (LM, 108, 98–99).

It is exactly such security, such a sense of ourselves, that Twain brings into question in "The Stolen White Elephant," as the relationship between figure and ground collapses in on itself. At the narrative point I have described (to be followed only by the final turn of the illogical and elliptic ending) the sense of that relationship—which is white elephant and which fog — has completely blurred. This may suggest the reason why the clash of figurative possibilities in the narrative does not function in any direct sense as a source of humor, as Gutwirth's theoretical probings suggest that it might. As readers, we end up half aware of such possibilities (that the elephant is to be read figuratively) but unclear about the relationship between figure and ground, uncertain which metaphoric or allegorical readings do apply and how we decide between them, or indeed whether we should be trying to read this narrative in such a figurative manner at all. We are uncertain quite on *what* level we should be taking both elephant and the larger narrative in which it figures. Twain dislocates his readers here: leaves us unsure of the base from which we are meant to be operating—unsure of *our* own ground. Just as the elephant merges with the fog toward the end of the tale, so too are its readers unable (metaphorically) to see the elephant: to see the point of the story, the nub of the joke. We can find immediate humor in the parody of the detective story, in the individual comic incident and incongruity within that story, in the burlesque of the detective business itself. We find further humor at a second and deeper level in the way we are caught between different kinds of response to the narrative. But we are still left puzzled by the sense that we still have not penetrated to its core and comic intention: that there is some kind of further level or larger meaning. We are left with the odd sense of being (like the narrator?) victims of a further hoax that we do not really understand.

This brings me finally back to the "pointedly pointless" aspect of this narrative with which I began. If Gutwirth discusses "uneasy laughter" as being "utterly incompatible with mirth" (LM, 108) and sees such laughter as a form of humor where we cannot be sure of our readerly ground, then "The Stolen White Elephant" seems to fit at least the last part of that description. Disorientation is a major theme in this story, a product of the (unanswerable) questions we are led to ask as we read — *has* this elephant, for example, actually been stolen at all and, if so, by whom and for what possible purpose? Further disorientation results from a lack of logic and connection in the narrative form and its rapid spatial moves. A geographic tracing of the elephant's path (exactly what Blunt does) suggests a principle of both randomness and uncertainty at work in terms of where it goes next, and how one can tell. In the course of a few hours, it is reported as being in New Jersey, New York, and Pennsylvania (21–22). But it might be in none of these places, and the reports of its presence may be false. The elephant certainly "does move around!" (21). The references to the directions it takes also tend to unmoor the reader: "Some say he went east, some say west, some north, some south, — but all say they did not wait to notice particularly" (22). Later, the elephant and the fog merge, and at the text's conclusion we are not quite sure what has happened or why. The more our eyes should be opened to what exactly is the case, and to what is the narrative intent, the less we actually see. The comedy in the story is built on a base of radical uncertainty.

Such uncertainties operate at a historical as well as an epistemological level. The notion of the precious (priceless?) white elephant ("rare in nature") opens questions of relative worth which, again undecidably, shadow the story. Oriental values (honor, worship, reverence, gratitude, 7–8) and hierarchies (the king and his subjects) are in implicit contrast with those of Twain's contemporary West. So, too, the elephant's worth (based on its "sacred" and symbolic properties) points to the different value scheme operating in the capitalist economy of postbellum America.[33] Blunt's actions are cash-centred: the $7,000 fee for Barnum's advertising, the $25,000 reward he straightaway has the main narrator put up. His apparent greed, self-interest, and deceit may function as an implicit critique of Gilded Age enterprise culture as a whole. But all such interpretation must remain speculative, for such thematic leads go undeveloped. The reader is left caught between sketchy information (of Siam) and extravagant burlesque (with any satire of American sharp practice clearly secondary to the story's main comic thrust). Cultural comparisons and questions of relative values are introduced, but there is no knowing quite where they lead.

To be human in a world that lacks logic, sense, even meaning, is to be unsure of one's bearings. To get the joke is to acknowledge such a fact. The references to the illogical and the absurd within the text might be extended beyond its margin to speak of the condition of the modern itself. The multitude of allusions to the factory, to photography, to telegrams, steamships, omnibuses, and railroads in the story may be particularly appropriate to a world (both textual and historical) where all that we can know is just how little we know; all we know of the ground on which we stand is just how uncertain it is. The motif of rapid modernization and the anxieties associated with such a process run (often covertly) through so much of the *Stolen White Elephant* book. It would not be surprising to find it in its title story.

This historical contextualization must, by necessity, remain tentative and undeveloped, for it is built on a thin textual base. It does, however, conform to the narrative's general sense of instability and undecidability. In "The Stolen White Elephant," the elephant crashes its way to the textual foreground. An uncontrollable and alien force, it stands out, in an anomalous and unsettling way, from the described background. But it also disappears into this background, leaving only traces of its presence, as the fog descends or as the focus switches to the detective seeking his clues. Foreground becomes background and vice versa, depending on the textual moment and on the perspective taken.

The detective is associated, at least in theory, with the impulse to gain logical control over a confused narrative. But in "The Stolen White Elephant," the elephant (and the principle of narrative chaos it symbolizes) gets equal attention: turning up unexpectedly and randomly, and disrupting all ordered sequence. The shifts of perspective and changes of focus suggest that attempts to categorize Twain's work easily run into difficulties. The relation between what is hidden or at the margins of his narratives and its central presence and premise is unstable and will differ from reader to reader depending on his or her emphasis and point of view. Thus this text can be read as a spoof on the detective business. It can also be read, though, as a type of philosophical speculation using the comic form to address entirely serious themes: the role of humor and its relation to social order and authority; the nature and strength of our grip on the reality around us. As he shifts ground in his story, turning (some of) his readers quite about, Twain upsets Gutwirth's distinction between uneasy laughter and mirth. In his work they often *do* coexist. Seeing the elephant, we may (uncomfortably) recognize uncertainty and dislocation as our human lot. But, at another level and at the same time, we can continue to "laugh heartily" over the brilliant comic "nonsense" Twain creates.

7
Merry Tales and *The £1,000,000 Bank-Note and Other New Stories*

> Berlin ... is a new city; the newest I have ever seen. ... The main mass ... looks as if it had been built last week, the rest of it has a just perceptibly graver tone, and looks as if it might be six or even eight months old.
>
> — "The German Chicago"

> Now how are you to tell when you are awake? What are you to go by? People bite their fingers to find out. Why, you can do that in a dream.
>
> — "Mental Telegraphy"

Twain's *Merry Tales* was published in 1892 and *The £1,000,000 Bank-Note and Other New Stories* in the following year. In this chapter I discuss them together. This is partly because of their close chronology and relative brevity. But there are other reasons, too. *Merry Tales* recycles a good deal of earlier material. Part of a cheap series ("Fiction, Fact, and Fancy") produced by Twain's own (struggling) firm, four of its seven stories and sketches are taken directly from *The Stolen White Elephant*. It contains only one new piece of any note, "The Private History of a Campaign That Failed."[1] *The £1,000,000 Bank-Note* seems an odd hodgepodge, with various generic types — fiction, travel essays, literary commentary, parapsychology, etc. — apparently randomly combined.

One of the general claims of this study, though, is that Twain's books of short writings usually reveal more of interest and value than their critical reception, and even sometimes a glance at their contents, might first suggest. And whatever the part Twain himself played in their process of compilation, the formal and thematic patterns within and between these collections, and their changes in tone and modes of humor, give them considerable importance as indicators of his overall literary development. In his afterword to the Oxford Mark Twain edition, Forrest G. Robinson rightly asks of *Merry Tales*: "Is there a book title in the Mark Twain oeuvre less readily recognized than this one?"[2] But even here, in "The Private History of a Campaign That Failed" (discussed in the next chapter), we have one first-class narrative: in Howells's words, "immensely amusing, with such a bloody bit of heartache in it, too."[3] I do not give a separate chapter to any piece from *The £1,000,000 Bank-Note*. The majority of critical work here, however, goes to that text.

Before *Merry Tales*, Twain had not published a collection of his short works for a decade. He had, though, written some of his finest fiction and nonfiction: *Life on the Mississippi*, *Adventures of Huckleberry Finn*, and *A Connecticut Yankee in King Arthur's Court*. He was at the peak of his writing career and, especially in the case of *Huckleberry Finn*, seemed to have regained his popular touch, too.[4] During that period, Twain's decision to play a major role in the publishing business seemed to have paid off. Twain and Charles Webster, his nephew by marriage, had been planning a partnership for some time. And just before Osgood's bankruptcy in May 1885, Charles L. Webster & Co. had been formally established, with Twain as the dominant business partner.[5] Earlier, in February 1885, when their partnership was still to be formalized, Twain and Webster pulled off their first and biggest coup in contracting to publish *The Personal Memoirs of Ulysses S. Grant*.[6] Grant's death immediately following the book's completion helped to trigger enormous sales, which quickly reached 300,000. As Hoffman writes: "Representing purchase by one American home in thirty, [the] sale earned a royalty of over $400,000 for Grant's heirs and a profit of about half that for the publishing company."[7] Taken together, the *Memoirs* and *Huckleberry Finn* meant immediate prosperity for Webster & Co. and a period of real "optimism and self-confidence" for Twain himself.[8]

However, by the time *Merry Tales* was published, Twain's professional and private lives had taken a downward turn. He would always find it difficult to combine his serious business interests and his writing. And business, anyway, had started to go badly. The financial state of Webster & Co. would fluctuate, but in 1894 the company would collapse. To read, in *Merry Tales* and *The £1,000,000 Bank-Note*, the list of books then advertised by Webster's is to be underwhelmed by their sales potential. The *Yale Lectures on Preaching* by the Rev. Nathaniel Burton and D. D. and R. L. Garner's *Speech of Monkeys* (on experiments with monkeys and speech theory) are just two examples. But a poor selection of titles and an overproduction of books were not the only factors to blame for the firm's problems. The decline in subscription publishing,[9] the expenses of selling the eleven-volume *Library of American Literature* by installment (see MTNJ3, 612–13), and a general cycle of economic depressions (espe-

cially the Panic of 1893) and consequent business collapses all contributed to the failure.[10]

Twain's mood during the Webster & Co. period shifted, too, between
boom and bust as circumstances changed. In early 1887 he is projecting
wildly about profits on just one book of a "dead-certain half-million" and
considering "the proper division of the swag" (MTLP, 213). By June
1891, he is writing of "the emergency of a constipated purse." And by
mid-1893 his deep financial anxiety and complete loss of business self-
confidence are obvious: "I am terribly tired of business. I am by nature
and disposition unfitted for it and I want to get out of it. . . . Do your best
for me, for I do not sleep, these nights, for visions of the poor-house."[11]

The 1894 Webster & Co. bankruptcy signaled Twain's own temporary
financial ruin. This was hastened by Twain's other disastrous business
investment, his "catastrophic gamble" on James Paige's typesetting machine.[12] There is no need to repeat this well-known story. It is enough to
say that from 1880 to early 1895, when he finally abandoned his investment and the machine, Twain had been backing Paige's invention, one
that was supposed to revolutionize the typesetting business. Exact cash
figures are hard to come by, but by early 1886 he was, it seems, supporting
Paige to the tune of $3,000 a month. And in August 1890 he would sign a
contract agreeing to pay $250,000 dollars within six months for all of
Paige's rights in the machine.[13] In 1891, his own attempts to form a stock
company for investment purposes failed (see MTNJ3, 572–73).

After the artistic (though not financial) success of *A Connecticut Yankee*,
the quality of Twain's literary work took a significant dip with *The American Claimant* (1892).[14] His domestic life, too, was on a downward spiral.
Both his mother and Olivia's died in the winter of 1890, and his daughter
Jean fell ill, possibly with her first epileptic attack. Twain himself suffered,
through 1891 and 1892, from severe rheumatism which badly affected his
writing ("My arm is howling," "I seem to be disabled for life," MTLP, 285,
297). In June 1891, Twain took his family to Europe, a move spurred by
his and his wife's poor health and by the high cost of running the family
house. The expatriation would last, off and on, for nine years, and the
family would never return to live in Hartford. A quoted remark appears
in Twain's notebook in spring 1891, possibly intended for inclusion in
The American Claimant. It is, nonetheless, prophetically accurate about
Twain's life from then on: "You git busted — in health or in money —. . .
land, but its (*sic*) long work, & up-hill to git back again — & you scacely
(*sic*) ever do" (MTNJ3, 609).

What is surprising is just how much writing Twain managed to keep
doing during these years. *Merry Tales* relies on material from the 1870s
and 1880s. "A Curious Experience" and "Mrs. McWilliams and the Light-

ning" are both taken from *The Stolen White Elephant*, and so are "The Invalid's Story" and "The Captain's Story" (both self-contained pieces drawn from "Some Rambling Notes of an Idle Excursion").[15] In terms of text space, then, half of the book is recycled material from that 1882 collection. Of the more recent material published here, "The Private History of a Campaign That Failed" and "Meisterschaft" had been published in *Century* in December 1885 and January 1888, respectively. "Luck" first appeared in the August 1991 *Harper's Monthly*.

But the work published in *The £1,000,000 Bank-Note* was mostly written in the early 1890s, some of it when Twain was having such trouble with his rheumatism. Only "A Petition to the Queen of England" (*Harper's*, December 1887) and "Mental Telegraphy" (first written in 1878 but unpublished until its revised version in *Harper's*, December 1891) were not new. "A Majestic Literary Fossil" was published in *Harper's* in February 1890. "Playing Courier" came out, under a fuller title and prior to American magazine publication, in the *Illustrated London News*, 19 and 26 December 1891. Its companion piece, "The German Chicago," was again first published episodically in the *Illustrated London News* on 24 September, 1 and 22 October 1892.[16] The book's title story appeared in *Century* in January 1893. "A Cure for the Blues" and "About All Kinds of Ships," both recently written,[17] were published for the first time in this collection. "The Enemy Conquered; or, Love Triumphant" was not Twain's own work but rather a transcription of the 1845 pamphlet romance by S. Watson Royston. Its positioning in the collection followed Twain's burlesque critique of it in "A Cure for the Blues." If the quality of Twain's work at this time was uneven, it was still a remarkably productive period. He also wrote *Tom Sawyer Abroad* in August and September 1892, and finished his first version of *Pudd'nhead Wilson / Those Extraordinary Twins* in December, with the final version the following July.[18]

Twain and his family began "an almost unbroken nine years of [European] exile" when they arrived at Le Havre on 14 June 1891 (MTNJ3, 574). It is no surprise, then, that he should play a relatively small part in the planning and preparation of the two books soon to come out. Twain was nonetheless in regular contact with Fred J. Hall. And if Hamlin Hill could write that "after 1891 . . . Hall was left substantially on his own" in the running of Webster & Co. (MTLP, 245), the letters between the two show that Twain continued to be concerned both with company affairs generally and the production and marketing of his own work. It is clear from their correspondence, too, that Hall was acting as Twain's agent at this time, forwarding material to various magazines and negotiating payments with them.

Merry Tales was issued as part of a Webster & Co. trade series, "Fact, Fiction, and Fancy," "designed to sell quickly and in large quantities to a popular audience." It cost seventy-five cents in cloth and just twenty-five cents in paper.[19] Twain was still convinced that pamphlets were a money-making proposition, and he was floating the idea of opening a new market for this type of paper-bound reprint, with newsboys licensed to do the selling. He proposed, in particular, another edition of "Jumping Frog," writing Hall on 7 November 1891:

I wish you would make such a pamphlet out of The Jumping Frog sketch and enough matter taken from White Elephant to fill up the pamphlet — print 3,000 and try it on. I believe that by the time you had 50 or 100 such pamphlets made up out of my stuff and uncopyrighted stuff of other people's, you would be able to pay all the firm's annual expenses . . . and have a profit left. *"The Jumping Frog," — by Mark Twain.*

A strong bold title-page like that ought to sell *just as easily as a newspaper.* I am satisfied that somebody will very soon introduce the 10-cent pamphlet. It is the coming form. Whoever gets in first may master the market. (MTLP, 290)

Hall was clearly interested in this scheme, but the idea modified into the more conventional trade series of books, with Arthur Stedman (son of poet and critic Edmund Stedman) as its general editor. Its first volumes were ready by the end of April 1892, and its launch coincided with a period of what Hall called "splendid business" for the firm as a whole (see MTLP, 298, 310).

Even though he was in Europe, Twain keenly followed Webster & Co.'s progress and helped plan the issue of his own work. Initially, Twain had thought to write and publish another full-length travel book. But he suggested to Hall that the six articles on Europe that he was immediately writing for the S. S. McLure syndicate should be produced meanwhile as "a 25 cent book of 35,000 or 40,000 words" ready "to throw onto the market when the last of the 6 is published."[20] Five months later, on 21 January 1892, Olivia (writing on Twain's behalf) noted his changed decision — that "it is not wise at present to publish the letters that after a time he will add something to these and make a dollar book."[21]

Twain's dialogue with Fred Hall continued, for just four days after the above letter he is laying out the details for a book of short pieces:

Yes, you can use my Century war article ["The Private History"]; also "Luck" (Harper's Monthly few months ago);
The Mental Telegraphy article (same magazine — December;) also A Letter to Queen Victoria (same magazine 3 or 4 years ago.)
"Meisterschafft [sic];"
Article about an old medical Dictionary (Harper — about 2 yrs. ago.)
There may be others but I don't recal [sic] them. (MTLP, 303)

We can assume that Hall and his associates were compiling a new collection or collections and making the necessary editorial decisions back in

America. Twain, however, was evidently playing a part in this process, both responding to Hall's suggestions and adding some of his own, in terms of what material might be used. But what is slightly confusing here is that half of the material Twain lists would appear in *Merry Tales*, the other half in *The £1,000,000 Bank-Note*. At this point it seems that, if the plans for the making of two separate books were now in place, Twain himself did not have complete knowledge of the details.

By October 1892, however, with *Merry Tales* having been out for six months, Twain was taking a much stronger and more informed role in the preparation of *The £1,000,000 Bank-Note* book. Thus he wrote to Hall on 13 October 1892:

I am sending to Harper's an article . . . entitled "A Curious Book." If they do not accept it, Mr. Alden will let you know, and you can send and take it away. . . .

The enclosed (enclosed with the literature itself in a big blue envelop [sic],) is Table of Contents of the proposed book—a book suitable for railroad and summer reading and such-like.

I'll explain the Table of Contents:

1. Preface — (if I conclude to write one.)
2. "A Curious Book" is the article I am sending to Harper.
3. "The Enemy Conquered" is the curious book unabridged—as you will see.
4. The Californian's Tale.
5. Meisterschaft

[the above two bracketed together with the words "herewith enclosed" appended]

6. About Ships—that's the Ship article you've already got. I don't care to publish it in any magazine or newspaper.
7. Playing Courier—(enclosed)
8. German Chicago—"
9. £1,000,000 Bank Note. . . .

If a little more matter is needed you can send me the syndicate letter which I wrote about the Beyreuth Musical festival, and I will correct it and return it to you. I have lost my copy. (MTLP, 322–23)

There are several things worth comment here. First, Twain lays out here — though not in its eventual order — most of the material (six of the nine pieces) that would appear in *£1,000,000 Bank-Note*.[22] And all the material included in the final collection and not named above *is* named in Twain's earlier January letter. The shape of the book, then, seems very much determined by Twain himself, though with Hall playing an important supplementary role. Second, it is curious to see Twain mention "Meisterschaft" here, when the piece had just appeared in *Merry Tales*. Though he made a practice of ruthlessly recycling his short work, the suggested immediate reuse of this piece indicates that perhaps Twain had not yet seen *Merry Tales* and was unaware of its final selection of material. Finally, Twain's reference to making corrections implies that his authorial part in the preparation of the final copy for the book may not have been

quite as minimal as is normally accepted. He does show a rather unexpected concern with the checking-over of previously published texts.

Twain too gave the collection its title. He wrote Hall on 12 December
1892: "*I*, for my part, prefer the *£1,000,000 Banknote and Other Stories*, by
Mark Twain as a title; but above my judgment I prefer yours. I mean
this — it is not taffy."[23] We see signs here of the author's general lack of
confidence just now in his own literary opinions and decisions. Thus, for
example, he wrote to Hall about the final version of *Pudd'nhead Wilson*: "I
will . . . get you to examine it and see if it is good or if it is bad. I think it is
good, and I thought the Claimant bad, when I saw it in print; but as for
any real judgment, I think I am destitute of it" (3 February 1893, MTLP,
337). It is clear that the various problems pressing in on Twain at this time
were affecting all aspects of his self-belief.

Twain was clearly not responsible for the title of *Merry Tales*. He wrote
to Harper's, when they were planning to reissue the book in 1897: "Please
squelch that title & call the mess by some other name — almost *any* other
name. Webster and Company invented that silly title" (see AF, 3). Twain's
dismissive attitude here ("the mess") is well founded. The material in the
collection is uneven in quality, and the book has more signs of being
hastily put together and carelessly planned than any other of Twain's
collections of short works.[24] Despite Twain's plea, however, *Merry Tales*
was retained as a section title when all its items (except "The Invalid's
Tale" and "The Captain's Tale") were republished as part of *The American
Claimant and Other Stories and Sketches*.[25]

The Fiction, Fact, and Fancy Series, of which *Merry Tales* was part,
evidently sold poorly despite the "bargain rates" at which the books were
offered.[26] In the Editor's Note to the book, Twain is described in terms of
the nationalistic qualities of his work: "to no writer can the term 'American' more justly be applied." But this generalisation conceals an increasingly problematic issue for Twain himself, as to just which particular
Americans he was writing for and to what end.[27] In 1882 he had published *The Prince and the Pauper*, which, as Louis J. Budd describes, had
"raised mild praise for its unexpected, scholarly side and a relieved acclaim for Twain's ability to express 'finer' sentiments and show reverence
for the morally deserving."[28] But, around 1890, he was still writing to
Andrew Lang as follows:

I have never tried in even one single little instance, to help cultivate the cultivated
classes. . . . I . . . always hunted for bigger game — the masses. . . . Yes, you see, I have
always catered for the Belly and the Members, but have been served like the
others — criticized from the culture-standard — to my sorrow and pain; because,
honestly, I never cared what became of the cultured classes; they could go to the
theatre and the opera, they had no use for me and the melodeon.[29]

In the moves between an identification with "genteel culture" and with populist entertainment, between instruction and amusement, between a reliance on and burlesque of popular forms, there lies a series of ongoing and irreconcilable tensions at the very roots of Twain's artistic identity.[30]

The role of literature and the responses of its audience, indeed, become a self-reflexive theme in these two collections. So, in one of the lesser-known stories in *Merry Tales*, "A Curious Experience,"[31] Twain echoes his friend William Dean Howells and his war against poor reading habits and in favor of "realism" and "the moral order he assumed [it] would disclose." Alan Trachtenberg borrows some of Howells's own words to describe the "zealous mission" he conducted against popular dime fiction and the sentimental romance: "Howells described [such 'injurious' literature] as 'the emptiest dissipation,' a kind of 'opium-eating,' drugging the brain and leaving the reader 'weaker and crazier for the debauch,' in 'dumb and passive need.' "[32] Howells, as Trachtenberg shows, was somewhat hoisted on his own ideological petard here. For the democratic spirit (a belief in a "republican equality and solidarity") which underlay his realist campaign, and the conception of literature that backed it up ("the authority . . . of serious fiction as a serious enterprise"), ran bang up here against the perceived failure of that civilized spirit and sound moral sense in the American masses. And Twain's story endorsed much the same message about the harmful nature of sentimental and dime fiction. It in effect dramatized what were "the deepest, most unsettling fears among respectable critics: that for the young readers of such sensational and fantastic fiction, the line between fiction and real life might indeed be entirely obliterated."[33]

"A Curious Experience" is a lengthy narrative and one that works as a type of hoax. The story concerns young Robert Wicklow, a drummer boy who enlists on the Union side at Fort Trumbull, Connecticut, during the Civil War. His mysterious activities and the letters he writes eventually lead his commanding officer — the main teller of this tale — to judge him a Confederate spy. The life both of the Fort and of the local community are highly disrupted as this occurs. Finally, though, this narrative of mystery, betrayal, and rebellion turns out to lack all substance, a product of Wicklow's invention alone:

It turned out that [the boy] was a ravenous devourer of dime novels and sensation-story papers — therefore, dark mysteries and gaudy heroisms were just in his line. Then he had read newspaper reports of the stealthy goings and comings of rebel spies in our midst, and of their lurid purposes and their two or three startling achievements, till his imagination was all aflame on that subject. . . . Ah, he lived in a gorgeous, mysterious, romantic world during those few stirring days, and I think it was *real* to him, and that he enjoyed it clear down to the bottom of his heart. (139, 141)

The only thing to fear, then, has been a boy's imagination and his bad reading practices. That Twain seems here directly to dramatize the warnings of Howells (and his fellow "respectable critics") about "sensation-story" fiction may not be surprising, given the closeness of their friendship. And his critique is in line with repeated attacks, from a realist perspective, on fraudulent sentimentality and romance throughout his work. Nonetheless, to have one of America's most popular humorists (who in the Lang letter says, "To simply amuse [my audience] would have satisfied my dearest ambition at any time")[34] critiquing the "low" and injurious appeal of other kinds of popular fiction does read somewhat oddly.

There are common motifs that run through *Merry Tales*, one of which is the repeated concern with military life in "The Private History of a Campaign that Failed," "Luck," and "A Curious Experience." We might indeed read "A Curious Experience" as in partial dialogue with the first and better known story. Both narratives were evidently based on fact, though "A Curious Experience" was the result of secondhand knowledge.[35] A shift of narrative levels takes place in this latter with the move from high seriousness to games-playing: from the major's account of a dramatic and adult intrigue of considerable political moment to his revelation that all this is the romantic fabrication of a fourteen- or fifteen-year-old "lad" (86). This also anticipates the similar movement—though reversed (from play to seriousness)—that occurs in "The Private History." The major of "A Curious Experience" describes the leaking of recruits from the Northern army: "The bounties [for joining up] were so prodigious that a recruit could pay a sentinel three or four hundred dollars to let him escape, and still have enough of his bounty-money left to constitute a fortune for a poor man" (86). This again compares with "The Private History," where we are given a matching account of those—this time on the Southern side—who "entered the war, got just a taste of it, and then stepped out again" (9). If financial opportunism in the former case contrasts with naive thoughtlessness in the latter, the final results (desertion) are the same.

The muddying of the lines between playful joke and serious social action has crucial thematic implications in "A Curious Experience." The commandant, fooled by the boy's apparent conspiracy, arrests a college president and a Western bishop's sister as Confederate spies and puts the local town under martial law. The boy himself is tortured, "triced . . . up by the thumbs" and shrieking in agony (132), even though he has absolutely nothing to confess. So, for instance, the blank sheets of paper suspected to be written over with "sympathetic ink" (114) are finally discovered to be just as empty as they look. Forrest Robinson suggests that "the solemnity and awe conventionally accorded military life are

subtly undermined" here by the boy's "harmless joke." For "grown men
... [are] stirred to suspicion, fear, anger, and violent action by a groundless fiction hatched in the overheated fantasies of a child."[36] As the narrative moves from spy/detective story to hoax, so the tricing up of a child by
the thumbs takes on a rather sinister aspect. Caught between stories and
worlds (a boy's fantasy and an officer's account of military treachery), we
are left unsettled, unable quite to sympathize with either. Twain here
describes just one brief and unimportant incident in a major historical
event. But in doing so he shows his ability to take us from one incompatible mental world to another and to open up for inquiry the series of
relationships that result. Reading is measured against reality. Authority
(the role of the commandant), law (the suspension of habeas corpus,
115), and cruelly repressive forms of discipline (torture) are set against
the rights and behavior of those of subaltern status. Such themes make
this story of more than marginal interest.[37] The narrative relies too much
on the melodramatic business of spying and the turn of plot that triggers
its collapse. Nonetheless, when Anne Bernays writes, "If only [Twain]
had let 'A Curious Experience' age a little longer, it might have become
one of his most interesting stories" (xlii), her claim does not seem
implausible.

In "A Curious Story," a volunteer in the Union army corresponds to
the volunteer in the Confederacy of "The Private History." In each story,
romantic illusions of different kinds meet up with the hard realities of
military life: torture and death. Both narratives tend to undermine military values and behavior. "Luck" is the third story of military matters in
the *Merry Tales* collection and one that again tends to "diminish the
heroic luster of military endeavors."[38] Like "A Curious Experience," this
was another secondhand tale, told to Twain by Joe Twichell and apparently repeated verbatim. In "The Private History" the narrator ("Mark
Twain") recounts the nadir and collapse of his military career. "Luck"
moves in an opposite direction, explaining how the name of its main
protagonist, Lord Arthur Scoresby, "shot suddenly to the zenith from a
Crimean battle-field, to remain forever celebrated" (66). This happened,
we are told, thirty years before the London banquet in Scoresby's honor:
the event that spurred the writing of this piece. It is at this retrospective
celebration that the narrator learns that Scoresby is "an absolute fool"
(67). His career advancement had always in fact been due to "lucky
accident" (69). This had climaxed in a blunder during the Crimean War
when, advancing to the left instead of retreating to the right as ordered,
he caused the whole Russian army to panic and lose the battle — and all
by blind luck. Throughout Scoresby's career, then, "everybody [had] ...
misinterpreted his performance" (72). His "noble gravity" (66) disguises
a "wooden-head," a "donkey" (70).

Twain first published this narrative in 1891 at the time when his own luck seemed to be running out and when events seemed to conspire against him.[39] In the stress on pure accident in this story, and the doubts thus raised about personal agency and its effectiveness, we see the development of a strand of thinking that would become insistent in his work. The notion of Scoresby's secret going undiscovered through misinterpretation ("Everybody had him focussed wrong," 72) returns us to the stress on relativism, especially in the move from one mind-set to another, apparent right from the start of Twain's career.

"Meisterschaft," "a burlesque in the form of a play" (xlii), is the last piece in *Merry Tales*. The interest in language and its difference here, and the possibilities for dialogue and discord in that difference, strike a familiar Twain note. But unless one reads German (see 183–97, for instance), the play, burlesquing the Meistershaft system of language tuition, is virtually unreadable. Even here, though, critics were unable to agree about the merits of the piece. When it came out in book form, the *San Francisco Chronicle* called it "that terribly tedious sketch . . . which the author may have thought funny, but which no one else ever did." The New York *Sun*, in contrast, said "nobody should miss [it] . . . with its beautiful German and its capable English, mixed."[40] Similarly, in a more recent critical context, Malcolm Bradbury introduces *The £1,000,000 Bank-Note and Other New Stories* (the book that followed *Merry Tales*) by calling it:

surely the most delightful of Mark Twain's later books . . . interesting, among other reasons, because it belongs so exactly to the moment before the final turn into darkness, when Twain's comedy still has a great deal to do with hope, joy and success. . . . The *£1,000,000 Bank-Note* is one of the chief comic pleasures these years . . . yielded. (xxxi, xl, xliv)

While James D. Wilson, writing the afterword, judges it quite differently as a "volume of largely pedestrian sketches" seemingly "hastily put together to turn a quick profit . . . [and] shamelessly padded to achieve volume length" (AF, 1–2). Such examples suggest that Twain's texts as a whole are marked by a particular interpretive undecidability.

When Wilson speaks of padding he is specifically referring to "A Cure for the Blues" and "The Curious Book Complete." But in putting together these two texts, Twain is continuing the defense of a Howellsian realism of "A Curious Story." His primary target here, though, is not so much the adverse effect that popular romantic fiction has on its reader as he or she negotiates an everyday world. Rather, it is the aesthetic and representational failures of such fiction on which he now focuses.[41]

The Enemy Conquered; or, Love Triumphant is in fact a direct reprinting of a short pamphlet romance published by S. Watson Royston in 1845 (though Twain changes the authorial name to G. Ragsdale McClintock).[42] Twain had first come across the piece in 1884 when George Washington Cable was recovering from illness at his home, and both men were taken by "the book's inflated sentimental language and unconscious humor" (MTNJ3, 47). Placed immediately before Royston's story, "A Cure for the Blues" shows Twain taking some delight in critiquing its overblown rhetoric, illogical plotting, and generic determinants. He focuses especially on the author's style, which "nobody can imitate . . . not even an idiot" (83), the "jingling jumble of fine words [that] seemed to mean something; but it is useless . . . to try to divine what it was" (90). As an example of the latter, he quotes the simile "like the topmost topaz of an ancient tower," which has, Twain says, not "a ray of sense in it, or meaning to it" (80). He goes on to describe the names of Royston/McLintock's fictional characters as ones which "fantastically fit his lunatics" (83), and draws particular attention to that of the heroine, Ambulinia Valeer ("It can hardly be matched in fiction," 89). Plot inconsistencies and absurdities are pilloried. So when the two lovers, Elfonzo and Ambulinia, hide among the orchestra to avoid being seen together at a village show, Twain writes: "This does not seem to be good art. . . . [O]ne cannot conceal a girl in an orchestra without everybody taking notice of it" (99). All this is of course particularly similar to, and preparation for, Twain's later and more vehement two-part critical assault on James Fenimore Cooper and his "Literary Offences" (1895).

It is Twain's belief in a realist aesthetic that underpins and motivates "A Cure for the Blues." Howells described realism's aim as "to picture the daily life in the most exact terms possible."[43] And Henry James spoke of Howells's own writing in terms of its "art of imparting a palpitating interest to common things and unheroic lives," adding that "the truth of representation . . . can be achieved only so long as it is in our power to test and measure it."[44] Twain critiques *The Enemy Conquered* for its complete divergence from just such principles:

The reader must not imagine he is to find in it . . . purity of style . . . truth to nature, clearness of statement, humanly possible situations, humanly possible people, fluent narrative, connected sequence of events —. . . or logic, or sense. No; the rich, deep, beguiling charm of the book lies in the total and miraculous *absence* from it of all these qualities. (78)

Twain's tone here — and in some contrast to "A Curious Story" — is one of comic pleasure rather than direct moral and aesthetic condemnation. But similar assumptions motivate both pieces.

Twain quotes liberally from *The Enemy Triumphant* as he writes "A Cure for the Blues." There is then something redundant about its consequent reprinting. In his essay, Twain fillets Royston's story to reveal its unconsciously comic highlights. The publication of its entire turgid narrative is a case of critical overkill (and I suspect most readers just skip it). Twain himself, though, apparently saw "A Curious Old Book" — that is, "A Cure for the Blues" and Royston's text taken together — as central to the collection, telling Hall, "The article 'A Curious Old Book' is the *important* feature, not the '£1,000,000 Note.' " He continued: "The 'Curious Old Book' is the most delicious thing that has been offered to a magazine in 30 years." Twain's delight in Royston's stylistic clumsiness, and his own commitment to a different set of literary standards, led him apparently to overvalue this section of his book.

But there is much interesting material in *The £1,000,000 Bank-Note*, and Wilson, despite his overall dismissiveness, is right to say that "collectively, and juxtaposed with one another, the diverse items in [it] illuminate the wide range of Mark Twain's intellectual, spiritual, and aesthetic interests, as well as the complexity of the late Victorian mind" (AF, 13). The collection can be linked to *The Stolen White Elephant* in its recurrent concern with the general issue of modernization, especially in the two sketches "About All Kinds of Ships" and "The German Chicago."[45] As the book circles round this (very large) subject, however, it shows a generally more positive attitude than in the previous collection, though with clear ambivalence still present. Twain's work on *A Connecticut Yankee* may well have influenced, and complicated, his responses here.

The best two pieces in this book are its title story and the comic sketch "Playing Courier." If the postbellum era in America can be approached in terms of what Martha Banta calls a "capitalist historiography,"[46] then "The £1,000,000 Bank-Note" helps trace some of the stages in that development, for this is a story about money and financial investment in an international context. Money, to adapt the saying, talks louder than either words or appearances in the London world in which the story is mainly set. "Henry Adams," the narrator and main protagonist,[47] like Hank Morgan in *A Connecticut Yankee*, is unexpectedly and suddenly (in terms of text time) transported from one (American) world to another (British) one. A penniless stranger in a strange land, he is picked, for his honest, intelligent looks and because he *is* a stranger, to receive one of the only two million-pound notes issued by the Bank of England. Adams — though he is ignorant of this fact until late in the story — is given the note to resolve a bet between two brothers over whether a man could "live thirty days, *any way*, on that million, and keep out of jail, too," or whether with "no way to account for his being in possession of it . . . he would starve to death" (11–12).

Adams goes into a tailor shop to replace his ragged clothes. Judged on the basis of his looks, his words (claiming not to have "any small change about me," 19) are met with sarcastic disbelief. When the bank note is handed over, however, the salesman's "smile froze solid, and turned yellow" (20) and his attitude is transformed. Money here is power. In this modern capitalist world, old feudal indexes of status vie with those based purely on financial worth (and see 24, 30–31). Twain also returns to one of his obsessive themes, the problematic nature of the outward signs of social identity, with the tailor's difficulty in telling the man he now takes to be an eccentric millionaire from a tramp.[48] The story is both a romance and a rags-to-riches narrative.[49] Adams rises swiftly in the London world and does so entirely on credit, for no one checks the substance behind the million pound sign he carries in his pocket. Indeed, so much value is indicated in that sign that none of those with whom he does business *can* check the substance (by offering change). The note's value is guaranteed by the Bank, but because of its size and rarity the note is also worthless: "he could n't offer it at a bank or anywhere else, because he would be arrested on the spot" (11). The awesome power of this token that Adams carries comes in time to constitute his public identity, for his nickname is the "vest-pocket monster" (28).

Twain works his tale around the conditions and contradictions of capitalist exchange and the different notions of worth in his nineteenth-century world. The conditions and assumptions that govern the narrator are those imposed by the market. This is, potentially at any rate, a boom and bust economy: living on credit now (by reason of that uncashable note) Adams judges "there was going to be a crash by and by" (23). The main business dealings noted in the text are international—between England and America. Again it is the relation between insubstantial indexes of worth (British financial investments in paper stocks) and actual material substance (the American mining of hard silver on which that investment would be based) which is at stake in those dealings. And Adams has a twinned figure in the tale, his friend Hastings, who has "come to England with . . . an 'option' to sell the Gould and Curry [silver-mining company] Extension for the 'locators' of it, and keep all he could get over a million dollars." But not "a solitary capitalist" (37) listens to him. So while Adams, to all outward appearance, becomes "a vast millionaire, and a colossal celebrity!" (28), Hastings is "defeated, routed, annihilated!" (35).

When Adams is apparently most successful, he still knows that his fortune rests on a fraudulent base, capital on which he cannot knowingly draw: "I was standing on a half-inch crust, with a crater underneath" (35). Twain writes both his hero and Hastings out of their crisis by having Adams stimulate investment in the Gould and Curry stock on the strength of his own "name," now put behind the project (38). Ironically, while the index of Adams's "name" rests on an insubstantial base (for he is a pauper), the Gould and Curry Company was (at least in the 1860s) "irreproachable" and hugely successful.[50] But the narrator's "cold . . . capitalist" scheme (38) works. False confidence makes the market move, and Adams gains £20,000 as a result.

Bradbury writes, "In the world of 'The £1,000,000 Bank-Note,' speculation and capitalism, along with love and ingenuity, still work fine. . . . American smartness and benevolent British capital make a happy marriage" (xlii). If this is roughly true in terms of the plot outcome, all kinds of doubts and hesitations about the workings of a capitalist system and the communities it breeds are built into this narrative. If Adams remains a hero, it is not because of the money that he makes or the way that he makes it, but the fact that such activity does not consume his mind and heart, for Portia, whom he marries, holds ten times more value for him than the bank-note that led him to her and facilitated their relationship.[51] Even this romance, though, contains an odd and disturbing element, with the language Adams uses to describe his wife's worth. The bank-note (now canceled) has been framed and placed "in the sacredest place in [the Adams] home." And when Adams repeatedly refers to it, he always says: "Yes, it's a million-pounder, as you see; but it never made but one purchase in its life, and *then* got the article for only about a tenth part of its value" (44). Adams's love for his wife and her central role in his life are clear. But to place the symbol of enormous wealth in a "sacred" place in the house and to describe his wife in terms of commercial and financial exchange (an "article" bought at bargain price) hints that the market may now make the man. Once engaged in capitalist enterprise, its assumptions and language have entered Adams's deepest modes of thought and being and form the gauge by which all aspects of his life are measured. Later texts, "The $30,000 Bequest" and "The Man That Corrupted Hadleyburg," return to the subject of what happens to intimate human relationships where money is involved and have far bleaker tales to tell. It may be that a hint of that bleakness is concealed even within the apparently positive note on which this story ends.

"Playing Courier" engages the modernization theme in a much more peripheral way. It is true that the power of the American dollar allowed, and indeed stimulated, the type of sojourn abroad represented in "Playing Courier," and the relative luxury (couriers, hotels, and first-class trains) in which it was carried out. But the strength of Twain's sketch lies not in its economic context but in the recovery of a comic poise missing from much of his recent work. The author returns here to the use of the "Mark Twain" persona and the comic gap between covert authorial presence and persona that this allowed.[52] In more and more of Twain's first-person work ("A Cure for the Blues" is an example) any comic projection of the authorial self is lost in favor of a more direct representation of that author (no longer covert), his opinions and experiences. In "Playing Courier," though, we are back to Twain at his comic best (and see xliii).

This sketch has further (loose) links to the general modernization motif in its play on qualities of efficiency, systematization, and rationalization synonymous with that term. Such qualities inform all areas of modern life, even those of leisure pursuits.[53] In Switzerland and having delayed in hiring a courier, the narrator of "Playing Courier" decides to do the job himself. He represents himself as "a great stickler for order and system" (199) as he goes about his job (and see 187). The comedy comes as the narrator's self-presentation is undermined by every detail of his brief career and in both the chain of blunders he makes and his attempts to mislead or mollify his "Expedition" concerning the outcome of his various tasks. The smooth order and efficiency with which the daily business of modern life (modern tourism in this case) normally functions is disrupted and disorganized by the narrator's comically naive and inefficient presence.

The main gap opened up here is between the projected controlled efficiency of this "Mark Twain" with his (precarious) sense of self-worth and his actual incompetence as measured by the outcome of his actions. This is nowhere better illustrated than when he goes to collect two of his party's members from their lodgings. They have in fact left some hours earlier, but the unknowing narrator sits in the horse-cab he has taken and, while he waits for his charges to descend from their rooms, decides to "muse during the fifteen minutes and take it easy." "A very still and blank interval" follows, then a policeman taps him on the shoulder. Looking up, the narrator sees "a good deal of a crowd, and they had that pleased and interested look which such a crowd wears when they see that somebody is out of luck." He then finds that his horse and driver are asleep and that all three of them (himself included) have been "hung . . . full" of the "gaudy decorations" (for the anniversary of the "Signing of the Compact" is being celebrated that day). What follows is predictable but nonetheless very funny:

The officer said:
   "I'm sorry, but we can't have you sleeping here all day."
   I was wounded and said with dignity:
   "I beg your pardon, I was not sleeping; I was thinking."
   "Well, you can think if you want to, but you've got to think to yourself; you disturb the whole neighborhood."
   It was a poor joke, and it made the crowd laugh. I snore at night sometimes, but it is not likely that I would do such a thing in the daytime and in such a place. The officer undecorated us, and seemed sorry for our friendlessness, and really tried to be humane, but he said we must n't stop there any longer or he would have to charge us rent. (199–201)

It is the sheer multiplicity and complexity of the narrator's chain of half-done tasks, confusions, and mistakes that produce the comic zest of "Playing Courier." Thinking he has lost his letter of credit, he visits the police authorities and the mayor. The officer on duty wants to hold him as "a suspicious-looking person," but the mayor resists, saying "he saw . . . nothing the matter with me but a wandering mind, and not much of that" (188–89). He practices his French on the policeman, "but he would n't have that. . . . It seemed to make him particularly bitter to hear his own tongue" (198). When he buys train tickets at a cigar shop, they turn out to be "lottery tickets . . . and . . . a lottery which has been drawn two years ago" (204). A professional courier is finally employed to sort out the mess the narrator has created. Accompanying him on his various tasks of restitution and reparation, "Twain" decides his next actions on the basis of this new courier's account of the general mood of his party: "He described the weather to me that was prevailing on the upper levels there with the Expedition, and I saw that I was doing very well where I was. . . . I stayed out in the woods till 4 P.M., to let the weather moderate" (208). The comic misadventures and strained relationships represented here, and the figurative wit with which they are described, effectively shape and drive forward the narrative throughout.

The essays "About All Kinds of Ships" and "The German Chicago" are the pieces in the collection most clearly focused round the modernization theme. Here, Twain uses a mainly nonfictional form. And here too we get a more direct celebration of modernity than anywhere in *The Stolen White Elephant* book or in most of Twain's fictional representations of that subject. In "About All Kinds of Ships," this celebration consists of Twain's account of his own experience on board the Atlantic liner *Havel*. Twain goes back to chart his adult personal history by way of sea voyages. First, in chronological order, he mentions the "sailing vessel" that was becalmed on his trip from San Francisco to the Sandwich Islands (181). Then he refers to the "little steamer . . . the excursion tub 'Quaker City,' " with its crew of forty and seventy passengers (159–60). This builds toward his most recent experience on the *Havel*—a "modern leviathan . . . built of steel" (157) with nearly eleven hundred people on board (160). Such developments in marine technology have rendered the sailing ship and earlier types of steamship "obsolete" (154) as far as ocean travel goes.

Twain also introduces a note of fictional burlesque into this essay as he taps into the larger history of sea travel to complement his own experiences. So he introduces an extended comic sequence about Noah and his Ark, playing with the idea of a contemporary German ship inspector subjecting Noah to examination concerning the seaworthiness of his boat and its compliance with safety regulations. Twain shifts tone here from reportage and commentary to a comedy based on the clash of conceptual and linguistic systems:

"What is your hull sheathed with — copper?"
"Her hull is bare — not sheathed at all."
"Dear man, the wood-boring creatures of the sea would riddle her like a sieve and send her to the bottom in three months. She *cannot* be allowed to go away, in this condition. . . . Just a word more: Have you reflected that Chicago [the reference here is to the 1893 Exhibition] is an inland city and not reachable with a vessel like this?"
"Shecargo? What is Shecargo? I am not going to Shecargo."
"Indeed? Then may I ask what the animals are for?"
"Just to breed others from . . . [for] the rest are going to be drowned in a flood. . . ."
"A flood?"
"Yes. . . . It is going to rain forty days and forty nights.". . .
"Privately — but of course not officially — I am sorry you revealed this, for it compels me to withdraw the option I gave you as to sails or steam. I must require you to use steam. Your ship cannot carry the hundredth part of an eleven-months' water-supply for the animals. You will have to have condensed water." (169–70)

Twain then turns to Columbus and his voyage, again burlesquing the events described (Columbus wearing "deep gauntlets of finest white heretic skin," 174) but now also making serious comparisons concerning the changing conditions of sea travel.

Modernization and its advantages form the core subject of the essay. Twain praises the "ingenuity of man . . . in this passing generation" and the "mastery" over nature that results: "the giant ship of our day does not climb over the waves, but crushes her way through them" (160). All the watchwords of a newly modernized world are called up here, for the construction of the modern ship is marked by a "complete efficiency" and its environment is one where "every comfort and convenience" can be enjoyed (156–57). Electric lights (that one can "burn . . . in one's room all night," 155) have replaced the dim candles of twenty years earlier. The modern steamer seems to operate independently of human agency: "The handling is . . . done . . . by signaling with patent automatic gongs . . . communicating orders to the invisible mates. . . . [T]he ship seems to land herself without human help." (158). "There is no wasted time" — for "that is the modern way" (161) — between the experimental trial of such things as a new ballast system and its practical adoption. The luxury and "cheeriness" of the modern ocean steam ship make it "the pleasantest place one can be in, except, perhaps, one's home" (177).

Despite this enthusiasm, Twain, like so many of his contemporaries, cannot quite fully endorse this new and modern world. And a deep ambivalence pervades the last parts of his essay. Modern-day tourism (using such ships as Twain has described) has diminished the sense of adventure and individualism previously associated with foreign travel: "everybody is a wanderer in the far lands now . . . there are no perils of the sea for him, there are no uncertainties" (180). More pertinently, "the romance of the sea" has now vanished (177). The "poetic element" of ocean travel — the sentimental songs, for instance, that offered such "fire and color to the imagination" — has disappeared in the face of the "unsentimental aspect and frigid attention to business" of recent marine developments (180). Twain's viewpoint here is an unstable one, since he also refers dismissively to the mawkishness (178) of such old songs. But when he speaks of the "very pleasant company of young people" on that early becalmed Sandwich Islands trip, he sounds another strongly nostalgic note, and his language takes on accordingly archaic forms: "I wonder where they are now. Gone, oh, none knows whither; and the bloom and grace and beauty of their youth, where is that?" (181). Twain then swiftly ends his essay with a good joke about barnacles fastening the becalmed boat to the Pacific floor. This move carries all the signs of a writer who realizes his text is drifting in contradictory directions and who wants to end it as quickly and effectively as he can.

The essay Twain writes on "The German Chicago" is similar to "About All Kinds of Ships" in both its celebration of modernity and the much briefer note of ambiguity discomposing that viewpoint. Twain lived through the period when the modern American city came into being. Chicago itself, for instance, "had grown from a village of 350 people in 1833 [two years before Twain's birth] to a city of over two million by 1910 [the year of his death]."[54] Yet American urbanization and its effects are not given much attention in his writing. As the comparative nature of its title suggests, however, "The German Chicago" does tackle contemporary urban experience and its modernizing processes in a way that applies both to a European and an American context. Despite important cultural differences on which Twain also focuses, the development of the modern city is a transnational phenomenon. The reflections on Berlin in this essay are, then, reflections on American urban modernity, too.

Twain starts off his essay with the significant words, "I feel lost, in Berlin" (210). The possibility of alienation in new urban surroundings is thus immediately raised. Unlike Chicago, Berlin had long been an established major city, but as in its American counterpart the pace of change had completely transformed the past environment. For the "dingy city in a marsh, with rough streets, muddy and lantern-lighted," with its "straight rows of ugly houses all alike" had "disappeared totally, and left no sign" in the making of this "new city; the newest I have ever seen." Contemporary Berlin then (and the urban life for which it stands) brings a whole new sign system into being. And, paradoxically, Berlin is even more modern that the American city with which it compared, for even Chicago, with its "many old-looking districts . . . would seem venerable beside it" (210).

Comparison, though, is initially more important than contrast as Twain describes the new urban scene. Both Chicago and Berlin are "giant" cities that have seen a "phenomenal swiftness of growth." Twain estimates current population as "say a million and a half" in each. Berlin is distinguished by the widespread (even "wasteful") use of gas and electric light and a "spaciousness" formed by its wide and straight streets and the accompanying "freedom from crowding." Again, and perhaps surprisingly, Twain makes a comparison with Chicago that focuses not on the latter's increasing number of tall buildings but on the "flatness of surface" it shares (211–12).

For most of the essay, Twain focuses specifically on Berlin and the particular signs of modernity it evidences. While much of what he says is not necessarily true of American city life at the time, Twain still shows remarkable prescience in identifying within this environment key features of what Max Weber would call "the reality in which we [as modern beings] move."[55] So he places great emphasis on the "method and system" observable in Berlin (seemingly "the most governed city in the world," 213). Order and system are, indeed, key words throughout the essay. The city is figured on one occasion as a type of living organism. The multicolored maps of the horse-car routes are "like pictures of the circulation of the blood" (221). But Twain's stress is mostly on the way in which orderly and efficient supervisory forms govern potential outbreaks of natural and social excess: 'the police do not like crowds and disorder here. If there were an earthquake in Berlin the police would take charge of it and conduct it in that sort of orderly way that would make you think it was a prayer meeting (220).

"Conflagrations and break-downs" in the urban material fabric are prevented by strong building regulations. "Systematic and frequent" sanitary inspections mean that overcrowded tenement houses (as in New York and Chicago) do not exist (216). The Berlin police act as a type of panoptic source of authority and control: any newcomer to the city must report his or her family's names, income, residence, and so on, "to the police immediately" (214). "Everything" in the city "is orderly" (216), from the way the firemen contain fires (again we see a concern here with forms of excess) to the cleaning of the streets. Twain's admiration for Berlin and the way it is governed is clear. He does note the points at which its systems break down: the street numberings and the horse-cars, for example (modernization, at least as far as the transport system goes, is clearly incomplete). But this serves as comic embroidery to what is a generally positive description of modern city life. Orderliness here is strongly beneficial rather than a potential threat to privacy and agency.

There is, though, an underlying note of anxiety about this life raised in the reference to alienation at its start and at one other significant point in the essay. This latter comes when Twain is commenting humorously on the irrational way that houses in Berlin are numbered:

> There are a good many suicides in Berlin; I have seen six reported in a single day. There is always a good deal of learned and laborious arguing . . . going on as to the cause of this state of things. If they will set to work and number their houses in a rational way perhaps they will find out what was the matter. (223)

Suddenly, and beneath the surface wit, we get an indication that modern city life is not without its (severe) alienating problems. Georg Simmel's comments in "The Metropolis and Mental Life" (1903) about the intensification of nervous stimulation in modern city living, and the qualities of "punctuality, calculability, and exactness" that mark its parameters, come to mind here.[56] So too do his accompanying warnings about "a retrogression in the culture of the individual with reference to spirituality, delicacy and idealism" (337). Though Simmel's analysis is contentious, his discussion of the "flat and gray color" of city life as seen through the eyes of those subject to constant overstimulation of the nerves (330), and of the "mutual strangeness and repulsion" between individuals which "self-preservation in the face of the great city" appears to demand (331), might stand as a form of explanation for the suicides of which Twain speaks. There is again clear indication of ambivalence on Twain's part as he explores the conditions of modern life and, specifically here, its urban forms.

Modernization and its effects, then, become a type of running motif throughout this collection. Not all the pieces in the book can be read in this way, but it is surprising just how many can. Thus "Mental Telegraphy," Twain's essay on thought transference and the "finer and subtler form of electricity" (66) by which he explains it, should be read in the context of developments in experimental psychology at the time.[57] His speculations in the essay also connect up, though, with the material conditions and changes of day-to-day life as, for instance, he discusses the simultaneous occurrences of inventions in entirely different places. As Bradbury writes:

> some interesting preoccupations derived from Twain's experiences in the nineties intrude into, or maybe are prefigured by, this earlier text [a first version was written in the 1878]. . . . [T]he piece ends, perhaps inevitably, with the expectation of a new popular invention. Surely what we need next are phrenophones — machines which can shoot thoughts from brain to brain, replacing the telegraph. You could say that in the pages of this volume the Internet was born. (xliii)

There is one other preoccupation that surfaces in "Mental Telegraphy" to take increasing importance as Twain's literary career progresses. Twain ends the essay not with the phrenophone idea (see 65–66) but with a consideration of the relationship between dreaming and waking (see the second forwarding quote to this chapter). He speaks of the investigations of the English Society for Psychical Research and refers to his own experience of being "asleep — at least wholly unconscious — for a time" without suspecting it has happened and without "any way to prove that it *has* happened" (73–74). This idea of a crossover from waking state to dream, and vice versa, and the difficulty (and perhaps impossibility) of distinguishing the two increasingly and crucially plays on Twain's literary imagination from henceforth. The epistemological uncertainty to be found right from the start of his career now takes a further and ontological turn. It is here that the posthumously published Dream Manuscripts have one of their sources.

"The Private History of a Campaign That Failed"

> I could have become a soldier myself, if I had waited. I had got part of it learned; I knew more about retreating than the man that invented retreating.
>
> — "The Private History of a Campaign That Failed"

Twain's literary response to the American Civil War, "the southern cataclysm," has generally been judged reticent and evasive.[1] The event stands relatively silently, so to speak, between Twain's detailed account of his days as an apprentice steamboat pilot in "Old Times on the Mississippi" and of his travels in the Far West in *Roughing It*. In "The Private History of a Campaign That Failed" (1885), he does briefly address that experience, but in terms of a personal (though not unrepresentative) act of evasion. He tells how he, like so many thousand of others, "entered the war, got just a taste of it, and then stepped out again, permanently" (9).[2] James M. Cox relates this last act to the construction of Twain's comic identity (in Nevada in 1863): "The discovery of 'Mark Twain' in the Nevada Territory . . . had quite literally been a way of escaping the Civil War past which lay behind him in Missouri. In effect, the humorous identity and personality of 'Mark Twain' was a grand evasion of the Civil War."[3] What we have in "The Private History," then, is apparently deeply suggestive. The one exception to Twain's general refusal as a writer to engage directly with the Civil War occurs in a narrative concerning his evasion of that war (an act crucial, for Cox, in defining its author's very literary identity).

This emphasis on evasion does not mean, however, that "The Private History" fails to address important social and cultural issues, for it stands in some ways as a twinned text to *Adventures of Huckleberry Finn* (1885),[4] a book that contained its own evasion episode. As is now generally recognized, that "evasion" is not without its historical meanings, having its crucial parallel in the events of post-Reconstruction America. It stands as a bleak — if oblique — commentary not just on the nature of Jim's final "freedom" but on that of the recently "emancipated" African American in the 1880s South. There has, in other words, been increasing acknowledgment of the indirect (evasive) methods Twain uses to approach the cultural anxieties of his time. And indeed, this applies to his treatment of the Civil War as a larger whole, for it is now accepted that he does address the subject of this war, though by roundabout means. So Neil Schmitz, for instance, claims the middle section of *Huckleberry Finn* (a novel set in the 1830s or 1840s) is "heavily freighted with Civil War experience." He sees a number of Twain's other works, too — "A True Story," *Life on the Mississippi*, and "The Private History" — as Civil War texts. And he sees Twain looking generally here "for ways to break out of the Southern imaginary (William Gilmore Simms, Sidney Lanier) into a Northern real (William Dean Howells, U. S. Grant)." Accordingly, he relates the "desertion of the cause of Confederate nationalism" in "The Private History" to the loss of "a usable Southern patriarchal literary tradition" in Twain's work as a whole.[5]

As with so many of Twain's stories, there is a general lack of critical consensus on "The Private History." Cox focuses on the climactic passage where the narrator describes the killing of the (assumed enemy) horseman (42–45) to find in it "the stock responses of the most maudlin melodrama," a "patchwork of clichés." And he describes the complete story as "a campaign that failed."[6] J. Stanley Mattson, on the other hand, calls the account of the stranger's death "a passage which Twain rarely surpassed." He judges the finished narrative a "cleverly written" deconstruction, directing "an arsenal of grape-shot at the entire concept of the glory of war."[7] Recent critics are similarly divided. Anne Bernays praises the story:

Unmatched in the care and handling of *tone*, [Twain] has produced in this merry tale about shattered innocence and slaughter an antiwar manifesto that is also confession, dramatic monologue, a plea for understanding and absolution, and a romp that gradually turns into atrocity even as we watch. (xxxii)

Neil Schmitz, though, follows Cox in seeing something "totally unconvincing" about the piece: "It wants to make a pacifist argument . . . but it can't. . . . Humor doesn't pull it off in the 'Private History,' is uncertain in its focus, doesn't admit the pain, evades it, puts into play the defense of the dead stranger, prevaricates, is contradictory."[8]

I recognize the contradictions in the story and the uncertainty of its final focus, but I see powerful meanings lying there. I follow a number of related critical paths to reach this concluding point. First I discuss the story in terms of its generic status, the way Twain blurs the boundary between nonfiction and fiction as he describes both the Civil War context and his protagonist's individual rejection of warfare. I then examine how in this narrative (as in *Huckleberry Finn*) an act of evasion does not mean the avoidance of social and cultural concern. At the most straightforward level, Twain (as both Mattson and Bernays suggest) uses the lens of personal reminiscence in "The Private History" to directly interrogate the militaristic values associated with the Civil War (and any war). But the story, and that interrogation, must be also read more obliquely. For it must be read not just in the context of the Civil War itself, but also in that of the 1880s (the time of its writing) and "the cultural debate over the remembrance and meaning" of that war that was then taking place.[9] The pacifist slant Twain brings to his narrative adds a particular twist to such later ways of reading the war. The tensions in the story's ending are of particular interest here, though. Twain circles around a series of (irresolvable) issues concerning evasion, military action, the construction of masculinity, national identity, the nature of the postbellum social order, and the relationship between private and public realms. As he does so, his narrative reflects the paradoxes of contemporary debate about the war but also revises the premises of that debate. An ongoing concern with the twinned questions of identity and modernity shadows the textual activity that occurs. That all this, however, can be read from the contradictions (and silences) of the last few pages of the story suggests both the amount of unresolved activity occurring beneath its surface and its cultural resonance.

I begin, though, by discussing the cross-generic status of Twain's account of his short time as a Confederate volunteer in the Marion Rangers: the status of the narrative as what Richard Peck calls " 'enriched' autobiography" or "heavily fictionalized 'autobiographical' essay."[10] "The Private History" was first published in December 1885 in *Century* in its "Battles and Leaders of the Civil War" series. Though the first-person narrator is not named, the story's original appearance under Twain's name in this nonfiction series and the use of some of its materials elsewhere mean that we can take its autobiographical base for granted.[11] "A Biographical Sketch" by Twain's nephew, Samuel Moffett, published in *McClure's* in 1899, gives further supporting evidence.[12] Here, the reader is told:

Brought up in a slaveholding atmosphere, Mark Twain naturally sympathized at first with the South. *In June he joined the Confederates in Ralls County*, Missouri, *as a Second Lieutenant under General Tom Harris*. His military career lasted for *two weeks. Narrowly missing the distinction of being captured by Colonel Ulysses S. Grant, he resigned, explaining that* he had become *"incapacitated by fatigue"* through *persistent retreating.* In his subsequent writings he has always treated his brief experience of warfare as a burlesque episode, although the official reports and correspondence of the Confederate commanders speak very respectfully of the work of the raw countrymen of the Harris Brigade.

The sketch then details the role taken by the "speedily reconstructed" Twain as assistant to his brother, Orion, who was appointed secretary of the Nevada Territory for his support of President Lincoln.[13] In fact, as he wrote all this, Moffett was working from notes supplied by Twain himself (the words emphasized in the quotation above are Twain's own, taken directly from those notes).[14]

The information Twain gives in "The Private History" generally accords with the biographical facts and with what we know of conditions and events in Missouri at the time. The narrator starts by describing conditions "Out West" (10) and the unsettled circumstances that ended when he decided to join the Confederate cause and "became a rebel." He then details the invasion of Missouri by Union forces, and Governor Claiborne Jackson's "proclamation calling out fifty thousand militia to repel the invader" (11). Following this is the account of Twain's visit to his boyhood Hannibal, the formation there of the Marion Rangers — a fifteen-strong military company — and their move under cover of darkness ("for caution and secrecy were necessary," 16) to New London, ten miles away.

There are several things to note here. Lorch shows that the chronology of events Twain gives does not quite add up but that his account of the conditions of the time does. Twain speaks of the way that, in that region, "men's minds . . . [leaned] first this way, then that . . . during the first months of the great trouble" (10). And it is clear that the question of divided sympathies was a very real one, both in Hannibal and in other parts of the South. J. Hurley and Roberta Hagood give a detailed picture of the tensions in the town and the military movements that took place there. Missouri itself was torn between Union and Confederate sympathies. In Marion County (where Hannibal was), Lincoln received only 235 of a total of 3,293 votes in 1860, suggesting a predominant Confederate presence. But the important railroad interests (the Hannibal & St. Joseph) in Hannibal were Unionists, and one of the railroad's officials, Maj. Josiah Hunt, took responsibility for organizing the Home Guard unit that began to drill on 31 May 1861. Federal support followed, due to fears of Confederate attack on the railroad, for the latter was of huge importance in the moving of Union troops and supplies. And from 8 June, when the Illinois Sixteenth Regiment arrived, increasing numbers of Union troops were stationed in Hannibal. Thus any Confederate activity there tended to be a type of guerrilla action. Those committed to fighting for the South had to make their way out of town in small groups to join units like the second division of the Missouri State Guards commanded by Gen. Thomas A. Harris.[15] This was the context for that necessary "caution and secrecy" of which Twain speaks.

We have little hard information about the exact composition and activities of the volunteer rebel group Twain joined. But the situation he describes and the broad outline of his brief career as one of its members seem generally accurate. Twain fills his narrative with the names of specific political and military figures — Harris, Claib Jackson, Colonel Ralls, Ab Grimes — and with references (mostly veiled by fictional names but sometimes only thinly so) to other young Hannibal men who took up the Confederate cause.

One of the more interesting of such cases is his description of the romantic "young fellow" Dunlap, who changes his name change to d'Un Lap to "ennoble" its formerly "plebian" quality (12–13). Twain is clearly having satiric fun here at the expense of John L. Robards, whom he had known since childhood and who did evidently serve in the Marion Rangers unit. In March 1885, Robards had written to Twain using the name RoBards. That this appealed to the author's comic sense is obvious from the note he put on the envelope: "This was always a poor well meaning ass — & at last has gone & stuck that big B in the middle of his name!" (MTNJ3, 112).

To read a fuller account, in RoBards own words, of that change of name is to realize that Twain might have made yet more comic capital from it. For if, as Schmitz suggests, one of Twain's intentions in his Civil War writings was "to break [the South's] narcissistic Sir Walter Scott trance," here was a person who evidently remained fixed in precisely that mentality.[16] Julian Street recounts a meeting with RoBards some three decades after Twain had written his story:

Colonel RoBards is still amiable. . . . Seeing that I was making notes, the Colonel called my attention politely to the spelling of his name, requesting that I get it right. Then he explained to me the reason for the capital B, beginning the second syllable.

"I may say, sir," he explained in his fine Southern manner, "that I inserted that capital B myself. . . . I am a Kentuckian, sir, and in Kentucky my family name stands for something. It is a name that I am proud to bear, and I do not like to be called out of it. But up here I was continually annoyed by the errors of careless persons. Frequently they would fail to give the accent on the final syllable, where it should be placed, sir — Ro*Bards*; that is the way it should be pronounced — but even worse, it happened now and then that some one called me by the plebeian appellation, Roberts. That was most distasteful to me, sir. *Most* distasteful. For that reason I use the capital B for emphasis."[17]

Twain builds into his supposed representation of Dunlap (or Robards) in 1861 details fresh in his mind from his 1885 correspondence. And as he elaborates here on the basis of his later knowledge, so he departs from his original factual base throughout the narrative whenever it suits his artistic and imaginative needs to do so. I give three further examples of the way in which this occurs.

Twain's speech at the Putnam Phalanx Dinner for the Ancient and Honorable Artillery of Massachusetts in Hartford in October 1877 illustrates the different ways Twain would embroider his Civil War experience. On this occasion, he opens in a less "modest" and "apologetic" (9) way than in "The Private History," declaring, "I did not assemble at the hotel parlors today to be received . . . as a mere civilian guest. . . . For I, too, am a soldier! I am inured to war. I have a military history." However, this first time round, the story of his "stirring campaign" takes a somewhat different shape than it would eight years later. Twain reports how at the start of the war he "slipped out of Hannibal," to join "a detachment of the rebel General Tom Harris's army" (he comments to his northern military audience at this point: "I find myself in a great minority here"). Though he describes how he becomes "Chief Mogul" of a company of eleven, he leaves Hannibal with just one friend, the only member of the unit ever mentioned by name: the nineteen-year-old Ben Tupper. Some details of Twain's speech accord with the later "Private History": the swearing in by Colonel Ralls, the horse (here it is Tupper's) that bites its sleeping rider's leg, and the rats in the corn crib. But here the insubordination that results from the imposition of military rank on those who consider themselves civilian equals is dramatized in a cruder way and one that, eight years later, Twain presumably found racially unacceptable. When Twain commands Tupper, who is swearing at the biting rats, to keep quiet, he replies: "Who was your nigger last year?" More tellingly, there is no mention of the episode that climaxes "The Private History," the killing of the stranger. Instead, "the boys" start grumbling because of the way they are kept " 'a-humpin' around so" and are threatened with court-martial for their general insubordination. As a result, "there and then, on the spot, my brigade disbanded itself and tramped off home, with me at the tail of it. . . . We were the first men that went into service in Missouri; we were the first that went out of it anywhere."[18] To compare Twain's later version of his military life with this one is to see the author reworking, elaborating, and imaginatively reconstructing as he rewrites. It is generally accepted, for instance, that the climactic shooting episode of "The Private History" is "almost certainly invented."[19]

Another aspect of the unstable relationship between fact and fiction here lies in the representation in "The Private History" both of the protagonist and comic persona, Mark Twain, and of "the boys" who accompany him.[20] As the author looks back on an earlier version of himself, he constructs both himself and his companions as foolishly naive and thoughtless figures:

[To Ed Stevens] this military expedition of ours was simply a holiday. I should say that about half of us looked upon it in the same way. . . . We did not think; we were not capable of it. As for myself, I was full of unreasoning joy to be done with turning out of bed at midnight and four in the morning [as a riverboat pilot], for a while; grateful to have a change, new scenes, new occupations, a new interest. In my thoughts, that was as far as I went; I did not go into details; as a rule one doesn't at twenty-four. (14–15)

In fact, Twain was well past twenty-five at the time of these events. And though one might argue that a year's difference is neither here nor there, the lowering of the age is of a piece with the general portrayal of the narrator and his fellow volunteers. For as John Gerber comments:

The more one reads [the story] the more [one] must conclude that it is primarily a literary rather than an historical document. . . . Twain and his cohorts all seem more like boys in their teens than they do like men in their mid-twenties. . . . Change the names and they would be Tom Sawyer's gang out on another adventure cooked up by Tom's fertile imagination.[21]

The distance between the author and the comic antics of his quasi-fictional persona is clear here and is (as in so many earlier Twain pieces) a central element in the text's dramatic effect. Indeed, one part of the thematic movement of the narrative, from innocence to experience, depends on it.

Gerber's reference to Twain's fiction indicates a third way in which "The Private History" imaginatively transgressed any firm factual boundary. The illustrations that accompanied the *Century* version of the narrative (not reproduced in *Merry Tales*) have close intertextual links with Twain's wholly imaginative works. Done by E. W. Kemble, who also illustrated *Huckleberry Finn*, the similarities between the two sets of drawings suggest the complementary nature of the two texts. Kemble's picture of the narrator of "The Private History" bears a close resemblance to Huck, while his illustration of "Farmer Mason explaining the principles of war" (page 200 in the *Century*) is very similar to the "Every one had a gun" drawing toward the end of *Huckleberry Finn*, when the farmers group to prevent the theft of Jim from Uncle Silas.[22]

In itself this may be thin evidence. But in terms of the story's content, too, it is clear that Twain's 1877 Hartford speech influenced his making of *Huckleberry Finn* and that his fictional work in that text then slid over into the writing of "The Private History." The difficulty of keeping text from text and fiction from nonfiction in clear and separate categories is indicated by Richard Peck when he writes of the 1877 speech:

A casual reader might . . . believe [its] plot elements . . . to be drawn from *Huckleberry Finn*, if only the characters' names were changed. [Twain] and Ben Tupper are clearly prototypes of Tom and Huck. . . . The farm itself; the nighttime escapades; Ben opposing [Twain's] romantic notions of military conduct with his clear common sense; and finally Ben deserting, fed up with the nonsense of it all: these fragments seem a literary rehearsal for the series of antics better developed in the concluding chapters of Huck's story.[23]

A series of overlaps can also be identified between the novel and "The Private History." Both first-person narrators speak and justify themselves (whether consciously or not) "from the vantage point of a social pariah."[24] Both stories move from their narrator's involvement in a series of increasingly complex incidents and entanglements to the physical escape and withdrawal that provide their closure. And Tom Quirk asserts that Twain "appropriated . . . [Huck's] 'sound heart' . . . as his own" in the "revulsion of feeling" the narrator of "The Private History" has to the stranger's death and in the "superior moral impulses" that then justify his desertion.[25]

Moreover, the stranger's shooting serves as "simply another version of Tom's being shot in the dark at the end of *Huckleberry Finn*, and [Twain's] response to it is of a piece with Huck's revulsion at the deaths he has seen along the river."[26] Even the language of the two texts corresponds. The "plaintive wailing of the spinning wheel . . . the most lonesome sound in nature" (34) that the narrator of "The Private History" hears at Mason's farm is echoed in chapter 32 of *Huckleberry Finn*, while his realization that "I had killed a man — a man who had never done me any harm" (42) recalls Huck and his response to Jim when he decides to steal his children out of slavery in chapter 16. The intertextual connections here are numerous. What is crystal clear from them, however, is that any attempt in "The Private History" to distinguish fiction from history fast runs into serious difficulty.

To say this, however, does not at all mean that we should read "The Private History" in a historical vacuum. Far from it, for the story engages both the context of the Civil War period and that of the cultural response, twenty years on, to the war's legacy. This response contained its own internal contradictions. And, as I go on to show, Twain's story gives a number of distinctive twists to the Civil War discourse of this later time.

In *The Romance of Reunion*, Nina Silber describes how "Americans [came] to grips with the new concept of nationhood" in the years following the Civil War. This meant confronting the dilemma that resulted from a northern victory that "had made the nation one" in political fact but "certainly not in terms of deep-rooted emotions and feelings."[27] Silber points to the growth of "an intensely sentimental discourse" in the Reconstruction years and beyond, the development of a concept of union built on "the emotions and sentiments of the heart" rather than "a superficial conciliation through laws and through force [the politics of Reconstruction]." This sentimental discourse rested on compassion, "not for the Confederate cause, but for the sacrifice and ultimate failure which that cause had generated."

As unionist bonds were reforged, there was, accordingly, a thrust on the northern part to "take the high ground of emotion as opposed to the low ground of party positioning. In this way they hoped to re-create the heartfelt, and supposedly more natural, foundations of a truly national community."[28] This could work in a number of sometimes paradoxical ways. The divergent emphasis on both memory and amnesia provides an example of this. In the institutionalization of the official celebrations of Memorial Day, for instance, the bravery and suffering of both Union and Confederate soldiers could be acknowledged, despite the misguided nature of the latter cause. And so joint memorial services became possible.[29] But there was also a move away from remembrance and toward "a policy of historical amnesia." Such forgetfulness tied in with the sentimental model (a compassionate victor refusing to dwell on prior southern wrongs), but it also "fit well with American notions of progress and expansion, notions which were often celebrated, albeit with a certain ambivalence, in the Reconstruction period." Other ways in which the "culture of healing and unity" of the period symbolically overcame sectional division were through "the increasingly popular genre of the reunion drama" and the significance of the "family metaphor" as part of "the rhetoric of reunion."[30] These both formed part of the historical rather than the amnesiac impulse.

The culture of reunion and forgetfulness, which Silber claims became "increasingly florid and maudlin" in the 1880s, brought other contradictions and ambiguities with it. The sentimental stress on reunion and "Americanism" could take in the optimistic version of an expansionist nation but could also, in its commitment to a unified and nationalistic ideal, serve as a counterforce to very real anxieties about social transformations and fractures ("an apparent multitude of social and cultural divisions") which became increasingly evident as the century continued.[31] And the reunionist stress on the manliness, bravery, and selflessness of those who had fought in the war provided a way for American men to identify with images of "power and virility" at a time when social upheaval and economic and industrial change were increasingly placing earlier versions of autonomous masculinity in crisis.[32] If Twain's narrative contains its own fractures, the most significant relate to, and further complicate, those operating at this larger ideological level.

The immediate context for the writing and appearance of "The Private

History" was the enormously popular series on "Battles and Leaders of the Civil War," which started in the November 1884 issue of *Century*.[33] This series contributed strongly to the culture of reunion but clearly bucked any amnesiac trend. A number of editorial commentaries, in the "Topics of the Time" section of the magazine, ran alongside the series and it is worth paying some attention to these. In October 1884, the series' aims and intentions were spelled out, with particular stress given to the need for mutual understanding between the country's two sections and the joint representation that its pages would provide. The papers to be published were expected "to prove of lasting value to the history of the most eventful period of our national life." The series would take as its topics, "decisive battles, the leading characteristics of army life on each side of the lines, and the lives of the most prominent commanders, North and South." The "authenticity and value" of the essays were guaranteed by the fact that they were "written by officers who wore either the blue or the gray."[34] Thus the lack of sectional bias was effectively announced three times in nine lines of the magazine.

This was followed by repeated stress on the importance of reunion. Emphasis was placed both on the shared experience of the participants and on the larger and apparently uncontrollable determinants that conditioned their actions. Steve Davis refers to the resulting sense of "impersonal causation": "fixing the blame for the conflict not on particular southerners but on general, inanimate social forces."[35] So, again, the introductory "Topics of the Time" editorial described the series' plan in the following terms:

to soften controversy with that better understanding of each other, which comes to comrades in arms when personal feeling has dissipated, and time has proven how difficult are the duties and how changeable are the events of war—how enveloped in accident and mystery. . . . No time could be fitter . . . for a publication of this kind than the present, when the passions and prejudices of the Civil War have nearly faded out of politics, and its heroic events are passing into our common history where motives will be weighed without malice, and valor praised without distinction of uniform.

Here political conflict was acknowledged, but overlaid by a stress on the integrity of the emotions and actions of the men on both sides of the dispute: "the generation which has grown up since the war . . . may now be taught how the men who were divided on a question of principle and State fealty . . . won by equal devotion and valor that respect for each other which is the strongest bond of a reunited people."[36]

I do not examine the later "Topics of the Time" sections in such detail. But it is noticeable how often an editorial return was made to the series and how clearly the message of mutual consideration and reunion was spelled out. So, referring to the contemporary debate on the reorganization of southern society in the May 1885 "Topics," the editor wrote of the "[m]utual respect, sympathy, knowledge" that were "indispensable" parts of that process. The same message was then applied to the effect of the Civil War series itself:

It is a help to mutual understanding and good-will that the North should know all that is admirable and desirable in Southern life and character, and much of this has been and will be recorded in these pages. It is important that the South should lay aside its prejudice, hold itself in the literary and human frame of mind.[37]

The death of General Grant stimulated another flurry of reunionist writing in the October edition of the journal. Here a number of elements came together. If Grant's death did not mean the forgetting of the past, it did bring a particular type of closure to it:

The war for the Union closed forever with the funeral of Grant . . . the solemn and memorable pageant at [his] tomb . . . where the leading generals of the living Union and of the dead Confederacy stood shoulder to shoulder and mingled their tears in a common grief — this historical scene marked the virtual conclusion of sectional animosity in America. . . . The South believes no longer in slavery, no longer in secession.

To a limited degree, this piece symbolically reopened that war by putting forward a political and sectionalist argument against government aid for "needy disabled ex-Confederate soldiers" (on the grounds that "their very act of rebellion" should not be made "an occasion of bounty"). But the focus of the piece soon shifted to a sentimentalist stress on the fine qualities and good motives of all those who had fought. And this served, in turn, as a prelude to a final paean both to Grant and to American nationhood:

Let the country join with General Grant in the noble spirit of the dedication of his "Memoirs" to the soldiers and sailors on both sides of the fateful struggle, and not withhold honor from those who fought conscientiously, bravely, and without stain upon either side. We can now all give thanks together to the Almighty that liberty was established and the nation saved, while we bury the last remnant of rancor in the tomb of the captain of the national armies.[38]

It is in the context of such editorials, the series they accompanied, and the mood of the time they reflected, that Twain's own narrative must be read.

Twain was the publisher of Grant's *Memoirs*. Grant completed the book shortly before his death (23 July 1885) and the first volume was issued in

December. Twain's business activities, then, fed straight into the strong cultural interest in Civil War material of the time. Twain's own relationship with Grant (who figures briefly in "The Private History of a Campaign That Failed") was complex. Justin Kaplan analyzes some of its "several levels" in terms of a series of connections, between

> the Rebel son and the punishing figure of power and authority (who, as President, later assumed a more explicitly paternal office); the parallel and ironic relationships of anti-hero . . . to hero. . . . And, reversing these relationships, the former Rebel son, now reconstructed, had become, as publisher, the strong and benevolent figure who rescues the Grant family from poverty.[39]

Twain's "Private History" was part of the same "Battles and Leaders" series to which Grant had also contributed. Twain's piece was unlike Grant's — indeed unlike most other contributions to the series — and had a "patently maverick" quality.[40] Robert Underwood Johnson, an editor for *Century*, had evidently expected Twain to write a straightforward account of his "actual experiences in the ranks." He hoped that, as "one of a literary group of 'eminent rebels,' " Twain's Confederate experience in Missouri would "supply a missing link in the Series." It was only when Johnson received Twain's first manuscript that he realized it contained much that was comic and fanciful. He responded, however, enthusiastically: "[It] is excellent — 'roarious."[41] J. Stanley Mattson, however, suggests that Twain's contribution was seen as "basically suspect," since "it alone was cut from the subsequently published four-volume edition of the collected essays of the Civil War series."[42]

Twain's narrative has other "maverick" qualities to it quite besides any fictional and comic aspects. These can be related to its role as part of that general response to the Civil War in the postbellum period that I have been discussing, for if Twain's story can be read in similar terms, there are nonetheless subversive and revisionist elements in it. Thus it skews and undermines the whole brand of heroic thinking associated with that response, though without undermining the accompanying reunionist message.

Much of Twain's article is antiheroic in tone, and it consistently ridicules notions of valorous military activity. So, for instance, the Marion Rangers' early "battle-scars" (31) result from "perhaps the most mortifying spectacle of the civil war" (29). "Stumbling along in the dark" (27) as they retreat from a rumored but invisible enemy presence, Twain and the boys finally reach their intended venue, the friendly Mason's farm. But then the farm dogs came "bounding over the fence, with great riot and noise, and each of them took a soldier by the slack of his trousers and began to back away with him" (29). Twain's story insistently focuses on the romantic expectations, comic inadequacies, clownish qualities (dogs hanging onto trousers), and lack of seriousness of these supposed "soldiers." Their predilection for "horse-play and laughing" and "holiday frolic" (18) is established, then interrupted by generally irrational and panicky fears of an enemy presence. The "town boys" (35) quickly show themselves unable to cope with the situations and adverse conditions they meet, except by complaint, internal bickering, and comically demeaning action.

The tone of the narrative abruptly shifts with the scene describing the killing of the stranger (a man assumed to be one of the enemy). But the move from farce to serious incident and argument has an artistic logic to it. Twain's "inside narrative" is the private history of an innocent abroad in a wartorn public world.[43] His ineffectual foolishness and panicky fears are measured against the people, language, and events that compose this world. Thus he listens in some confusion to Colonel Ralls, "veteran of the Mexican War" and Confederate recruiter, and the absurd military rhetoric he delivers:

we listened to an old-fashioned speech from him, full of gunpowder and glory . . . and windy declamation which was regarded as eloquence in that ancient time and that remote region; and then he swore us on the Bible to be faithful to the State of Missouri and drive all invaders from her soil, no matter whence they might come or under what flag they might march. This mixed us up considerably, and we could not make out just what service we were embarked in; but Colonel Ralls, the practiced politician and phrase-juggler, was not similarly in doubt. (18–19)

Later, the company's "horse-play and school-boy hilarity" (40) are cooled as a type of military engagement does occur. Rumors of an enemy approach climax with the appearance of a man on horseback. He is shot — the fact that six shots are fired at once make exact culpability impossible to determine. The narrator, "helplessly stroking" the stranger's forehead as he dies, is deeply affected by the "reproachful look" the stranger seems to give him, by the thought of the man's family now also tragically harmed, and by doubts about the rightness of his own actions. Although the man was "killed in fair and legitimate war," the boys now have sorrowful second thoughts, "saying that if it were to do over again they would not hurt him unless he attacked them first." For the narrator, this means: "My campaign was spoiled. It seemed to me that I was not rightly equipped for this awful business; that war was intended for men, and I for a child's nurse. I resolved to retire from this avocation of sham soldiership" (43–45).

The Marion Rangers then fall back to a series of camps, one run by "a profane old blacksmith of sixty" who has furnished his recruits "with gigantic home-made bowie-knives, to be swung with the two hands, like the *machetes* of the Isthmus." The narrator comments: "It was a grisly spectacle to see that earnest band practicing their murderous cuts and slashes under the eye of that remorseless old fanatic." Soon after, with the prospect of a Union regiment at hand, the narrator finally decamps: "Half of our fifteen, including myself, mounted and left on the instant" (46–47). He quits both the narrative and the Confederacy with what Neil Schmitz calls "a nonsequitur, humorously put, cowardly speech par excellence."[44] Having told the story of his "failure," he then changes tack to suggest a different possible outcome. Projecting a continued military career, he bases it on exactly the evasions he has just comically represented: "I could have become a soldier myself, if I had waited. I had got part of it learned; I knew more about retreating than the man that invented retreating" (49–50).

The militaristic values that stand squarely behind the whole *Century* series are, to considerable degree then, metaphorically shot to tatters here. As Mattson says,

The wonder is that Mark Twain's "Private History" should ever have reached the press, particularly within the context of a series so patently military. . . . For, by Mark Twain's own definition, every campaign and battle treated throughout the entire series was nothing less than "a campaign that failed."[45]

So Ralls's traditional rhetoric of war is described as "windy declamation," and those who put its premises into practice, such as the blacksmith, are fanatics who train innocent raw recruits to imitate their own "remorseless" murderousness. The farcical behavior of the Marion Rangers, however childish it may be, is constructed as preferable to the supposed adult and rational behavior (the killing of a man in battle) that replaces it. The "social conscience [that] shrinks to vestigial proportions . . . in war"[46] is measured negatively against the narrator's individual moral choice not to fight: "The taking of that unoffending life seemed such a wanton thing" (44). And his female self-identification (as child's nurse) is set in direct opposition to the power and virility conventionally associated with man and warfare: qualities now associated with senseless violence and unnecessary death. As Steve Davis says, this single killing of the stranger prompts us paradigmatically "to characterize the whole war as one big massacre."[47]

I have previously shown how one strand of a reunionist discourse emphasised the heroic valor of the soldiers of both Union and Confederate sides. The womanly values and sentimental language ("helplessly stroking," "pitying interest," "sincerely mourned," 43–44) of his narrator mean that Twain undermines such masculine and military values. Nonetheless, "A Private History" still speaks to the culture of healing and unity I have identified.[48] Twain blurs the lines between Union and Confederate in his narrative and stresses shared frameworks of knowledge and experience. What happened to me, he seems to say (and the direct intimacy of the first-person voice adds to this impression), could equally and easily have happened to a young Northern recruit. He prompts us to see the young men of both sides as subject to similar circumstance, their encounters with the war imaginatively interchangeable.

The passage where Colonel Ralls juggles his phrases and confuses the boys considerably with his talk of driving invaders from the soil, no matter under what flag they might march, hints at such interchangeability. Fine rhetorical sounds distort specific meanings and clear comprehension here, but Ralls's words serve as a reminder of the forms of rhetoric and patriotic language used by *all* sides in war. And right at the start of "The Private History," Twain takes a cross-partisan line in identifying his own experience with the "thousands" like him who only participated briefly in the war. He also alludes to the "confusion in men's minds" at the time: what Mattson describes as "the largely inconsequential considerations that played so large a part in making one man go 'Rebel' and another 'Yankee.'"[49] So Twain's narrator and his Mississippi "pilot-mate" (a New Yorker by birth) are both initially "strong for the Union," then for the Rebels, only to end up on opposing sides (10–11). The apparently accidental and capricious nature of sectional choice encourages a reading of war as that "impersonal causation" discussed earlier: men caught up in a given series of events almost despite their best conscious intentions. The generalizations made in the final sections of the narrative — that "this war-paper of mine . . . is a not unfair picture of what went on in many and many a militia camp in the first months of the rebellion" (49) — once more tend to reinforce the shared nature of the experiences Twain recounts.

Twain recalls not the bravery and suffering of his soldiers (the common basis for reunionist sentiment) but their fright, cowardice, and stupidity ("rabbits," 49). In doing so, he still contributes to reunionist discourse but in a completely unexpected way, "by de back" as it were. The conventional valuations of bravery and cowardice, masculinity and femininity, are turned topsy-turvy here. Assumed versions of the Civil War, and the norms associated with it, are thrown into disarray in a subtle yet subversive way.

But there is another and more complex side to all this. James M. Cox and Neil Schmitz are both right in saying that Twain's narrative moves in more than one direction and contains unresolved contradictions. Cox analyzes the comic effect of the story in terms of its "genuine merger" of "burlesque aggression" and "apologetic defense." As he incisively puts it:

the apologetic defense which was the ostensible motive for the narrative becomes the narrator's extravagant narrative of his own innocent and incompetent participation in the private history. . . . [Thus] the apologetic defence of not having been a good soldier is transformed into the humorous offence of displacing the public history of the Civil War with his private history.[50]

Cox, though, sees burlesque incompetence and irreverence as compromised by other elements in the story. Twain, he says, found it impossible to resist his culture's shared "reverence" of the Civil War. "The *real* sacred cows of Mark Twain's time — as indeed they seem to be of our whole history — were the Civil War and its heroes." The narrative's final reliance on "moral sentiments" (the death of the stranger sequence and its "revelation about the senseless brutality of war") and its reference in the last few pages to General Grant are consequently presented in a "serious" way. He sees this as an undermining of the very comic identity on which Twain's art relied.[51]

Cox's concern here is with the way Twain's engagement with a public event of such cultural weight adversely affects his comedy.[52] The paradox he notes comes from this and involves a shift from the use of the Mark Twain persona to a more direct authorial voice. Twain's most successful work does occur where the authorial presence is least evident, where Mark Twain is a constructed comic persona or where a fictional protagonist is used. But this is not necessarily to dismiss as a "failure" a text where more "serious" subject matter is set alongside comic representation.[53] Indeed, I see the burlesque elements of the narrative as providing an appropriate preamble to the more "serious" material (the death of the stranger) that follows. But it is Cox's comment on the relation between private and public history that particularly interests me here. I return to this subject shortly.

The reference to General Grant at the end of the narrative raises a different issue and sense of paradox than that concerning comedy and seriousness, and it is Grant's presence in the story that rightly bothers Neil Schmitz. He notes the narrative's "pacifist argument," its desire to "represent all the deserters," and its illustration of the fact that "Mark Twain left the war because . . . he was horrified by killing, hated killing." He continues, "but [the text] can't finally face down . . . the grimly fearless, coolly self-controlled U. S. Grant. It turns abruptly from the pacifist pieties given over the corpse of the slain stranger to glorify Grant and the killing power of well-trained modern troops."[54] Schmitz's words here appear to be based on several textual passages. One is where the narrator speaks about those who, unlike him, *did* stay in the military and "afterward learned the grim trade" of war: "learned to obey like machines; became valuable soldiers; fought all through the war, and came out at the end with excellent records" (37–38). Another is the narrator's direct reference to Grant:

In time I came to know that Union colonel whose coming frightened me out of the war . . . — General Grant. I came within a few hours of seeing him when he was as unknown as I was myself; at a time when anybody could have said, "Grant? — Ulysses S. Grant? I do not remember hearing the name before." It seems difficult to realize that there was once a time when such a remark could be rationally made; but there *was*.[55]

Finally, there is the description of mere "rabbits" being changed into "soldiers" as a result of "the steadying and heartening influence of trained leaders" and of "the invaluable experience of actual collision in the field" (48–49).

Twain clearly implies Grant's heroic status here, and it is difficult to read his comments about the "invaluable experience" of war and the "valuable soldiers" it produced as ironic. The antimilitaristic message of the narrative is consequently quite undermined. Twain seems caught here between two responses that he cannot reconcile. We might begin to explain this by remembering what the war meant, to both author and audience, at a public level. The Civil War was "the pivotal period of our history," the time when "the nation [was] saved."[56] The general postwar emphasis on reunion and Americanism, as well as Twain's own politics,[57] mean that the narrative's more positive references to warfare and its allusion to General Grant should come as no real surprise. Looking back from the 1880s it would have been difficult to read that history more than one way. The winning of the Civil War had determined all that followed: the concept of nationhood as it existed at that later time depended on that war for its very being.

In other words, Twain's apparently positive references to Grant and the "killing power" of his troops are an inevitable element in Twain's larger endorsement of the making of the modern and unified American nation, in which the "grim trade" of war played its necessary part. And if Twain is contradictory here, again this is understandable. He is hardly alone in finding it difficult to reconcile a hatred of warfare — its confusion, unnecessary killings, and false rhetoric — with an acceptance perhaps of its necessity and certainly of its long-term historical benefits.

But other implicit (and unresolvable) contradictions open up here between various versions of male selfhood and between public history and private thoughts, feelings, and actions. In "The Private History" (Twain's very title draws our attention to the different types of history he engages), Twain dramatizes his doubts about military values and their effect from a skeptical and antiauthoritarian position. He accomplishes this by giving a countervoice to the deserter and coward: one who resists compromising his "sturdy independence" (36) in enforced service within a hierarchical body; who prefers to follow his own conscience rather than accede to the demands of a dubious public morality; and whose involvement with a particular side is, to a degree, arbitrary rather than a convincing and deliberate political choice. The fact that, at the point of writing, this deserter has gained a national repute similar to that of the military commander against whom he almost fought helps endorse the value of the person he then was and the decision he then took. There are other ways than Grant's, Twain appears to say, of being decisive and of being male.[58] Public history and a discourse of national unification are set against private history, the need for independence and integrity, and for evading the powerful social forces and pressures that surround the individual subject.

Here, Twain echoes but also repositions the ambivalences in reunionist thought previously discussed. He represents the Civil War itself — rather than the postbellum period — as the time when such ambivalences, and the anxieties underlying them, were produced. Reunionist thought moved between support for the nation that the war brought into being and disquiet about the conditions of day-to-day living consequently produced. In "The Private History" the positive reference to Grant implicitly endorses the violent making of the modern American nation signified in his textual presence. But the thoughts and actions of Twain's deserter reveal, even at that earlier historical point, an unbridgeable gap between private need and large-scale social force. As an impersonal and incorporated world increasingly impinged on the subject in the late nineteenth century, and as social and cultural conditions made the notion of a shared national identity more problematic, such a separation of private and public realms would become increasingly marked.[59]

Similarly, and related to this, the reunionist emphasis on the heroic manliness of Civil War soldiers as a response to the later fractures and anxieties in American social and industrial life is anticipated here but also (and paradoxically) both revised and undermined. There is a clear sense of admiration both for Grant's virility and manliness and for the achievements of the "valuable soldiers" in the ranks. But countering this we have, on the one hand, the sympathetic feminization of the first-person protagonist and, on the other, fighting men described as "machines": a dehumanizing term that resonates beyond its immediate context to point toward the rationalizations and efficiencies of the postbellum social and industrial order. In this latter allusion Twain might be seen to anticipate Stephen Crane in suggesting that it was the Civil War itself (and, again, not the later period) that saw a crisis in masculinity, the manly qualities of the common soldier not released there but rather placed under erasure.[60] Twain goes beyond the majority of his 1880s contemporaries then, not only in implying the earlier date and occasion for such a crisis but also in questioning the meaning of manliness itself.

I am aware that I am basing my interpretation here on just a few textual details (especially the use of the word "machines"). I am aware, too, of the series of questions that my reading leaves unanswered. Some of these circle around the representation of boyhood (the state associated with Twain's protagonist for most of the narrative), masculinity, and manhood in the story.[61] Others relate more specifically to the twinning of Grant and Twain and to the various versions of the latter. For instance, how can we link the narrator's necessary step outside the scan of public action to the fact of the author's later national celebrity?[62] I see this text not as smoothly coherent but as riven — especially at its end — by tensions that are apparent, paradoxically, only in its gaps and silences and that are never fully explored. The question of whether Twain himself was conscious of such fissures and contradictions, or whether he was using a form of evasion as a deliberate literary tactic, remains necessarily open. But certainly the power and importance of this story lies in the way Twain uses perhaps *the* central event of nineteenth-century American history to introduce themes and contradictions of the very deepest social and cultural resonance.

9

The Man That Corrupted Hadleyburg
and Other Stories and Essays

> Do I seem to be preaching? It is out of my line: I only do it because
> the rest of the clergy seem to be on vacation.
>
> — "About Play-Acting"

The Man That Corrupted Hadleyburg and Other Stories and Essays was published by Harper and Brothers in June 1900. Twain's personal and professional life was now on something of an upward curve again after the two
crippling disasters of the 1890s. The first of these was the bankruptcy of
Charles L. Webster and Company in 1894. The second was the death of
Susy, his twenty-four-year-old daughter, in August 1896 while Twain was in
England following his round-the-world lecture tour described in *Following the Equator* (1897). The tour itself was made to pay off the debts owed
to the Webster creditors, and Twain had managed this, with the astute
financial assistance of his recent friend and business adviser, Standard Oil
magnate Henry Huttleston Rogers, by early 1898.

Twain and his remaining family lived in Vienna and then in London
and Sweden from September 1897 to October 1900, so all the planning
for the *Hadleyburg* book took place across the Atlantic. The Vienna resi-
dency was partly for reasons of economy and partly for the development
of the musical education of his daughter Clara.[1] To read the correspondence with Rogers during the period is to note Twain's continued attraction to business speculations and his attempts to interest Rogers in the
various "big fish" he thinks to have landed.[2] The letters show, too, his now
overwhelming concern for the safety and closeness of his family: "We
cannot divide the family again after our disastrous experience" (CHHR,
351). What is most striking, however, is to see the recovery of Twain's
spirits as Rogers invested his capital to good effect and the financial losses

of recent years were at last reversed. Thus he calls Rogers "a magician who can turn steel and copper and Brooklyn gas into gold," and notes with admiration and wonder the rapid rise in value of his acquired stocks (CHHR, 389). Indeed, his own literary activities are treated as of little account in such a context. So he writes Rogers: "Let us get back on the financial platform, now, and do another tour. It is much better than literature. Literature is well enough, as a time-passer, for the improvement and general elevation and purification of mankind, but it has no practical value" (CHHR, 386). A $10,000 profit in Federated Steel earned in a single week has Twain responding: "We have been gay. . . . We are resembling the long-vanished Clemenses of 10 years ago. God knows what we should be resembling if it had not been for you" (CHHR, 384).

Despite his dismissive comment about literature, Twain was in fact highly productive in this period. Indeed Jeffrey Rubin-Dorsky says that he "was in a publishing frenzy in the 1890s," with fifteen books coming out between 1889 (*A Connecticut Yankee*) and 1900, when the *Hadleyburg* collection appeared.[3] A number of those books included short stories, sketches, and essays. *Tom Sawyer Abroad; Tom Sawyer, Detective and Other Stories* (1896) contained the two Tom Sawyer novels/novellas of the title bulked out with most of the contents of *The Stolen White Elephant* collection (though "A Curious Experience" and "Mrs. McWilliams and the Lightning Rod" were replaced by "Map of Paris" and "Letter Read at a Dinner").[4] *How to Tell a Story and Other Essays* (1897) contained only essay material.[5] *The American Claimant and Other Stories and Sketches* was issued in 1897 as part of the Uniform edition of Twain's works with most of the material from *Merry Tales* and all of *The £1,000,000 Bank-Note* added to the title novel.[6] *Literary Essays* (1899) contained most of the *How to Tell a Story* collection (omitting only the title essay) and four essays that would soon reappear in *Hadleyburg*.[7] It included three other pieces ("Saint Joan of Arc," "In Memoriam" and "Mark Twain: A Biographical Sketch" by Samuel E. Moffett) subsequently published in the 1906 collection, *The $30,000 Bequest and Other Stories*.[8] We see here something that had always marked Twain's literary career but that became increasingly noticeable from around this time: the recycling and remixing of significant amounts of his literary materials for new book publication, primarily for commercial reasons. Twain and his publishers were always highly aware of the literary marketplace and made it carry as much as, and often perhaps more than, it could bear. Such thinking underlies Twain's letter to Rogers regarding Frank Bliss's edition of his collected works: "Whenever a Uniform and a De Luxe [edition] can be marketed, *that's* the time to do it; a delay of a year can be fatal, for a literary reputation is a most frail thing — any trifling accident can kill it; and its market along with it" (CHHR, 349).

Twain did not merely recycle old material during this period, however. Carl Dolmetsch says that, despite certain uncertainties about the direction of his writing,[9] Twain's Vienna period was marked by "a joie de vivre and new vigor in his work [as well as his business] plans." And the summer of 1898 spent in Kaltenleutgaben, a spa town just outside Vienna where the family went for Olivia and Jean's health, was particularly fruitful, bringing "the last great creative surge in . . . Twain's long career."[10] Here he worked on *What Is Man?* "The Man That Corrupted Hadleyburg," "Wapping Alice," "The Great Republic's Peanut Stand," "The Great Dark," "The Chronicle of Young Satan," and vignettes for his autobiography. The time spent in Vienna itself was also productive, with the content of *The Man That Corrupted Hadleyburg* collection made up of "mainly Viennese pieces."[11] This suggests, too, that we might expect to find a relatively unified and thematically coherent set of materials in that book.

Twain — and this is becoming a familiar motif — played a larger part in the planning and putting together of *The Man That Corrupted Hadleyburg and Other Stories and Essays* than has previously been recognized. The generally accepted view is that, after the Webster and Company bankruptcy, Twain had little directly to do with the publishing process. Thus Hamlin Hill ends his edition of *Mark Twain's Letters to His Publishers* in 1894, saying:

Twain continued to write books [after this date] — and occasionally to write his publishers, but the great majority of his letters concerning his publications went through H. H. Rogers, who served as intermediary and informal business agent. . . . Mark Twain [was] badly scarred from his close contact with the publishing of his own books.[12]

Twain, it is true, was often casual, to say the least, about the planning and production of his books. Lewis Leary comments on the laconic tone of his March 1898 note to Frank Bliss about the planned uniform edition of his work: "Oh, as to the books that are to go into the Uniform Edition? *Begin* with Innocents Abroad, and put in all the books that have been published by you and by Webster and by Harper" (CHHR, 339). But Hill's summary is somewhat misleading. Despite his use of Rogers as an agent, Twain continued (at least in the case of the *Hadleyburg* collection) to take a real, if inconsistent, interest in the publication of the book.

By the late 1890s Twain had come, in some ways, full circle with the production of his books. Frank Bliss, Elisha's son, was the publisher of *Pudd'nhead Wilson* (1894) and *Following the Equator* (1897), and both were issued as subscription books through the American Publishing Company, which Frank now ran.[13] The initial sales figures of the travel book had been disappointing (see CHHR, 317–19). But Twain was also publishing with Harper's by this time, under a contract Rogers had helped to negotiate. *Tom Sawyer Abroad; Tom Sawyer, Detective and Other Stories, Personal Recollections of Joan of Arc* (1896), *How to Tell a Story and Other Essays*, and *The American Claimant and Other Stories and Sketches* all came out under their imprint. And in October 1903 Twain would tie himself (through Rogers) to Harper as his exclusive publisher and cut loose from Bliss's firm. Before this date, though, and at the time Twain was writing the stories and essays that would appear in *The Man That Corrupted Hadleyburg*, he was in dialogue with both publishers. He was involved, too, in the complex negotiations between them over the publication of a uniform edition of his writing and how that would relate to the continued separate publication of his new books. The arrangements he made, which lasted until the 1903 Harper contract, gave the American Publishing Company the right to publish the uniform edition of Twain's works (in Autograph, Royal, Japan, De Luxe, and Popular versions). Harper meanwhile — and this was something that seemed to have happened as a result of circumstance rather than being built into any contract — published all the new single volumes that were issued.[14]

To follow the publication history of the *Hadleyburg* book is to see Twain's part in it. Initially it seems he was unsure quite who would publish the proposed new collection. He wrote Bliss on 10 December 1898:

By & by there will be matter enough for a volume of Sketches — say by next summer — if it goes to Harper, tell me how soon thereafter you would want it for the Uniform, so that I can take care of that feature.
You couldn't run a volume of Sketches by subscription, could you?[15]

Apparently he must have received a positive reply from Bliss, for two months later, on 2 February 1899, Twain was giving more details and speaking of him as the book's "owner":

There's as much as 100,000 words for the volume of Sketches. . . . Half of it has not yet been in print and half of *that half* is especially good, and ought to be put into a magazine but I don't much care, one way or another, as to that, provided *you* publish the book. *New* is important to you but not to the Harpers.[16]

On 31 March, the project still seemed on course with Bliss as the assumed publisher. Twain mentioned to Bliss the articles on Christian Science he had been writing and said, "I think [the one now being written] may as well go into the vol. of Sketches without first appearing in a magazine," adding the postscript, "Perhaps "*Christian Science, Etc*" should be the *title* of the new book. Good selling title."[17]

These discussions with Bliss, however, must have fallen through, for the book went not to him but to Harper. On 14 September 1899, Henry Alden of Harper informed Twain:

> The Messrs. Harper are on sharp look-out for some new books from you. In the first place it seems about time for a new book of short stories. "The Man Who Corrupted Hadleyburg," which is to appear in our Christmas Number [of *Harper's Magazine*], is a capital story — a splendid *piece de resistance* for a new volume.

Suggesting other stories that could then be added ("Is He Living or Is He Dead?" and "Eskimo [sic] Maiden's Romance"), Alden proposed another collection too:

> [T]he making of an interesting book from articles recently published in magazines: "Stirring Times in Austria," "At the Appetite Cure," "The Austrian Edison Keeping School Again," "About Play-Acting," "From the *London Times* of 1904," "Concerning the Jews." Etc.

Twain seems to have rejected the Bliss option around this time. Perhaps Alden's final words had an effect: "You, of course, have literary work in quite immediate prospect, and I trust you will give us the first refusal of it. We are on the top-wave both in magazine and book enterprise, and our situation is one promising the best results to authors as well as to us."[18] Perhaps Twain saw a certain logic in leaving the uniform edition sets to Bliss and the subscription business, while he continued to publish single volumes through the trade with Harper. And as both the 1 October 1899 letter to Harper (see note 14) and the letter to Rogers on 4 October ("I think I *will* let Harper issue a new volume of short things . . . if he says Bliss won't be hampered in using the vol. in the Uniform edition," CHHR, 413) suggest, certainly Twain saw himself easing the way for Bliss and the uniform edition — for which he had great financial hopes — if he favored Harper over the new book.

It is clear, too, that Alden's words in the 14 September letter at least approximately complemented Twain's own previous thinking about the type of book (or books) that should now appear. Independently, both Twain and Harper had been planning a new collection of short works. From this point on, they worked together. One of Twain's Notebook entries for the period has a list of stories and articles and their word lengths and this may constitute an initial plan for the contents of the collection. In a letter to Alden on 30 October 1899 (reproduced in part here) he sent a close version of this list:

			Words
Lively times Aus. Parliament, '98 (H)			12,000
From London Times 1904.	Century '98		4,000
Appetite Cure	"Cosmop"	'98	4,300

About Play-Acting,	"Forum"	'98	5,000
The Great Republic's Peanut Stand" (MS.)			13,000
Concerning the Jews, Harpers	'99		9,000
Austrian Edison as School Teacher (Century)		'98	1,000
The Hornet Shipwreck	(Century)	Oct. '99	13,500
My Rebel Campaign	(Century)	1896?	7,000
Man Corrupted Hadleyburg			22,000
Diplomatic Pay and Clothes	(Forum)		4,650
Christian Science	(Cosmop)	'99	8,000
" "	(MS)	12/10/99	8,500
My First Lie and How I got out of it	(World)		3,250
My Boyhood Dreams	McClure	Jan. 1900	2,600
In Memoriam	Harper	Nov. '97	2,000
			119,800[19]

Twain here implicitly rejected Harper's plan for two new collections in favor of a single mixed volume. Harper, though, held to the original scheme. A letter of 4 December from J. Henry Harper "enclose[s] herewith our plan for dividing the two volumes of Mr. Clemens' articles, stories, etc., which we are proposing to publish in the Spring." One volume (of 58,150 words) was to contain mainly essays, the other (61,550 words) mainly fiction. Harper does largely follow Twain's list (above) of suggested contents, though necessarily reorders them. But he omits "My Boyhood Dreams," lists three (rather than two) Christian Science papers, and adds two more fictions, "Is He Living, or Is He Dead?" and "Eskimo [*sic*] Maiden's Romance." A note by Twain on the letter agrees to the use of these short stories. Twain added a further annotation, putting the words "A postscript" after the named "Austrian Edison" and noting that it should follow "London Times of 1904."[20]

A final and unexpected stage in the making of this book seems to have occurred in April 1900, though lack of full documentation (at this point) makes it impossible to give a definitive version of what then happened. Twain wrote to Col. George Harvey of Harper on 4 April 1900. I follow the description and partial reproduction of this letter in the Mark Twain Papers. We can assume that Twain is speaking of the English and German edition of the *Hadleyburg* book here, for he asks that "the article on copyright [presumably 'The Great Republic's Peanut Stand'] should be left out and replaced by 'My Campaign' (in the Civil War); the short story 'Luck' and . . . 'Meister Schaft.'" And the first and last of these three named pieces appeared in the European but not the American edition of the book.[21] But, significantly, Twain asks here that "the proposed *two* books should be compressed into one." In the absence of any documentation on Harper's own decision to issue the American edition of *Hadleyburg* as one volume, we cannot know whether this request influenced or merely echoed that decision. But clearly, at some point between November 1899 and the printing of the book, Harper's original plans for it changed. Twain also asked in the letter to Harvey that "2 sets of these amended proofs . . . be sent to me," though he also tells the Colonel, "Further compression can be made by leaving out *anything you please*" (CU-MARK*). This seems entirely typical of Twain in the handling of his short works: at one moment showing real concern with the shape and content of his book, the next putting things entirely in the hands of his publisher.

A last letter of 12 April clearly follows on from this previous correspondence. In it, Twain writes Harvey with "a copy of the Table of Contents as I have arranged it for the London and Tauchnitz editions." He says, "I have knocked out 42,000 words & left 130,000 — an over-abundance still," and finishes by again ceding final control to Harvey: "Go on & knock out anything you want to; and leave *in* anything you please." There is the suggestion here that the American edition may not have been finalized at this point, for Twain writes that his table of contents "may be useful *on the other side*, on account of the sandwiching of grave & gay which it furnishes" (my emphasis).[22]

There are gaps in my account of the making of the *Hadleyburg* book. The final collection, though, is closely modeled on an amalgam of the two books proposed by J. Henry Harper in his 4 December 1899 letter (itself written in the knowledge of Twain's own earlier proposed list of contents). The first seven pieces in the book are exactly those planned for the second volume Harper projected. "How to Tell a Story," mentioned in none of the earlier plans, is then inserted. That is followed by four of the pieces, in their original order, planned for the first volume in the Harper letter. Five pieces (three papers on "Christian Science," "In Memoriam," and "Great Republic's Peanut Stand") have now been omitted, but three additional pieces — "Travelling with a Reformer," "Private History of the 'Jumping Frog' Story," and "My Boyhood Dreams" — have been added right at the end of the book. What is clear in my reconstruction is how closely Twain was in touch, even as he uses Rogers as a mediating figure, with his publishers during this period. To repeat, this is not the version of his role that has traditionally been given.

Indeed, the part Twain played in the publication of *The Man That Corrupted Hadleyburg and Other Stories and Essay* may well account for the relative coherence of the collection. This is not the rag-bag of disparate materials we might expect, especially given the speed with which Twain was churning out books at the time. In his afterword to the Oxford edition, Jeffrey Rubin-Dorsky dismisses all but three of the stories and essays in the collection as "periodical literature . . . written for the moment and for money" (1).[23] While that may be a fair assessment, it fails to take account of the cumulative impact of the book, for Twain circles round a number of themes here. Some are continuations and developments of those already familiar from his previous work, but others are specific to this period. Some are prompted by his increasingly bleak philosophical outlook; others make a direct response to the political conditions of the time (the one tending to reinforce the other).[24] All in all, this gives a unity and textual coherence to the book that is noticeable though — and this will be no surprise to those who know Twain's work well — far from fully consistent or absolute. The next chapter consists of an analysis of the dialogic relationship between the title story and what is generally recognized as the best nonfiction piece in the book, "Stirring Times in Austria," examining one such set of textual connections in more detail and showing, too, the cross-generic transactions involved.

The thematic links between material in the *Hadleyburg* book should not be surprising given the recent composition of many of the pieces in it. Though "My Début as a Literary Person" is based, as the title suggests, on Twain's earliest magazine piece (written in 1866), this retrospective essay, first published in the *Century* in November 1899, also contained much reworked material.[25] Two of the fictional pieces in the book, "Is He Living or Is He Dead?" and "The Esquimau Maiden's Romance" — both brought into the collection on Harper's suggestion — were first published in 1893, in the September and November *Cosmopolitan*. "Travelling with a Reformer" first appeared in the December issue of the same magazine. "Private History of the 'Jumping Frog' Story" was taken from the April 1894 *North American Review*, and "How to Tell a Story" from *Youth's Companion*, 3 October 1895. But the rest of the stories and essays in the book were of recent date. "Stirring Times in Austria" was published in *Harper's Magazine* in March 1898. "The Austrian Edison Keeping School Again" was in the August 1898 *Century*, and "At the Appetite Cure" appeared in *Cosmopolitan* that same month. "About Play-Acting" first appeared in the October 1898 New York *Forum*, and "From the 'London Times' of 1904" in November's *Century*. "Concerning the Jews" and "The Man That Corrupted Hadleyburg" came out in *Harper's Monthly* in September and December 1899, respectively. "My First Lie and How I Got Out of It" was in the New York *World* Sunday supplement, 10 December 1899; "My Boyhood Dreams" was in *McClure's* in January 1900. Looking back at the publication history of the *Hadleyburg* book traced in the previous section, we can infer that Twain himself wanted his most recent work in the new collection whereas Harper wanted to bring in material covering the period since February 1893, when *The £1,000,000 Bank-Note* had come out.

One of the noticeable things about Twain's collections of short writings is the author's increasing turn to the essay form. Though the use of this genre by no means precluded humor, it is fair to say that the balance between the comic and the serious in Twain's work had by this point tilted overall in the latter direction. Indeed, even when he was writing fiction, as in the longest (title) work in this book, it was often marked by a type of sardonic irony and/or thematic bleakness distinctively different from the comic exuberance of much of his earlier work. This is not to say, however, that such exuberance was completely abandoned, as the study of "A Double-Barreled Detective Story" in my final chapter will show. And Twain's continued interest in comedy and its forms of expression is still evident in this collection in nonfiction form. In "How to Tell a Story" he writes an illuminating study of the subject.

In this essay Twain makes a distinction between the humorous story, which he defines as an "American" art form, and stories both of the English "comic" and the French "witty" kind. The effect of the humorous story, he says, depends on the "manner" of its telling, the other two on the "matter" (225). The "high and delicate art . . . of telling a humorous story," Twain continues, "was created in America":

The humorous story is told gravely; the teller does his best to conceal the fact that he even dimly suspects that there is anything funny about it . . . the teller will divert attention away from [the story's] nub [or "snapper"] by dropping it in a carefully casual and indifferent way, with the pretence that he does not know it is a nub. . . . To string incongruities and absurdities together in a wandering and sometimes purposeless way, and seem innocently unaware that they are absurdities, is the basis of the American art. (226, 230)

This is as good a description of Twain's own comic techniques, both on the lecture platform and in short stories like "The Jumping Frog," as one will find.

As we have previously seen, though, there is another level to Twain's *written* comic performances that depends on their more complex manipulations of narrative and on the different relationship between the teller and his audience. And when Twain returns once more, in "Private History of the 'Jumping Frog' Story," and tells again the story that launched his comic career, it is the various gaps and mediations that occur between oral performance, written text, and translations and repeated versions of that text, to which he draws attention.[26]

As Twain focuses on the difference between oral and written text, he reminds us of the sometimes narrow—and even undecidable—line between the comic and the serious. And, if we trust these later authorial comments, the author now clears up something of the problems I discuss in chapter 2 in deciding how to read and interpret the original "Jumping Frog" tale. Speaking of his own first hearing of the narrative (in Angel's Camp) from the vernacular figure he would reinvent as "Simon Wheeler," Twain says:

I heard the story told by a man who was not telling it to his hearers as a thing new to them, but as a thing which *they had witnessed and would remember.* He was a dull person, and ignorant; he had no gift as a story-teller, and no invention; in his mouth this episode was merely history . . . and the gravest sort of history, too; he was entirely serious, for he was dealing with what to him were austere facts, and they interested him solely because they *were* facts. . . . [H]e saw no humor in his tale, neither did his listeners. [N]one of the party was aware that a first-rate story had been told in a first-rate way, and that it was brimful of a quality whose presence they never suspected — humor. (376–77)

Solemnity and humor exist in twinned relationship here, the difference between them a matter not of content but of imagination, interpretation, and point of view.

Twain's discussion of the foundations of American humorous performance and of the origins and diverse versions of his own earliest comic success within the *Hadleyburg* collection are evidence of his ongoing concern with humor and its effects. Indeed, he would show continued confidence in its transforming potential in the renowned passage from *The Chronicle of Young Satan* where the power of laughter is celebrated as a weapon that could blow "colossal humbug . . . to rags and atoms at a blast."[27] By 1900, however, Twain's own comic outlook had been strongly affected by the growing seriousness and cynicism of his general view of life. And in *The Man That Corrupted Hadleyburg* it is the "colossal humbug" of his world that most concerns Twain, described mainly in a serious and sardonic manner. By and large, the possibilities of powerfully effective and affirmative forms of humor are very much reduced here.

Twain's increasingly pessimistic social and political perspective at this time — despite the upturn in his personal circumstances — is suggested by another comment made in the summer of 1900: "The time is grave. The future is blacker than has been any future which any person now living has tried to peer into."[28] In terms of recent political events, Twain comments particularly on the Dreyfus case in this book, making direct reference to it on four occasions (144–46, 170, 270, 388–89). Captain Alfred Dreyfus, a French army officer, was court-martialed and convicted in 1894 for selling military secrets to Germany. Dreyfus's treatment, and the injustice and anti-Semitic prejudice it revealed, became an international cause célèbre in the period, fanned by Emile Zola's 1898 open letter of support and the consequent 1899 retrial, which again found him guilty.[29] Clearly Twain was both angered and intrigued by the case and was aware of its wider significance. So even a story like "The Man That Corrupted Hadleyburg" itself, which nowhere mentions Dreyfus (but which was written in Vienna in 1898, the same year Zola published "J'accuse"), should be read in its context. As Cynthia Ozick comments in her introduction:

the notion of a society — even one in microcosm, like Hadleyburg — sliding deeper and deeper (and individual by individual) into ethical perversion and contamination was not far from a portrait of a Europe undergoing the contagion of its great communal lie. The commanding theme of "The Man That Corrupted Hadleyburg" *is* contagion; and also the smugness that arises out of self-righteousness, however rooted in lie it may be. (xxxv)

Ozick's reference to the "communal lie" echoes the idea of the "colossal National Lie" (180) that Twain analyzes in "My First Lie, And How I Got Out of It." Twain revisits old philosophical ground in this sketch. He develops the idea of the "silent lie" and the concept of lying as a universal practice, earlier proposed in "On the Decay of the Art of Lying" (*The Stolen White Elephant*). Here, again, he claims that "all people are liars from the cradle onward" and that this is "the eternal law" of human behavior (168–69).[30] Twain at first takes a comic and an autobiographical approach to his subject. But as he proceeds he focuses in a more serious vein on the wider political effects of what he calls "the lie of silent assertion" (169). In essence, he is speaking of the hegemonic here: the way that people silently assent to dominant sociopolitical values and practices despite the moral injustices that may be at stake. Twain's optimistic stance (that laughter can demolish "humbug") is consequently countered in this essay, in an ironical statement of similar rhetorical power.[31] For here, such humbug, as expressed in everyday forms of social and political injustice, is seen as having more or less absolute sway: "The silent colossal national Lie that is the support and confederate of all the tyrannies and shams and inequalities and unfairnesses that afflict the peoples — that is the one to throw bricks and sermons at. But let us be judicious and let somebody else begin" (179–80).

Despite these words, Twain does preach his own sermon against such political tyrannies in "My First Lie." Almost every word of the essay, though, confirms its predominantly ironic and pessimistic thrust. Interestingly, this is one of the few places in his published books where Twain *explicitly* recognizes that the slave regime of the antebellum South had been a great moral wrong. He chooses, though, and in line with the general tenor of his argument, to concentrate on national rather than the regional culpability in his comments on the early days of abolitionist activity and the way it was rendered ineffective:

It would not be possible for a humane and intelligent person to invent a rational excuse for slavery; yet you will remember that in the early days of the emancipation agitation in the North the agitators got but small help or countenance from any one. Argue and plead and pray as they might, they could not break the universal stillness that reigned, from pulpit and press all the way down to the bottom of society — the clammy stillness created and maintained by the lie of silent assertion — the silent assertion that there wasn't anything going on in which humane and intelligent people were interested. (169–70)[32]

Twain uses two further examples to illustrate "the universal conspiracy of the silent-assertion lie . . . hard at work always and everywhere . . . in the interest of . . . sham" (170). One is that of contemporary British policy in South Africa. The other, again, is the Dreyfus case (the essay was written in the year of Dreyfus's retrial). Twain writes how "all France, except a couple of dozen moral paladins, lay under the smother of the silent-assertion lie that no wrong was being done to a persecuted and unoffending man" (170).

Twain, then, in this collection focuses on the moral shabbiness of both the American and the European political and social order. Partly because of his own expatriation, he casts his eye wide here and is repulsed by what he sees. The Dreyfus case and the anti-Semitic sentiments it aroused also figure in one of the more contentious pieces in this collection, "Concerning the Jews." It was not just Dreyfus that prompted this essay but Twain's own recent experiences in Austria, too.[33] Even at the time, "Concerning the Jews" had a mixed reception. Frank Bliss called it "a bang-up thing . . . one of the best serious articles you have ever done."[34] But in the year following its publication, Rabbi M. S. Levy would write that Twain's "many statements . . . regarding the various traits of the Jews . . . are not only tinged with malice and prejudice, but are incorrect and false."[35] The essay was clearly intended as a rebuttal of anti-Semitic prejudice. While Twain reluctantly accepts that "the race prejudice [against the Jews] cannot be removed," he speaks sharply on the nature and scope of such prejudice: "By his make and ways [the Jew] is a substantially a foreigner wherever he may be, and even the angels dislike a foreigner. I am using this word foreigner in the German sense — *stranger*. Nearly all of us have an antipathy to a stranger, even of our own nationality" (278). Twain distances himself from such forms of behavior: "I have no race prejudices, and I think I have no color prejudices nor caste prejudices nor creed prejudices." He then collapses his developing argument about comparative racial/ethnic difference in the shift to reductive and sardonic generalization: "I can stand any society. All that I care to know is that a man is a human being — that is enough for me; he can't be any worse" (254).[36]

What is clear in reading the essay is that though Twain's intentions in defending the Jews from prejudicial attack may have been admirable, his essay runs into difficulties in its tendency (as Cynthia Ozick puts it in her introduction) to repeat "the old myths [about Jewishness] . . . for an airing in the American idiom" (xlvii).[37] Sander L. Gilman gives perhaps the fairest assessment of the piece in calling it:

one of the most complex documents written against anti-Semitism in late nineteenth-century America. . . . The shifting, sometimes contradictory positions concerning the Jews which Twain espoused were recognized by his contemporaries. What is important and has not been noted by the critics . . . is that Twain shifts the underlying rhetoric of his argument about the Jews from one which sees the nature of the Jews as immutable to one which understands it as socially constructed.[38]

"Concerning the Jews" was, in part, stimulated by the response Twain received to his essay "Stirring Times in Austria." Here, too, he had raised the question of anti-Semitic prejudice, though this time in the context of contemporary Austrian politics. His representation of the effects of such prejudice in that essay, though relatively brief, provides a more startling and prophetic approach to the subject. I give more detail in my next chapter.

The *Hadleyburg* collection is marked by the amount of serious social and political commentary and analysis it contains. It also provides a forum where Twain expresses the general bleakness of his philosophical outlook at this stage of his life, despite the easing of his immediate material circumstances. The type of sardonic comment as that quoted above from "Concerning the Jews" can thus be seen as symptomatic of a more general pattern in the book, and clearly connects up with the thematic emphasis of the title story itself. One of the most important essays in the collection for revealing Twain's mindset at this time is "About Play-Acting." Here, he discusses a "remarkable" Austrian play he has seen in Vienna, *The Master of Palmyra* by Adolf von Wilbrandt, praising it as "a great and stately metaphysical poem" (235).

It is not just the metaphysics of the play, though, that interest Twain. He also uses his essay to comment on the state of the theater in America. Here again we see evidence of that conflicted attitude toward high and mass culture noted in previous chapters. Twain attacks the American theatre audience for its lack of seriousness:

You are trying to make yourself believe that life is a comedy, that its sole business is fun. . . . You are ignoring the skeleton in your closet. . . . America . . . neglect[s] what is possibly the most effective of all the breeders and . . . disseminators of high literary taste and lofty emotion — the tragic stage. To leave that powerful agency out is to haul the culture-wagon with a crippled team. . . . What *has* come over us English-speaking people? . . . Comedy keeps the heart sweet; but we all know that there is wholesome refreshment for both mind and heart in an occasional climb among the pomps of the intellectual snow-summits built by Shakspeare [sic] and those others. (248–51)

Such words might take somewhat aback those readers who remember Twain's earlier identifications with the "factory hands and farmers" of his

country and with their tastes and comic preferences. He was always ambivalent, though, about the motives and meanings of art and about the
status of his own comic popularity. And here a further and clearly self-
reflexive element impinges on his words. For Twain is unable to forget
the (metaphorical) skeletons in his own closet among which were bankruptcy, family ill health, and the death of Susy. His comic sensibility and
general outlook on life were affected accordingly.

The themes and plot of *The Master of Palmyra* itself closely reflect
Twain's own developing view of reality. No doubt that is why he thought
the play so important. It explains, too, why his celebration of the play has
such a peculiarly familiar feel to it for those who know his late work well.
Twain's essay foregrounds subjects and perspectives to which he would
often return in his own writing, both fiction and nonfiction. All the
characters in the play suffer the "decay of age" except the hero, Appelles,
who, granted his wish for a "deathless life," remains "young, handsome,
vigorous . . . through the long flight of years covered by the five acts."
"Death, in person, walks about the stage in every act" and this "black
figure with the corpse-face . . . always . . . made the fussy human pack seem
infinitely pitiful and hardly worth the attention of either saving or damning" (238–40). Twain, as he describes the play, shifts tone and point of
view. A philosophical detachment regarding the worthlessness of human
life gives way, in the course of the analysis, to pathos and a deep sense of
personal devastation. This occurs as Twain describes Appelles's loss of
friends and of family, particularly that of his dear son: "At length he is
wholly alone in the world; all his friends are dead; last of all, his darling of
darlings, his son, the lad *Nymphas*, who dies in his arms. His pride is
broken now" (241). Death is described as "the healer of sorrows . . . man's
best friend" (240) and Appelles is eventually granted a final boon and
allowed to die. Twain sums up the drama:

This piece is just one long, soulful, sardonic laugh at human life. Its title might
properly be "Is Life a Failure?" . . . [T]he episodes in the piece seem to be saying
all the time, inarticulately: "Note what a silly, poor thing human life is; how
childish its ambitions, how ridiculous its pomps, how trivial its dignities . . . how
wearisome and monotonous its repetition of its stupid history through the ages."
(242–43)

The move in Twain's description of the play between pathos and pessimism, and between the sardonic and the deterministic (for there is
nothing Appelles himself can do to alter his fate), anticipates that of his
own late work. And Twain also gives here — as reflected through the
play — a far darker view of human nature and history than that held
earlier in his literary career.[39] By this point, any belief in "natural" human
goodness (Huck Finn's essentially good heart) has been replaced by a

bleaker point of view where "natural" has instead become synonymous with "barbaric": "in our day the spectacle of a shipwrecked French crew clubbing women and children who tried to climb into the lifeboats suggests that civilization has not succeeded in entirely obliterating the natural man even yet." Twain's description of the slaughtering of Christian by Pagan, and then of Pagan by Christian, in the play, presents a similarly negative view of human history. Its circular rather than linear and progressive pattern illustrates what Twain calls the "picturesque failure of civilization" (243–44).

Twain's account of the themes of "The Master of Palmyra" can then be superimposed on his own later work with scarcely a join visible. And a good number of the essays in this collection reflect the general pessimistic tenor of much of late Twain. But hints of such obsessive concerns are present even in "My Début as a Literary Person," Twain's revisiting of a much earlier essay.[40] This would suggest the lines of connection that can be identified right across the spectrum of Twain's writing even as important differences of emphasis and tone occur.[41] In "My Début," Twain looks back on — and repeats — the report he brought in 1866 from Hawaii to San Francisco of the wreck of the clipper *Hornet*. He uses the diaries of the fifteen men who survived "after a voyage of forty-three days in an open boat, through the blazing tropics, on *ten days' rations* of food" (85) to give his own account its immediacy and its strong narrative drive.

"My Début" anticipates Twain's late dream tales (and *The Great Dark* and *The Enchanted Sea-Wilderness* in particular)[42] in the stress on the loss of bearings, disorientation, and alienation as he recounts the shipwreck and the lifeboat's progress. Thus Twain describes the dangers of the doldrums, "a watery perdition, with winds which are wholly crazy, and blow from all points of the compass at once" (94–95). Then, once the lifeboat's journey is under way, other descriptions follow that emphasize dislocation, relativism, and the collapse of certainties.[43] The shipwrecked men are met with "baffling winds" (101). Their boats (there are originally three of them) are described as a mere "speck" (107) on the ocean. And they "*sai[l] straight over*" islands on the map that are "said to be doubtful" but prove in fact to be completely nonexistent (113). Henry Ferguson, whose diary Twain quotes extensively in the sketch, reports on their eventual rescue that "we were too happy to sleep; would keep the reality and not let it turn to a delusion — dreaded that we might wake up and find ourselves in the boat again" (121).[44] As Twain reread and reused Ferguson's diary entry, that must have struck a particularly resonant chord, for he would himself obsessively explore the dream-reality borderline and its permeability in his late and unfinished work (and especially in the *No. 44, The Mysterious Stranger* manuscript). Realist assumptions of stable subjectivity and ontological certainty were undermined as he did so. Twain's reference to the "literary gold" and "eloquence" (126) of this section of Ferguson's diary suggests just how strongly he responded to it.

"My Début as a Literary Person" begins as personal history, about the making of Twain's own literary reputation and the "currency" (84) of his nom de plume. His early dreams of literary glory, he explains, were dashed by the article's publication not under the name of "Mark Twain" but of " 'Mike Swain' or 'MacSwain,' I do not remember which" (85). This may be only a passing mention, but it does introduce a self-reflexive concern with literary (or artistic) reputation, and the gains (and costs) associated with it, which recurs at a number of points in this collection. Twain returns to this subject in the rather curious fiction "Is He Living or Is He Dead?"[45] His narrator tells here how the painter François Millet fakes his own death with the help of artist friends and takes on a new identity and how his works then rise phenomenally in price. This is in accord with the "law . . . that the merit of *every* great unknown and neglected artist must and will be recognized, and his pictures climb to high prices" but only "after his death" (188).

The story can be read biographically in a number of ways. It can be interpreted in terms of some buried desire on the author's part to shuck off his name and fame and the burdens they carried, to go where he will be anonymous and unhindered by public recognition. Or it can be seen as a fictional exploration, at a time of acute financial anxiety (1893), of the question of the "value" of his literary persona, for it raised questions, when applied to the author's own self, as to how Twain as "known" literary celebrity ranked with other (perhaps unknown) talents, and whether the market value of his work accurately reflected, or fell considerably below, his "true" artistic worth.[46] If, however, we read the story from the first of these interpretive perspectives, we recognize a complicating and contradictory element to it. The representation of Theophile Magnan (the renamed Millet) does not suggest any blessed release from the demands of fame, but rather speaks of anxieties about the loss of established identity and the estrangement that his change of life brings with it. Magnan/Millet is now apparently "alone in the world, for he always looks sad and dreamy, and doesn't talk with anybody" (182). Despite the financial rewards that now come his way, he goes (it seems) ungreeted even by his previously "doting" and "inseparable" friend (184), who tells the narrator his story. Such alienation anxieties are repeated, in different ways, over and over in Twain's late work.

In both this story and "My Literary Début" Twain is concerned with the "currency" of the literary or artistic name, both in terms of its status (as unknown or famous) and its financial value. And the theme of cur-

rency, exchange value, and the possibility of some firm "gold standard" — in the last two cases that of artistic merit — is also a repeated one
in the collection as a whole. So, in "The Man That Corrupted Hadleyburg," what appears to be "gold coin" (4) turns out to lack any authen-
ticating substance and is in fact just "virgin lead" (67). And throughout
the story, too, a metaphoric analogy is made between gold and language,
the fraudulence of the one paralleled by the falsity of the other.[47]

The question of currency and of relative value also stands as the central
theme of "The Esquimau Maiden's Romance." This is one of the few
pieces in the whole collection where the comic exuberance of his earlier
work resurfaces. In the story, ethnocentric assumptions are in part undermined with the representation of cultural difference that occurs.[48] Twain
relies on the humor of defamiliarization and incongruity as, from the
start of the narrative, two systems of value are measured against each
other. "Mark Twain" (for the author returns to the use of that narrative
persona here) describes the Eskimo maiden, Lasca, as she "absently
scrap[es] blubber-grease from her cheeks with a small bone-knife," as "a
beautiful creature. I speak from the Esquimaux point of view. Others
would have thought her a trifle over-plump" (197–98). The rest of the
story then switches back and forth between the different standards and
values of Eskimo and American culture. Thus the narrator, for instance,
describes Lasca's amazement on hearing that Vanderbilt, "almost the
richest man in the whole world" (201), has not even a single slop-tub in
his drawing-room (a key sign of status and wealth in her tribe). He also
expresses his own astonishment when Lasca tells him of the "prejudice
against soap" her tribes *used* to have, until she clarifies: "Yes — but that
was only at first; nobody would eat it" (205).

If this seems the standard stuff of ethnocentric humor, Twain also
emphasizes the "honest" and "natural and sincere" (197–8) qualities of
Lasca, this "little provincial muggins" (203). And the most damning
criticism of the narrative is aimed not at her but at the "ways of millionaires" (213) and the social divisiveness, conspicuous consumption,
and avaricious mentality brought with them. Though Twain here refers
in the first instance to Eskimo culture, he is clearly turning his humor
back, in a Veblenian manner, on his own late nineteenth-century American world.[49] It is a western import, too, "the debasing iron fish-hooks of
the foreigner" (213), that constitutes the foundation of Lasca's father's
fortune. Financial worth is equated with a moral and cultural corruption that comes apparently from without, from the narrator's western
"home." The criticism of the "ways of millionaires" has everything to do
with American culture and, in terms of any identifiable social reality, little
to do with the Eskimos. The story may not be profound, and its moves
between sentiment and satire are a touch uneasy.[50] But the ungrounding

of the reader, caught in a type of cultural in-between place where neither Eskimo or American world is finally favored, is typical of one relativistic strand of Twain's comic vision. And the story bounces along with an exuberance and a playfulness that is unusual in this collection as a whole.

The Man That Corrupted Hadleyburg is by no means a fully unified collection of stories and essays, nor would we expect it to be so. Its thematic and formal moves lead in a number of different directions. But its content is both more coherent and more interesting than the odd casual comment from critics, and the fact that the collection has been almost completely overlooked in assessments of Twain's work, would indicate. Much of the material in this book comes out of Twain's highly productive Austrian period, and as such it provides a strong representation of many of the thematic and philosophical concerns that interested the author both then and in the later part of his literary career as a whole.

Carnival in "Stirring Times in Austria" and "The Man That Corrupted Hadleyburg"

Rather than concentrating on the complexities of the political situation of the time, Twain is primarily concerned with the absurdity of a spectacle like something in fiction

— Walter Grünzweig

Noise and tumult all over the House.

— "Stirring Times in Austria"

This chapter sets one of Twain's best-known short works, "The Man That Corrupted Hadleyburg," against the political essay "Stirring Times in Austria," where he describes the series of events that took place in the Austrian parliament in late 1897. The juxtaposition illustrates both the textual patterns that connect the apparently disparate parts of the *Hadleyburg* book and the way such connections cut across generic boundaries. Twain's moves between fiction and non-fiction serve only to reinforce the common basis of the particular themes he develops and his underlying view of human nature and behavior at this time (circa 1898). I build here on Cynthia Ozick's insight as she makes an initial exploration of the complementary relationship between the two texts. She speaks of the Austrian parliament, as Twain represents it, as "a non-homogeneous Hadleyburg corrupted well past mere greed into the contagion of chaos and contumely" (xxxix). Twain does not refer specifically to the Hapsburg Empire in "Stirring Times." Nonetheless, the trace of the word Hapsburg in Hadleyburg helps to reinforce the connection being made here.[1] Ozick's introduction, together with Bruce Michelson's stimulating analysis of the Hadleyburg story, form the twin points of departure for my own critical work.[2]

Hadleyburg is a small American community, though Twain never precisely locates the town geographically. The townsfolk, with names of Richards, Burgess, Wilson, Goodson, and the like, seem to come from the same ethnic background. At first glance there would appear to be little in common between such a fictional setting and that of "Stirring Times in Austria," for, in the latter, Twain focuses on the Hapsburg parliament and its nineteen national groupings, to describe the political disunion of the time. Ozick, though, notes the similarity between the two groups, since in Hadleyburg the citizens' "interests conflict as if they held nothing in common" (xxxix).[3] For her, the shared "crux" of each work lies in their treatment of the issue of language (xl). In "Stirring Times in Austria," Twain explains how the ratification of the Ausgleich, the treaty that formally held together the Austria-Hungarian Empire, was jeopardized. This resulted from the deal Count Bedani, the leader of the government, made with the Czechs, "making the Czech tongue the official language in Bohemia in place of the German. This created a storm." The German-speaking minority, "incensed" (292) by this move, accordingly obstructed government business — and that of the Ausgleich ratification in particular — until the status of their own language should once more be restored. Ozick proceeds to compare the nineteen states in the Austrian parliament to the nineteen worthies in Hadleyburg, and she sees the way both parliamentarians and leading citizens "furiously compete" as analogous: "We can recognize in Hadleyburg the dissolving Austria-Hungary of the 1890s" (xl).

Ozick's critical work is valuable. It is noticeable, however, that her comparative treatment of the language theme in the two texts is undeveloped. And she remains curiously blind to their main point of comparison: the way in which description of the sessions of the Austrian parliament structurally mirrors that of the Hadleyburg town meeting. Prompted by the use of Bakhtinian terms in Michelson's analysis of "The Man That Corrupted Hadleyburg" (though he never uses the Soviet theorist's name),[4] I use Mikhail Bakhtin's work as a lens through which the public meetings at the center of both texts can be analyzed. My critical intentions are thus limited here. And the conclusions reached concerning social and political hierarchies and the way they work, and the view of human nature represented, will come as no surprise to those familiar with Twain's late work. They serve, though, to further illustrate the very close relationship between these two "Austrian" texts.[5] Walter Grünzweig's note that "The first mention of the ['Hadleyburg'] story can be found in the *Notebook*, in an entry dated December 1, 1897, only a few days after the events described in 'Stirring Times in Austria' had taken place" serves as a further indicator of this connection.[6]

Bakhtin's notion of *carnivalization* provides a useful model to apply to "The Man That Corrupted Hadleyburg." It can also be applied to "Stirring Times in Austria," though its relevance in that case is less immediately obvious. The theorist's name comes to mind in Ozick's reference to a shared concern with language in the two texts and the furious competition between individuals and groups there represented. His consistent emphasis is on the way language serves as a site of conflict and registers power relations in any particular society. Bakhtin's ideas can be briefly glossed in the context of my present critical concerns. Conflict, for him, inevitably occurs as one "social speech type" — that is, the voice of a particular professional, regional, ethnic, age-related, or other social or political group—meets another in any given cultural context.[7] His sociopolitical model is one in which authoritarian and hierarchical forces, associated with what he calls the centripetal, are in constant dynamic tension with liberating and centrifugal ones. The centripetal is the unhealthy urge toward the closed system and "cultural centralization": the establishing of a single officially recognised language and value system.[8] The centrifugal, in contrast, "endlessly develop[s] new forms which parody, criticize and generally undermine the pretensions of the ambitions toward a unitary language."[9] In his favoring of the centrifugal, Bakhtin asserts his commitment to social diversity and change, for a culture is not for him something fixed, rigid, and ordered. He emphasizes rather its many-languaged aspects, assigning qualities of health and vitality to the ongoing forces of disunity that the authorities and ruling classes of any society would try to deny and destroy.

Carnivalization is a key term for Bakhtin and one that directly relates to the centripetal-centrifugal axis. It is the model of carnival festivity "transposed into the language of literature," life turned upside-down as conventional hierarchical barriers are removed.[10] Bakhtin's preference for "low" languages over "high" is evident in carnival's emphasis on the comic overturning of official systems of life and thought by an unofficial folk culture and the energies thereby released. Carnival is a time of masquerade, as masks and false identities are assumed which blur the boundaries between high and low and upset authoritative systems and structures. And carnival is associated with public space (especially the public square) where normal hierarchies are suspended as the festival runs its course and where all types of people can meet and mingle freely and easily together. Carnivalization primarily means laughter: a laughter "directed toward something higher — toward a shift of authorities and truths." What results is the relativizing of "all structure and order, of all authority and all (hierarchical) position."[11] In communal performance — the very essence of carnival — the language and structure of officialdom (law, prohibition, and restriction) are overturned on behalf of the vital and indecorous folk energies there allowed release.

The version of carnival that occurs in "Stirring Times in Austria" is grotesque and life-denying. The language and structure of officialdom are subject to contest and potential overthrow, with energies loosed that are normally harnessed. However, such action takes place primarily in a limited arena, and any sense of life-affirming folk culture — "the folk as an untamable, rebellious, and regenerative force that will destroy the status quo" — is completely absent.[12] That absence points forward to "The Man That Corrupted Hadleyburg" and the bleak view of human behavior and of the way social hierarchies function that it too ultimately shares.

The setting of the parliamentary meetings described in "Stirring Times" differs from the town meeting in "The Man That Corrupted Hadleyburg," but the centrality of these public assemblies in both texts is highly significant.[13] The parliament in "Stirring Times" is not the carnival area (the public square) where all types of people can mingle freely together. It is, however, a *type* of public forum — a microcosmic version of the pluralistic Austria-Hungarian entirety, with a membership drawn "from all the walks of life and from all the grades of society" (316) and representing "peoples who speak eleven languages" (292). Moreover, the sense of the multilayered communal whole indicated here (something we might expect in a representative body) is reinforced in the way Twain carefully structures his essay to draw links between what occurs within the parliament, where most of the main events happen, and outside it. Indeed, the essay starts with a striking metaphor of diffuse electrical energy, where this connection is immediately made: "The atmosphere is brimful of political electricity. All conversation is political; *every man* is a battery, with brushes overworn, and gives out blue sparks" (284, my emphasis). Despite public confusion about the real nature of the political situation,[14] energies within the parliament have their counterpart on the streets outside. "Stirring Times" both starts and finishes with public restlessness, the final references to "a popular outbreak or two in Vienna," and rioting elsewhere (340), a direct result of the parliamentary turbulence described at the essay's core.

Parliamentary events, then, are linked in the essay to the release of disordering energies in the larger public community. And within the parliament, elements of the carnivalesque are clearly apparent. As government authority is challenged, so events take on (sporadically) a masquerade quality, with formal debate drowned in the "general exuberance" (320) that bursts forth. Dr. Lecher, an opposition member, gives a "memorable" (295) twelve-hour filibustering speech holding up the government's attempt quickly to push through the Ausgleich.[15] Though he finally gets a hearing for his words, he commences in "pantomime," his voice drowned out by the "wild and frantic and deafening clamor" (299–300) from the house floor. Later, Lecher and Wolf (another key opposition figure) "spoke at the same time, and mingled their speeches with the other noises, and nobody heard either of them" (308). All types of wild energies are loosed as language (reasoned or otherwise) is drowned out, first by "explosions of yells" (299), later by the "slam-banging" of desk-boards (305), and then by a form of music, as Wolf "struck the idea of beating out a *tune* with his [desk-] board" (308). This festive overturning of officialdom, as normal parliamentary business is disrupted, is continued in the next sitting of the house. Here "ceaseless din and uproar . . . shouting and stamping and desk-banging" (320) are followed by the bursting forth of personal insults, first singly, and then in the form of communal song:

in their rapture [the Christian Socialists] flung biting epithets with wasteful liberality at specially detested members of the Opposition; among others, this one at Schönerer: "*Bordell in der Krugerstrasse!*" Then they added these words, which they whooped, howled, and even sang, in a deep-voiced chorus: "*Schmul Leeb Kohn! Schmul Leeb Kohn! Schmul Leeb Kohn!*["] and made it splendidly audible above the banging of desk-boards and the rest of the roaring cyclone of fiendish noises. (325)

The unruly nature of these parliamentary events clearly have a carnival element to them, but the urge toward heterogeneity and the celebration of communality Bakhtin associates with the term are denied here. Laughter is present (see, e.g., 325) but far outweighed by forms of irony and abuse. There is, in this context, no clear antithesis between authority systems and a festive and pluralistic community. The government is associated with an extra-legal exercise of power (the president "persistently ignoring the Rules of the House in the interest of the government side," 320). But it is *also* identified with the centrifugal impulse, since it is the very fact of "*dis*union which has held [this Austria-Hungarian] empire together" (285). And not just the opposition but the government benches too share in the carnival nature of the events taking place, in their own use of "pure noise" (308) to short-circuit the legislative process. Most crucially, given Bakhtin's celebrations of linguistic diversity and social difference, it is the government that, as a means of retaining its authority, works toward linguistic pluralism (allowing Czech as the official language in Bohemia). It is the opposition that fights for centripetal linguistic purity: "that the country's public business should be conducted in one common tongue, and that tongue a world language — which German is" (293).

The boundaries, then, are blurred in this microcosmic parliamentary context between the imposition of authority and the carnivalistic sense of release. And expected Bakhtinian relationships between the demand for a unitary official language system and the acceptance of heterogeneity are reversed. This completely undermines any note of celebration concerning the positive expression of diversity, the regenerative nature of communal performance, and the fulfilling release of folk energies we might otherwise (from this same Bakhtinian perspective) expect.

Indeed, it is the more sinister and pessimistic side of this essay that remains most strongly with the reader. The dark carnival Twain describes, with energy loosed to no positive end, may be no more than an accurate (if selective) report of events. But the reference to German as a "world language" and the racial intolerance loosed within the parliament are, from a later historical perspective, chilling.[16] As Ozick says:

the 1897 parliamentary upheaval [Twain describes] . . . is an indelible precursor that not merely portends the profoundly unforgettable Viennese mob-events of 1938, but thrusts them into our teeth with all their bitter twentieth-century flavor. Here is no déjà-vu, but its prophesying opposite. Or, to say it otherwise: a twenty-year-old rioter enjoying Mark Twain's Vienna easily becomes a sixty-year-old Nazi enjoying *Anschluss* Vienna.[17]

Carnival (or its approximation) is swiftly ended in the parliament with the sudden introduction, on the government's command, of "an invasion of brute force . . . a uniformed and helmeted battalion of bronzed and stalwart men marching in double file down the floor of the House" (339). This is soon followed by the collapse of the government and by public riot. The mix of racist and anti-Semitic abuse within parliament ("You Jew, you!" "East-German offal tub!" 321, 325) is supplemented to become open violence on the streets. Events inside and outside the parliament thus complement each other. For this violence is no open expression of a folk energy but its corrupt, narrowly nationalistic, and antihumanistic underside (the uses to which Hitler would put the celebration of "the folk" come quickly to mind).[18] So Twain reports that, in the outbreaks that take place (in Vienna, Prague, and elsewhere), "in some cases the Germans [were] the rioters, in others the Czechs — and in all cases the Jew had to roast, no matter which side he was on" (340). Twain's figure of speech provides another example of that prophesying opposite of déjà-vu to which Ozick refers, as images of festivity, entertainment, and laughter associated with carnival are entirely obliterated in the anti-Semitism, racial hatred, and mob destruction then released.

The events Twain describes in "Stirring Times in Austria" are nonfictional and occur in a turbulent European political setting. Nonetheless,

both the parliamentary scenes in his essay and its general tone significantly foreshadow "The Man That Corrupted Hadleyburg."[19] "Hadleyburg" is one of Twain's best-known stories. Indeed, as Cynthia Ozick
suggests, it may seem overly familiar to a contemporary readership, so
often has its ironic fable of "the stealthy despoliation of an idyllic town by
a cunning stranger" now been retold and reformulated by others (xxxvi). The story has also received much critical attention, perhaps in recognition of Twain's "firmness of tone and narrative control over his material," perhaps because of the power of its theme. As Tom Quirk says, the
story "is among one of the most devastating comments on the desire for
riches to be found in American literature" (SSF, 103, 108). I focus here
primarily on the third section of the story (38–71), the town meeting,
and how events there can be compared with those in "Stirring Times."
But first I give a brief and selective summary of the narrative.

"The Man That Corrupted Hadleyburg" focuses on a single town, "the
most honest and upright . . . in all the region round about . . . synonym for
incorruptible" (1, 21). Twain's theme, as one might guess from this description, is temptation and corruptibility. A "passing stranger" who has,
in some unknown way, been offended by this proudly self-sufficient town
that "cared not a rap for strangers or their opinions" (2) looks to gain his
revenge. Accordingly some eighteen months later he sets a communal
trap. Returning to the town, he leaves a heavy sack and a letter in the care
of Edward Richards, the local bank cashier. The sack, he writes in the
letter, holds $40,000 of gold coins as a gift for the citizen who had (and
this is fabrication) done him, as a "ruined gambler," "a great kindness."
This kindness had taken the form of a twenty-dollar handout and the
giving of a certain piece of advice. The narrative plot hinges on this
remark, supposedly made by the donor. For the letter, directly alluding to
the town's reputation, says: "my benefactor . . . will be found. This is an
honest town, an incorruptible town, and I know I can trust it without fear.
This man can be identified by the remark he made to me [as he made his
original gift]; I feel persuaded that he will remember it" (4–5).

Each of the nineteen principal citizens of the town then privately gets a
second letter. This contains the information that it was Barclay Goodson
(the only man in the town capable of such generosity, and now dead)
who made the said remark. The key words are then given, on the basis
that the letter's recipient had once (so the writer seems to remember his
benefactor telling him) done Goodson a "very great service." If this was
in fact true, he should claim the money as the latter's "legitimate heir"
(26). The crucial town meeting then follows, where it is discovered (in
front of a large audience) that eighteen of those principal citizens have
claimed the gold and have written down the supposed remark to give to
Reverend Burgess, the long-disgraced local minister chairing the meet-

ing. One by one, Burgess reads out the series of names and the quoted remark ("You are far from being a bad man: go, and reform") to the growing derision of the audience. The town's reputation for honesty and incorruptibility is killed stone dead. A further note from the stranger, explaining his motives and his plan — "to corrupt Hadleyburg the Incorruptible" by testing its "virtue in the fire" (63) — is then also read out.

But there are a series of other twists involved. The main protagonist of the story is Edward Richards, the man to whom the sack is originally entrusted. He succumbs to the same temptation as his fellow citizens, but Burgess protects him, concealing the fact that he too has written down the given remark. The sack of gold — which in fact has turned out to contain "gilded disks of lead" (65) — is auctioned on Richards's behalf to recognize his "invulnerable probity" (69). After further intervention by the original (but unrecognized) "stranger," who is now present at the town meeting, it is purchased by Clay Harkness, one of the disgraced eighteen. Harkness then uses his purchase to defeat his opponent, the banker Pinkerton, in the upcoming local election by stamping the latter's name on the bogus coins, together with the "go and reform" remark quoted by all the claimants. He then distributes these coins among the voters: "Thus the entire remaining refuse of the joke was emptied upon a single head. . . . Harkness's election was a walk-over" (77). Richards's reputation has been protected by Burgess, who believes that the former once "saved [him] in a difficult time" (76). Plagued by guilt and paranoia, however, Richards and his wife fall ill and die, though Richards publicly admits his own failure to withstand the temptation offered by the stranger before this last happens. The narrative ends as follows:

The last of the sacred Nineteen had fallen a prey to the fiendish sack; the town was stripped of the last rag of its ancient glory. Its mourning was not showy, but it was deep.

By act of the Legislature . . . Hadleyburg was allowed to change its name to (never mind what — I will not give it away), and leave one word out of the motto that for many generations had graced the town's official seal.

It is an honest town once more, and the man will have to rise early that catches it napping again. (83)

A representation of the town seal then follows, with the former motto — "Lead us not into Temptation" — altered by the omission of the middle word.

The town meeting in this story can be compared to the parliamentary sequence in the "Stirring Times" essay. Carl Dolmetsch briefly alludes to the connection between them when he writes:

Depicting the same atmosphere of "delightful pandemonium," the scene is theatrically staged, with the chair attempting to keep order while raucous taunts and insults are exchanged and speaker after speaker is jeered or shouted down by a "storm," a "cyclone," or a "tornado" of voices, the same imagery [Twain] had used in "Stirring Times."[20]

But there is more to the comparison than this. Both narratives have public (or semipublic) meetings at their centre. In "Stirring Times" this takes a representative form, with a certain separation between parliamentary members, the crowded viewing galleries inside the House, and the general public outside. In the small town of Hadleyburg, however, the whole community pack into the town hall. Indeed, its numbers are further boosted by a variety of "strangers" who also attend, including "a strong force of special correspondents who had come from everywhere" (38) (for the case has generated nationwide publicity), and even a representative from Barnum's (66). But the form and progression of both meetings are similar. In "Hadleyburg," too, ordered process gives way to pandemonium, and reasoned discussion to "all manner of cries . . . scattered through the din" (53–54), as the dishonesty of the chief citizens is revealed. And, once more, individual speech is replaced first by "*Many Voices*" (58) acting as a communal chorus, and then by outbreaks of musical festivity. Such festivity, as the local worthies are mocked, takes the form of religious parody, "a massed and measured and musical deep volume of sound (with a daringly close resemblance to a well-known church chant)" (59), and of a travesty of light opera:

"Hooray! hooray! it's a symbolical day!"
Somebody wailed in, and began to sing this rhyme (leaving out "it's") to the lovely "Mikado" tune of "When a man's afraid of a beautiful maid"; the audience joined in, with joy [adding further lines to that first]. . . . Then the happy house started in at the beginning and sang the four lines through twice, with immense swing and dash. (55–56)

If the transition from speech to uproar to song is similar in both texts,[21] the version of carnival represented in "Hadleyburg" is a fuller and more positive one. Bruce Michelson suggests this in describing how, here: "A too-settled social order gives way to folklife, to a springtime of human society in which collective talk and humor flow free, overcoming repression, inhibition and decorum. It is a springtime with power and identity residing nowhere and everywhere."[22] In the town meeting, the established social order is turned upside down. The discredited and "best-hated man" (9) in the community, the Rev. Mr. Burgess, is given authority as chairman. And the chief citizens of the community are derided as their greed and hypocrisy is exposed. During the meeting, the "monolithically serious" life of this firmly hierarchical community is undermined by the typical form of carnival laughter, where "ridicule [is] fused with rejoicing."[23] "The pandemonium of delight" that follows banker Pinkerton's humiliation is, we are told, "of a sort to make the judicious weep. Those whose withers were unwrung laughed till the tears ran down" (53). Laughter becomes king here (as it never fully is in "Stirring Times") and the jester who shares its crown is Jack Halliday, the town's "loafing, good-natured, no-account, irreverent" (22) who helps instigate the festival that the meeting becomes.[24] As the Town Hall becomes the meeting place for the variety of social types that make up the community, and as eighteen of the "nineteen principal citizens and their wives" (21) are reduced from beaming self-congratulation to public humiliation while indecorous folk energies find expressive release, the conditions of carnival literature appear successfully complete.

If the use of Bakhtin is more explicit, the analysis proposed here has much in common with Bruce Michelson's. His main interest, though, differs from my own. He is concerned with the nature of the gap between the dissolve of individual identity (in a foundational version of folk life) and a countering awareness of the way selfhood is defined both by the nature of external events and by social and psychological circumstance. I am interested in Twain's representation of social diversity. In discussing "Stirring Times in Austria," I noted how any opposition (in the way parliament functioned) between centralizing and decentralizing impulse was blurred. So, and to an extent analogously, the portrayal of social hierarchy in "Hadleyburg" is less clear-cut than first it seems. Both this fact, and the narrative closure that follows the town hall meeting, undercut the impact of the celebration of communal energy in that scene. The conclusions reached here do not significantly differ from those of prior critics. The focus, though, on the issues of class and authority, and the ironic attitude toward folk culture identified, help to twin this text thematically with the Vienna essay and also to suggest its relationship to other Twain texts (particularly *Huckleberry Finn*) that can be read from a similar thematic perspective.[25]

Carnival depends on the upsetting of established hierarchies, and at first view this is exactly what happens in "The Man That Corrupted Hadleyburg." At the public meeting, eighteen of the town's principal citizens are exposed as "liars and thieves" (64) by the "stranger."[26] And as exposure occurs, these eighteen "Symbols of Incorruptibility" (54) become the object of complete public ridicule, the rest of the community loosing their voices in exuberant mockery of them. So, to quote Bakhtin, "the *joyful relativity* of all structure and order, of all authority and all (hierarchical) position" occurs as the "high" town authorities are brought low (the first three men exposed are the Deacon, Lawyer, and Banker), and as "mass actions" and the "outspoken carnivalistic word" are given their day.[27]

The social reversal that takes place here is compromised, however, by the role of the main protagonists in the narrative, Edward and Mary Richards. Edward is one of the nineteen principal citizens of the town. He receives one of the letters sent by "Stephenson," and it is he alone who is left unexposed, his own written claim for the gold sack going publicly unread. This happens because of Burgess's debt to him: Edwards warned Burgess on the occasion of his unspecified "disgrace" of the town's "plan to ride him on a rail" (11). The fact that the "town" as a whole is, early on, identified with a violent act against an innocent man (for Burgess is not guilty of the supposed crime) warns us not to take the opposition between "the authorities" and "the folk" too seriously here. And if the town is socially mixed (both the town hatter and its tanner, we are told, cannot get recognition as members of the Nineteen), any clear gap between high and low is interrogated by the Richards's role in the story.

Edward Richards, as the local bank cashier, is neither rich nor success-ful. His working life consists of being "[a]lways at the grind, grind, grind, on a salary—another man's slave" (6). Richards's very name, moreover, would appear to signal his membership of the general mass (the sup-posedly untainted folk) and not the upper social echelon.[28] What he is doing here among the town's "aristocracy" (65) is never explained. Earl F. Briden describes Richards as "the town's representative conscious-ness."[29] But the very notion of social hierarchy and difference is collapsed in that remark. Both Richards's membership (despite his lowly occupa-tion) among the town's nineteen first citizens and his sharing of their greed act to deconstruct the opposition Twain appears to construct be-tween the classes, and between town authorities and folk life, to suggest instead a lack of essential difference between them. We recall here the statement from "Concerning the Jews" about Twain's own lack of social and religious prejudice: "All that I care to know is that a man is a human being—that is enough for me; he can't be any worse" (254). This can be applied, I would suggest, to the entire community of Hadleyburg, with the possible exception of Sam Halliday and the dead Barclay Goodson. Class difference and social status matter very little if to be a human being is, in turn, to be a self-interested hypocrite. Any positive conception of folk life collapses with this equation.

Even Sam Halliday, unbound by the social constraints of others in the town, is by no means an entirely positive folk figure. The mocking laugh-ter identified most strongly with him, then shared by others, brings no sense of communal renewal. Moreover, despite his position on the fringes of the community, he does not see entirely clearly. This text is one where human behavior remains largely impenetrable and where the "free fa-miliar contact" of carnival is never really achieved.[30] The story has a striking early image of Halliday carrying "a cigar-box around . . . playing that it was a camera, and . . . [saying], 'Ready! — now look pleasant, please' " (24), but the Howellsian idea of realist transparency does not work. Halliday is puzzled by the changing expression of the nineteen couples' faces at various stages following the receipt of Stephenson's letters, "and didn't know what to make of it" (37). "Stephenson" himself, the initial manipulator of events, is fooled by the apparent innocence of Richards. Burgess does not know Richards, either. The warmth of his feelings for him is based on partial ignorance, for Richards had proof that Burgess was innocent of his supposed crime, and he "could have saved him" (10) from his disgrace had he chosen to do so. And Richards, in turn, does not know Burgess, seeing the latter's concealment of his letter as an act of vengeance and not of gratitude. Finally, at the end of the narrative, the townsfolk know Burgess little better than at the beginning, as his "impassioned" denial of the motives attributed to him in Richards's death-bed confession fall "on deaf ears" (83). In a community where the thoughts and motives of others are rarely transparent, the full expression and free familiarity of carnival are never properly achieved, neither in the town meeting nor in the subsequent behavior of the town's inhabitants.

Indeed, any celebration of the folk spirit seems well and truly quashed by the narrative's end. If Bakhtin, in his celebration of carnival, tends to underestimate the fact that such festivity only *temporarily* upsets established hierarchies, Twain does not. As the town meeting concludes, Harkness uses the bogus coins to ensure his election to the legislature. In doing so, he "revive[s] the recent vast laugh" (77), but directs it away from himself to his political opponent, Pinkerton. Thus the festivity that has occurred is finally ended, with the public energies that have been released channelled to selfish and power-oriented ends. For what is at stake in this election are the "two or three fortunes" to be made by already wealthy individuals (like Harkness) in the routing of a new railway (70). That the election itself is contested by two of the discredited eighteen suggests that nothing fundamentally has changed in the town despite the humiliation that has occurred and that social hierarchies have been immediately restored.

The claim that a change in moral sensibility results from the carnival that has taken place (Gary Scharnhorst, among others, sees the story as "Twain's parable of the Fortunate Fall")[31] also seems highly dubious. The final line of the story, "[Hadleyburg] is an honest town once more, and the man will have to rise early that catches it napping again," might rather be seen, in James D. Wilson's words, as "fraught with irony." As Wilson explains:

The first clause is patently absurd, for Hadleyburg was never an honest town; furthermore, the syntax suggests a restoration, not a transformation — a return to pride in a deceptive, misconceived self-concept. The second clause . . . implies not that Hadleyburg has changed morally but that it is simply cleverer, less naïve — no one will catch "it napping again."[32]

The final focus on the town as a collective whole, moreover, undermines the sense of conflict between "the folk" and the "aristocracy" which gives the scene of the town meeting its energy. Such a stress on community may seem logical if we read the story to illustrate how folk values have helped to reform the whole town (and one might use the final illustration of the changed town seal to argue such a case). But if we take the more ironical option sketched above, the very notion of a life-giving folk energy is placed under erasure, as *all* town members are represented as a collective and unimproved social and moral unit.

The structural movement of "Stirring Times in Austria" is from populace to parliamentary meeting, and thence back to public riot and racial hatred. The events that take place in that central representative forum contain strong elements of the carnivalesque. In "Hadleyburg," the carnival structure is even more pronounced and the idea of community renewal appears initially to carry much more positive resonance. But the folk laughter released in the story turns out, under close analysis, to lack transformative power. And indeed the very difference between folk values and those of the authorities they would upset is subject to question. The essay and the story can then (despite obvious differences in genre, location, and subject matter) be read as twinned texts, both of which hinge on public meetings and their loosing of types of carnival. If the one text ends with everything back in its ordered social place, and the other with the possibility of political revolution, neither conclusion has much of a positive ring. The attitude toward democratic values and folk energies is ambivalent even in Twain's earliest works. By this stage of his writing career, it has darkened very considerably.

The $30,000 Bequest and Other Stories

The "help" are all natives; they talk Italian to me, I answer in English;
I do not understand them, they do not understand me, consequently
no harm is done, and everybody is satisfied.

— "Italian Without a Master"

We have named it Cain. She caught it while I was up country trap-
ping on the North Shore of the Erie. . . . It resembles us in some ways,
and may be a relation. That is what she thinks, but this is an error, in
my judgment. The difference in size warrants the conclusion that it is
a different and new kind of animal — a fish, perhaps, though when I
put it in the water to see, it sank, and she plunged in and snatched it
out before there was opportunity for the experiment to determine
the matter. I still think it is a fish, but she is indifferent about what it
is, and will not let me have it to try. I do not understand this. . . . Her
mind is disordered — everything shows it. Sometimes she carries the
fish in her arms half the night when it complains and wants to get to
the water. At such times the water comes out of the places in her face
that she looks out of, and she pats the fish on the back . . . and betrays
sorrow and solicitude in a hundred ways. I have never seen her do
like this with any other fish, and it troubles me greatly.

— "Extracts from Adam's Diary"

The trade edition of *The $30,000 Bequest and Other Stories* was published by
Harper in September 1906, and was the last authorized collection of
short stories and sketches to come out during Twain's lifetime. Twain had
celebrated his seventieth birthday the previous December with a banquet
at Delmonico's arranged by George Harvey (of Harper).[1] In the speech
he made there, Twain described this birthday as "the Scriptural statute of
limitations. After that, you owe no active duties . . . the strenuous life is
over."[2] Indeed, by this period in his life he had already become, in Justin
Kaplan's words, "a major celebrity, and a semi-retired man of letters."[3]

He still wrote and still published, but to more limited extent and less driven by financial need than in earlier times.[4] Thus Howells would write of Twain in 1901: "What a fame and a force he is! It's astonishing how he holds out, but I hate to have him eating so many dinners, and writing so few books" (MTHL2, 735).

Twain continued more or less to "hold out" despite the huge blow to his domestic life that was to come with the death of his wife Olivia, near Florence in Italy, on 5 June 1904. Twain did manage a type of recovery from this loss. In terms of his private life, this was helped by his heavy reliance first on his secretary, Isabel Lyon, and then on his biographer, Albert Bigelow Paine, both of whom, in their turn, took the role of his live-in companion as well as employee and work assistant.[5] In public, the enjoyment of his "incomparable celebrity" helped to mask whatever "private loneliness" he felt.[6] But there was no denying that his life was wrenched apart with Olivia's death. Twain's letters at the time clearly show his distress: "Our life is wrecked; we have no plans for the future. . . . It is an awful blow . . . and we do not rally very well" (CHHR, 569, 572). His daughter Clara was so affected by the death that she needed a series of "rest cures" to recuperate. His other surviving daughter, Jean, started having those epileptic seizures that previously seemed to have been stemmed. By the end of the year, "It had become clear that Jean would never be completely well again — nor would [Twain] himself."[7] And however Twain was able to present himself in public, he was privately subject to deep depressions. Paige reports him saying to Rogers at about this time: "I think I have had about enough of this world, and I wish I were out of it" (see CHHR, 576).

Given all this, it is unsurprising that Twain's part in the preparation of the *$30,000 Bequest* collection seems to have been small. Indeed, documentary sources relating to the shaping and production of this book seem scarcer than with any of Twain's previous collections of short works, except possibly *Merry Tales*.[8] This may be because, by this point in time, Harper & Brothers had complete autonomy as far as the publishing of Twain's books went. In 1903 the protracted dispute between Harper and the American Publishing Company had been settled, with the copyrights on those Twain books owned by Bliss's firm now being sold to Harper (with Twain himself paying half the $50,000 costs). Harper now had first option to publish everything the author wrote. As Twain wrote in his notebook: "The contract . . . concentrates all my books in Harper's hands, and now at last they are valuable: in fact they are a fortune."[9] One result of this was a type of "market saturation" as Harper published a whole series of Twain's stories and essays, in their various magazines, in single textual form, in book-length collections, and in their Uniform and author's national editions of his works.[10]

But the American Publishing Company continued to publish Twain, too. Its previous — more or less — sole prerogative to produce a uniform edition (as described in chapter 9) was ended with the 1903 agreement. Afterward, any further volumes in its series could only be published at Harper's discretion. For example, volume 23 of the American Publishing Company's uniform edition, *My Début as a Literary Person with Other Essays and Stories*, came out in April 1903 before the revised contract. But when volume 24, *The $30, 000 Bequest and Other Stories*, was published in 1907, a note appeared opposite the table of contents that read: "This edition is printed by Harper & Brothers, the exclusive publishers of Mark Twain's works, as an accommodation to purchasers of earlier volumes with a view to making their sets uniform." And while the American Publishing Company had been issuing its different versions of the uniform edition since 1899, Harper only commenced issuing the Hillcrest edition in 1903.[11]

All this impacts on the publishing history of the *$30,000 Bequest and Other Stories* collection. Harper, too, would issue the book of this title as volume 24 of its Hillcrest series, but at a slightly earlier date than Bliss, in 1906.[12] This Uniform Edition volume was a thinner version of the Harper trade edition (the single and separate volume) of that title issued in the same year. A letter from Major Leigh of Harper on 24 July 1906, at a time when the material for the Uniform Edition had evidently already been chosen, explains what was happening.[13] Writing to Twain, Leigh says:

> Colonel Harvey turned over to me the matter of the proposed contents for the new volume of the Hillcrest and Trade book, and, as I understand it, the contents proposed for the Hillcrest volume is O.K.
> Now, it is proposed to make the Trade volume which will sell for $1.75, by adding to the contents of the Hillcrest volume, the following articles:
> 1. The Invalid's Story
> 2. The Captain's Story
> 3. Biographical Sketch of Mark Twain, by S. E. Moffett
> 4. In Memoriam
> 5. The Belated Russian Passport
> 6. Two Little Tales
> 7. Diplomatic Pay & Clothes
> 8. Extracts From Adam's Diary
> 9. The Death Disk
> 10. Double Barrelled Detective Story
> 11. Same Contents proposed for Vol. 24, Hillcrest Edition.
> The Colonel tells me that you are anxious that none of these articles shall duplicate. None of them do duplicate in the sense of being in any $1.75 volume.
> 1. The Invalid's Story   :
> 2. The Captain's Story   : are in vol. 22
> 3. Biographical Sketch of Mark Twain   : Hillcrest Ed.
> 4. In Memoriam   :
> 5. The Belated Russian Passport   :
> 6. Two Little Tales   :

7. Diplomatic Pay & Clothes   : are in vol. 23
8. Extracts from Adam's Diary   : Hillcrest Ed.
9. Death Disk
10. Double Barrelled Detective Story.[14]

Leigh then goes on to discuss the status of "Extracts from Adam's Diary" and "A Double-Barreled Detective Story." These, he acknowledged, had previously been published as separate books "in a cheap unique way with illustrations." But that, he said, was not a reason to prevent their being reproduced in "the regular Trade books" (of which the proposed volume was to be one). "[F]rom my standpoint," he closes, "none of the stories duplicate." If Twain saw through the rather forced logic of that last remark, he was evidently happy to go along with Harper's plan. For a handwritten comment at the bottom of the letter reads:

To Col. Harvey
Mr Clemens agrees with Maj. Leigh that there is nothing to object to in his proposal as in his letter of July 24. (CU-MARK)

To sum up, it appears that Harper editors were exploring all avenues at this time in exploiting their newly acquired "property." Twain's selected stories and sketches were being published in the Uniform Edition. At the same time, some of his more recently written short stories and essays (based mainly on Volume 24 of the Uniform Edition but bulked out with material from the two prior volumes in the series) were published in a trade volume. The assumption clearly was that there were two quite separate markets here. There is little available evidence that Twain himself had much to do with the planning and selection either of the trade volume or the Uniform Edition version of *The $30,000 Bequest* collection. I would tentatively conclude that it was a Harper editor who was primarily responsible for putting together these books.[15]

Despite the apparent lack of authorial control here, however (and this does of course make a large difference), we can still assess *The $30,000 Bequest* on its merits as a collection. As we do so, we should keep in mind its close relation to the books in the Uniform Edition and the selective but cumulative nature of that latter project (as far as Twain's shorter pieces went). But there is something conclusive about this particular collection both in its bringing together of an appreciable selection of Twain's late short work, and in the fact that its title story was, in James D. Wilson's words, "the last substantial fiction [he] was to complete and publish during his lifetime" (RG, 259).

When Isabel Lyon wrote a much later note recalling the publication of *The $30,000 Bequest*, she focused first on its poor public reception:

At the time of its publication this book was quarreled with by the reading world as a hodge-podge; some of it taken from "Sketches Old and New," and even from the old Galaxy "Memoranda" published before 1871. The title led the world to believe that here was a new book by Mark Twain, for so it was advertised, and it was bought in good faith. Letters of complaint and censure came booming in, which Mr. Clemens replied to through me, referring the writers to Harper & Bros. who were the chief offenders.[16]

Contemporary reviews of the book, however, though thin on the ground, do not seem to have been so harsh. It was taken by some reviewers just as the "latest addition to the uniform edition" and, as such, "full of chuckles . . . from cover to cover."[17] And their general tone seems to have been positive: "with Twain we are at least sure of entertainment. . . . As a humorist he stands alone, his reputation secure."[18] There is some fair amount of early Twain material in the book, and it is here that its adaptation from the retrospective Uniform volume is most obvious. Thus, for instance, "Advice to Little Girls" was first published in the *California Youth's Companion* of June 24, 1865, "General Washington's Negro Body-Servant" in the New York *Galaxy* for February 1868, and "A Burlesque Biography" in 1871 (as the booklet, *Mark Twain's (Burlesque) Autobiography*).[19] The book's older pieces originated between 1865 and 1872, with particular use made of *Galaxy* material. But there are also four stories — "A Telephonic Situation," "Edward Mills and George Benton: A Tale," "The Captain's Story," and "The Invalid's Story" — that had been published between 1877 and 1882 (the first three in the *Atlantic Monthly*).[20] The majority of these early sketches and stories had not, however, previously appeared in any of the six main collections on which I have focused in this book.

If readers did complain, as Lyon suggests, about the book, those complaints may not have had a great deal of justification, at least in terms of its recycling of older material. Half the book's contents — nineteen pieces — and by far its majority in terms of sheer textual volume come (in terms of first publication) from the period 1900 to 1906 and had not previously appeared in any of Twain's collections of short works.[21] All these later pieces had already appeared in magazine format (in *Harper's Weekly* or *Harper's Monthly*) but this was normally the case with Twain's published collections. There may have been some cause, though, for readerly dissatisfaction in the fact that four of the book's stories — "A Double-Barreled Detective Story," "Extracts from Adam's Diary," "A Dog's Tale," and "Eve's Diary" — had all been previously published by Harper in separate book form (in April 1902, April 1904, September 1904, and June 1906, respectively).[22] Even despite this, the book still contained a very considerable amount of "new" material and so forms a fitting ending to Twain's career as a writer of short genres (stories, essays, sketches, etc.).

One distinctive feature of *The $30,000 Bequest* is "Mark Twain: A Biographical Sketch," positioned rather oddly some three-fifths of the way through the book.[23] Pulled into the collection from volume 22 of the Uniform Edition, the sketch, written by nephew Samuel E. Moffett, provides a retrospective overview of Twain's life history. The sketch, however, is based on briefer notes written by Twain himself. By comparing the two versions of the sketch — Twain's own handwritten notes and the published version — we can both recover Twain's own autobiographical summation of his career to this point (with whatever distortions it may contain) and see how Moffett then supplemented it. I highlight a few salient details. The comment on how Twain's early efforts at journalism, produced for his brother Orion's Hannibal newspaper when he was thriteen, riveted "the town's attention, 'but not [according to Orion] its admiration' " (333) comes from the author's own account.[24] And the explanation of his nom de plume as adopting "the old Mississippi leadsman's call for two fathoms (twelve feet) — 'Mark Twain' " (340) is also drawn more or less directly from the same source.[25] The description of the dealings with Paige is also worth noting. Moffett writes:

[Twain] was spending great sums on a type-setting machine of such seductive ingenuity as to captivate the imagination of everybody who saw it. It worked to perfection, but it was too complicated and expensive for commercial use, and after sinking a fortune in it between 1886 and 1889, Mark Twain had to write off the whole investment as a dead loss. (347)

Twain's own words here had originally read: "In 1886–89 M.T. spent $170,000 on a type-setting machine, the invention of one James W. Paige, a fraud. The money was all lost." Twain's wife Olivia then altered this, replacing the specific sum given with "a large amount of money." She also struck out the hostile reference to Paige ("the invention . . . a fraud") and added in its place the phrase "which was a failure" (to immediately follow "a type-setting machine") (CU-MARK). Moffett both justifies Twain''s actions and recounts more fully their disastrous consequences in the third version of events that he creates. In the notes for this sketch, then, we have one more autobiographical source for our reading of Twain's life.[26]

To examine the more recent of Twain's stories and essays in the collection is to see clear connections with the previous *Hadleyburg* book. Indeed, the title story, "The $30,000 Bequest," forms a sequence with the title stories of both his previous collections, "The £1,000,000 Bank-Note" and "The Man That Corrupted Hadleyburg," in its central concern with money and its effects. It is most closely twinned with the latter, however, in the irony produced in the gap between the focalization (point of view) of the main protagonists — Saladin and Electra Foster — and the generally neutral and detached tone of the story's third-person narrator. The story is also strongly linked with "Hadleyburg" in its main theme: the moral collapse that an obsession with money brings.[27] And both narratives end on a bleak note, their main protagonists (the Richards and the Fosters) dying, man and wife together, as a result of the mental torture their experience has brought them.

In all three stories in this sequence it is the intervention of a stranger that drives the plot. In "The $30,000 Bequest," the Fosters receive a letter from a distant and dying relative of Sally (Saladin Foster's nickname) promising the named legacy on the condition that Sally "made no inquiries concerning the moribund's progress towards the everlasting tropics, and had not attended the funeral" (4). Sally and Aleck (or Electra) then wait for the bequest to be realized, for they receive no further word telling of the death of their "benefactor." Meanwhile they gradually move into a fantasy world where the investing and spending of the imaginary money becomes the main pleasure and driving motivation of their lives. Aleck, with her business mind, makes and loses "a cold million" (29) on the stock market. Sally meanwhile "pollut[es] himself with a gay and dissipated secret life in the company of other fast bloods, multimillionaires in money and paupers in character" (36). As their imagined wealth increases, so their moral structures and Christian values collapse. Thus the narrator ironically comments: "They had lived to prove . . . a sad truth which had been proven many times before in the world: that whereas principle is a great and noble protection against showy and degrading vanities and vices, poverty is worth six of it" (28).

The Fosters' imaginary speculations abruptly go awry, affected by the turn in national economic circumstance brought by the "record crash . . . when the bottom fell out of Wall Street" (45). They console themselves, however, in the fact that they still retain their original $30,000 stake. It is at this point, though, that they finally discover that their donor relative is long-since dead and that they have been the victims of a hoax — for he was in fact penniless and has left them nothing. As they are told: "He hadn't anything to leave but a wheelbarrow. . . . It hadn't any wheel, and wasn't any good" (47–48).[28] Mental collapse ("they . . . began to twaddle to each other in a wandering and childish way," 48) and death follow this revelation.[29] And Sally, in the final words of the story, is still caught in the grip of the constructed illusion that has motivated his and his wife's behavior from the first loosing of the hoax. As "consciousness was fading from his brain," he mutters that:

with base and cunning calculation [the "benefactor"] left us but thirty thousand, knowing we would try to increase it, and ruin our life and break our hearts. Without added expense he could have left us far above desire of increase, far above the temptation to speculate, and a kinder soul would have done it; but in him was no generosity, no pity, no —. (49)

The effectiveness of this conclusion is noted in Judith Yaross Lee's astute comment in the afterword that "clear-sighted in its economics but mad in both psychology and values, [it] keeps the irony of the tale alive to the end" (AF, 11).

If "The $30,000 Bequest" recalls "The Man That Corrupted Hadley-burg," it does have significant differences. There is something far more solipsistic about this story, as suggested by the marginal part played in the narrative by the community of Lakeside, the "pleasant little town" (1) where the Fosters live. In "Hadleyburg," the focus is on the whole com-munity as well as the central couple. Two things could have helped to cause this shift in emphasis. First, as a number of critics have suggested, there may be an autobiographical impulse driving the tale.[30] There is a peculiar gender reversal in the text, with Saladin given the "curious and unsexing . . . pet name" of Sally, and Electra (Aleck) described as the "calculating business-woman" of the family (3). This may reflect Twain's own anxieties about his own "masculine" role around this time: the awareness of his own failures as a businessman and investor, the some-time dependency on his wife's inheritance,[31] and the placing of his copy-rights, after the Webster & Co. business failure, in her name. The compo-sition of the Foster family and the parental concern over the daughters' marital futures can also be taken as self-reflexive.

A second possible explanation for the solipsistic thrust of this story may lie in its mirroring of one of the central and obsessive concerns of Twain's late writings: a deep ontological insecurity concerning the very nature of external reality and its relationship to the internal world of dreams. Something of the narrative development and tension comes from the opposition that builds up between the Fosters' "sordid and plodding Fact-life" (34) and the "glowing and continuous and persistent excite-ment" of their "Dream-life" (35).[32] As the latter overwhelms the former, a confusion between these realms comes to take over the story. And the narrator's summary comment, "how soon and how easily our dream-life and our material life become so intermingled and so fused together that we can't quite tell which is which, any more" (20–21), directly anticipates the late dream tales as a whole.

There are wider connections, though, between The $30,000 Bequest and Other Stories and the previous Hadleyburg collection. In both, we can note the increasing philosophical strand to Twain's later short pieces. This becomes all the more obvious in *The $30,000 Bequest* in the contrast with sketches reprinted from the early stages of the author's career. Thus the 1872 squib, "Deception," is merely an excuse for a brief account of the comic discomforting of "Mark Twain" in his role as a lecturer.[33] Twain acts as attempted "benefactor" to a young gentleman distressed at the fact that his uncle "seemed to have grown permanently bereft of all emotion." He pulls out all the stops during the lecture he is giving to try and make the prominently seated uncle laugh. At the lecture's conclusion, he is left "bewildered and exhausted," with no success despite his best efforts. It is then Twain realizes he has been hoaxed when a third party explains his failure, telling him that the man he has "peppered" with jokes is in fact "deaf and dumb, and as blind as a badger" (255–6). This is a typical early piece, very short (two pages), making use of the gullibility of the "Mark Twain" comic persona, and depending for its humor on a physical infirmity taken together with the expressive force of the simile that describes it.

The very subject of deception at the core of this sketch forms a connection and contrast with Twain's later work. In "Was It Heaven? Or Hell?" (first published in *Harper's Monthly* in December 1902) Twain uses the same theme not for light comic purposes but to serious philosophical ends. In doing so, he reprises the subject matter of "My First Lie, and How I Got Out of It" from the *Hadleyburg* book and its focus on "the lie of silent assertion." "Was it Heaven? Or Hell?" — unlike "My First Lie" — is a fictional narrative rather than an essay. It is based on the separate deaths from typhoid of a mother (Margaret) and her sixteen-year-old daughter (Helen), and the care given them by the mother's "maiden aunts" (69), Hannah and Hester. The emotional center of the tale lies in the two deaths; its moral and intellectual focus in the behavior of the aunts.

The story starts with a lie and ends with the consequences of a series of other lies. The two aunts are described as strict, uncompromising, and austere moralists by training but "by nature — and inside — . . . utterly dear and lovable and good" (69).[34] In their former role, they judge all lies harshly as morally "unthinkable" (70). It is the aunts' discovery of a lie by Helen, and their insistence that she confess the sin to her sick mother, that starts the narrative. For their doctor — a frank, independent, and tough-speaking individual[35] — arrives on the scene at this point to spur the core debate in the story about the nature of lies and lying. His position is similar to the author's own in the earlier "My First Lie". He attacks the aunts' contention that "*All* lies are sinful" in two ways. Most immediately, he suggests that there is a "difference between a lie that helps and a lie that hurts" (78). And he calls the aunts, and others like them, "moral moles" for their failure to recognize that silent lying is a universal human practice:

you lie from morning till night, but because you don't do it with your mouths, but only with your lying eyes, your lying inflections, your deceptively misplaced emphasis, and your misleading gestures, you turn up your complacent noses and parade before God . . . as saintly and unsmirched Truth-Speakers. (82)

He then gives, as illustration of one of their silent lies, the fact that they would have hidden the sickroom scene from his knowledge had he not surprised them there, "to keep me from finding out your guilt; to beguile me to infer that Margaret's excitement proceeded from some cause not known to you" (83). His repeated message to the aunts in this sequence is, "Reform — and learn to tell lies!" (80).

And this is exactly what Hannah and Hester do. The story runs on a heavily sentimental model from this point as the aunts, "hearts . . . breaking . . . but their grit . . . steadfast and indestructible" (86), nurse mother and daughter separately. They find that they cannot help but lie, as they follow the instincts of their "tortured heart[s]" (87) to protect the mother from the knowledge of the daughter's impending death, and vice-versa. When the girl dies, Twain depends — as so often in this story — on pathos for his effects: "At last came that kindly friend who brings healing and peace to all. The lights were burning low. . . . The dying girl lay with closed lids" (95). Hester allows her comforting presence to be mistaken for the girl's mother in Helen's final moments. The girl's death is consequently concealed from the mother until she also dies. The story ends with an angel appearing, to whom the aunts confess their "sin" and "human weakness," but say that they would similarly lie again were the circumstances reproduced. The angel then "whisper[s] the decree" — for he has previously said that "liars" shall "burn in the fires of hell." The final section of the narrative then contains only the title words: "Was it Heaven? Or Hell?" (101–2).

Much of this is standard sentimental fare. But one intriguing thing about the story is the "uncanny resemblance" it bears to Twain's own personal situation, for later in the year he wrote it, with both wife and daughter Jean seriously ill, just such evasions were to be practiced within Twain's own family.[36] We can, moreover, use the story (and other sentimental narratives like "The Californian's Tale") to again identify a clear difference within the collection between Twain's early and late work: this time in terms of the approach taken toward death. In "Post-Mortem Poetry," for example (first published in the *Galaxy* in June 1870), Twain approaches death, via a concern with newspaper obituary verse, only with scoffing and impersonal wit:

"Our little Sammy's gone
His tiny spirit's fled;
Our little boy we loved so dear
Lies sleeping with the dead. . ."
. . . There is an element about such poetry which is able to make even physical suffering and death cheerful things to contemplate and consummations to be desired. (251–52)

Twain would never lose his sharp eye for clichéd language and forms of sentimental indulgence, but parts of his own late work undoubtedly conform to such patterns.[37] The tales of loss, broken families, separation, and death scattered throughout this book, and throughout the late work as a whole, are clearly a response to personal circumstance and experience. It makes for uneasy reading nonetheless, despite the difference in verse forms, to set "Post-Mortem Poetry" against the mournful cadences and archaic forms of "In Memoriam," the poem written by Twain himself to commemorate the "vast disaster" (352) of the death of his own daughter Susy.

In "Was It Heaven? Or Hell?" Twain's philosophical concern with the nature and moral status of lies is developed in a type of fictional fable. Though he was then to revise the story, his own first verdict of "Too much sermon: it is a millstone around the story's neck" (CHHR, 492) remains one that many readers might share. Lee notes the contrast between the "literary seriousness" (AF, 9) and moralistic tone of many of the more recently written pieces in *The $30,000 Bequest,* and the early work reprinted there which "exploits opportunities for jokes in almost any subject, the more solemn the better" (AF, 6). And while we should not forget that there is plenty of "serious" material in Twain's earlier work, too, that comparison remains generally true.[38]

Thus "The Five Boons of Life," first published in *Harper's Weekly* on 5 July 1902, echoes *Hadleyburg's* "About Play-Acting" with its pessimistic view of human life and its view of death as a "precious" gift. In this fable, "the good fairy with her basket" comes "in the morning of life" (159) to offer the male protagonist her gifts. Pleasure, Love, Fame and Wealth, the traditional human desires he chooses first, turn out to prove "but temporary disguises for lasting realities—Pain, Grief, Shame, Poverty" (164). So love, for instance, leaves him finally sitting "by a coffin in an empty home . . . desolation after desolation" sweeping over him (161). When he is ready to accept the final gift of death — "that sweet and kindly one, that steeps in dreamless and enduring sleep . . . the shames and griefs that eat the mind and heart" (164) — it is unavailable to him, given instead to "a little child" that trusted the fairy to choose on its behalf. The protagonist is left instead only with "the wanton insult of Old Age"

(165). An obsession with death, in one form or another, is a continuing motif in this collection. And this particular story shows Twain's outlook on life in these, his late years, at perhaps its briefest (the piece is composed of five very short sections) and bleakest.

There is a tendency in this late work to speak as a moralist and philosopher. But another voice Twain assumes here is that of one who by his celebrity and reputation has earned the right to pronounce on matters of public interest. Thus in "Diplomatic Pay and Clothes" (first published in *Forum*, March 1899) Twain ironically critiques the ideological stance of democratic unpretentiousness by which the American nation justifies the undistinguished nature of the formal dress worn by its ambassadors abroad:

the ambassador's official clothes — that boastful advertisement of a Republican Simplicity which manifests itself at home in Fifty-thousand-dollar salaries to insurance presidents and railway lawyers, and in domestic palaces whose fittings and furnishings often transcend . . . [those in] the palaces of the sceptred masters of Europe. (412)

Attacking the shabby pay and conditions of American public servants in foreign lands, his argument, if couched at times in comic manner, is that of a national spokesperson and moral commentator, whose judgments can be expected to carry considerable public weight. Twain's later nonfiction is increasingly marked by such a tone.

There is evidence in *The $30,000 Bequest* of Twain's continued ability to sharply penetrate the façade of Victorian social and moral pieties. His own fiction does, however, here lapse at times into such conventional and formulaic attitudes and values. The heavily sentimental strand in the collection is an example of this. "A Dog's Tale," first published in *Harper's Monthly* in December 1903, was apparently written to support his daughter Jean's antivivisectionist sympathies.[39] Some critics see allusions to slavery in the story's depiction of the dog's devoted serving of its master and the inhumane treatment received in return, but the formulaic nature of the narrative prevents such references from having any but the most superficial of effects. The cloying sentimentality of the story is its most noticeable feature. The first-person narrative is told by Aileen Mavourneen, a dog whose puppy is subject to a deadly experiment conducted by the "renowned scientist" (57) who heads the family that owns her. The dog's response to the puppy's demise is typical of the narrative's dominant tone: I ran at once to my darling, and snuggled close to it where it lay, and licked the blood, and it put its head against me, whimpering softly, and I knew in my heart it was a comfort to it in its pain and trouble to feel its mother's touch, though it could not see me" (65).

As so often in Twain, though, there is more to this work than such excessively worked appeals to the emotions of his readers. He also produces some effective comic moments in the story, mainly based around Aileen's mother and her use of a sophisticated human vocabulary to impress the "dogmatic gathering[s] in the neighborhood." And he commences the narrative with what Frederick Busch calls "one of the great opening sentences" (IN, xxxiv): "My father was a St. Bernard, my mother was a collie, but I am a Presbyterian" (50). Twain here both burlesques the conventions of standard autobiography, and handles the surreal category shift he introduces, with a long-practiced comic authority.

If Twain's fictions in this book sometimes lapse into conventional Victorian sentimentality, his representations of gender are often similarly predictable. Thus the father in "A Dog's Tale" is a scientist, "business-like, prompt, decided, unsentimental, and with that kind of trim-chiselled face that just seems to glint and sparkle with frosty intellectuality!" (56–57). Sadie, the little girl of the family, is given the traditional "feminine" quality of tender-hearted emotional concern: "She was crying; my name was falling from her lips all broken, poor thing" (62). The sentimental tradition was built on such gender stereotypes, and they are repeated throughout this collection.[40] Thus, for example, from the start of "The Death Disk" (first published in *Harper's Magazine*, December 1901), Abby, "a curly-headed little figure in nightclothes" (431) conforms similarly to the pattern of the innocent and treasured child, the small enchantress who brings sweetness and emotional relief to a careworn "masculine" world.

Similar conventions are engaged, though this time in terms of husband-wife relations, in "The Californian's Tale" (first published in 1893). Frederick Busch speaks of its representation of "late-nineteenth- and early-twentieth-century immutabilities," which include "the beauty and light generated by sylphlike young wives" (IN, xxxvi). So, too, the wifely role is idealized in "Eve's Diary." This story, written the year after Twain's wife died, and published in *Harper's Monthly* in December 1905, was seen by his biographer to be full of the author's "love, his worship, and his tenderness for the one he had laid away."[41] This tenderness and the irredeemable sense of loss that accompanies it are captured in Adam's final elegiac words at Eve's graveside: "Wheresoever she was, *there* was Eden" (310). As Susan K. Harris describes, such female characters as these act as a "symbolic outlet" in Twain's fictions providing an "emotional centering" for the men in whose "psychic landscape" they alone provide a "secure object." Twain joins many of his contemporaries in representing women in this way, for

this is one of the functions of the Angel in Victorian literature; by always being the same, she represents continuity and innocence in a world of flux and corruption.

For Twain's protagonists she provides a way to escape not only the anxieties of their public lives but also the anxieties of their private lives.[42]

Twain's representation of gender in the cases mentioned above is formulaic and unsurprising, and conforms to patterns that can be found in his fiction as a whole. I draw attention to the issue, however, because of the presence of other narratives here where such conventions start to break down. As we have come to expect with Twain, apparently straightforward assumptions rarely go entirely unchallenged. I have already mentioned the reversal of expected gender attributes in "The $30,000 Bequest." Similarly, something rather strange occurs with the gender roles represented in "The Belated Russian Passport," first published in *Harper's Weekly* on 6 December 1902. This narrative is built round the relationship between two men, the energetic and forceful Major Jackson and the passive and weak-willed American student Alfred Parrish.

The plot of the story depends for its effect mainly on the tensions built up concerning Parrish's possible fate and the sudden reversal of the ending. Parrish is apparently about to be condemned to ten years in Siberia for finding himself in Russia without a passport, as a result of the over enthusiasm of the Major, who sees all difficulties as surmountable. But his skin is saved by the unexpected line of questioning taken by the secretary at the American legation, who asks about Parrish's boyhood home and a particular picture hanging there. The narrative ends with Alfred's description of his father's view of that painting ("the hellfiredest nightmare he ever struck!" 381), the secretary's revelation that it was he who painted that picture, and his consequent issuing of a new passport on the basis of the confirmation of identity accordingly made. Twain here reverses the paradigm of sudden upset — from happiness and stability to disaster and nightmarish alienation — to be found in many of his other late works. He also plays, though lightly here, on two of the dominant themes of his late years: the role of a mysterious stranger (beneficial or harmful?) and the problematic of identity (how do we prove we are who we say we are?).[43]

But hints of transgression of normative gender role also appear in this story of the crossing of forbidden frontiers, even if finally they remain undeveloped and peripheral to its main theme. Parrish's nickname in childhood was "Miss Nancy" and, as he explains to his fellow students, "I reckon I'm that yet — girlish and timorous, and all that. I ought to have *been* a girl" (354).[44] In direct contrast is the Major, whose brisk energy is described through barely veiled sexual allusions. Introduced as "full of steam — racing pressure — one could almost hear his gauge-cocks sing" (355), he later speaks of himself as " as cocky as a buck angel" (375). The Major metaphorically sweeps Parrish off his feet, making the latter's "mouth water and his roused spirits cry out with longing" as he describes the attractions of the Russian capital. And he has the boy "quivering with eagerness" (356) as he agrees to the unexpected journey there. The Major then acts the role of bridegroom on the trip itself. He proves "an adorable travelling companion . . . full of accommodating ways" (365) to the boy, comforts him from his trembling unease over the absent passport by "kindly pettings and reassurings," and offers his "supporting arm" when Parrish consequently slumps "limp and helpless to the ground" (366). There is little disguising the transgressive sexual subtext to these sequences despite their inconclusive nature. Both here and in "The $30,000 Bequest" we have signs of certain anxieties concerning the limits of, and assumptions concerning, Victorian gender norms and stereotypes. These anxieties, though, remain undeveloped, to be more fully explored in other texts, many of which would remain unpublished until after Twain's death.[45]

There is much in the *$30,000 Bequest* collection that would support a reading of the late Twain as overly concerned with "pensive recollection and philosophical speculation" (RG, 132), strongly influenced by immediate personal circumstance, and increasingly caught within the conventional patterns of a Victorian sentimental tradition. But there is also a great deal in the book that works in quite different fictional and nonfictional ways. And the power of Twain's comic imagination is still clearly evident here, serving as a powerful countering influence to the textual bathos and pessimism, and modifying (and sometimes disrupting) the "literary seriousness" on display.

Nowhere is the humor more sustained than in the various texts that focus on the theme of language and representation. For Twain's interest in the relationship between word and object, and in the process of translation from one word to its (foreign) other, is a recurrent and distinctive comic feature of this book. In "A Dog's Tale," Twain (perhaps influenced by Anna Sewell's *Black Beauty*, 1877) uses the literary convention that gives the first-person voice of an animal control of the narrative. As the reader suspends disbelief on entering this textual world, the author quickly creates a further dislocating effect by then focusing precisely on the gap between human speech and animal comprehension and making this the source of humor. So the dog-narrator's mother, despite her lack of understanding, has a fondness for the long words she hears her human owners using, and fires them off (with an invented meaning at hand) to impress her fellow canines. The word she uses to cover any "emergency" then arising is "the word Synonymous." Thus:

When she happened to fetch out a long word which had had its day weeks before and its prepared meanings gone to her dump-pile, if there was a stranger there of course it knocked him groggy for a couple of minutes. . . . [W]hen he'd hail and ask her to cash in, I (the only dog on the inside of her game) could see her canvas flicker a moment — but only just a moment — then it would belly out taut and full, and she would say, as calm as a summer's day, "It's synonymous with supereroga-tion," or some godless long reptile of a word like that, and go placidly about and skim away on the next tack, perfectly comfortable, you know. (51–52)

Here it is the lack of fit between the mother dog's words and their mean-ing, her assumption of social and intellectual superiority on these fraudu-lent terms, and the apt metaphoric wit of the narrator (and supposedly linguistic inferior) in describing her mother's actions, that create the comic effectiveness of the sequence.

The comic play over language and representation fades out, however, as "A Dog's Tale" turns to its main antivivisectionist theme. In contrast, "Italian Without a Master," published in *Harper's Weekly* on 2 January 1904, foregrounds the subject of language and translation throughout.[46] Here the "Mark Twain" persona — the illustrations in the piece clearly depict Twain himself — reappears, as comedy is created in the gap be-tween the narrator's linguistic naivete and the author's more knowledge-able perspective. The sketch opens with the narrator's humorous com-ments on the impossibility of dialogue with his foreign "help" (see the first introductory quote to this chapter). Such linguistic solipsism launches the movement of the whole sketch that depends on Twain's deliberate and studied ignorance of the Italian language:

I have no dictionary, and I do not want one; I can select my words by the sound, or by orthographic aspect. Many of them have a French or German or English look, and these are the ones I enslave for the day's service. That is, as a rule. Not always. If I find a learnable phrase that has an imposing look and warbles musically along I do not care to know the meaning of it; I pay it out to the first applicant, knowing that if I pronounce it carefully *he* will understand it, and that's enough. (172)

But the humour also depends on Twain's clever play on exactly those aspects of linguistic similarity and difference suggested in the above pas-sage. A word's sound, spelling, and meaning may form a translatable connection but will not necessarily do so, and can indeed compose an entirely arbitrary sequence. The translation of the newspapers Twain reads forms the main business of the sketch.[47] Thus he takes the words, "Il ritorno dei Beati d'Italia/Elargizione del Re all' Ospedale italiano," to mean "that the Italian sovereigns are coming back — they have been to England. The second line seems to mean that they enlarged the King at the Italian hospital. With a banquet I suppose. An English banquet has that effect" (175).[48] Again, "Inaugurazione della Chiesa Russa" is trans-lated as "the Inauguration of a Russian Cheese," a remark that Twain says "oversizes my hand" (177).[49] The narrator explains the pleasure he gets from his activity:

You can never be absolutely sure of the meaning of anything you read in such circumstances; you are chasing an alert and gamy riddle all the time, and the baffling turns and dodges of the prey make the life of the hunt. A dictionary would spoil it. Sometimes a single word of doubtful purport will cast a veil of dreamy and golden uncertainty over a whole paragraph of cold and practical certainties. (180)

In one sense, we are taken back here to Twain's early work in *Innocents Abroad* (1869) and the comedy at the expense of the foreign cultures and languages to be found there. But the xenophobic quality of that early work is replaced here by a gentler form of humor based on linguistic relativism, on a pleasurable understanding of the gaps between signifier and signified, and on a preference for the qualities of speculation and imagination — however inaccurate they might eventually prove — over the world of "cold and practical certainties."[50] In this last detail we might even see something of the general tenor of Twain's thought at a time when such a "practical" world was becoming increasingly difficult for him to endure, for he wrote this sketch as his wife was dying, lying "gravely ill" in a nearby room.[51]

Twain's comic — and intellectually sophisticated — interest in the subject of language and representation is also evident in "Extracts from Adam's Diary" and "Eve's Diary." These stories were published on 3 June 1893 (in *Niagara Book*) and in December 1905 (*Harper's Monthly*), respectively, and can both be seen as part of a larger long-term project: "Twain's ... attempts to rewrite or to supplement biblical accounts of the Creation, the Fall, and the Flood."[52] These twinned stories have received significant critical attention from such critics as Stanley Brodwin, who focuses on the relation between Eve's compassion and Adam's humor, and Susan K. Harris, who examines Adam's "sexual and aesthetic development" (as he responds to Eve's presence) and the "rhetorical fluidity" that accompanies it.[53] Here, and treating the two narratives interdependently, I focus briefly on the language theme: an unsurprising one given the version of the return to human origins that the texts describe.[54]

The process of naming and categorizing is an ongoing and unifying motif in both texts. Eve, who feels like "an experiment" (287), has to make sense of her world from new. She responds to her environment with a perceptual consciousness unmoored from standard ways of understanding subject-object relations and the larger contexts that determine them. In this respect, she is somewhat like Faulkner's Benjy, in *The Sound and The Fury*, though the estranged simplicity of her understanding of the world is marked by a different (sentimental) type of poeticism than we find in Faulkner's text: "The moon got loose last night, and slid down and fell out of the scheme — a very great loss. . . . I wish I could get some [stars] to put in my hair. . . . I tried to knock some down with . . . clods . . . but I never got one. It was because I am left-handed and cannot throw good" (288–89). Adam, in his diary, uses the word "we" straight away, but he gets it from Eve, "the new creature with the long hair" (414). In her diary, "the sociable 'we' " (293) only gradually comes into use. For hers is a gradual negotiation of words and their relation to meaning, initially categorizing Adam as "a reptile," or possibly as "architecture" since "when it stands, it spreads itself apart like a derrick" (290–91).

Both Adam and Eve make the naming of things an important part of their diaries. Eve, however, is more directly associated with the use and development of language: "always talking" (415) and with "a rage for explaining" (417), her naming "goes recklessly on, in spite of anything [Adam] can do" (415). Eve believes in an intuitive and natural relationship between words and things:

The minute I set eyes on an animal I know what it is . . . the right name comes out instantly. . . . I seem to know just by the shape of the creature and the way it acts what animal it is.
    When the dodo came along [Adam] thought it was a wild-cat — I saw it in his eye. But I saved him. . . . I just spoke up . . . "Well, I do declare, if there isn't the dodo!" (293–94)

Adam, though, is more sceptical. It seems that he recognizes the arbitrary nature of the relationship between language and reality and is capable, accordingly, of playing with the slippages and punning possibilities of words as he speaks:

The new creature names everything that comes along, before I can get in a protest. And always the same pretext is offered — it *looks* like the thing. There is the dodo, for instance. Says the moment one looks at it one sees at a glance that "it looks like a dodo." . . . Dodo! It looks no more like a dodo than I do. (414)[55]

One of the differences between Eve and Adam is the contrast between her aesthetic sensitivity and his belief in "practical value" (302). So while Eve "revel[s] in the flowers, those beautiful creatures that catch the smile of God out of the sky," Adam calls them "rubbish" (297). Twain generally explores the theme of gender difference and here confirms expected norms. Much of the humor of the latter part of Adam's diary, though, rests on the return Adam himself makes to the language and categorization issue, as he now tries to puzzle out the status of his son, Cain (see the second introductory quote to the chapter). Cain, he decides, cannot be a snake as "it doesn't crawl." Instead, Adam concludes, "the short front legs and long hind ones indicate that it is of the kangaroo family, but it is a marked variation of the species, since the true kangaroo hops, whereas this one never does" (424). And as Adam (as more children arrive) gradually realizes their identity as his "boys" and "girls," and comes to value Eve more and more, so he too comes to share the warmth and sensitivity that initially belongs to her alone. His diary ends: "After all these years, I see that I was mistaken about Eve in the beginning; it is better to live outside the Garden with her than inside it without her. At first I thought she talked too much; but now I should be sorry to have that voice fall silent and pass out of my life" (429).

If the recurrent concern for language, categorization, and representation in these texts sometimes works (and particularly in Eve's sections) at a whimsical level, nonetheless Twain's comic touch is generally sure here. And he shows a sharp understanding of the theoretical issues at stake.

Any judgment of Twain's later writings in terms of his use of a distancing irony and as "the imaginative product of the author's despair and bitterness" clearly only tells one part of a more complex and multidimensional story.[56] The *$30,000 Bequest* collection is patchy, it is true, but it contains material that shows the wide range of Twain's concerns and the variety of his fictional and non-fictional modes even at this stage of his career. In my final chapter, on "A Double-Barreled Detective Story," I return to the subject of humor and its continuing expressive presence in this collection. I make some concluding comments on its relationship to the deep seriousness that had always formed a part of his work, but which, in these last years, had become an increasingly distinct component of it. These comments also provide a framework for a retrospective glance at his writing career as a whole.

12

Comic Intentions in
"A Double-Barreled Detective Story"

> ... far in the empty sky a solitary oesophagus slept upon motionless wing.
> — "A Double-Barreled Detective Story"

Mark Twain's "A Double-Barreled Detective Story" is given little critical attention these days. Tom Quirk briefly mentions it as "an antic and funny (if somewhat rambling) burlesque of Arthur Conan Doyle's detective fiction" (SSF, 112). Frederick Busch notes the "double and triple switches of identity" in its last sections. He comments, too, on Twain's "metafictional mischief" as he responds to earlier magazine readers concerning his use of the word "oesophagus" at the narrative's structural halfway point (see above). [1] And, like Quirk, he picks up on the spoofing references to the Sherlock Holmes stories, seeing one of Twain's possible primary intentions as "to wreak a kind of vengeance on Conan Doyle" as he writes. However, in then immediately asking, "At whom does [Twain] discharge the barrels?" of this double-barreled story, Busch suggests that such commentary does not resolve his interpretive uncertainties about the text. His overall judgment, too, is dismissive: "Its plot is not only labyrinthine, it is often unfollowable. . . . [It] is a tale not many sophisticated readers can take seriously."[2]

Judith Yaross Lee takes a more sympathetic approach. Showing how Twain targets "the melodramatic revenge tale" as well as the detective story here, and describing the intertwining of the two detective plot strands in the story, she says that "the pile-up of parodies leaves many readers perplexed, especially considering that the melodramatic opening chapter lacks any signs of burlesque."[3] She is, though, more confident in her reading of the text's multiple effects, briefly showing how "the double barrels in Twain's story . . . extend beyond plot and narrative structure to encompass sources and targets, as well." Lee also shows her awareness of the links between this narrative and the serious recurrent concerns of Twain's later fictions when she notes that the story "raises questions of identity, doubles, and heredity familiar to readers of *Pudd'nhead Wilson*." And her comment that it "points up the increasing distance between humour and theme toward the end of Twain's career" is one that bears particular relevance in light of my own prior analysis of the *$30,000 Bequest* book as a whole and the reading of this particular story that now follows (AF, 12–13).

Lee also refers back to Hamlin Hill's earlier comments on the tale and the way that he, too, sees it connecting up with the main body of Twain's fiction. Disconcertingly, however, the "major themes" Hill identifies — "The Southern 'code' of revenge, the Western mining camp and its special argot, the lynch mob and the courageous spokesman for reason and order" — appear, at first glance, quite different in kind from the identity/doubles theme that Lee describes. It is, of course, quite possible for any narrative to be composed of a multiplicity of themes. Moreover, the *Pudd'nhead Wilson* comparison might be helpful (at least if we also bring *Those Extraordinary Twins* into consideration) in suggesting at least some connection between such diverse concerns, for both the revenge motif and lynching also figure in those twinned texts. Hill's final verdict on "A Double-Barreled Detective Story" is a curiously divided one, though. A "substantial work of fiction," it is also "a veritable Gatling gun of ideas, modes of writing, and crossed purposes," its lack of coherence showing that "the raw materials on which Mark Twain had established his reputation were no longer malleable." For Hill, in short, the story would seem to be both evidence of Twain's ability to produce major work and proof that he could no longer do so.[4]

The paradox contained in Hill's assessment and the general critical uncertainty and lack of consensus, as far as narrative theme and authorial intention go, gives this story a curiously indeterminate status. The publishing evidence, however, shows that Twain or his publisher (most probably the latter) thought highly enough of it not only to publish it in two installments of *Harper's Magazine* in early 1902, and later to include it in *The $30,000 Bequest and Other Stories*, but also to publish it as a separate book immediately following its magazine appearance, in April 1902.[5] While such publishing activity was often based as much on financial as on aesthetic considerations, and while the repeated use of the same Twain material was not uncommon, this still serves to distinguish this story from the general mass of his work.

In the rest of this chapter I explore some of the "double-barreled" effects of this narrative in detail, showing the descriptive limits of that phrase for a text that moves in *multiple* formal and thematic directions. I also take up the analogy Lee makes between this story and *Pudd'nhead Wilson* more fully. Thus far, I have mostly stressed the textual connections within Twain's collections of short works. This story provides a strong reminder of the relationships that also exist between Twain's shorter pieces and his novels. I also consider the difficult question of comic intention, contending that there are other ways to read this narrative than those which focus on its "incoherence" and which see the interpretive uncertainties it produces as a sign of artistic failure. To take such responses and turn them on their critical heads might be to see Twain engaged here in deliberate comic dislocations; casting his readers adrift as they try to bring firm meaning and interpretation to a text that takes some delight in resisting such procedures. We know what Busch means when he critiques the story as one not many readers can take seriously, but his words are themselves open to double meaning, for this is a *comic* tale and Twain's intentions do not have to be "serious."[6] My intention in writing this final chapter has one further dimension. In establishing a way of approaching Twain's humor and its variable relation to the social and cultural issues that are also so important to his writing, I hope to bring focus to a subject that has been simmering beneath the surface for much of this study. In a number of ways, then, this chapter forms an apt conclusion to my book.

One thing noticeable is the degree to which critics have reused or embroidered the firearms metaphor in the title of "A Double-Barreled Detective Story." Thus Busch's words, as he asks at what target Twain "discharge[s] the barrels" of his narrative, are similar to Hill's as he discusses the story as "a veritable Gatling gun of ideas." Both critics take the connotations of violence in the title and allow them, in their own choice of language, further figurative release. The form of such release, however, differs as we move from the idea of specific and limited damage (two barrels) to that of general mayhem. The latter, indeed, recalls Hank Morgan's use of thirteen gatlings at the end of *A Connecticut Yankee at King Arthur's Court* to randomly "vomit death" into the ten thousand knights opposing him (565).

Humor is, of course, often associated metaphorically with forms of violence, and Twain's comic writing in particular has often been seen in such terms. Marcel Gutwirth talks of humor as "a field of force-on-the-loose" (LM, 107). And we recall Howells's comments on the "glorious" episode of "Some Rambling Notes of an Idle Excursion" that "nearly killed Mrs. Howells." Bruce Michelson, speaks more generally of Twain's "unrestricted war against seriousness."[7] We can take Gutwirth and Michelson's words together to suggest again that, if it is difficult to pin down a specific main target for Twain's comedy in "A Double-Barreled Detective Story," we may find a key to his intentions in the very multifaceted nature of the text and the comic effects there realized. Twain's delight in attacking that abstract quality "seriousness" on all fronts and with not just two but a multitude of metaphorical (gun) barrels, may help to explain and unlock a narrative that has previously seemed just too random and diffuse to be taken "seriously." We may be entering a type of Catch 22 interpretive world here where we expect comic writing, and especially Twain's comic writing, to address specific social and cultural issues while, at the same time, we are aware that one possibility for humor is to playfully deny the very concept of such "importance"; to radically dislocate what Michelson calls "the grounds of culture, common sense, and identity."[8] Indeed, it may be that Twain himself was caught between two such responses to the world that he represented and was unable completely to square them.[9]

The title of "A Double-Barreled Detective Story" encourages us to focus on its theme of doubleness. It is here that we can return to the links with *Pudd'nhead Wilson* (1894). This story forms, in many ways, a twin text to the earlier novel. First, it is prefaced by an ironic maxim that could be easily mistaken for one of Pudd'nhead Wilson's Calendar entries: "We ought never to do wrong when people are looking" (447). The same is true of the further remark at the head of chapter 4: "No real gentleman will tell the naked truth in the presence of ladies" (468). Indeed, half way through the narrative, Twain seems to give a clue to the connection between the two texts. We learn that the man assumed to be Jacob Fuller—the object of the "hounding" that occurs in the text (of which more later)—has become an ˋalien figure who "keeps quite to himself, consorting with no one" in the new community in which he moves. And he has taken on the name of *David Wilson* (my emphasis, for this is Pudd'nhead's real name, too) as his disguise (464).

More important, this narrative reintroduces many of the same thematic issues as *Pudd'nhead Wilson*. Jacob Fuller is refused permission to marry by his would-be father-in-law (the marriage takes place, nonetheless, without such permission). Part of his resulting anger stems from the judgment that is made on him then and passed on to his bride-to-be: that, as Fuller repeats it, "my character was written in my face; that I was treacherous, a dissembler, a coward, and a brute without sense of pity" (450). Such a belief in the transparency of signs—that surface appearance reveals deep truth—is likely to be unreliable in Twain's fiction. Here, in a slight twist on that connection, it appears that in dismissing Jacob on the basis of such apparent evil traits, the father-in-law may have helped to bring them into being. It is at this stage in the story that Jacob decides to revenge such insult: to "kill [his wife's father] by inches" through his treatment of his daughter, "his idol" (450). And so he does, lashing his wife to a tree on the public road at midnight, setting his bloodhounds on her until she is naked, her clothes torn off, and then leaving her forever, the father dying of a broken heart as a consequence (451–52).

However, that phrase "my character was written in my face," with its assumption of an easily read knowledge of others, raises deeper issues. A transparency of character and identity is implicit here: we know who others are, and can judge them on the basis of their outward physical features. This is challenged, though, by the deep uncertainties about the nature of identity—where selfhood lies, and how it can be measured, confirmed, and defined—that obsess so many of Twain's late fictions and *Pudd'nhead Wilson* in particular. The question of how we tell Tom from Valet, black from white, and (if we include *Those Extraordinary Twins*) Siamese twin from twin has been the subject of extensive critical discussion, and there is no need to rehearse it again here.[10] In "A Double-Barreled Detective Story" we have a partial reflection of the earlier novel in a number of ways. Issues of false identity and disguise pervade the narrative. The protagonist, Fuller's son, was apparently conceived on the night that his father abandoned his mother. His mother named him Archy Stillman. It is he who carries out his mother's "stern plan" for revenge: to track his father down wherever he goes: "relentlessly . . . poisoning his life . . . you will make of him another wandering Jew; he shall know no rest any more, no peace of mind, no placid sleep; you shall shadow him, cling to him, persecute him, till you break his heart as he broke my father's and mine" (457–58). As Stillman pursues his father, both men take on disguises. Just as Tom Driscoll "blacked his face" before robbing his uncle, so Archy darkens his complexion to disguise himself from Fuller. As Tom puts on a "suit of girl's clothes" after the murder that then occurs, so Fuller cross-dresses (but as an "old woman," 463) as he tries to evade Archy.[11]

Issues of authentic and false identity, then, circulate in both texts. Tom Driscoll is finally known for who he is (Valet de Chambre) by his fingerprints and Archy knows Fuller by his handwriting—as long as he "does not disguise it too much" (465). But even the identification of crime by fingerprint can be unreliable. There is detailed analysis available in Ritunnano, Kraus, and Baetzhold of the way that Twain burlesques the Sherlock Holmes stories, especially *A Study in Scarlet* (1887) and the first magazine installment of "The Hound of the Baskervilles" (August 1901).[12] But another Holmes story is relevant to my immediate argument about identity and its proofs.

In "The Adventure of the Norwood Builder" (1903), the Scotland Yard man, Lestrade, is convinced of John McFarlane's guilt by the bloody "well-marked print of a thumb" on the whitewashed hall wall of the house where the apparent murder has been committed. Since this matches the "wax impression of young McFarlane's right thumb," it is seen by Lestrade, and also by Dr. Watson, as "final" proof of criminal identity. Holmes, however, reveals that Oldacre, the supposed murder victim (who fakes his own death to get "crushing revenge upon his old sweetheart," McFarlane's mother) has also faked this evidence. He has got McFarlane, at a previous meeting, to put his thumb on the soft wax of a package to secure it: "It was [then] the simplest thing in the world for him to take a wax impression from the seal, to moisten it in as much blood as he could get from a pin-prick, and to put the mark upon the wall during the night."[13]

I am not arguing here (despite the similar revenge motif) that Twain was influenced by this Holmes story. Dates of publication make that impossible. But I am suggesting that to "authenticate" criminal identity by fingerprints is not necessarily straightforward. And, transferring that argument to *Pudd'nhead Wilson*, such identifications are (at least potentially) similarly suspect. Wilson's conviction that "I never labeled [fingerprints on a strip of glass] carelessly in my life" (277) is what allows him to "put things right" at the end of the novel: to reveal Tom as Valet, and vice versa. But just say Wilson slipped up on that one occasion some twenty years earlier and had wrongly labeled the fingerprints of Valet and Tom as babies. Then the "crime" would have remained unsolved. Tom would stay "Tom" and Valet, "Valet," even though in neither case was that true. Such speculations may seem unwarranted, for they rewrite Twain's book. But they do suggest that we may pursue Twain's uncertainties concerning identity in *Pudd'nhead Wilson* even further than critical analysis has generally allowed. If in that novel, in the struggle to distinguish original from copy, identity is reduced to a minimal form (there is absolutely no way there to tell two individuals apart except by the lines on their skin), then even this way of telling person from person cannot be guaranteed. Science (fingerprinting) can be affected by circumstance — as in the Holmes story. Indeed, the content of one of Pudd'nhead Wilson's Calendar entries says exactly this: "Even the clearest and most perfect circumstantial evidence is likely to be at fault, after all, and therefore ought to be received with great caution" (263). Conventional views of the self as "unique, distinguishable, irreplaceable" are placed in even further doubt here.[14]

And similar themes haunt "A Double-Barreled Detective Story." The problematic relationship between original and copy (we might recall Twain's own anxieties about "the impostors who performed as Mark Twain")[15] is humorously introduced in Ferguson's imitation of the actions and deductive processes of Sherlock Holmes at the end of the narrative. The action has now moved to a silver-mining camp, Hope Canyon, and Holmes himself has been introduced as a character in the text. When one of the western audience tells Ferguson (the local Wells-Fargo man) that "you've got [Holmes] down to a dot. He ain't painted up any exacter to the life in the books. By George, I can just *see* him," another validates this response with the words, "You bet you! It's just a photograft, that's what it is" (494). This imitation scene recalls, to a degree, that in *Pudd'nhead Wilson* when "the old deformed negro bell-ringer" (69) follows in Tom's wake, both mimicking and exaggerating the airs, graces, and dress Tom has assumed while at Yale.[16] The confusions about identity that are introduced in that book stem from the further resonances of the action. An old black man imitates a young white man. But that young white man (the "real" Tom Driscoll) is in fact being imitated by a young black man (he who is assumed to be Tom) who is in fact not black — in terms of physical coloration — at all. In the scene from "A Double-Barreled Detective Story," the question of imitation takes a different guise. But the dizzying relation between actuality (the real Sherlock Holmes), literary representation (Holmes "painted up . . . to the life in the books"), authenticity, translation, and visualization (as mimed version of supposed behavior conjures up absent original: "I can just *see* him") engages similar issues. The use of the phrase "just a photograft," and the phonetic mistake that concludes it, brilliantly manages linguistically to muddy any line that exists between copy and original (graft: "to insert or fix in or upon something, with the result of producing a vital or indissoluble union," OED).

The problematic nature of identity, then, is a recurrent concern in "A Double-Barreled Detective Story," too. Fuller can be known by his handwriting, although handwriting can be altered or indeed forged. But it turns out that the Fuller who is so known is not the "real" Fuller at all. At an early point in the narrative (less than a quarter way through) the tale of revenge is stalled and replaced by one of attempted restitution, when Stillman discovers that (as he writes to his mother): "God forgive us . . . we are hunting the *wrong man*! . . . *This* Jacob Fuller is a *cousin* of the guilty one" (464). The man, then, who "efface[s] himself with a new name and a disguise" (465) and who is driven to madness by the pursuit that occurs, is innocent.[17] The guilty cousin has already changed his name (to Flint Buckner) following his "fiendish deed" (464). We are in a shifting textual world here, where name, appearance, identity, and even character are all in a state of flux.

If all this reminds us of *Pudd'nhead Wilson*, so too does the concern with doubles and doubling that runs through the text. Pudd'nhead Wilson's early joke about the yelping dog ("I wish I owned half of that dog. . . .

Because I would kill my half," 24) metaphorically instigates the thematics of doubling and inseparability—Tom and Valet, white and black, free man and owned property—which underlies the entire narrative. In "A Double-Barreled Detective Story" that joke is curiously literalized, for Archy Stillman (note the double pun on his name) is also, it seems, half a dog. Fuller's act of revenge on his wife, her nakedness, the blood-hounds' presence, and her consequent pregnancy all imply bestiality. Twain watches his language here, and the hints at such sexual abuse are elliptic, comically contained within the broad parody of melodrama that occurs. But when Archy's mother learns of his extraordinary sense of smell, she exclaims: "It's a birthmark! The gift of the bloodhound is in him" (454).

Obviously one of Twain's intentions here is to parody Conan Doyle and the character of Jefferson Hope in *A Study in Scarlet*, who, determined on vengeance, pursues his male prey like a "human bloodhound."[18] Still-man literally sniffs out his quarry. But his half-a-dog status ("I am . . . part dog," 466) also connects up with the metaphoric resonances of the phrase in Twain's earlier novel. Here, too, a series of individuals are twinned with one another, joined in symbiotic connection. Thus Archy's fate and identity as manhunter are entwined with the two Fullers who become his twin quarry. Archy, we have seen, is told by his mother to make Fuller "another wandering Jew . . . [who] shall know no rest any more." But in searching the "whole globe" to find (the other, innocent) Fuller whom he has forced to flee, Archy finds himself in the exact posi-tion of his supposed victim: "Do you see, mother? It is *I* that am the Wandering Jew" (465). Both men become homeless wanderers, doubles, their fates interconnected.

Twain's concern with the problematic nature of identity and with fig-ures locked in twinned relationships is strongly reminiscent of *Pudd'n-head Wilson*. But this narrative works in a very different way overall. And what is most noticeable is the way that Twain uses the motif of the double, and the proliferation of plot strands based on that motif, as a comic effect in its own right, rather than as a pathway into the searching cultural analysis of the earlier novel. Twain and his friends evidently used the "double-barreled" form as something of a private joke (AF, 12), and here the spiraling nature of that joke seems to become an end in itself, for the doublings introduced pile one upon the other. Archy and Jacob are twinned figures in the revenge story being played out. But that story itself is then doubled as another revenge tale is told: of Fetlock Jones, the English youth, on the vicious Flint Buckner for the "insults and humilia-tions" (473) he has endured.

This latter story, and that of the murder that follows—the Hope Canyon section of the tale — is formally marked off by the change of narrative tack that occurs at the start of chapter 4. This, in turn, duplicates Conan Doyle's *Study in Scarlet* and the double-barreled nature of that text. The detective abilities of Archy are set against those of Sherlock Holmes (Jones's uncle), who has unexpectedly arrived in the village. So not only are detectives doubled here but literary form itself is disrupted (divided?) as any pretense that we could take the narrative seriously, as relating — in whatever minimal way — to realistic representation, is shattered by this metafictional device: the entry of another author's fictional construct into the story.[19] Jacob Fuller (the misidentified, rather than the actual, criminal) then further twins the two detectives. He is convinced, in the insanity to which he has been driven, that it is not Archy but Holmes, with his "superhuman penetration and tireless energies" (519), who has pursued him. Double then piles upon double, to the total confusion of any reader looking for a single and sustained "meaning" to this text. The doubling becomes, rather, a form of comedy — an extended joke — in its own right.

Indeed, what starts off with twinned or doubled figures and plot sequences leads to a type of multiplicity effect as different characters, scenes, relationships, and themes combine profusely to dislocating readerly effect. So too with genre. Twain moves from a parody of melodrama in the opening part of his story, "then burlesques detective fiction in the second barrel" (RG, 57). But there are more than two generic barrels at play here. The sentimental tradition, on which Twain places such reliance elsewhere in this collection, is parodied in the story of the lost Hogan child (used to illustrate Stillman's detective skills) and the mother's response to her child's safe recovery: "The mother hugged it with a wild embrace . . . the grateful tears running down her face, and in a choked and broken voice she poured out a golden stream of that wealth of worshiping endearments which has its home in full richness nowhere but in the Irish heart" (487). Such shifts, together with the moves made between third-person narrative, first-person epistolary form, and even the story within a story, have the reader thrown constantly off balance, not sure at any one point just where the narrative leads or to what end.

The closure of the story, indeed, reinforces this sense of pointless misdirection. First, in a scene reminiscent of *Huckleberry Finn* (but which also owes something to the ending of *Those Extraordinary Twins*), another "extraordinary" (502) person, Sherlock Holmes, is threatened with lynching and saved only by the intervention of the sheriff, who confronts and disperses the cowardly mob.[20] This is followed by a very brief chapter where Archy learns, from "Sammy" Hillyer with whom he cabins, that Buckner (now murdered by Jones) was in fact the "real" Jacob Fuller. The whole revenge/detective motif has by now been rendered absurd by

Archy's "farcically ineffective" actions, the "havoc" he has brought about in "his bungling pursuit of the wrong man" (RG, 57). Twain continues here the critique of the assumptions underlying the detective fiction genre to be found in *Pudd'nhead Wilson*, too. In that book, Twain's irony is directed at the way the detective's powers of rational analysis are connected to the hegemonic workings of the social order. The disruptive and morally scandalous fact that cannot be hidden from sight (racial inequality and its results) is entirely overlooked in the shift of focus to the puzzling out of clues in a particular murder mystery. The detective ends up being celebrated by a community that fails to see his or its blindness. Similarly here man's reasoning abilities and intellectual skills are revealed as something of a joke, with instinct (Archy's hound-nature) triumphing over (Sherlock Holmes's) reason, and the genre's assumptions of "life as a place where justice prevails and where events fall into meaningful patterns" is subjected to deep mockery.[21]

"Meaningful patterns" are difficult to pin down in "A Double-Barreled Detective Story," as Twain shifts (sometimes wildly) between a variety of themes and forms. Twain takes great comic delight in individual incident and especially the burlesque of Conan Doyle, playing, for instance, on Holmes's reappearance in *The Hound of the Baskervilles* after his supposed death in the Reichenbach Falls in an earlier story.[22] Thus Sherlock Holmes's "awful gravity" and "paleness" are explained by the fact that "he's been dead four times a'ready. . . . Three times natural, once by accident. I've heard say he smells damp and cold, like a grave" (490). But the main source of Twain's comic effects in this text is the sheer pleasure taken in the very lack of formal or thematic consistency. Any potentially identifiable serious target or motif in the narrative tends to dissolve in what is comic play for its own sake: what Michelson calls the "Big Bang . . . theory of humor" which in its "collision of models and thought-systems . . . achieve[s] liberation from everybody, including the model-happy interpreter."[23] As we look for interpretive meaning here, we are caught between multiple responses to a comic text that deliberately defies such sense-making process.

This brings me back, however, to the thematic links I have previously identified between this story and *Pudd'nhead Wilson*. And this in turn relates to my comments in the last chapter about the different modes of Twain's short writings in this late period. In the earlier novel, the identity/doubling themes operate not to broad comic effect but to serious social ends. A recent theoretical book by Susan Purdie helps to distinguish further between the various forms of humor involved here.

In *Comedy: The Mastery of Discourse*, Purdie distinguishes between serious intention and involvement in a comic text and mere joking. She uses the term "implication" to designate "any response which carries some sense of being involved with the effects of an utterance — the precise opposite, in fact, of the response to whatever is taken as a joke."[24] She goes on to distinguish different types of implication. It might be "affective," where "we sympathise, or even empathise, with the people concerned" (77). Or it might be "ideological," where "a value system has been mobilised," and where we judge represented behavior (which is now "disturbing rather than funny") as "having effect in its world" that must be "judged morally." Such judgments parallel the judgments we operate in reality (83). In such terms, our amusement at the comic discussion of Sherlock Holmes's paleness detailed above involves what Purdie would call, in contrast, "an unimplicated attention" (78). We take it as a joke and little else.[25]

Purdie's way of looking at things, however, is by no means black and white, for she recognises that "it is perfectly possible for texts to be unserious (= funny) and serious (= important)" at one and the same moment. Noting the prevalence of "seriously implicating moments" in comic texts, she consequently recognizes that "some mixture of address is so common in joking texts that a definition of "comedy" which points *only* to its funniness must be so restrictive as to be virtually useless" (113–14).

Certain problems are raised here in the move made from the oppositional (implicated versus unimplicated) to the complementary ("unserious and serious at one and the same moment"). But we might start to solve them by seeing comedy in terms of a spectrum with unserious "joking" at one end, highly serious social concern (presented through a humorous lens) at the other, and a large area in-between where the funny/serious balance is subject to considerable variation.

Such a model, with the contrasts it establishes at either end of this spectrum, is useful for any consideration of Twain's humor, whether in his short works or his novels and travel books. Throughout this book we have noted Twain's swings from playful and surreal forms of comedy and a delight in relativistic uncertainty to writing — both comic and otherwise — of more serious social and moral intent. But the contrasts I identify have particular force when applied to his writing from the early 1890s onward. The differences between *Pudd'nhead Wilson* and its immediate twinned text, *Those Extraordinary Twins*, can serve as a paradigm for the parallel contrast between *Pudd'nhead Wilson* and "A Double-Barreled Detective Story." And similar differences in comic approach apply, too, between the latter and a narrative like "The Man That Corrupted Hadleyburg" (1899). A significant pattern becomes apparent here.

Twain, as is well known, pulled *Puddn'head Wilson* and *Those Extraordinary Twins* apart. Caught between different stories and literary modes, he made what was intended as a single work into two separate texts. I have argued elsewhere that—in terms of literary form—this separation suggests that Twain could no longer manage to reconcile a repressive social reality with the use of an anarchic and extravagant humor.[26] Thus, on the one side (*Pudd'nhead Wilson*), we have a sardonic (implicating) irony that operates around a series of targets including the nature of fixed racial categories, the assumption of autonomous subjectivity, and the connection between moral principle and community practice.[27] On the other (*Those Extraordinary Twins*), we have farce—unserious joking—as Twain takes obvious delight in the absurdist potential of his twinship device. Thus he describes the tired and wet Siamese twins undressing in a comic and deliberately dehumanising turn of figurative phrase, when he says "the abundance of sleeves made the partnership-coat hard to get off, for it was like skinning a tarantula" (327). Jokes like this carry the narrative that follows: an exuberant and apparently unserious "extravaganza" (317) about the Siamese " 'freak' — or 'freaks' " (311).

The differences between *Pudd'nhead Wilson* and "A Double-Barreled Detective Story"—the latter with its high proportion of unserious "joking"—operate similarly. And the contrast between "A Double-Barreled Detective Story" and narratives like "The Man That Corrupted Hadleyburg" and "The $30,000 Bequest" works to like effect, with (again) a corrosive satire and irony acting as the dominant textual feature in the last two named stories. In pieces like "The Five Boons of Life" it is, rather, a bleak philosophical pessimism that predominates, with humor completely dropped from the picture. While I would not want to suggest that Twain's art only operates in such a polarized way, it does seem that a significant gap between different forms of humor, and between the comic and the serious, has opened up here and that this gap is suggestive of underlying and incompatible tensions in Twain's later artistic vision.[28]

There is one important qualification I want to introduce to this account, however, that relates back to the whole range of Twain's work. I have argued that what we see in Twain's writing is a comic imagination that veers from having "strong implicating intentions" (Purdie, 116) to having very few. So while the themes of doubling and false identity in *Pudd'nhead Wilson* stimulate serious cultural analysis, in "A Double-Barreled Detective Story" (as in *Those Extraordinary Twins*) they have little "implicating" extratextual resonance, becoming rather part of a primary comic pattern of confusion and circularity that leads, apparently, nowhere beyond itself. To repeat an earlier comment, serious motifs tend to dissolve in comic play for its own sake.

But Twain's delight in the comedy of patent absurdity can rarely be completely divorced, however much it might *seem* the case, from some type of "implicating" effects. The "solitary oesophagus" description in

"A Double-Barreled Detective Story" may be, as Twain writes to a respondent, a "joke . . . the whole paragraph . . . [has] not a vestige of sense in any detail of it" (470). But all those other textual "jokes" about doubling, detection, and identity cannot quite be dismissed as lacking a serious base. As in *Those Extraordinary Twins*, a series of anxieties about agency, identity, personal responsibility, law, communal order, and violence do emerge and cannot be entirely ignored, despite the broad comic effects (parody, burlesque, farce, and a narrative emphasis on pointless misdirection) that both contain them and deflect much of their implicating force. Even when it appears at its most "unserious," then, Twain's comedy here still retains something of its "serious" side.

My comments in this chapter have primarily been concerned with Twain's work in the 1890s and early 1900s. However, as I have suggested above, the tension between implicated and unimplicated humor that Susan Purdie explores is well suited to an analysis of Twain's writing as a whole and his short works in particular. His comedy is composed of an unstable mixture of components. If one part of him was increasingly attracted to serious social themes, the other was engaged in a comic ungrounding of seriousness, a comic play that converted sense to a type of nonsense, and that delighted in a dislocation of all codes, values, and ways of understanding ourselves and our world, that playfully denied both common sense and coherent meanings.[29] His humor, then, ranges *between* the implicating and the nonimplicating, with such comic forms mixed within and between his various texts, and indeed sometimes even from one sentence to another within the same text. It is in such moves, and such unexpected combinations, that his comic imagination was formed and fired.

Conclusion

> Come on, you sniveling thieves! Fall into ranks and blast away with
> your rotten [criticism] at an unoffending people! Do your worst and
> vamose — scatter — git! Say your say and then stop your yowling
> forevermore.

I take liberties with Twain's words here,[1] inserting my "criticism" to replace his original "poetry." I do so, and use this passage, in part to direct
the reader back at this concluding point to Twain's own short writings
rather than to my secondary critical analysis of them. One of the main
findings of this book is just how much of Twain's work — and particularly
the shorter pieces — has been overlooked or forgotten and what a wealth
of material it represents. If some of Twain's short writing (though by no
means all) is patchy in quality, there is — as Emerson Everett says in his
Authentic Mark Twain — nearly always something that repays the reader's
attention even in the most minor story or sketch.[2] The collections of
short writings provide an alternative entry point to Twain's literary career
to the one (via the book-length works) normally taken. In them, the
quality of his comic imagination, his engagement with the changing social and cultural issues of his time, and his own artistic and philosophical
development can be clearly traced.

The other reason for using this quote, though, is to remind my reader
just how much of Twain's short work is now scattered between various
often inaccessible sources or is still not available at all. The "San Francisco Letter" from which the passage is taken appears neither in the
Works of Mark Twain: Early Tales & Sketches volumes (which have not yet
reached this chronological point) nor in the Library of America two-
volume *Mark Twain: Collected Tales, Sketches, Speeches, & Essays*. Indeed, it
was only reprinted for the first time in 1999 in a journal with very limited
circulation.[3] The full versions of the articles and sketches Twain wrote for

the *Buffalo Express* have only just been reprinted (in Joseph McCullough and Janice McIntire-Strasburg's edition of *Mark Twain at the Buffalo Express*, 1999). We can expect more of Twain's short writings, particularly those from his early career, to continue to appear. These, no doubt, will prove a rich source of comedy and social comment and further our knowledge about both the author and his literary career.

I have ended this book with the last collection of short writings published before Twain's death in 1910. In doing so, I stop short of all the short works, both finished and fragmentary, that appeared posthumously. This is in no way to downplay the importance of that work or its artistic merits.[4] But my project has been a discrete one: to focus on an examination of the short works that appeared in collected form in Twain's lifetime. I leave any further examination of the posthumous and unfinished short works to others.

Any conclusions now made are tentative for, from such a range of material written over so many years, it is difficult to summarize without limiting and even misrepresenting their variety. For the most part I let my separate chapters and their developmental logic stand for themselves. But I focus very briefly on two main issues.

First I return to Twain's humor, a subject round which I have been circling for much of my book. Twain's use of the playful and the ludicrous runs in different comic directions from the satiric and ironic.[5] The movement of my argument between chapters 3 and 4 (on *Sketches, New and Old*) and chapters 11 and 12 (*The $30,000 Bequest*) suggests that a vying for authority between the two forms — one a broad and often absurdist comedy, the other a humor expressly directed to the ends of serious social or moral critique — takes place throughout Twain's career, though alongside the use of a whole series of other comic tactics, too. In his early work Twain moves much more easily from one type of humor to the other and indeed often manages to combine them within the confines of a single work. By the end of his career, the swings between the two forms have become both more pronounced and more irreconcilable. An earlier comic flexibility — that which also distinguishes his best-known full-length work, *Huckleberry Finn* — becomes increasingly difficult to capture toward the end of his career.[6]

But to see Twain's humor just in such terms is to do it less than justice. Often it is exactly the indeterminacy of the comedy and the difficulty of interpreting it in a single way and from a single point of view that creates its resonant effects. Thus, as in "The Stolen White Elephant," the relation between the playful (sheer nonsense) and the serious (a narrative about social repression and the very role of humor) can be highly unstable. Such instability is then increased in the further movement between those prior responses and a type of existential black comedy, in reading the story as a type of allegory of a world that lacks all logic, sense, and meaning. In such stories, the contradictions between such comic forms never fully surface due to the very undecideability that Twain (whether consciously or not) builds into them.

Even to say what I do here, however, becomes reductive. I hope one of the things my book shows is that there are other ways to approach Twain's humor and that the very number of the forms he uses and the range of his thematic interests will condemn any critic who tries to straitjacket it to definitional failure. I only hope my own efforts have helped to illuminate at least some of his multiple effects. But there is plenty more work to be done on this subject.

I have identified, however, a certain loss of comic pliancy in Twain's later writings, and this connects with my second general point. I do not wish to make too many comparative value judgments about Twain's later work as it develops from, and contrasts with, that done earlier. And it is, of course, difficult always to firmly distinguish — as far as thematic content and modes of humor go — between early, middle, and late in such a categorization. But it is apparent that Twain's short works become, to use a word from Mikhail Bakhtin, increasingly monologic (or single-voiced) as his career proceeds. The use of the "Mark Twain" persona and the opportunities it afforded for comedy in its construction both of a range of different poses and a productive gap between such poses and the authorial figure and value scheme do increasingly disappear as Twain's short-writing career progresses. Increasingly, too, it is the philosophizing, didacticism, and cultural pronouncements, made by a firmly identified authorial voice that feature in his collections. And a certain generic rigidity (Twain's late use of the sentimental mode would be an example) comes to take over at least some of his writing, and this too adds to the monologic effect. Twain becomes, not unsurprisingly, a different type of writer as his career progresses.

I do not want to paint a one-dimensional picture here but just to identify a general trend. As my references in chapter 11 to such works as "Eve's Diary," "Extracts from Adam's Diary," and "Italian Lessons Without a Master" show, Twain remained able right to the end of his career to produce relativistic, multidimensional, and extremely effective forms of comedy almost at will. My chapter on "A Double-Bareled Detective Story" shows that the part of Twain that delighted in comic nonsense and an inspired absurdism also remained strongly in evidence. Robert Giddings borrowed Twain's own phrase "a sumptuous variety" for the title of the collection of essays he edited on Twain's work.[7] The same phrase would do well to describe Twain's own collections of short writings. Together they constitute a valuable and much underexplored resource for any understanding and appreciation of Mark Twain and the nature of his artistic achievement.

Notes

Introduction

1. One of the best brief general studies of Twain's short stories is Alan Gribben, "Samuel Langhorne Clemens (Mark Twain)," in Bobby Ellen Kimbel, ed., *American Short Story Writers Before 1880, Dictionary of Literary Biography* (Detroit: Gale Research, 1988), 74: 54–83. Gribben's definition of the short story is broad, but he offers a valuable overview both of Twain's resistance to generic constraint and of the various thematic strands of his short writings.

2. For instance, in the introduction (xli) and afterword (12) to Mark Twain, *The $30,000 Bequest and Other Stories* (1906), both Frederick Busch and Judith Yaross call "The Double-Barreled Detective Story" a novella. R. Kent Rasmussen uses the same term to describe "The Man That Corrupted Hadleyburg," AZ, 300.

3. William Dean Howells's review in the *Atlantic Monthly* 36 (December 1875) is reprinted in CR, 151–52. This book is invaluable in its recovering of original critical responses to all the collections I am examining.

4. See James D. Wilson, AF, *The £1,000,000 Bank-Note and Other New Stories* (1893) 2. "The Enemy Conquered," a third fictional piece in the book, was not written by Twain.

5. Douglas Tallack critiques such modernist assumptions in *The Nineteenth-Century American Short Story: Language, Form, and Ideology* (London: Routledge, 1993). His alternative position is by way of Fredric Jameson and the notion of "generic discontinuities" (xi). Thus he focuses on the flexibility of movement between the conventional boundaries of a genre (the short story) and the deconstruction of such orderings as elements from alternative genres (the sketch, the novel) intrude and challenge such limits. His especial interest is in the way that a novelistic urge to address "social and historical concerns" (193) presses against the formal demands of the short story genre. He does not, however, consider Twain's short works. Other concerns prevent me here from following up the theoretical question of genre definition in any large-scale way. Tallack's approach may, however, be one useful way forward in the consideration of Twain's extraordinary and slippery generic range.

6. See *Newsletter of the Friends of the Bancroft Library*, Spring 1999, 13. Thanks to Bob Hirst for bringing this letter to my attention.

7. The matter of my overall book length was also an issue here. I would, however, note David Bradley's introduction to the Oxford Mark Twain edition of this

volume and particularly the account (IN, lvi) of Twain's influence (via these literary essays) on Bradley's own thinking concerning "the racial dynamics of aesthetics."

8. Quoted in Norris Yates, *The American Humorist: Conscience of the Twentieth Century* (Ames: Iowa State University Press, 1964), 11.

9. "Jim Smiley and His Jumping Frog" was first published in the New York *Saturday Press* on 18 November 1865. Twain revised the title to include the "Celebrated" when the story was reprinted in the San Francisco *Californian* (16 December). The adjective changes to "Notorious" by the publication of *Sketches, New and Old* (1875).

Chapter 1. The Celebrated Jumping Frog of Calaveras County, and Other Sketches

1. Twain's work — and many of the sketches in this first collection — can usefully be read in the light of Randall Knoper's comments on how his "writerly performances . . . were rehearsals of white masculine identities, and dramatizations and negotiations of the uncertainties that fractured these identities in the later decades of the nineteenth century." *Acting Naturally: Mark Twain in the Culture of Performance* (Berkeley: University of California Press, 1995), 24. It is particularly in the early sketches that Twain invokes "a working-class masculinity of aggression, mockery, posing, and braggadocio," which he sets against "the sincerity and emotional expression of supposedly classless bourgeois domesticity" (35). But it is Twain's cultural ambivalences, and the resulting popularity of his work, on which Knoper mainly focuses: "his [overall] ability to poise his writing in the divide between the middle class and its others" (32).

2. See ETS1, 543. Twain's letter was written on 30 April 1867.

3. Letter of 19 and 20 October 1865, MTL1, 324.

4. In pirated editions by Routledge and John Camden Hotten. Total sales of the various versions of the book in England by Hotten, Routledge, and Chatto & Windus between 1867 and 1902 (barring those resulting from the latter's sale of the book's plates in 1874) were nearly 98,000. American sales by the end of 1868 were only about 2,200 copies, "a disappointing record," whereas Routledge had issued 8,000 copies in that same period. See ETS1, 545, 547, 548, 555. British sales were boosted by the publication of *The Innocents Abroad* (1869), while in America, Twain's dissatisfaction with the *Jumping Frog* book and greater control over the publishing of his work meant that a mere 4,076 copies were printed before, in December 1870, he bought the plates and destroyed them. See Robert H. Hirst, "A Note on the Text," *The Celebrated Jumping Frog of Calaveras County, and Other Sketches.*

5. However unstable such affluence would be. Twain was not good at holding on to his money, and the financial instabilities of his time did not help in this respect.

6. An apparently unsent version of a letter to Andrew Lang, circa 1890, CU-MARK.

7. See MTL1, 322. The original article, on American humor and the "little known" status of Californian writing in the East, was in the *Round Table* of 9 September 1865, ETS1, 31–32.

8. See also Edgar M. Branch, " 'My Voice Is Still for Setchell': A Background Study of 'Jim Smiley and His Jumping Frog,' " in David E. E. Sloane, ed., *Mark*

Twain's Humor: Critical Essays (New York: Garland, 1993), 18, especially on the explicit value Twain placed on laughter and humorous writing in his May 1865 piece, "A Voice for Setchell."

9. Letter of 19 April 1867, MTL2, 27–28.

10. Frederick Anderson, Michael B. Frank, Kenneth M. Sanderson, eds., *Mark Twain's Notebooks & Journals*, vol. 1, *1855–1873* (Berkeley: University of California Press, 1975). See 302 (the "bloated aristocrats" reference) and 307–8. Twain's Sandwich Island letters were commissioned by the Sacramento *Daily Union*. He traveled from 7 March until 13 August 1866. In *Mark Twain: Social Philosopher* (Bloomington: Indiana University Press, 1962), Louis J. Budd writes of the intermittent "suspicions about mass man" that "had assailed Twain almost from the start" and of his "brooding about the democratic process" (62). See also his comments on *Roughing It* (46).

11. Louis J. Budd, "Mark Twain as an American Icon," in Forrest G. Robinson, ed., *The Cambridge Companion to Mark Twain* (Cambridge: Cambridge University Press, 1995), 12.

12. The spirit of Edgar Allan Poe seems to shadow Twain's work on a number of occasions. Here *The Narrative of Arthur Gordon Pym* comes to mind.

13. This argument is developed in Peter Messent, *Mark Twain* (Basingstoke, Hants.: Macmillan, 1997). That book focuses mainly on Twain's novels.

14. Budd, "Mark Twain as an American Icon," 13.

15. ETS1, 29. Richard Bucci speaks of Twain's involvement with the *Californian* as "a milestone in his literary career. . . . [T]his work is more purely literary than any other body of writing he did in the West. It is no surprise . . . that when they came to make the Jumping Frog book, author and editor selected from the *Californian* more frequently than from any other source." See Richard Bucci, AF, *The Celebrated Jumping Frog*, 14.

16. Letter of 1 May 1867 in MTL2, 39. Hirst, in ETS1, notes that when he revised the *Frog* book in 1869, "he corrected sixteen substantive errors in that sketch alone" (541).

17. See MTLP, 70; MTEB, 85–87; ETS1, 545n.

18. MTL2, 369–70. Part of Twain's vehemence can be explained by his cultural circumstances as he wooed a member of the wealthy, liberal, and cultured Langdon family. But, in addition, Hirst speaks of Twain's "basic dissatisfaction with the book . . . with the accuracy of the texts and even with the choice of sketches," ETS1, 555–56.

19. I paraphrase Hirst here and take the quote from him. See ETS1, 542.

20. In that same letter, Twain says of the projected book, "I want to know whether we are going to make anything out of it, first."

21. Twain, especially in these early years, would commonly project a self-image of carelessness and laziness. He says in one letter, for instance, "I am the genius of Indolence." See MTL2, 329.

22. See "A Note on the Cover," in *The Celebrated Jumping Frog*.

23. Randall Knoper, *Acting Naturally*, 59. But see here, too, other like influences in the "host of monolinguists and comedians who, as it was frequently put, specialized in being funny without seemingly realizing it."

24. John Camden Hotten, introduction to *The Complete Works of Artemus Ward* (London: Chatto & Windus, 1905), 35, 36.

25. *Artemus Ward, His Book* (New York: Carleton, 1862), 41–42.

26. Introduction to ETS1, 53–54. Branch is speaking of the period before 1871.

27. A significant issue that affects both these books is their general lack of

textual reliability, the nonauthorial interventions in their production. I address this question in my following two chapters.

28. Throughout this chapter, I take the narrator of the *Jumping Frog* sketches to be "Mark Twain," in one of his various guises.

29. This sketch also satirizes the genre of the sentimental romance as it proceeds. Don Florence notes, too, the identity theme raised here, the speculation about "what constitutes the self. At what point does the unfortunate young man, losing his bodily parts one by one, cease to be the man Aurelia originally loved?" See *Persona and Humor in Mark Twain's Early Writings* (Columbia: University of Missouri Press, 1995), 42.

30. For a useful summary of the "extraordinary range" of Twain's "literary repertoire" in the early work (which includes the shifts of narratorial identity assumed), see Edgar Branch, introduction to ETS1, 52–53. See also Don Florence, *Persona and Humor*.

31. Though he does rely here more on orthographic misspellings than in the "Jumping Frog" sketch. So, e.g., "The within parson, which I have sot to poetry . . . warn't a man to lay back and twidle his thums" (37).

32. Though in some sketches, such as "The Story of the Bad Little Boy," the narrator becomes almost invisible.

33. See ETS2, 125–27. Twain specified *Harper's Weekly* as the source of such "sickly war stories" on first publication of this sketch (128).

34. Roy Blount remarks that this gleeful mocking of sentimental narratives about wartime casualties was "pretty audacious," given its timing and Twain's own Civil War record. See IN, xxxiv.

35. Knoper, *Acting Naturally*, p. 27.

36. And two of the three sketches referred to here would be reprinted in *Sketches, New and Old*.

37. Mark Twain, *Roughing It* (1872), 506–11. And see Richard Bridgman, *Traveling in Mark Twain* (Berkeley: University of California Press, 1987), 39–48. The sketch, like a number in the collection, is a heavily edited and shortened version of Twain's original piece as published in the *Californian* on 26 August 1865. The number of local references in the second half of the original sketch helps to explain the cuts now made. See "The Facts," ETS2, 250–61.

38. Bridgman's analysis of the Greeley letter as an embodiment of "precisely the enigma that Twain himself had to deal with: a scrawled world that yielded a variety of uncertain . . . interpretations" is illuminating here. *Traveling in Mark Twain*, 41.

Chapter 2. Indeterminacy and "The Celebrated Jumping Frog"

1. A number of critics — including Kenneth Lynn in *Mark Twain and Southwestern Humor* (Boston: Little, Brown, 1959), David E. E. Sloane in *Mark Twain as a Literary Comedian* (Baton Rouge: Louisiana State University Press, 1979), and Henry B. Wonham in *Mark Twain and the Art of the Tall Tale* (New York: Oxford University Press, 1993) — see the roots of Twain's humor as extending beyond the bounds of a Western regional tradition. Randall Knoper, in *Acting Naturally*, traces the influence on Twain of a nationwide theatrical tradition, both working and middle class.

2. ETS2, 282–88. Louis J. Budd uses this same text in TSSE1, 171–77.

3. ETS2, 282. Whether it was Webb or Twain himself who changed this opening for the *Jumping Frog* book cannot be firmly established. The evidence, though, points to Webb. See ETS1, 527.

4. That version of the story was evidently "set from a revised copy of [*Mark Twain's Sketches. Number One* (1874)], now lost." Twain revised, but did not extensively alter, the story for that small twenty-five-cent sketchbook. See ETS2, 672 and ETS1, 613.

5. ETS2, 667. See here, too, for plans for a future volume of *Early Tales & Sketches* to include a version of the tale incorporating revisions made by Twain as late as 1874. In his tinkering, Twain would concentrate particularly on the use of dialect terms.

6. ETS1, 556–57. Similar or identical changes did, however, appear in texts issued in 1872 and 1873.

7. Looking at Twain's revisions of the clippings that served as printer's copy for the book, it would seem that this change may well have been Webb's. See ETS1, 533.

8. See ETS2, 288, and Mark Twain, *Sketches, New and Old* (1875), 35. This latter ending, in turn, is a close version of the Doheny version of the text (ETS2, 682). Michelson notes the various changes of title Twain gave the sketch, and nicely comments that "in both name and substance this tale stayed appropriately restless in the retelling." Bruce Michelson, *Mark Twain on the Loose: A Comic Writer and the American Self* (Amherst: University of Massachusetts Press, 1995) 25.

9. Such editorial problems (though most apparent in the *Jumping Frog* book and *Sketches, New and Old*) recur throughout Twain's publishing career. Only in the case of my extended analysis of the particularly problematic "Jumping Frog" story do I give an alternative textual version. I encourage my reader, though, to be aware of the alternative published versions of the short texts. ETS and TSSE use the first printing of a story or sketch as their editorial base.

10. "Mark Twain" is identified only in the *Saturday Press* version of the story. I continue to posit "Mark Twain" as the narrator's identity in line with the construction of the first-person voice in the *Jumping Frog* collection as a whole. The substance of my argument can stand without this identification, though. For convenience, I generally refer to the story simply as "The Jumping Frog" in this chapter and elsewhere. I do not refer further to alterations made to the story's opening and closing following its first printing. Nor do I note in my main text the change from the "Boomerang" of the first printing to Angel's Camp: "Angel's" became standard from an early date. Indeed one cannot now easily think of the sketch without the presence of that distinctive name.

11. I do not note small punctuation differences between the first printing and this textual version. "*O,* curse" in the former becomes, for instance, "*Oh!* hang" in the latter.

12. S. J. Krause sees "at least eight levels of story interest" in the narrative and describes its design in terms of "a nest of boxes." See "The Art and Satire of Twain's 'Jumping Frog' Story," *American Quarterly* 16 (Winter 1964): 563.

13. This would be the fourth level if we take Twain's authorial presence into account. For the moment I am taking the tale as a self-enclosed entity. The move from first to second level occurs with the shift of first-person voice from present to past.

14. The closest critical cousin to my own analysis may be the short but sparkling section in Michelson, *Mark Twain on the Loose*, 25–33. My own reading was devel-

oped separately: an early version of this chapter, "Caught on the Hop: Interpretive Dislocation in 'The Notorious Jumping Frog of Calaveras County,' " came out in *Thalia: Studies in Literary Humor* 15, 1 and 2 (1995): 33–49.

15. See especially "Artemus Ward as Pioneer Funnyman," a chapter in Sloane, *Mark Twain as a Literary Comedian*, 29–44. But the deadpan style was in widespread use in nineteenth-century America and, in Randall Knoper's words, "obviously engaged social conditions that had made trickery and self-betrayal special concerns" (58). For more on this and on Twain's use of deadpan humor as a pivot between "the respectable and the vulgar" (64), see *Acting Naturally*, 55–73.

16. Mark Twain, "How to Tell a Story," in *The Man That Corrupted Hadleyburg and Other Stories and Essays* (1900), 226–27, 230.

17. Kenneth S. Lynn, *Mark Twain and Southwestern Humor*, 146.

18. For further material on the tall tale as a genre, see Henry B. Wonham, *Mark Twain and the Art of the Tall Tale*. He describes the tall tale as one that works through comic exaggeration and plays the boundary between "plausible statements and outrageous assertions." It is the "culturally binding force" of the genre (traditionally an *oral* performance) that particularly interests him: the tall tale as "a comic ritual capable of affirming . . . collective experience, often at the expense of cultural outsiders" (7, 33, 22). For critique, see Messent, "Caught on the Hop."

19. I am very aware of the clumsiness of speaking of Mark Twain as the author of the sketch and of "Mark Twain," a constructed and part-fictional version of the author, as its protagonist. This still, however, seems the best way to proceed in referring to the single-named author, narrator, and protagonist who appears here and in so many of the early sketches and books.

20. Henry B. Wonham, *Mark Twain and the Art of the Tall Tale*, 23. The anonymous voice from outside the building (18) is the only evidence of any other human presence in Angel's Camp.

21. James M. Cox, *Mark Twain: The Fate of Humor* (Princeton, N.J.: Princeton University Press, 1966), 30. Gillman, too, says that "because Simon Wheeler never breaks his own deadpan presentation, we never know exactly who is the duper and who is the duped." Susan Gillman, *Dark Twins: Imposture and Identity in Mark Twain's America* (Chicago: University of Chicago Press, 1989) 22. In written form, deadpan leads to interpretive ambiguity, without clear authorial signalling otherwise. And the same can also be true (though Wonham tends to overlook it) of oral performance.

22. Memory and retelling here might function only as random and eccentric assertions of the self in the context of present dilapidation (8), both of this mining town and perhaps its occupant.

23. I treat "Mark Twain" here as he is represented within the story. A more complex reading could consider further the readers of the story and their variable knowledge of the author and his history.

24. Stuart Hutchinson, *Mark Twain: Humour on the Run* (Amsterdam: Rodopi, 1994) 39. We are then left with the (highly problematic) question of how to distinguish affectation from authenticity. The linguistic uncertainty between standard and vernacular forms in Twain's various versions of the stranger's language (p'ints/points) reinforces the difficulty in, and perhaps the impossibility of, locating his origins.

25. And see the final section of this chapter.

26. Wonham, *Mark Twain and the Art of the Tall Tale*, 35.

27. Paul Baender, "The 'Jumping Frog' as a Comedian's First Virtue," *Modern*

Philology 60 (February 1963): 196. Though the first narrator retrospectively notes the "ridiculous or funny" aspect of Wheeler's performance, the "exquisitely absurd" gap between his serious demeanor and his "queer yarn" (9), no such recognition is visible in his immediate response. And even here the "exquisite" part of the comedy is seen to lie in the nature of the latter gap, rather than in the content of Wheeler's tales. Moreover, the reference to a comic element in Wheeler's story does not apparently lead the first narrator to reconsider his first response ("bore[d] nearly to death," 7–8).

28. It does not matter here if Wheeler's humor may (quite possibly) not be deliberate, for the first narrator nonetheless proves his incompetence as a listener. Twain plays here on the gap between our readerly recognition that this is comic material, *whatever* Wheeler's intentions, and the first narrator's impatience, his very fleeting recognition of this quality.

29. Hutchinson, *Humour on the Run*, 39.

30. This is to trust the tale rather than the teller. See my comments on Twain's later explication of his story in chapter 9.

31. In the tall tale, an audience of "cultural insiders" enjoys the telling of a fictional and hyberbolic narrative. Only the "outsider," lacking "either cultural experience or experience of the genre, or both," is taken in by what at first is the apparent plausibility of the tale. The hoax differs in that "by thoroughly concealing its fictional nature behind the guise of realistic presentation, [it] treats its entire audience in the same way that the tall tale treats only its naïve victim. . . . [T]he perpetration of a hoax occurs at the expense, rather than for the entertainment, of its audience." Henry B. Wonham, *Mark Twain and the Art of the Tall Tale*, 35, 24, 33. See also discussion of "The Stolen White Elephant" in chapter 6.

32. Michelson, *Mark Twain on the Loose*, 31.

33. Thus adding another element to the divisions and victimizations in the narrative and potentially undermining the East-West contrast.

34. "I have a lurking suspicion that your Leonidas W. Smiley is a myth. . . . If that was your design, Mr. Ward, it will gratify you to know that it succeeded" in the *Saturday Press* version.

35. See Michelson's suggestion that the first narrator, "Mark Twain," also plays deadpan here: that we hear "a deadpan narrator telling a tale about another deadpan narrator telling a suspect tale." *Mark Twain on the Loose*, 31.

36. Twain plays throughout the story with notions of inside and outside and their relative (assumed and real) superiority and inferiority. Such categories are continually being turned topsy-turvy.

37. This assumes an analogy: that the first narrator is unwitting victim of Wheeler's tall tales. And see note 27.

38. James Cox's remark that "the stranger's secret act of 'fixing' the jumping contest corresponds to the artist's 'secret' structure which becomes apparent to the reader only after he has been taken in" is apposite here. However, Cox does not develop, and indeed seems to rather fudge, his point. See *Mark Twain: The Fate of Humor*, 29.

39. As the narrator is (possibly) having the wool pulled over his eyes by Wheeler, and as Smiley is (certainly) by the stranger.

40. This possibly happens only right at the end of the tale when we are given the first narrator's final response to Wheeler. Possibly it occurs prior to that point, as we see textual space disappearing on us, without our getting further in terms of narrative progression than a sequence of apparently irrelevant stories, and as we take in the full implications of the first narrator's opening remarks. Even if we

realize much earlier that Wheeler's tales are *one* of the points of Twain's story—and, led by the title, that the frog story is central among these — our full understanding of another of its points can only come with the first narrator's final response to Wheeler and the form that the conclusion to the tale takes.

41. Bruce Michelson, *Mark Twain on the Loose*, 34.

42. Michelson notes: "If others pioneered and even perfected the Southwestern tale, it was Mark Twain who perfected the Southwestern *meta*-tale, the story of a story . . . frame tale stories about being confounded by stories and storytellers, about stories not even getting told, tales and tellers derailing ordinary business, normal thinking, and basic assumptions about identity and real life" (ibid., 26).

43. See Henry B. Wonham, *Mark Twain and the Art of the Tall Tale*, 34–35, 39–40, 54.

44. Ibid., 63. Wonham is discussing one of Twain's earlier 1861 letters from Nevada here, but his words can be applied to this different context.

45. "Anvil" becomes "church" in the 1869 Doheny version and *Sketches, New and Old*.

46. For both quoted meanings of "cavort," see *The Compact Edition of the Oxford English Dictionary* (Oxford: Oxford University Press, 1971), 1: 362. Note that the first meaning of the word (riding in a heedless or purposeless way) is given as tentative.

47. In terms of the reversal motif, the very premise of a man educating a frog to jump dislocates expected norms and categories (animal/human, teacher/pupil, nature/culture, etc.).

48. Edgar M. Branch, " 'My Voice Is Still for Setchell,' " 601. I suggest here, following the first narrator's prompt, that for Wheeler there may be no distinction finally to be made between community insider and outsider and between he who loves games of chance for their own sake and he who coolly exploits the naivete of others to fix the odds in his own favor. This relativism fits the overall frame of my general argument. We are left between options here — as far as models of human behavior go — with any idea of the normative in considerable question.

49. The description of this "mining camp" as "ancient" (8) has been changed to "decayed" by *Sketches, New and Old*.

50. Hutchinson, *Humour on the Run*, 40.

51. See Pascal Covici, *Mark Twain's Humor: The Image of a World* (Dallas: Southern Methodist University Press, 1962), 51, and Lynn, *Mark Twain and Southwestern Humor*, 146–47.

52. See Hutchinson, *Humour on the Run*, 39–40.

53. S. J. Krause, "The Art and Satire of Twain's 'Jumping Frog' Story," 568. Branch, in " 'My Voice Is Still for Setchell,' " suggests that Krause overstates his case. His comment that Twain's references to Webster before 1865 "are not politically hostile" (596) is particularly relevant.

54. Krause, "The Art and Satire of Twain's 'Jumping Frog' Story," 567–68, 576.

55. Lynn, *Mark Twain and Southwestern Humor*, 147.

56. Quote taken from website ⟨www.npg.si.edu/exh/brady/gallery/08gal. html⟩.

57. Neil Schmitz, "Mark Twain, Henry James, and Jacksonian Dreaming," *Criticism* 27 (Spring 1985): 155, 159.

58. Ibid., 159.

59. Wonham, *Mark Twain and the Art of the Tell Tale*, 69.

Chapter 3. Sketches, New and Old

1. ETS1, 617. Twain would continue to reuse some early work, especially "The Jumping Frog." But he would no longer extensively mine this work to build new collections.

2. The sheer mass of this early material, together with the difficulties of recovering it all, means that even the most authoritative texts we have — ETS1 and 2 and TSSE1 and 2 — do not give a complete run of the work.

3. See, for instance, Robert Hirst in ETS1, 635.

4. To William Wright ("De Quille"), circa March 29, 1875. Quoted in ETS1, 618. See, too, Richard Bridgman, *Traveling in Mark Twain* (Berkeley: University of California Press, 1987), 1–13. Note especially the comments on the importance of Twain's newspaper training (2) and his use of the associative mode (9–10) in his travel books.

5. Edgar M. Branch in ETS1, 38. The book sold some 40,000 copies in its first six months of publication (ETS1, 557–58).

6. Hirst, ETS1, 640, 617, 640–41. The book, though, also contained versions of eleven of the twenty-seven pieces in the *Jumping Frog* book. This (*Sketches*) was the only early collection of short pieces to become part of the (later) official Writings of Mark Twain (see ETS1, 617).

7. For discussion of the copyright issue, including the beneficial effects for Twain of these early piracies, see ETS1, 548–53. Twain expended much energy on the matter of proper copyright throughout his life: see, e.g., indexed references to "copyright and piracy" in Andrew Hoffman, *Inventing Mark Twain: The Lives of Samuel Langhorne Clemens* (London: Weidenfeld & Nicolson, 1997) and (for another angle on the issue) Susan Gillman, *Dark Twins*, 182–88.

8. All page references in this section to Robert Hirst in ETS1 unless otherwise noted.

9. For a fuller history of Twain's publishing relations with Bliss, see MTEB.

10. Twain's initial motives may have been to ensure that material he had not in fact written, or with which he was now dissatisfied, would be withdrawn from, or revised for, the British market. He was soon, however, to replace Routledge with Chatto & Windus as his authorized British publisher.

11. TSSE1 generally relies on ETS1 and 2. Usefully, it includes many sketches that have still to appear in the *Early Tales & Sketches* series, in the form in which they will then be published.

12. Thus the more genteel "cuspidor" replaced "spittoon," "d——d" became "hanged," etc. See ETS1, 606–7. Hirst also shows how, as Twain revised sketches from Hotten's *Jumping Frog* book for the 1874 *Humorous Works*, he "often found that they needed more . . . pruning than later material did" (607).

13. Hirst himself is reluctant to abandon the value of this book, arguing for the need for "a critical edition" in order to retain "the selection and revision of sketches which Mark Twain shrewdly if somewhat carelessly offered in [it]" (657). I accept the problematic textual status of this and the *Jumping Frog* collection but give my reasons for using them, given the absence of the type of editions that Hirst and I would like available. In this chapter, I retain the book text as published. Again, though, I would direct my reader to ETS1 and 2 and TSSE1 for comparison with the earlier and what Louis J. Budd calls "the freshest and most biting versions" of these texts (TSSE1, 998).

14. See ETS1, 618–19. Other factors were involved, too. See, e.g., Twain's brother, Orion Clemens, and his attack on Bliss's "double-dealing" over *Roughing*

It (MTEB, 64–67). Twain's negotiations with Osgood started in 1872, but it was in the winter of 1874–75 that Twain began seriously to prepare the volume of sketches (ETS1, 619).

15. Hirst points out how far this book differed from *The Innocents Abroad* in Bliss's editorial interventions. Here, but only here, "Bliss clearly felt free to revise a text merely to meet the physical and aesthetic demands of the page" (ETS1, 644).

16. This, where Twain had left a sketch unrevised. "Because [the editions of *Humorous Works* and *Sketches*] evolved independently, their texts are almost never identical" (ETS1, 643).

17. The sketch is still listed in the contents of the Oxford Mark Twain reprint, but it has been removed from the main text.

18. As in this case, the titles given at the head of the sketches and stories themselves do not always match those printed in the book's table of contents. For consistency, I use the former.

19. Don Florence, *Persona and Humor in Mark Twain's Early Writings* (Columbia: University of Missouri Press, 1995). 11, 21.

20. Ibid., 7, 33.

21. Thus Florence's view of *Roughing It* (1872) as the culmination of such aspects of Twain's early comic talents can be contrasted with the reading of the novel given in Peter Messent, *Mark Twain*, 44–64, contrasting the narrative's "interpretive indeterminacy" with its "clear sense of history, unmuddied by any sense of interpretive disablement" (57).

22. See CR, 151.

23. Florence, *Persona and Humor in Mark Twain's Early Writings*, 56, 2. I do not explore here the relationship of sameness and difference between the authorial Mark Twain and his creator Samuel L. Clemens.

24. Though my later analysis of this piece suggests how the two (author and narrator/character) then swiftly diverge.

25. The author's voice is silent but implicit. I note, however, in this case, the difficulty, and perhaps impossibility, of interpreting what is in essence a double deadpan. A naive narrator "fronts" for an authorial figure whose own attitude (dismissively racist or humanely satirical) to the Indian remains unknown within the sketch's frame.

26. Where "Twain" is not named, the illustrations nonetheless identify him.

27. "Tadpole" breaks the illusion of a coherent narrative voice and lets us know definitively that this is burlesque. As Twain projects a persona then, he also authorially undermines it. Twain's original pieces for the *Buffalo Express*, "the best of [which] were reprinted in *Sketches New and Old*" (xliii), are collected in Joseph B. McCullough and Janice McIntire-Strasburg, *Mark Twain at the Buffalo Express: Articles and Sketches by America's Favorite Humorist* (Urbana: University of Illinois Press, 1999). There are some considerable variations between newspaper and book versions. Thus while "My Watch — An Instructive Little Tale" is virtually the same in each printing, the book version of "A Visit to Niagara" is very different from that which appeared in the *Express*. The introduction to McCullough and McIntire-Strasburg's book (xiii–xlvii) provides useful critical and contextual material.

28. The sketch is better known as "Personal Habits of the Siamese Twins" (as in the table of contents. See Clark Griffith, *Achilles and the Tortoise* (Tuscaloosa: University of Alabama Press, 1998), 21–52, for commentary on this story and the implications of the comedy of twinship in Twain.

29. See also 211–12. I return to the subject of twinning and the relationship between comedy and matters of more serious cultural concern in my final chapter on "A Double-Barreled Detective Story." If this present sketch showed more sign of taking itself seriously, there would be a temptation to read the "which . . . the captor, and which the captive" sequence as a possible allegorical reference to the North-South Siamese connection in the Civil War and after.

30. Florence, *Persona and Humor in Mark Twain's Early Writings*, 5.

31. In the chapter on *The Innocents Abroad* in *Mark Twain*, 22–43, I examine the shifting and slippery nature of "Mark Twain's" identity in one of his full-length narratives.

32. Twain reports that "Susie is croupy" to Howells on 15 January 1875 (MTHL1, 60). He seems then to have written the story before his 12 February letter to Osgood (see ETS1, 623, 625).

33. This is Twain's only book of short works, among those I examine here, that is fully illustrated (by True Williams), and this makes considerable difference to the reader's reception of the text. See Beverly R. David and Ray Sapirstein, "Reading the Illustrations in *Sketches, New and Old*" in the Oxford Mark Twain edition, AF, 23–24. David's commentary on the book in *Mark Twain and His Illustrators*, vol. 2 (Troy, N.Y.: Whitston, 1999) can also be usefully read alongside my chapter. The *New York Times* review of the book (29 October 1875) noted that it "abounds with illustrations, some of which are almost as funny as the text." See CR, 150.

34. Twain's early tales often have a violent element to them. Readings are pertinent here that locate Twain in the tradition of frontier literature and/or "a style of rowdy . . . masculinity" (Randall Knoper, *Acting Naturally*, 41).

35. This, in turn, was a thin cover for James Nye, the other Nevada senator. Nye's name is given in full in the first published version of the sketch.

36. Any such judgment is necessarily subjective.

37. In fact, Twain refers to "The Petrified Man" as burlesque (239), satire (240), swindle and humbuggery (241), but not as a hoax. This suggests both the flexible nature of the humor and the overlapping nature of these terms.

38. This, in turn, seems fraudulent: Budd finds no evidence of its appearance in the *Lancet*. See TSSE1, 1049. Twain writes about other hoaxes here, in "A Ghost Story" and "Legend of a Capitoline Venus." The former was based on the successful Cardiff Giant hoax of the 1860s. The Giant can still be seen in the Farmers' Museum at Cooperstown, New York.

39. Thus Don Florence writes: "Twain's hoaxes . . . at times . . . suggest a vision of the world. . . . Twain implies there are no sure standards of knowledge by which to determine what is false . . . and what is true." *Persona and Humor in Mark Twain's Early Writings*, 32–33. See also Bruce Michelson, *Mark Twain on the Loose*, 14–17, and Susan Gillman, *Dark Twins*, 14–16.

40. Bruce Michelson, *Mark Twain on the Loose*, 15.

41. Indeed we might see satire and hoax as coexistent but incompatible forms here. Only the reader who is, or becomes, aware of the hoax can fully appreciate the satire.

42. See his letter to Orion and Mollie Clemens on 21 October 1862 (some two weeks after first publication), speaking of the sketch as an "unmitigated lie, made from whole cloth," MTL1, 242.

43. Again see *Mark Twain on the Loose*, 15–16. Michelson's comments on the anonymity of the author in the original version of the sketch are also relevant here.

44. See Maria Ornella Marotti, *The Duplicating Imagination: Twain and the Twain Papers* (University Park: Pennsylvania State University Press, 1990) 31–32 .

45. The M.T. in brackets seems to be yet a further version of the Twain persona, more closely related to the narrator than to the authorial figure we might expect. And see Twain's letter to his wife, Olivia: "Got a French version of the Jumping Frog—fun is no name for it. I am going to translate it *literally*, French construction & all (apologising in parenthesis where a word is too many for me) & publish it in the Atlantic as the grave effort of a man who does not know but what he is as good a French scholar as there is — & sign my name to it, without another word. It will be toothsome reading." Dixon Wecter, ed., *The Love Letters of Mark Twain* (New York: Harper, 1949) 183.

46. Florence downplays this, suggesting, for instance, that where we find a satiric voice in the early sketches it has a tendency to "erup[t] into such nonsense that absurdity may overwhelm satire," *Persona and Humor in Mark Twain's Early Writings*, 41.

47. Such stances are not always consistent. The varying times of narrative composition often explain this fact (see my next chapter). Sometimes, as in the area of race and ethnicity, Twain's prejudices and sympathies can vary widely from group to group, particularly in this early period

48. Though we can identify satire here, it is — as so often — difficult to comment on its relation to Twain's own life. He may be recognizing personal culpability in such generally accepted financial practices. If so, the critique still remains.

49. See Susan K. Harris, *The Courtship of Olivia Langdon and Mark Twain* (Cambridge: Cambridge University Press, 1996), 146–48.

50. See his "Map of Paris" (1870) and Twain's own comments on the "periodical and sudden changes of mood in me, from deep melancholy to . . . cyclones of humor" that resulted from his and his wife's wretched personal circumstances at the time. See Jeffrey Steinbrink, *Getting to Be Mark Twain* (Berkeley: University of California Press, 1991) 136–38. Susan Harris refers to a similar outburst of comic wildness as a form of "carnivalesque release" in *The Courtship of Olivia Langdon and Mark Twain*, 148.

Chapter 4. "A True Story" and "Some Learned Fables, for Good Old Boys and Girls"

1. He is referring to "The Experiences of the McWilliamses with Membranous Croup," "Some Learned Fables" (both published in 1875), "A Curious Pleasure Excursion," and "A True Story" (both from 1874). For a list of the most recently written pieces contained in the book and first publication details, see AF, 11–12.

2. This is another case where the relation between authorial voice and projected fictional persona becomes difficult to distinguish. If the sketch is fictional, the lesson learned by the narrator — that "a healthy . . . cheerfulness is not necessarily impossible to *any* occupation" (249) — seems direct authorial comment on human nature.

3. See Huck's use of "warn't particular" and the composite "I took a . . . stretch, and . . . laid there . . . comfortable," in *Adventures of Huckleberry Finn* (1885), 19, 58, 61.

4. Neil Schmitz, "Mark Twain's Civil War: Humor's Reconstructive Writing," in Forrest G. Robinson, *Cambridge Companion to Mark Twain*, 82. Schmitz's brief analysis is a stimulating one, and I use it as a springboard for my own critical work.

5. MTHL1, 22–26. This was Twain's first publication in the highly respectable literary journal. In December 1874, in a letter to Howells, he famously referred to

the *Atlantic* readers as "the only audience that . . . don't require a 'humorist' to paint himself stripèd & stand on his head every fifteen minutes" (49).

6. Even though, in the same memoir, he mentions that the owner of the *Atlantic Monthly* had "always believed that Mark Twain was literature." See MTHL1, 26.

7. There may also be something of that tendency toward "hypercanonization" that Jonathan Arac speaks of (in relation to Twain's much-celebrated novel) in *Huckleberry Finn as Idol and Target: The Functions of Criticism in Our Time* (Madison: University of Wisconsin Press, 1997).

8. See, for instance, Herbert A. Wisbey, Jr., "The True Story of Auntie Cord," *Mark Twain Society Bulletin* 4, 2 (June 1981): 1–5.

9. Shelley Fisher Fishkin quotes a previously unpublished memoir on the impact the story had on Twain: "[Mary Ann Cord] told me a striking tale out of her personal experience . . . & I will copy it here — & not in my words but her own . . . strong & simple speech. . . . I wrote [her words] down before they were cold." See *Lighting Out for the Territory: Reflections on Mark Twain and American Culture* (New York: Oxford University Press, 1996), 85. But Makoto Nagawara points out inconsistencies in various reports of the story's composition in " 'A True Story' and Its Manuscript: Mark Twain's Image of the American Black," *Poetica: An International Journal of Linguistic Literary Studies* 29/30 (1989): 144.

10. SSF, 59. I would recommend caution in such an identification. Not all Twain's readers would have known his identity as Samuel Clemens. Schmitz implicitly refuses the connection: "The interlocutor is a Northern liberal gentleman who didn't request the story he receives, doesn't even want to hear it." "Mark Twain's Civil War," 82.

11. See Wisbey, "The True Story of Auntie Cord."

12. Unpublished memorandum, 13 August 1982, by Emory G. Evans, University of Maryland, following an interview with Leon Condoll (spelled as Condol in Wisbey and Fishkin), Cord's great-grandson. Evidently the plantation owner, a Mr. Crumle, "took [Henry] into his home." The implication of this memoir is that Henry escaped from Crumle's, *and there is no reference here or in Wisbey to any auction scene.* Wisbey reports that the real-life recognition scene between Cord and her son also depended on an exchanged ring (3). Evans's memorandum gives a slightly different version of this, confirms the detail of the ring, but adds that it was given to Henry by Crumle's wife (CU-MARK).

13. Justin Kaplan, *Mr. Clemens and Mark Twain* (Harmondsworth: Penguin, 1970), 277.

14. See Nagawara, " 'A True Story' and Its Manuscript," 144, 145.

15. Neil Schmitz asks, "What are the familial traces? What are the documentary texts?" in this "African American family history." "In 'A True Story,' " he responds, "there is just a saying. . . . And a scar, to recognize." "Mark Twain's Civil War," 83.

16. The original words are deleted and not easy to read. Nagawara, I think, misinterprets them in " 'A True Story' and Its Manuscript," 151. I work here from a copy of the manuscript in the Mark Twain Papers. Mark Twain's previously unpublished words are copyright © 2001 by Richard A. Watson and Chase Manhattan Bank as Trustees of the Mark Twain Foundation, which reserves all reproduction or dramatization rights in every medium. Quotation is made with the permission of the University of California Press and Robert H. Hirst, General Editor of the Mark Twain Project. Subsequent quotations from previously unpublished words by Mark Twain are also copyright © 2001 and are signaled by an asterisk (*) in their citation.

17. SSF, 59. Quirk sees the use of an unmasked personal presence as "remov[ing] the armor of his literary persona [Mark Twain] in order to absorb more completely the guilt and humiliation that properly belongs to him." An alternative reading with an anonymous first narrator is entirely justified, and still allows a provisional reconstruction of the authorial value scheme.

18. "[T]he outrageous ignorance/innocence of the interlocutor's casual remark . . . abruptly cuts Aunt Rachel's uproarious laughter off. . . . [T]he lie of the euphemism ['trouble'] . . . snaps into sharp focus her relation to Misto C and his family, her alienated difference." Neil Schmitz, "Mark Twain's Civil War," 82.

19. Ibid., 83.

20. See Alan Trachtenberg, *The Incorporation of America: Culture and Society in the Gilded Age* (New York: Hill and Wang, 1982), 190. And see 184–93 generally.

21. Thus Neil Schmitz says: " 'A True Story' . . . redirects Southern writing, turns comic dialect sketch into serious testimony," "Mark Twain's Civil War," 83.

22. Ibid., p. 82.

23. That is, if we allow for Quirk's autobiographical reading, at least in the northern liberal context of Quarry Farm, Elmira.

24. Makoto Nagawara shows how Twain revised the manuscript to place emphasis on Rachel's "poses and gestures." " 'A True Story' and Its Manuscript," 146.

25. Prolepsis is anticipatory: the telling of a story-event that is to happen later. This is information denied to Aunt Rachel at the time of the event now being retold.

26. The spatial dynamics of the piece become a little problematic at this point given the prior "towered above." Presumably, Rachel is now stooping as she acts out her role.

27. Eric Lott, in "Mr. Clemens and Jim Crow: Twain, Race, and Blackface," suggests that Twain's "very language of race" was "furnished" by blackface minstrelsy (149) and that, consequently, his fiction generally is marked by an ambivalent and contradictory representation of race. See the *Cambridge Companion to Mark Twain*, 129–52. In "A True Story," Rachel and her mother's comic dismissal of other lower-class "niggers" as "trash" could be seen in this light.

28. The considerable influence that Olivia Langdon's family and its circle had on Twain in this matter is generally accepted. The fact that the incident on which the story is based took place at the Elmira home of Susy Crane, Olivia's adopted sister, is thus not merely coincidental. The story, too, starts to take Twain back to the subject matter, time, and place of his southern boyhood. He was writing *Tom Sawyer* at exactly the same time (summer 1874). The memories into which he was tapping, and the different approaches to his material (for in *Tom Sawyer* slavery is not a major issue), may suggest stages in a process toward the writing of *Huckleberry Finn*.

29. MTHL1, 24. The Sisyphus/Atlas reference does not appear in the *Sketches, New and Old* version of the story. Smith and Gibson suggest that "Clemens probably revised the piece" before this book publication (MTHL2, 863).

30. MTHL2, 863. Smith and Gibson comment that the story "is not up to Mark Twain's best or even his average standard, and it does contain possible grounds of offence." I would disagree with the first half of this statement. As to the second, the same can be said of much of the best comic writing. The quote attributed to Professor Wood-louse is wrongly made: it is part of the expedition's official report.

31. The two satiric strands in the narrative are partly brought together at its end. See where the "obscene" Tumble-Bug links human scientific knowledge to

the impulse to know and understand divine purposes (148). In his valuable essay, "Mark Twain on Scientific Investigation: Contemporary Allusions in 'Some Learned Fables for Good Old Boys and Girls,' " Howard Baetzhold pins down the numerous "hidden allusions to people and events actually featured in the news shortly before and during the time that Twain was writing his story" (136). See Robert Falk, ed., *Literature and Ideas in America: Essays in Memory of Harry Hayden Clark* (Athens: Ohio University Press, 1975), 128–54. Baetzhold sees Twain's satire as aimed not at "science and scientists *per se*" but at "human presumption and gullibility" as a whole (151–52).

32. See the public interest in 1873 and 1874 "over international plans to observe the rare astronomical phenomenon, the transit of Venus across the face of the sun, which was to occur on December 8, 1874." Baetzhold, "Mark Twain on Scientific Investigation," 138.

33. See Beverly R. David and Ray Sapirstein, "Reading the Illustrations in *Sketches, New and Old*" (AF, 22) in the Oxford Mark Twain edition.

34. See Howard Baetzhold, "Mark Twain on Scientific Investigation," 145–46.

35. Barnum's five-story American Museum contained, as one of its many exhibits, "a collection of wax figures — some, like the one of Queen Victoria, notoriously bad." A. H. Saxon, *P. T. Barnum: The Legend and the Man* (New York: Columbia University Press, 1989), 93.

36. See "Mark Twain on Scientific Investigation," 149. Baetzhold suggests Alfred Russell Wallace as a possible source, as well as Darwin himself.

37. Sherwood Cummings, *Mark Twain and Science: Adventures of a Mind* (Baton Rouge: Louisiana State University Press, 1988), 13.

38. See Baetzhold, "Mark Twain on Scientific Investigation," 150.

39. See chapter 10 of this book, as well as my comments on *Huckleberry Finn* and the carnivalesque in Peter Messent, *New Readings of the American Novel* (Houndmills, Basingstoke: Macmillan, 1990), 212–14.

40. The status of this log is not fully explained at this stage of the narrative. Later reference is made to an "official report" (141) but presumably this incident would not be included there.

41. For Mikhail Bakhtin, carnival is associated with a laughter directed "toward a shift of authorities and truths" and the relativisation "of all structure and order, of all authority and all (hierarchical) position." Something of this occurs in this scene, if the carnivalistic process (with its switching of social roles) remains incomplete. See *Problems of Dostoevski's Poetics*, trans. Caryl Emerson (Manchester: Manchester University Press, 1984), 127, 124.

42. The Tumble-Bug reports pragmatically what he sees. But the (countering) necessary human need to construct organizing and general systems of knowledge is also emphasized.

43. Mark Twain, *A Connecticut Yankee in King Arthur's Court* (1889), 224–25.

44. My reading here borrows from Richard Boyd Hauck, *A Cheerful Nihilism: Confidence and "The Absurd" in American Humorous Fiction* (Bloomington: Indiana University Press, 1971), 137–38.

45. Letter VII, in Mark Twain, *Letters from the Earth*, ed. Bernard DeVoto (New York: Harper and Row, 1962), 30. According to R. Kent Rasmussen, "Letters from the Earth" was "the last substantial manuscript that Mark Twain wrote." Written in 1909, it was unpublished during Twain's lifetime. AZ, 280–82.

46. "Was the World Made for Man?" in *Letters from the Earth*, 212–13, 215–16. See also "The Lowest Animal," 176. DeVoto tentatively dates the material from this section of the book between 1897 and 1909 (see 292).

47. *Three Thousand Years Among the Microbes*, in John S. Tuckey, ed., *Mark Twain's Which Was the Dream? and Other Symbolic Writings of the Later Years* (Berkeley: University of California Press, 1967), 497.

48. Hauck's discussion of Twain in *A Cheerful Nihilism*, 133–66, is of relevance here, though I do not always agree with his conclusions.

49. As I have shown in my previous chapter, the comedy of relativism and indeterminacy marks Twain's humor from the first. But it is in the late work that we see the particular focus both on moves between alternative universes and on concepts of history and evolutionary change that spur my comparisons here.

50. See also my general analysis of Twain's late works in chapter eight of Messent, *Mark Twain*.

Chapter 5. The Stolen White Elephant, Etc.

1. Everett Emerson, *The Authentic Mark Twain: A Literary Biography of Samuel L. Clemens* (Philadelphia: University of Pennsylvania Press, 1984), 118. See also MTEB, 123.

2. Bernard De Voto, ed., *Mark Twain in Eruption* (New York: Harper, 1940), 158. Contemporary reviews were (perhaps predictably) mixed. So the *Chicago Inter Ocean* was relatively positive about the book: "the humor [in some of these sketches] is of the rollicking kind that takes a man by force" (24 June 1882, 10). The *New York Tribune* was more critical: "[Twain's] humor veils its flame; retires, in fact, to the intellectual attic, and draws up the ladder" (18 June 1882, 8). See CR, 224, 222.

3. See RG, 183. Also MTEB, 123 ("Mark Twain had a problem").

4. Frederick Anderson, Lin Salamo, and Bernard L. Stein, eds., *Mark Twain's Notebooks & Journals*, vol. 2, *1877–1883* (Berkeley: University of California Press, 1975), 3–4.

5. Everett Emerson, "The Strange Disappearance of Mark Twain," *American Literature* 13 (Autumn 1985): 143–55. Emerson sees the "old authentic Western Mark Twain" (152) and the language and points of view associated with that persona virtually abandoned in this period. See also Emerson's *Mark Twain: A Literary Life* (Philadelphia: University of Pennsylvania Press, 2000) — a book that comments usefully, though usually briefly, on a good number of Twain's short stories and sketches. In fact, the "Mark Twain" persona was still used, but not so frequently nor to such diverse effect.

6. See, e.g., Twain's letter to Osgood in November 1881 about the possible journal publication of "Mental Telegraphy": "Now here is my idea: send it . . . but strike out the nom de plume, and sign it *S. Langhorne*. . . . There is not a statement in the article which is . . . untrue. . . . Yet there isn't one in it which would be believed, with my nom de plume at the bottom." MTLP, 145.

7. Justin Kaplan, *Mr. Clemens and Mark Twain*, 325. Kaplan's comment here refers to the "portents of declining creativity" which he too identifies with this period.

8. Slote's firm produced and marketed Twain's scrapbook. And it was Slote who involved Twain in his heavy investments (which were to lose him some $50,000) in the Kaolatype process for making engraved printing plates. See AZ, 268, 432.

9. For further details, see Merle Johnson, *A Bibliography of the Works of Mark Twain, Revised and Enlarged* (Westport, Conn.: Greenwood Press, 1974), 32.

10. Merle Johnson, in *A Bibliography of the Works of Mark Twain*, gives no details of

this or of any other collections of Twain's stories and sketches where no American publication of the same title is involved. See, though, Robert M. Rodney, *Mark Twain International: A Bibliography and Interpretation of His Worldwide Popularity* (Westport, Conn.: Greenwood Press, 1982) to help fill such gaps.

11. Letter from Chatto and Windus to Osgood and Company, of 25 May 1882, CU-MARK. And see Dennis Welland, *Mark Twain in England* (London: Chatto and Windus, 1978), 108. In fact, six of the eighteen items overlapped. The longest item in *An Idle Excursion* is "Old Times on the Mississippi."

12. Subscription publishing was the avoiding of normal trade outlets (in theory, though not always in practice) in favor of large numbers of agents with prospectuses. These agents made direct contact with potential customers throughout the country, especially in isolated communities, and took orders for the books they promoted both in advance of and following publication. For further details, see MTEB.

13. MTEB, 121, 125. The story of Twain's relationship with Osgood would be complicated by the role of Charles L. Webster, Twain's nephew by marriage and an employee of both Osgood and Twain. Webster was responsible for organizing the new subscription side of Osgood's firm. See MTLP, 129–31.

14. See De Voto, *Mark Twain in Eruption*, for Twain's later comments on the "mighty botch" (157) Osgood made of subscription publishing (with reference to *Life on the Mississippi*). The writer's own part in the botch goes unrecognized, as might be expected. Twain writes: "I should have continued with Osgood after his failure with *The Prince and the Pauper* because I liked him so well, but he failed and I had to go elsewhere" (158).

15. MTLP, 152–53. Isabel Lyon, in Twain's employment from 1902 until 1909, and his private secretary from 1904, would later dismissively remark: "Twenty years after 1882, how Mr. Clemens would have hated this cheap attempt at a humorously ungrammatical letter. . . . It would never have been sent, had Mrs. Clemens seen it" (note dated 9 July 1936, CU-MARK).

16. This resumé by Mark Twain is copyright © 2001 by Richard A. Watson and Chase Manhattan Bank as Trustees of the Mark Twain Foundation, which reserves all reproduction or dramatization rights in every medium. It is published here with the permission of the University of California Press and Robert H. Hirst, General Editor of the Mark Twain Project.

There are two pages to the resumé. Page 1 ends with "make *two* books." The lines (reproduced here) separating the sections of the first page are Twain's. Twain's reference in the March 4 letter to both the envelopes and the 93,000 words suggests his "resumé" was written at that time. But a letter from Osgood to Twain on 15 March 1882 somewhat muddies the picture of the selection process. Osgood speaks here of exploring "the '*Atlantic*' files for your short articles." He names thirteen of these, some of which overlap with Twain's own list ("Carnival of Crime," "Mrs. McWilliams and the Lightning," etc.), some of which had already appeared in *Punch, Brother, Punch!* (e.g. "Some Rambling Notes"), and some of which had been published in previous Twain books (*A Tramp Abroad* and *Sketches, New and Old*). He also refers to other stories and sketches about which Howells had told him (including "nuggets in 'The Contributor's Club'"). He says, "I have ordered all the Atlantics—do you want me to send them?" This letter seems to have had little impact on the selection process. CU-MARK, and see MTHL1, 398.

An undated letter from Twain to Osgood reads: "I reckon I can get the Sketches ready in time, though publishing books don't pay for the trouble of writing them—only this one don't *have* to be written," MTLP, 155. This would seem logically to precede his March 4 letter, but Hamlin Hill places it later, between letters of April 7 and June 9.

17. "Speech on the Babies" replaces the "Speech at a Dinner of the Knights of St. Patrick" of *Punch, Brother, Punch!*

18. CU-MARK. The editors of MTHL1 apparently did not have this letter available. Their conclusions on page 400, therefore, need modifying. Some of the final parts of Howells's letter are difficult to read, but I am reasonably confident this transcription is correct. The slight muddle over numbers here (see 10 and 12, and the two 16s) is carried over from Howells's letter. The numbers given are those (in pencil) to which Howells refers.

19. An editorial note then reads, "The rest of the letter is missing." See MTHL1, 400. Nothing in Howells's letter indicates the eight pieces that might be omitted, though his numbering might imply them. It may be that the two men had spoken together about the matter.

20. "The Great Revolution in Pitcairn" was also first intended for *A Tramp Abroad*. See RG, 141.

21. I do not give such details in chapters 1 and 3 because of the sheer number of sketches included (in the latter case) and because of the availability of ETS1 and ETS2 and the critical work they contain. For more detailed information on first publication details of many of the pieces to which I refer, see the two TSSE volumes.

22. "On the Decay of the Art of Lying" and "Speech on the Babies" were also first published in the collection.

23. The joke Howells refers to is the following: "We went ashore and found a novelty of a pleasant nature: there were no hackmen, hacks, or omnibuses on the pier . . . and nobody offered his services to us, or molested us in any way. I said it was like being in heaven. The Reverend rebukingly and rather pointedly advised me to make the most of it, then" (66–67). In the Howells quote I condense two separate responses. Andrew Chatto, Twain's English publisher, also evidently enjoyed the articles. MTHL1, 185, 190, 193.

24. MTHL1, 179. A tripartite relationship emerges here between Twain the public personality, Twain the traveler (with the assumed name), and the use of the Mark Twain persona in the sketch.

25. This type of humor, focusing on death, physical disability, etc., is common in Twain's early writing and still occurs at this stage of his career. See, e.g., the gratuitous comment on the "man with the hare lip" in this travel piece (89). The influence of Howells, his wife Olivia, and others, would increasingly modify, though not obliterate, this side of Twain. Marcel Gutwirth's comments on taboo and the way that "the culture's unspoken anxieties are rehearsed, made manageable in . . . laughable exhibition" provides an analytic point of entry to this kind of comedy. See LM, 48.

26. See Richard Bridgman, *Traveling in Mark Twain* (Berkeley: University of California Press, 1987) for perceptive discussion of Twain's use of the travel writing form.

27. Emerson, "The Strange Disappearance of Mark Twain," 148.

28. John Seelye, introduction to *The Adventures of Tom Sawyer* (London: Penguin, 1986), xi.

29. For further unpacking of this double reading of the book see Peter Messent, *Mark Twain*, 65–85.

30. I do not use quotation marks here to distinguish author from narrator-

protagonist. This is partly for convenience, partly (in the context of Twain's prior work) because of the comparatively reduced nature of that gap.

31. The quote is from Ronald T. Takaki as he discusses *A Connecticut Yankee* in *Iron Cages: Race and Culture in Nineteenth-Century America* (London: Athlone, 1979), 166. Also see 169–70.

32. A third such possibility might be found in the creation and function of humor itself. See my brief comments on this subject as I discuss "The Facts Concerning the Recent Carnival of Crime in Connecticut." See, too, my next chapter.

33. Quirk makes an astute connection between this narrative of private life and Twain's public role. He recalls the letter to Howells about not needing to "paint himself stripèd & stand on his head" for an *Atlantic* readership, to say: "This remark is all the more poignant when one remembers that not long after that letter, Twain wrote the first of [the McWilliams stories], each story picturing a man going through just these sorts of antics." SSF, 62–63.

34. The phrase is Twain's own. See Gladys Bellamy, *Mark Twain as a Literary Artist* (Norman: University of Oklahoma Press, 1950), 135.

35. At several points in this chapter (and see Howells's response to the joke that "nearly killed" his wife) the transgression of social mores is expressed in two registers that invoke each other: humor and murder. Can one detect here, however obscurely, the idea in Twain that there is something fundamentally violent about writing, joking, making people laugh? And what happens to the *self* when it is constantly killing everybody with fatal jokes? A sense of terrible loneliness lurks here. I am in debt to Sam Halliday and his response to a draft version of this chapter.

36. SSF, 64. Quirk gives a good short analysis of the story, 64–69. And see Gregg Camfield, *Sentimental Twain: Samuel Clemens in the Maze of Moral Philosophy* (Philadelphia: University of Pennsylvania Press, 1994), 116–20, for discussion of Twain's juxtaposition of conflicting ideas about conscience in the story.

37. And see, too, Twain's recent reading of a book that would heavily influence his thinking, W. E. H. Lecky, *History of European Morals from Augustine to Charlemagne* (1869).

38. Andrew Hoffman says Twain's own consumption of cigars was typically thirty a day. *Inventing Mark Twain*, 344.

39. One crucial aspect of the story is this perversity of conscience: its status as a "master" driving its human "slave" (115), able to make the latter feel guilty whatever the nature of his actions. I leave this subject undeveloped as it forms something of a side issue to my present concerns. But it does counter any notion of conscience as a measure of essential right or wrong.

40. See especially T. Jackson Lears, *No Place of Grace: Antimodernism and the Transformation of American Culture, 1880–1920* (New York: Pantheon, 1981). Twain is writing here in the period just prior to that Lears considers. The latter's arguments, however, can still be applied.

41. As critics have previously noted. See, e.g., Howard G. Baetzhold, *Mark Twain and John Bull: The British Connection* (Bloomington: Indiana University Press, 1970), 45.

42. Twain's satire, however, is aimed in two directions. As in *A Connecticut Yankee*, the tale, which was written following Twain's reading of Carlyle, suggests (despite its ending) a "contempt for the ignorance and political incapacity of the masses" (142).

43. In my use of material on Beard and technology here and below, I am indebted to an M.A. dissertation, "Electricity and American Modernity: Electrical Science and Technology in Nineteenth-Century American Culture," by a former student, Sam Halliday. This is now in the library at the University of Nottingham. I thank the author for his permission to quote from it.

44. George M. Beard, *A Practical Treatise on Nervous Exhaustion (Neurasthenia): Its Symptoms, Nature, Sequences, Treatment* , ed. A. D. Rockwell (London: H. K. Lewis, 1890 [1869]), 31.

45. "Electricity and American Modernity," 11.

46. George M. Beard, *American Nervousness: Its Causes and Consequences* (New York: G. P. Putnam, 1881), 99. Beard is writing about the human body and Edison's electric light, and tracing connections between them.

47. Ibid., vi.

48. Based on Twitchell, as in "Some Rambling Notes."

49. See also Wolfgang Schivelbusch, *The Railway Journey: The Industrialization of Time and Space in the Nineteenth Century* (Leamington Spa: Berg, 1986), chap. 7, "The Pathology of the Railroad Journey." Schivelbusch quotes Russell Reynolds, "Travelling: Its Influence on Health" (1884): "There is pulling at the eyeballs on looking out of the window; a jarring noise, the compound of continuous noise of wheels, and this conducted into the framework of the compartment; with the obligato of whistle and of the brake dashing in occasionally, and always carrying some element of annoyance, surprise, or shock. . . . The eyes are strained, the ears are dinned, the muscles are jostled . . . and the nerves are worried by the attempt to maintain order" (118).

50. Halliday, "Electricity and American Modernity," 12. He borrows his final term from Anson Rabinbach, *The Human Motor: Energy, Fatigue, and the Origins of Modernity* (Berkeley: University of California Press, 1990).

51. Frank Baldanza, *Mark Twain: An Introduction and Interpretation* (New York: Holt, Rinehart and Winston, 1961), 100.

52. See Floyd R. Horowitz, "Mark Twain's Belle Lettre in 'The Loves of Alonzo Fitz Clarence and Rosannah Ethelton.' " Horowitz describes the type of phone Twain features and its rapid consequent development. See *Mark Twain Journal* 13, 1 (Winter 1965–66): 16. The telephone was patented by Alexander Graham Bell in 1876.

53. The phrase is Halliday's in "Electricity and American Modernity," 1, although he is not referring just to the 1870s.

54. See David E. Nye, *Electrifying America: Social Meanings of a New Technology, 1880–1940* (Cambridge, Mass.: MIT Press, 1990), 2. Nye's discussion of electrification and the erosion of the "lines between separate [private and public] spheres" (278) is also of relevance.

55. Karl Marx, *Grundrisse: Foundations of the Critique of Political Economy (Rough Draft)*, trans. Martin Nicolaus (Harmondsworth: Penguin, 1973), 524. Marx is specifically discussing the relationship of capital to markets here.

56. Horowitz, "Mark Twain's Belle Lettre," 16.

57. The science-magic relationship would be raised again in *A Connecticut Yankee*.

58. See Mark Seltzer, *Bodies and Machines* (New York: Routledge, 1992).

59. This has also to do with Burley's imitative skills. However, the distortions of the telephone (a shriek sounds like "the sharp buzzing of a hurt gnat" because of the loss of power "in travelling five thousand miles," 301) would presumably make disguise and pretence accordingly easier.

60. See Louis J. Budd, " 'An Encounter with an Interviewer': The Height (or Depth) of Nonsense," *Nineteenth-Century Literature* 55, 2 (September 2000): 226–43.

Chapter 6. Seeing the Elephant? "The Stolen White Elephant"

1. Don L. F. Nilsen, "Detective Fiction," in J. R. Le Master and James D. Wilson, eds., *The Mark Twain Encyclopedia* (New York: Garland, 1985), 214.

2. For further discussion of this issue, see Peter Messent, *Mark Twain*, 1–21 (an earlier version of this chapter). The author thanks Palgrave for permission to use material from this Macmillan Press book. See, too, Messent, *Studies in American Humor* 3, 2 (1995): 62–84.

3. This latter burlesque is, though, of detective *fiction*. "The Stolen White Elephant" refers both to a specific detective case (see note 18 of this chapter) and more generally to Allan Pinkerton's written accounts of the cases in which he was involved.

4. Tom Quirk, SSF, 80. Quirk is right in suggesting the problems many contemporary readers have in seeing all the humor of this tale. Some of my critical work is aimed at recovering a necessary context.

5. *Literary World*, 29 September 1882, 195–97. Quote taken from Louis J. Budd's papers, housed in Elmira College Library. My thanks to Professor Budd and to Mark Woodhouse (librarian in charge of the Mark Twain collection) for allowing the use of this material.

6. Private letter to the author.

7. The term is borrowed from Gerald Mast's comment on the films of Buster Keaton, and is quoted in LM, 157. I acknowledge my reliance on Marcel Gutwirth's theoretical models in this chapter.

8. Gutwirth discusses "frustrate[d] expectation" in his description of the comic. He links it with another phrase that is particularly provocative once applied to Twain's comic work: a "rupture [in] determinism." See LM, 92.

9. My move from first person-singular to plural, and the related identification between first-and third-person "reader," indicates that in reconstructing the reader's role I let my own response stand as representative. For my recognition of the problems involved in such a tactic, see the chapter on reader response in my *New Readings of the American Novel*, 130–61.

10. I reapply here the phrase Gutwirth uses to discuss Samuel Beckett's *Waiting for Godot*. See LM, 184. The appropriateness of the implied analogy will emerge later in the chapter.

11. Robinson comments: "So the manifest absurdities of plot and character are presented as having been scrupulously but in the event unnecessarily held from publication pending 'verification' of their nonsense," AF, 9.

12. There are a lot of chance railway encounters in Twain's short fiction. The formal possibilities of their strange combination of intimacy and reserve obviously appealed to him.

13. My comments on the move between the tall tale and the hoax in "The Jumping Frog" (chapter 2) are also relevant here. For economy's sake, I do not now return to that subject. But I would suggest that the form of reader response in both tales is very close.

14. Susan Gillman, *Dark Twins*, 14–15. Twain's fictional elephant has the same name, Jumbo, as the giant elephant (with its fifteen-foot head, ear tip to ear tip)

Barnum bought from London Zoo for $10,000, and which arrived in the United States on 9 April 1882. Either Twain was remarkably prescient or he made last-minute adjustments to his story, since it was originally written three and a half years before Jumbo's American career. In "Seeing the Elephant: Constructing Culture in Britain and the United States After Jumbo" (*Symbiosis: A Journal of Anglo-American Literary Relations* 4, 2 [October 2000]: 111–32), Tim Lustig gives a penetrating account of the sale of Jumbo to Barnum in the larger context of transatlantic cultural relations. He goes on to read "The Stolen White Elephant" against (my) allegorical grain (elephant as comic principle) and in the broader context of the mobility and variety of culture itself ("The more one attempts to *define* the elephant systematically, the more it eludes one"). My thanks to him for the advance copy of his essay and for his helpful comments on my own chapter.

15. Forrest G. Robinson, " 'Seeing the Elephant': Some Perspectives on Mark Twain's *Roughing It,*" *American Studies* 21, 2 (Fall 1980): 55–56.

16. My use of the words "seem" and "appear" suggests the difficulty of any definitive reading of a (hoaxing) text where the line between deception and the hiding of deception is problematic. So often in Twain, we cannot be sure who is hoodwinking whom, nor quite at what level we are meant to be reading and responding.

17. Additionally, once we realize that the story does not work satisfactorily as a conventional hoax, we may look for another narrative or allegory that will allow us to make more sense of it. My following sections illustrate what happens when we do so.

18. In his valuable study of the sources of Twain's story, "Of Detectives and Their Derring-Do: The Genesis of Mark Twain's 'The Stolen White Elephant,' " *Studies in American Humor* 2 (January 1976): 183–95, Howard G. Baetzhold describes its specific base in the Alexander T. Stewart grave-robbery case of 1878. Twain's contemporary audience would have been aware of the theft of the corpse of the wealthy dry-goods merchant from St. Mark's churchyard in New York City on 7 November 1878 and the absurdities of the investigation that followed. Despite reports of a ransom paid and of the body's recovery in 1880, the question is open, even now, as to whether the remains were in fact ever returned. See Baetzhold, 188–89. Twain's story thus operates first and foremost as burlesque: "when the detectives were nosing around after Stewart's loud remains, I threw a chapter into [*A Tramp Abroad*] in which I have very extravagantly burlesqued the detective business — if it *is* possible to burlesque that business extravagantly." See MTHL1, 246. The "loudness" of these remains and the "nosing around" of detectives after a body in a state of two and a half years' decomposition — which rendered it, in the words of police inspector Dilks, in charge of the case, "so offensive that [it] cannot be concealed" (Baetzhold, 186–87) — clearly parallels Twain's depiction of the comic nature of the elephant-detective relationship in his story. There are a series of other connections and parallels that might be made here. They do raise the question of how Twain came to have such close knowledge of the case (were daily newspapers sent to him?) given that he was in Italy and Germany at the time of the described events. I note, though, a few of the many such correspondences. The illiterate letters of Bridget Mahoney and Mary O'Hooligan (31–32) are echoes of various reported correspondence received in the Stewart case. Thus a letter dated 10 November 1878 read: "jents I caled at your offic. . . . I did not stele Mr Stewouts boddy I got it or wanted it for a feller who red of it in the post and herald." The finding of the elephant's body in the "vaulted basement where sixty detectives always slept" (33) was perhaps triggered by the "awful

suggestion" made by a woman that Stewart's body "may be buried in the cellar of the nearest Police-station, 'way down deep in a damp place.' She adds that 'people must not think because men are plicemen [sic] they are all right.' " The wild moves in Twain's story between the realm of the possible and that of the ridiculous and absurd might be seen as a partial mirroring of similar (unexpected) shifts in the Stewart case, where the regular investigative process was interrupted by such reports as that of the lunatic who visited police headquarters, "carrying a citrate of magnesia bottle filled with some milky fluid smelling slightly of carbolic acid.... The man gave his name as H. Zelinski, and said that the bottle contained the body of A. T. Stewart, which he had reduced by means of a white powder.... He left the bottle behind him and did not ask for any reward." (All from reports in the *New York Times*, 12 and 15 November 1878.) There is more to be written about such connections.

19. One significant strand of my overall analysis focuses on the problematization of binary relations of all kinds (visible and hidden, literal and metaphorical, comic and serious) and at all levels in this story. Twain anticipates postmodernist tactics and concerns here.

20. Twain's use of foreign names for comic ends indicates his attraction to common forms of ethnocentric humor. See my "Racial and Colonial Discourse in Mark Twain's *Following the Equator*," in *Essays in Arts and Sciences* 22 (October 1993): 67–83. The nub of Twain's joke here, however, lies in the reductive move from the formal complexity of the long, ornate, and polysyllabic Indian name to what has now become the most common and mundane of elephant nicknames. This is a common technique in Twain's comic armory — that sudden overturning of expectation; the deflationary shift from one level of discourse to another (so-called lower and vernacular) level.

21. We should remember that Blunt is presumably playing a double game as he "cons" the narrator out of $142,000 (35). Franklin Rogers shows how Twain "pour[s] ridicule" on the "major devices in detection" used by the Pinkerton Detective Agency. These include "the accumulation of exhaustive details both relevant and irrelevant, [and] the constant [and indiscriminate] surveillance of the suspect by detectives." Although Rogers is discussing *Simon Wheeler, Detective*, his comments are also relevant here. Introduction to *Simon Wheeler, Detective* (New York: New York Public Library, 1963), xxii.

22. The notion of an allegorical reading of the white elephant tempts speculation on a possible relationship between this story and Herman Melville's *Moby Dick*. The connection with Edgar Allan Poe and his use of absence and presence in "The Purloined Letter" might also be pursued.

23. See LM, 50–51, 58, 57. My argument here extends that begun in my discussion of "The Facts Concerning the Recent Carnival of Crime in Connecticut."

24. Mark Twain, *The Mysterious Stranger*, ed. William M. Gibson (Berkeley: University of California Press, 1969), 166.

25. See Baetzhold, "Of Detectives and Their Derring-Do," 192. "What seems to have irked [Twain] most," Baetzhold writes, "was the assumption of infallibility implied in the badge and motto, and in Pinkerton's books themselves."

26. See, e.g., Michael Denning, *Mechanic Accents: Dime Novels and Working-Class Culture in America* (London: Verso, 1987), 118–48. Denning describes how dime novelists quickly capitalized on the Molly Maguires case and, accordingly, how the figure of the detective became common in American popular fiction of the 1870s and 1880s. Allan Pinkerton's fictionalized versions of the cases involving his own agency were to appear from 1874 onward.

27. Lester Velie, *Labor U.S.A.* (New York: Harper, 1958), 123. James Mackay in *Allan Pinkerton: The First Private Eye* (New York: John Wiley, 1966) is more sympathetic to the Pinkertons, particularly in the case of the Molly Maguires. See 212–14. I should note at this point Twain's own prejudice against the unions and the Molly Maguires in particular—he called them "a powerful, numerous and desperate . . . devilish secret organization": see Louis J. Budd, *Mark Twain, Social Philosopher*, 71. But gaps between Twain's public politics and the implicit meanings of his artistic works are not unusual.

28. See Paul Smith, *A Reader's Guide to the Short Stories of Ernest Hemingway* (Boston: G. K. Hall, 1989), 208 (he is quoting from other critics here), and Richard Godden, *Fictions of Capital: The American Novel from James to Mailer* (Cambridge: Cambridge University Press, 1990), 67. Both refer to Ernest Hemingway's story "Hills like White Elephants," a later American narrative that operates around the divergent meanings of this term.

29. And see Lillian S. Robinson: "The only place where the [main] narrator's viewpoint could be interpreted as anything more sinister than extraordinary credulity is in his opening description of how the King of Siam came to be sending a white elephant to Queen Victoria, with its bland papering-over of assumptions too ingrained even to be called an apologia for the excesses of British imperialism. Even this may be read as an aspect of the character Twain is introducing, of whom it may be said that if he unquestioningly swallows the line that the rulers of small undeveloped countries knuckle under in disputes with colonial superpowers because they realize that the stronger country was right all along, then he will indeed swallow anything, AF, 9.

30. Such cultural relativism cuts against the ethnocentric humor previously footnoted (note 20).

31. At the same time, we are aware that part of Twain's joke lies at a simpler level, precisely in the making literal of a figure of speech (something which dreams often do) and the comic move between conceptual boundaries (the real and the surreal) which then follows.

32. This relates to Gutwirth's rabbit/duck example, with its quality (as we try to separate figure from ground) of now you see it, now you don't.

33. I recognize, in line with my previous argument, that other readings are possible. My earlier references to the Pinkertons do connect with a possible critique of the practices of monopoly capitalism.

Chapter 7. Merry Tales *and* The £1,000,000 Bank-Note and Other New Stories

1. "New," here, in terms of book publication.

2. *Merry Tales*, AF, 4.

3. MTHL2, 541. See also Anne Bernays, *Merry Tales*, xl, xxxii.

4. On March 14, 1885, Charles L. Webster wrote Twain, "I have *sold* 39,000 *books*," adding that none of the author's previous books had sold so well in such a short time. Twain replied on March 16, "Your news is splendid. Huck certainly *is* a success." See MTLP, 184–85.

5. See MTLP, 129, 169–71. Hill quotes Twain's letter to the editor of the Elmira *Herald*: "I am Webster & Co., myself, substantially." Andrew Hoffman gives a useful account of the Twain-Webster relationship and the publishing of Grant's *Memoirs* in *Inventing Mark Twain*. See his index.

6. "[T]his project absorbed [Twain's] every waking thought. He regarded pub-

lishing Grant's memoirs as the most significant achievement of his life." Hoffman, *Inventing Mark Twain*, 326.

7. Ibid., 328.

8. MTNJ3, 176. And see MTLP, 170.

9. MTLP, 333–34. But see note 19 below.

10. See Fred J. Hall's letter to Twain of 2 June 1893: "You can scarcely conceive of the condition of business generally . . . there has been failure after failure . . . a constant succession of crashes since you left. . . . We cannot collect money from our very best customers. It is like pulling teeth to get any money at all." And on 9 June 1893: "I am worried half to death. . . . [S]ince you left the whole bottom seems to have dropped out of everything and there has been a succession of crashes. . . . [I]n the banking business along during the month of May there were more than *ten times* as many failures than there were last year," CU-MARK.

11. MTLP, 277, 343, 355. I condense passages from two letters in the last quote. Both letters are to Fred J. Hall, who by February 1888 had replaced Webster, the "perfect scapegoat" for the then near-insolvency (243), as Twain's business partner.

12. Justin Kaplan, *Mr. Clemens and Mark Twain*, 463.

13. See AZ, 350, and MTNJ3, 571. Twain's intention as he made the 1890 contract was to attract the support of other investors in the machine.

14. I argue elsewhere that despite the "frustratingly uneven" quality of the novel, Twain "is wrestling . . . with crucial themes which lie at the very centre of his relationship to American culture and of his own identity as an artist." See *The American Claimant* (1892), AF, 18.

15. We see some of the difficulties in pinning Twain down generically, where such material can appear either independently or as part of a longer narrative.

16. My thanks to Ken Sanderson for his help in tracing first publication details.

17. In the case of "A Cure for the Blues," this seems to have been the case; see MTLP, 322. Twain had, though, planned such an article from 1884: MTNJ3, 47.

18. He also began *Personal Recollections of Joan of Arc* in this period.

19. Forrest G. Robinson, AF, 2. Webster & Co. increasingly moved to trade publishing, especially after the poor sales of *A Connecticut Yankee* (23,000 copies in the first seven months). "By the time of the completion of *Pudd'nhead Wilson*, Charles L. Webster & Co. was to have no subscription apparatus with which to sell it," MTLP, 262, 244–45.

20. Letter of 24 August 1891, MTLP, 282; see also 279–80, 283.

21. Letter from Olivia L. Clemens to Hall, MTLP, 302. Twain was ill, suffering from congestion of the lungs. Apart from "Playing Courier" and "The German Chicago," the other travel pieces Twain wrote in this period would not appear in book form until after his death (in *What Is Man? and Other Essays* [1917] and *Europe and Elsewhere* [1923]).

22. In a later letter, he also responds to an apparent suggestion from Hall that "Mental Telegraphy" be included, with the words: "Yes, get the 'Mental Telegraphy' into the book, even if you have to leave something out to make room," MTLP, 329. He himself ruled out "The Californian's Tale" from the collection (328).

23. MTLP, 328. It is clear that Twain himself was not overly concerned with the matter of this book's appearance or presentation. All he wrote to Hall concerning its production was, "Make it $1.50 book or $1 book as shall seem to you best. Put no expense on it." See letter of 24 November 1892, in MTLP, 326.

24. Though contemporary reviews were far from damning. The *Cincinnatti*

Commercial Gazette reviewer wrote that "merry indeed are the yarns that are spun by the head and brain of that master weaver" (2 April 1892). See CR, 13.

25. In the 1897 edition. The volume also contained all the material from *The £1,000,000 Bank-Note*. Harper's at this point were trying to get a Uniform edition of Mark Twain under way, using initially books whose copyright Twain controlled.

26. See Forrest G. Robinson, AF, 2. *Merry Tales* is advertised alongside *The German Emperor and His Eastern Neighbors* by Poultney Bigelow, *Selected Poems* by Walt Whitman, and *Don Finimondone: Calabrian Sketches* by Elisabeth Cavazza, in the series list placed at the front of Twain's book.

27. See the Editor's Note on publishing "the better class of native literature at moderate prices." The aim of the series, it seems, was to appeal to a mass readership but at a superior level, thus contrasting with earlier rivals which had distributed "a great deal of rubbish . . . to the undoubted injury of our popular taste." The concern here with "classes" of literature and their effect on different American social classes matches Twain's own.

28. Louis J. Budd, "Mark Twain as an American Icon," in Forrest G. Robinson, ed., *Cambridge Companion to Mark Twain*, 14.

29. Albert Bigelow Paine, *Letters of Mark Twain* (New York: Harper, 1917) 527–28 (some slight changes made after referring to CU-MARK). See Leland Krauth, *Proper Mark Twain*, for full-length treatment of "the bounded Twain . . . who honors conventions, upholds proprieties, . . . maintains the order-inducing moralities," etc. (3). Also see Krauth (14–16) on the ambiguities contained in this letter to Lang.

30. See Krauth, *Proper Mark Twain*, 5, 13.

31. The story is reprinted from *The Stolen White Elephant*.

32. See Alan Trachtenberg, *The Incorporation of America*, 192, 196, 199.

33. Ibid., 200, 193, 197.

34. Paine, *Letters of Mark Twain*, 289.

35. James D. Wilson gives details of the story's lack of originality. The very vagueness of these details is, however, a reminder of the common difficulty of pinning Twain down as he moves between fiction and nonfiction. See RG, 31–32.

36. AF, 8–9. The same undermining occurs in "The Private History," though in a different way. This notion of the "harmless joke" might be used to counter my first Howellsian reading. The text is unstable and can be read in different—and perhaps coexistent—ways depending on our critical construction of the relation between author and narrator.

37. Anne Bernays's aside that "There's something of Billy Budd in Wicklow" (xlii) deserves more attention as far as the conflict between a patriarchal military (and state) authority and a peculiar type of childish naivete goes. Twain's discourse and focus in fact at times anticipates Melville's: "The musicians are down on him" (94), "I felt like a father who plots to expose his own child to shame and injury" (101).

38. AF, 7. This, as so often with Twain, was one part of a more complicated picture. He made no secret, for instance, of his deep admiration for Ulysses S. Grant (though see next chapter).

39. See SSF, 89–90, for a biographical reading of the story.

40. *San Francisco Chronicle*, 10 April 1892; *New York Sun*, 7 May 1892. For the first reference, see CR, 323. The second is taken from the Louis J. Budd papers at Elmira College.

41. Targeted, we should remember, throughout Twain's career, from his earliest burlesques onward.

42. See MTLP, 329–30. Twain also had last-minute worries after writing "A Cure for the Blues" about whether Royston's book was originally intended as a hoax (339).

43. Quoted in *The Incorporation of America*, 186. I take issue with Michael Davitt Bell here. In *The Problem of American Realism: Studies in the Cultural History of a Literary Idea* (Chicago: University of Chicago Press, 1993), Bell argues that "it simply will not do to imagine that Twain's scattered critical writings reveal a realist in principle" (45).

44. Quoted in Tony Tanner, introduction to William Dean Howells, *A Hazard of New Fortunes* (London: Oxford University Press, 1965) ix.

45. I use the term "modernization" to refer to social and economic processes, to a post-Civil War America and the problems it faced in a time of rapid and disorienting change.

46. Martha Banta, "The Boys and the Bosses: Twain's Double Take on Work, Play, and the Democratic Ideal," *American Literary History* 3, 3 (Fall 1991): 489.

47. Ricki Morgan sees a play here on the original Adam, tempted here by money. But this Adam(s) does not "fall," remaining free from the "greed and money worship of the society surrounding him." See "Mark Twain's Money Imagery in 'The £1,000,000 Bank-Note' and 'the $30,000 Bequest,' " *Mark Twain Journal* 19, 1 (Winter 1977–78): 7. I have some trouble with such an allegorical view. There is another resonance, for as Malcolm Bradbury notes, Twain, "surely mischievously, grants (the narrator) the splendid name of America's greatest contemporary historian." IN, xl.

48. Adams is in fact (if temporarily) the tramp. But Twain catches us in a double-bind, for if we take the note as a guarantee of financial substance, Adams *has* now become a millionaire. The question of what exactly the note guarantees is at the core of things.

49. A romance in the mode of Alger and Franklin, for Adams is down to the last dollar in his pocket when he arrives in London (9).

50. ETS1, 322. By the start of 1863, Gould and Curry was "the richest incorporated mining company in the West, and by July its stock had soared to $6,300 a share" (458). This may suggest a chronology for the story. See also Twain's matching account in *Roughing It* of his own missed chance over the enlisting of "New York capital" in "a big mining speculation" (427, 421).

51. See Ricki Morgan on the symbolic resonance of Portia's name, "Mark Twain's Money Imagery," 8.

52. We take the first-person narrator of "Playing Courier" to be "Mark Twain" both by the autobiographical references (remembering that this is one of a series of travel pieces written at the time) and the close fit with prior constructions of that persona

53. Indeed, the formal separation of the realms of leisure and play from that of work is very much a product of modernization. See Michael Oriard, *Sporting with the Gods: The Rhetoric of Play and Game in American Culture* (Cambridge: Cambridge University Press, 1991).

54. Douglas Tallack, *Twentieth-Century America: The Intellectual and Cultural Context* (London: Longman, 1991), 17.

55. Quoted in Ibid., 11.

56. Georg Simmel, "The Metropolis and Mental Life," in *On Individuality and Social Forms: Selected Writings* (Chicago: University of Chicago Press, 1971), 328. Page references henceforth follow quotes.

57. See Susan Gillman, *Dark Twins*, 49–50, 147–48.

Chapter 8. *"The Private History of a Campaign That Failed"*

1. See Steve Davis, "Mark Twain, the War, and *Life on the Mississippi,*" *Southern Studies* 18 (1979): 231. Davis does, however, argue for *Life on the Mississippi* as a key source of "insight into Twain's attitudes on the war."

2. Fred W. Lorch writes that there was "widespread defection from [military] units, probably both Rebel and Union" during these early days of the war. He focuses, though, on the specific case of Governor Claib Jackson's rebel army and the consequences of its 17 June 1861 defeat at Boonville ("up the Missouri River") for other rebel units, including Twain's, in the area. See "Mark Twain and the 'Campaign That Failed,' " *American Literature* 12 (1940–41): 468–69.

3. James M. Cox, *Mark Twain and the Fate of Humor* (Princeton, N.J.: Princeton University Press, 1966), 196.

4. See especially Tom Quirk, "Life Imitating Art: *Huckleberry Finn* and Twain's Autobiographical Writings" in Robert Sattelmeyer and J. Donald Crowley, eds., *One Hundred Years of Huckleberry Finn: The Boy, His Book, and American Culture* (Columbia: University of Missouri Press, 1985) 41–55; and Richard Peck, "The Campaign That . . . Succeeded," *American Literary Realism* 21 (1989): 3–12.

5. Neil Schmitz, "Mark Twain's Civil War: Humor's Reconstructive Writing," in Forrest G. Robinson, ed., *Cambridge Companion to Mark Twain,* 85, 81.

6. Cox, *Mark Twain and the Fate of Humor,* 194, 197.

7. J. Stanley Mattson, "Mark Twain on War and Peace: The Missouri Rebel and 'The Campaign That Failed,' " *American Quarterly* 20, 4 (Winter 1968): 790, 791, 794.

8. Schmitz, "Mark Twain's Civil War," 88.

9. Ibid., 80.

10. Peck, "The Campaign That . . . Succeeded," 10, 5.

11. Fred W. Lorch, in "Mark Twain and the 'Campaign That Failed,' " gives details of three other accounts of Twain's war experiences. He supplies, on that basis, a chronology of events for the period. See 455–56 and 459–62. John Gerber, in "Mark Twain's Private Campaign," *Civil War History* 1 (1955): 37–40, also uses "the chief primary sources of information" (both autobiographical and otherwise) to reconstruct Twain's and the Marion Rangers' activities. Neither source gives a complete record.

12. *McClure's* 13, May–October 1899. Also published in *The $30,000 Bequest and Other Stories* (1906). The sketch was written to accompany Frank Bliss's uniform edition of Twain's works.

13. Samuel E. Moffett, "Mark Twain: A Biographical Sketch," in *The $30,000 Bequest and Other Stories,* 338–39.

14. CU-MARK. Privately printed by Merle Johnson in 1916.

15. See J. Hurley Hagood and Roberta Hagood, *Hannibal, Too: Historic Sketches of Hannibal and Its Neighbors* (Marceline, Mo.: Walsworth, 1986), 113–32. See also R. I. Holcombe, *History of Marion County Missouri* (Marceline, Mo.: Walworth, 1979 [1884]), 357–549, 929–35.

16. Schmitz, "Mark Twain's Civil War," p. 81.

17. Julian Street, *Abroad At Home: American Ramblings, Observations, and Adventures of Julian Street* (New York: Century, 1916), 250–51.

18. The speech is reprinted in Paul Fatout, ed., *Mark Twain Speaking* (Iowa City: University of Iowa Press, 1976), 106–9. In another speech, "An Author's Soldiering," made on 8 April 1887 (after the publication of "The Private History"), the killing of the stranger does again feature as "the only battle in the history of the

world where the opposing force was *utterly exterminated*" (219–21). See also "Remarks as Chairman," 381–83.

19. Richard Peck, "The Campaign That . . . Succeeded," 9. Twain's own notes for the story foreground its comic aspects:

2 weeks campaign (umbrella) with Ed Stevens & Sam Bowen. "What you lack (to Bowen) is stability of character."
Horse used to bite Sam's legs while he was asleep. . . .
Cut loose from Tom Harris & all other authority, to have their own way. . . .
Sam took mosquito blisters for a mortal disease.
Used to sit on his horse in prairie on picket duty & cry & curse & go to sleep in hot sun.
Sent our washing to town because didn't like country washing. (CU-MARK*)

There is still no mention in these notes of the killing of the stranger.

20. The intertextual recall of *The Innocents Abroad* is suggestive.

21. Gerber, "Mark Twain's Private Campaign," 42–43. In fact Twain did consider writing a fictionalized version of the story using Tom Sawyer. A notebook entry runs: "Put Huck & Tom & Jim through my Mo. campaign & give a chapter to the Century." See Peck, "The Campaign That . . . Succeeded," 6.

22. See Peck, "The Campaign That . . . Succeeded," 10. Kemble's illustrations tended, though, to conform to a certain type. So compare both the last-named illustrations above to that on page 195 of the June 1885 *Century* ("In and Out of the New Orleans Exposition").

23. Peck, "The Campaign That . . . Succeeded," 5–6. Peck goes on to show a tripartite relationship between the texts: "The conclusion of the *Adventures of Huckleberry Finn* draws upon and modifies [Twain's] 'War Experiences' [an alternative title for the 1877 speech]. 'The Private History of the Campaign That Failed' draws upon and modifies the conclusion of *Huck Finn*" (11).

24. That of the deserter in the case of "The Private History."

25. See Quirk, "Life Imitating Art," 51, 54.

26. Peck, "The Campaign That . . . Succeeded," 9.

27. Nina Silber, *The Romance of Reunion: Northerners and the South, 1865–1900* (Chapel Hill: University of North Carolina Press, 1993), 44.

28. Ibid., 48, 55.

29. Silber refers to Cincinnati's 1875 Decoration Day as one of the first such occasions (61). And see ibid., 96–97, on the 1880s.

30. Ibid., 61, 62, 95, 94, 63. The reunion drama focused on romantic love (usually between Southern woman and Northern man) threatened, but unsuccessfully, by sectional division.

31. Ibid., 97, 159–62. As I present my condensed version of Silber's account, I am aware of flattening out the chronological sequence of events and responses as she describes them. I also draw my own analytic conclusions from the information she presents.

32. Ibid., 167.

33. J. Stanley Mattson says it was "one of the most successful features in the history of the journal. . . . [I]nterest in the series . . . never flagged until its conclusion three years later." Mattson, "Mark Twain on War and Peace," 783.

34. "Topics of the Time," *Century* 28 (October 1884): 943. In the December 1884 edition, the Grangerford-Shepherdsons Feud section of *Huckleberry Finn* (one which could clearly be read in the context of the Civil War) appeared. It was followed directly by the second part of Warren Lee Goss's "Recollections of a

Private." "Jim's Investments, and King Solermun" followed in January 1885 in the same volume as George Washington Cable's "The Freedman's Case in Equity."

35. Davis, "Mark Twain, The War, and *Life on the Mississippi*," 234.

36. *Century* 28 (October 1884): 943–44. We see here a paradoxical blend of amnesia and recollection, where the aspects of the war that can best be used for purposes of present reconciliation are most emphasised.

37. *Century* 30 (May 1885): 164–65.

38. *Century* 30 (October 1885): 965.

39. Justin Kaplan, *Mr. Clemens and Mark Twain*, 423.

40. J. Stanley Mattson, "Mark Twain on War and Peace," 784.

41. Johnson's correspondence is quoted in Mattson, "Mark Twain on War and Peace," 784–85. The episodes of Warren Lee Goss's "Recollections of a Private" did provide an earlier version of a "bottom-up" and (occasionally) deflating view of the war in the series. His account of the recruitment process and of "one old lady, in the innocence of her heart, [bringing] her son an umbrella" (*Century* 29 [November 1884]: 108) may have had some influence on Twain's own thinking for his own article and the note, "2 weeks campaign (umbrella)," he made.

42. Mattson, "Mark Twain on War and Peace," 785. Possibly it was cut because it did not fit into the clear nonfictional category of the other essays. But there is another possible explanation: that Twain may have reserved the copyright for himself.

43. The term "inside narrative" is Tom Quirk's in "Life Imitating Art," 50. He is quoting Melville's *Billy Budd*.

44. Schmitz, "Mark Twain's Civil War," 88.

45. Mattson, "Mark Twain on War and Peace," 794.

46. Ibid., 789. Mattson's analysis runs along roughly similar lines to my own. He usefully points out that any pacifist message in "A Campaign That Failed" is contradicted by Twain on other occasions (793).

47. Davis, "Mark Twain, the War, and *Life on the Mississippi*," 239. Davis says the mysterious stranger is "presumably an innocent citizen." This is actually left in complete doubt, though see note 58.

48. That Twain does this at the same time as he distances himself personally (as Neil Schmitz describes) from the Southern cause is not necessarily problematic.

49. Mattson, "Mark Twain on War and Peace," 787.

50. Cox, *Mark Twain and the Fate of Humor*, 192.

51. Ibid., 195, 197. Cox argues that in Twain's previous work, as for instance in *The Innocents Abroad*, with its comic representation both of Europe and the pious American pilgrims, Twain chose "the popular cause . . . he was not with the minority but with the majority." The "costs of being a humorist" were revealed once this situation changed (196).

52. Cox fails to recognize that the pacifist message to the text may at least provide a partial challenge to this "sacred cow."

53. Cox, *Mark Twain and the Fate of Humor*, 195. In fact the final status of the "Mark Twain" persona in "The Private History" is problematic. The narrator suffers "morbid thoughts" and "a diseased imagination" (45) following the death of the stranger. This suggests a gap between the author and that (overly sentimental?) earlier version of him. It is clear, however, that we are to take the response to the death "seriously" as amending the earlier portrayal of comic ignorance and naivete.

54. Schmitz, "Mark Twain's Civil War," 88. Schmitz also finds fault with the final sentence of the story, comparing it to a similar passage in *Huckleberry Finn*. He

finds it to be "apologizing where Huck is not . . . obsequious where Huck is simply decisive." And he, too, sees the story in terms of its comic failure.

55. It is the news of Grant and his regiment's proximity that spurs the narrator's final retreat from the war. According to Lorch's chronology, Twain is fictionalizing: "It is . . . likely that by the time Grant reached Florida [Missouri, where General Harris's rebel camp was situated] Sam and Orion Clemens had already left St. Louis for the West." Lorch, "Mark Twain and the 'Campaign That Failed,' " 463.

56. *Century*, October 1884, 944; October 1885, 965.

57. Steve Davis says that "in mid-1862 [Twain] underwent a remarkable conversion. He sloughed off his former loyalties and became an ardent supporter of the Northern cause." Davis, "Mark Twain, the War, and *Life on the Mississippi*," 232.

58. In an intriguing short essay, "A Private History: Moments in the Friendship of Mark Twain and Ulysses S. Grant," Rachel Cohen points out that Twain's dead horseman "bears a striking resemblance to Grant's description of himself at that time in Missouri." She also recalls that Twain thought of calling his narrative "My Campaign Against Grant." "Buried in [the story of the killing of the lone horseman] . . . is the suggestion that the moral failure is not Twain's for killing one Grant and fleeing the battlefield, but Grant's for staying in the war and causing the deaths of a thousand Twains." See ⟨www.doubletakemagazine.org/issues/21/cohen/index.html⟩.

59. Such an impingement is indicated, for instance, by Ronald Takaki as he discusses Twain's slightly later *Connecticut Yankee*: "As [the 'enterprising' men of white America] built their 'America by design' . . . they were substituting technology for the body and . . . channelling men, women, and children into factories, and reducing them to machine attendants," *Iron Cages; Race and Culture in Nineteenth-Century America* (London: Athlone, 1979), 169–70. That Twain was writing his narrative in the 1880s may well, of course, have affected his representation of the earlier period.

60. *The Red Badge of Courage* was published a decade after Twain's story in 1895. The historicist readings of that Civil War text by Amy Kaplan and Bill Brown, however, usefully complement my own work on "The Private History." See Kaplan, "The Spectacle of War in Crane's Revision of History" in Lee Clark Mitchell, ed., *New Essays on "The Red Badge of Courage"* (Cambridge: Cambridge University Press, 1986), 77–108, and Brown, *The Material Unconscious: American Amusement, Stephen Crane, and the Economics of Play* (Cambridge, Mass.: Harvard University Press, 1996), 125–66.

61. The early narrative focus on the "boyishness" of his narrator may be read as a type of evasion of the grimness of male adulthood in war, of the "father" (Grant?). But is a "sturdy independence," if that is what the narrator finally possesses, preferable to that boyhood state? And does that independence then come to mean an acceptance of the more "feminine" aspects of the male self? If so, that still leaves us with two conflicting versions of masculinity, Grant's and the narrator's, at the story's end.

62. One reading of the Twain-Grant connection might be in terms of two exceptional figures who have managed in opposite ways to circumvent larger conditioning forces. Thus Grant was not a soldierly machine but a true war hero. And Twain's own celebrity stems from his autonomy, his evasion of institutional co-option, and his speaking of such evasions and resistances in his comic writing. But this is to resolve what is unresolved and oppositional in the narrative itself.

Chapter 9. The Man That Corrupted Hadleyburg and Other Stories and Essays

1. See Carl Dolmetsch, *"Our Famous Guest": Mark Twain in Vienna* (Athens: University of Georgia Press, 1992) for an authoritative account of Twain's intellectual life during this period.

2. He is referring here to a designing machine for carpet weaving invented by Jan Szczepanik. But see also his enthusiasm for cloth made partly out of peat and for Plasmon health food. See CHHR, 327–32, 335–39, 342–43, 439–42.

3. Jeffrey Rubin-Dorsky, AF, 1–2. Twelve more of Twain's books were issued between 1902 and 1909.

4. *Tom Sawyer Abroad* had previously been published as a single book in 1894

5. Beside the title story, the collection contains "In Defence of Harriet Shelley," "Fenimore Cooper's Literary Offences," "Travelling with a Reformer," "Private History of the 'Jumping Frog' Story," "Mental Telegraphy Again," "What Paul Bourget Thinks of Us," and "A Little Note to M. Paul Bourget." See the introduction for my reasons for not discussing this book further.

6. "The Invalid's Story" and "The Captain's Story," from *Merry Tales*, are not reprinted. There is a tricky question of terminology here. Twain referred to the American Publishing Company editions (Autograph, Royal, Japan, Hillcrest, etc.) as the uniform edition of his works. But "the only edition actually called 'The Uniform Edition of Mark Twain's Works' is the set of unnumbered volumes in red cloth, stamped gilt, that began to be issued in 1896 by Harpers and that were issued by them for many years thereafter" (private correspondence from Ken Sanderson: my thanks again for his generous help).

7. "Stirring Times in Austria," "Concerning the Jews," "From the 'London Times' of 1904," and "At the Appetite Cure."

8. "The Invalid's Story," "The German Chicago," and "About All Kinds of Ships" were also republished here. See AZ, 292. The 1900 American Publishing Company uniform edition of *How to Tell a Story and Other Essays* differed slightly from this *Literary Essays* collection. It added "How to Tell A Story" and "The Captain's Story" but omitted "The German Chicago," "About All Kinds of Ships," and "Saint Joan of Arc." Later Harper editions of *How to Tell a Story and Other Essays* (named *Literary Essays Etc.* on the book spine) repeated this last format.

9. Twain's plans changed from the writing and translating of plays ("I resolved to stop book-writing and go at something else"), to the writing of material "for publication when I'm dead, mainly," to a concentration on short stories ("I mean to write as much as ever, but only *stories*—and not print very often"). See variously in CHHR, 318, 340, 345, 358, 365, 372.

10. Dolmetsch, *"Our Famous Guest"*, 149, 244.

11. Ibid., 72. Dolmetsch is speaking here of the British (Chatto & Windus) and German (Tauchnitz) variants of the book *The Man That Corrupted Hadleyburg Etc.* But his words apply to the American edition too.

12. MTLP,·366. Hill gives other reasons for Twain's distancing himself from the publishing business, in particular the end of "the single subscription book" and his age and status. These last factors worked against the repeating of the kind of "wildcat operations which had provided the real spice of [his] relationships with Bliss, Osgood, Webster, and Hall."

13. Bliss had returned to the company after his father's death. Twain wrote to Rogers on his decision to publish *Following the Equator* with Bliss: "Harper publishes very high-class books and they go to people who are accustomed to read. That class are surfeited with travel-books. But there is a vast class that isn't—the

factory hands and the farmers. *They* never go to a bookstore; they have to be hunted down by the canvasser. When a subscription book of mine sells 60,000, I always think I know whither 50,000 of them went. They went to people who don't visit bookstores," CHHR, 249.

14. These negotiations were complex and indeed initially were planned to work in exactly the opposite manner, with Harper as publisher of the Uniform Edition. Indeed Harper did issue six titles in 1896, 1897, and 1898. The American Publishing Company published the first twenty-one volumes of its uniform set in 1899; volume 22, *How to Tell a Story and Other Essays*, in 1900; and volume 23, *My Debut as a Literary Person with Other Essays and Stories*, in 1903. Twain's own correspondence shows him acting as a middle man in this situation, ensuring that Bliss was able to publish his new, as well as his old, work in the uniform edition. Thus, for instance, he writes to Harper on 1 October 1899 (with a copy sent to Bliss): "Yes, *I* think, too, it is nearly time for a new book, but if I place it with you you mustn't give me a lot more trouble with Bliss. He wants to put the Jew article in his last Uniform volume — & why shouldn't he? Why should he be afraid you will object?" (CU-MARK*). See appendices B, C, and D in CHHR (678–87) for the 1896 and 1898 contracts between Harper, the American Publishing Company, and the Clemenses. Again, thanks to Ken Sanderson for help in sorting out some of this tangle.

15. CU-MARK*. Two months earlier, on 1 October, Twain had written to Rogers about a new collection, saying, "I want to put this book into *your* hands, you to give it to Bliss or to Harper, whichever you please." In the same letter, he says he is "pretty well along" with the story that would later become the title piece of the new book, "The Man That Corrupted Hadleyburg." At this point, though, he says, "I am not expecting to get *that* into [the new] volume. It won't be long enough for a book by itself, perhaps, yet too long to crowd into that one." On 2 November, Twain is asking Rogers to advise him as to "whether to give [the new volume of sketches] to Bliss (in case he should *want* it) or to Harper," CHHR, 367–68, 372–73.

16. CHHR, 388. Twain goes on to say that Bliss and Rogers together can negotiate with Harper, and that if Harper takes the book, Bliss can gain other concessions accordingly (probably with regard to the uniform edition): "You see you can consider the book your *own*, and that puts you in shape to dicker." See also the footnote to the letter to Rogers of the same date.

17. CU-MARK*. The British and German editions of *The Man That Corrupted Hadleyburg Etc.* did contain a long piece on "Christian Science and the Book of Mrs. Eddy."

18. CU-MARK. Harper's business failure in late 1899 rather gave the lie, however, to these words. Twain wrote Howells in January 1900: "Harper will issue two volumes of [the short things] in the spring. I consented a couple of weeks before their smash. They decline to give them up, now," MTHL2, 715.

19. CU-MARK*. Twain precedes this list with a letter of explanation and comment. He says, "If you should find and add anything that is not in the enclosed list, I should be glad to know the titles in order to make sure that I want it printed." The date of "My Rebel Campaign" is clearly a mistake: Twain refers to *Century* publication "about 1885 — or '86" in the body of the letter. Other dates too are incorrect. The list of titles in the letter to Alden clearly updates that in the Notebook.

20. CHHR, 421. The reordering Twain requested was never done.

21. CU-MARK*. Though I have no explanation why the content of the two editions differed, such variations are not atypical with Twain's books. Kenneth M. Sanderson annotates the relevant documentation: "It is worth noting that Clem-

ens was leaving to George Harvey, head of Harper & Bros. . . . the selection of pieces to be included in a book to be issued by Chatto & Windus, his English publisher. . . . [I]t may be that [Twain] was simply deferring to Harvey's good business judgment."

22. CU-MARK*. The table of contents to which he refers seems no longer extant. But Twain's work does not seem to have affected the American edition. The English and German editions of *Hadleyburg* contain all the material in the American edition except "How to Tell a Story" and "The Austrian Inventor Keeping School" (despite the instructions in the letter of 4 December 1899). The order of the contents, though, is quite different. This edition also contains "Christian Science and the Book of Mrs. Eddy," "Diplomatic Pay and Clothes," "Luck," "The Captain's Story," "My Military Campaign," "Meisterschaft," and "In Memoriam."

23. The exceptions, for Rubin-Dorsky, are the title story, "Concerning the Jews," and "Stirring Times in Austria."

24. Contemporary critics noted Twain's increasingly serious turn: "He is more than a humorist nowadays; he is a satirist, a philosopher" ("Books of the Day," *Boston Post*, 1 July 1900); "Mark Twain's humor has grown more quiet with the passing of the years, but more subtle as well, more philosophical, with a substratum of wisdom that gives a higher value to the fun" (*Book Buyer*, September 1900). See CR, 487, 490.

25. The original article is composed largely of the diary and log of Samuel and Henry Ferguson. The *Hadleyburg* version has much more authorial comment/paraphrase.

26. What prompts the essay is the issue of originality and repetition raised by Twain's learning that a version of the frog story was first told in ancient Greece (as written down, a footnote tells us, in Sidgwick's *Greek Prose Composition*). In fact it later emerged that the textbook had borrowed Twain's story to use for its own teaching ends. Twain uses the occasion to repeat material about the French translation of the story: see *Sketches, New and Old*.

27. *The Chronicle of Young Satan*, in William M. Gibson's edition of Mark Twain, *The Mysterious Stranger by Mark Twain* (Berkeley: University of California Press, 1969), 166. This passage was apparently written between June and August 1900: see Gibson's dating of the manuscript in his introduction, 5–7. Gibson also notes connections between *The Mysterious Stranger* materials and "Stirring Times in Austria" (12), "About Play-Acting" (17), and "Concerning the Jews" (18).

28. Quoted in Gibson, *The Mysterious Stranger*, 24. Such factors as the Boer War, the Boxer Rebellion in China, the recent Dreyfus case, the events in the Austrian parliament in late 1897, the 1898 assassination of the empress of Austria, and Twain's increasing opposition to British and American imperialism in general may have caused such a response. My reading here works against that of Bruce Michelson who, in *Mark Twain on the Loose*, argues for a turbulent and liberating quality to Twain's late writings and against the traditional "slide into despair" thesis (175, 253n.3). I place more emphasis on Twain's sardonic pessimism, though I agree that his writing moves in a number of often contradictory directions in these years.

29. Dreyfus was then pardoned by the president of the Republic in order to resolve this highly uncomfortable political issue. Only in 1906 was he finally cleared of his "crimes." Twain plays on some of the legal absurdities of the case in "From the 'London Times' of 1904." He also alludes in that story to the case of Oberlin Carter ("the American Dreyfus"), who was also tried twice for the same crime. In Carter's case, this was conspiracy to defraud the government (over

engineering projects). See Philip W. Leon, *Mark Twain and West Point* (Toronto: ECW Press, 1996), 102–4.

30. In "On the Decay of the Art of Lying," he wrote: "the Lie, as a Virtue, a Principle, is eternal. . . . Everybody lies — every day; every hour; awake; asleep; in his dreams; in his joy." See *The Stolen White Elephant Etc.*, 217, 219.

31. Even in "The Esquimau Maiden's Romance," the most comically expansive piece in the book (and written earlier, in 1893), humor is associated with the corrupting nature of power and money rather than effectively countering it. "Everybody laughs and cackles" at the "dismal" jokes of Lasca's wealthy father; they are rendered "cringing and obsequious" by his wealth and status (213).

32. The fact that slavery *was* abolished casts a more positive light both on human nature and on Twain's own attempts to preach to its improvement. As so often in late Twain, ironic and deterministic critique and a belief in human agency and capacity for self-improvement exist (often within the same text) in contradictory relationship.

33. See Cynthia Ozick, IN, xli–xliii.

34. Letter of 15 September 1899, CU-MARK.

35. Cited in Philip S. Foner, *Mark Twain, Social Critic* (New York: International, 1966), 231, and see Foner's larger discussion of Twain and Jewishness (221–36).

36. Jeffrey Rubin-Dorsky draws an unexpected but pertinent connection between Twain and Woody Allen's writings on Jewishness here, seeing their use of humor as similar. Thus Twain too introduces humor as "a form of distraction . . . blunt[ing] the thrust" of more serious (but "conflicted") arguments about anti-Semitism and what he sees as Jewish strengths and weaknesses, AF, 7–8.

37. For Jeffrey Rubin-Dorsky, it is Twain's own "warring attitudes" toward his subject that underpin the "fiery intensity" of his essay, AF, 7.

38. Sander L. Gilman, "Mark Twain and the Diseases of the Jews," *American Literature* 65, 1 (March 1993): 95–96. Before the publication of her introduction, Ozick's fierce criticisms of the Twain essay in the May 1995 *Commentary* led to strong debate on this subject. See Carl Dolmetsch, Sholom J. Khan, and Cynthia Ozick, in "A Tale of Two Scholars," *Commentary* (August 1995): 10–14.

39. I see the thematic ambivalences of *A Connecticut Yankee* as paving the way for such a view. See Messent, *Mark Twain*, 110–33.

40. In the title and opening paragraph of this essay, Twain looks back on a report originally written in 1866. As he does this, we see again his concern with a distinctively "literary," rather than merely popular, reputation.

41. Such a difference might seem to emerge in the more positive view of human nature than that described in "About Play-Acting" as Twain stresses the manliness of the chief mate (98–9) and "the mastery of . . . spirit" (122) of the captain himself. Any exceptional human qualities in "About Play-Acting" are submerged by the "blight" and "failure" (246) that overwhelm all human lives. But Twain's work cannot be reduced to easy uniformity, for he continued to retain his belief in heroic behavior despite the contradictions involved in his view of human nature. See, e.g., the figure of Captain Davis in *The Great Dark*.

42. Narratives that describe doomed encirclings, strangely unsettling events, and (in *The Great Dark*) a dizzying relativism as different worlds collide. The motif of shipwreck and disaster at sea was to become a dominant trope in Twain's late fiction. Even in his 1866 piece, the sources he quotes and their focus on such disorientations obviously struck a responsive chord in Twain.

43. Twain's report, with its account of shipwreck and the long sequence of trials that follow (including "missing" islands and the possibility of cannibalism), is

reminiscent of Edgar Allan Poe's *Narrative of Arthur Gordon Pym* (1838), another text which profoundly dislocates both its protagonists and its readers.

44. Twain must have been surprised to hear — over thirty years after the events described, and following the publication of the magazine version of this piece — from Henry Ferguson himself. Ferguson was particularly worried about Twain's use of the names of identifiable people. Twain edited the essay as Ferguson suggested, omitting the names at issue. See the letter from Ferguson to Twain of 8 December 1899, CU-MARK. See too CHHR, 435–36.

45. Curious in its use of the name of the real artist, François Millet, as its main protagonist.

46. Twain's letters around this time often return to the subject of the market rate of his work and his anxiety about being undervalued. On 17 October 1900, George Harvey of Harper would write to Rogers offering to take anything "of whatever character" Twain should write for the coming year at the fixed price of $100 for 1,000 words (CU-MARK). See also Tom Quirk's variation on my own analysis of this story in SSF, 98–100.

47. See Ozick, IN, xxxviii–xxxix.

48. As Horst H. Kruse shows in "Mark Twain and the Other: 'The Esquimau Maiden's Romance' in Context," in *Essays in Arts and Sciences* 27 (October 1998): 71–82. Though the comic intent behind the narrative is undeniable, the irrationality and unfairness of the "trial by water" that Kalula — the beloved of Lasca (the Eskimo maiden) — undergoes reminds us again of Dreyfus. And the story of his assumed death and of their doomed love is steeped in pathos.

49. A connection Quirk develops in SSF, 98. Alan Gribben's comment about the story and Twain's "perceptible drift toward the forms of the fairy tale and fable" in the final decades is also worth noting. See Gribben, "Samuel Langhorne Clemens (Mark Twain)," 76.

50. See Emerson, *The Authentic Mark Twain*, 189.

Chapter 10. Carnival in "Stirring Times in Austria" and
"The Man That Corrupted Hadleyburg"

1. Grünzweig, in "Comanches in the Austrian Parliament: Austria as a Metaphor for Mark Twain's Disillusionment with Democracy," *Mark Twain Journal* 23, 2 (Fall 1985), also briefly notes the "kinship" between "Stirring Times" and "Hadleyburg" and the relationship between the parliamentary sessions and town-meeting (7–8). Grünzweig's main focus, however, is on the connection between "Stirring Times" and Twain's "negative view of democracy" both at home in the United States and in general. Focusing especially on Twain's use of figurative language, he assesses the essay finally not as straightforward non-fiction but as a "semi-fictional piece of prose" (9). An earlier version of this chapter appeared in *Studies in Short Fiction* 35 (1998): 211–26. Reprinted by permission.

2. Michelson, *Mark Twain on the Loose*, 175–88.

3. Her distinction then between an implied homogeneous Hadleyburg and a "non-homogeneous" Austria-Hungary does not entirely hold.

4. It is his use of terms like "festival" (180) and "folklife" (182) that strongly indicate Bakhtin's influence.

5. Carl Dolmetsch's *"Our Famous Guest": Mark Twain in Vienna* is an invaluable resource for this period of Twain's life.

6. Grünzweig, "Comanches in the Austrian Parliament," 8.

7. See M. M. Bakhtin, *The Dialogic Imagination: Four Essays*, trans. Caryl Emerson and Michael Holquist (Austin: University of Texas Press, 1981), 262. I necessarily radically condense Bakhtin's complex arguments here, particularly the importance he gives to the literary text.

8. Ibid., 271.

9. David Murray, "Dialogics: Joseph Conrad, *Heart of Darkness*," in Douglas Tallack, ed., *Literary Theory at Work: Three Texts* (London: Batsford, 1987) 119.

10. Mikhail Bakhtin, *Problems of Dostoevsky's Poetics*, 122. My discussion here adds to my previous brief comments on the subject in chapter 4. For a short but pertinent discussion of carnival in a contemporary literary context, see Brian McHale, *Postmodernist Fiction* (New York: Methuen, 1987), 171–75.

11. Bahktin, *Problems of Dostoevsky's Poetics*, 127, 124.

12. Katerina Clark and Michael Holquist, *Mikhail Bakhtin* (Cambridge, Mass.: Harvard University Press, 1984), 310–11. They are commenting here on the way Bakhtin "consistently idealizes the folk" in his work. The status quo (the Badeni regime) is, as I describe, finally upset in "Stirring Times" but to no positive "folk" end. What Bakhtin says about the decline of carnival life (and the cutting off of carnival forms from their folk base) is relevant to the argument that follows. See Bahktin, *Problems of Dostoevsky's Poetics*, pp. 130–31.

13. For a more detailed analysis of the structure of "Stirring Times," and of Twain's skillful literary control of his materials, see William R. Macnaughton, *Mark Twain's Last Years as a Writer* (Columbia: University of Missouri Press, 1979), 65–71.

14. Due to repressive mechanisms employed by the political authorities, especially the censorship of the public press (287–92). See also Cynthia Ozick, IN, xli, and Walter Grünzweig, "Comanches in the Austrian Parliament," 4.

15. "[T]he longest flow of unbroken talk that ever came out of one mouth since the world began" (296).

16. The words "Schmul Leeb Kohn" quoted earlier evidently translate as "Jew flunky." Grünzweig, "Comanches in the Austrian Parliament," 5.

17. IN, xlii–xliii. Jeffrey Rubin-Dorsky's incisive account of the shift in tone of the essay from "Marx Brothers movie" to "Lenny Bruce nightmare" is also relevant to my discussion (AF, 10).

18. Another way of approaching this would be to say that Bakhtin's political value system (based on positive valuation of the "folk") is questionable. This in turn relates to Twain's own ambivalent response to the common populace.

19. "Stirring Times" was completed on 9 December 1897. "Hadleyburg" was finished in Vienna late the following year (Dolmetsch says in October). See *"Our Famous Guest"*, 72, 232.

20. Ibid., 234.

21. Bruce Michelson also notes the thematic tension between writing and oral discourse in "The Man That Corrupted Hadleyburg." While "Written words . . . prove part of Hadleyburg's crisis," Michelson sees the "*oral* discourse, of talk and song" linked to a "dream of primordial freedom — from social conformity, from culture-founded ideas, and from selfhood as a modern construct." See *Mark Twain on the Loose*, 183.

22. Ibid., 182.

23. Mikhail Bakhtin, *Problems of Dostoevsky's Poetics*, 125, 127.

24. But see Michelson, 182, on the "tide of namelessness" that comes to take over the text as "even Halliday disappears."

25. See, again, Peter Messent, *New Readings of the American Novel*, 204–42, and

Mark Twain, 86–109, where the status of carnival and folk energy in *Huckleberry Finn* are variously discussed.

26. The only name we have for the stranger is "Howard L. Stephenson," signed to the letter whose fictional content puts the plan of revenge into action.

27. Bahktin, *Problems of Dostoevsky's Poetics*, pp. 124, 123.

28. Where we are given the full names of the other members of the Nineteen, like those of lawyer Thurlow G. Wilson and L. Ingoldsby Sargent, they are significantly different in kind. The name Edward Richards may then signify his status as a type of everyman. All the names in the story are clearly of WASP lineage.

29. Earl F. Briden, "Twainian Pedagogy and the No-Account Lessons of 'Hadleyburg,' " *Studies in Short Fiction* 28 (Spring 1991): 131.

30. Bahktin, *Problems of Dostoevsky's Poetics*, 123.

31. Gary Scharnhorst, "Paradise Revisited: Twain's 'The Man That Corrupted Hadleyburg,' " *Studies in Short Fiction* 18 (Winter 1981): 64.

32. RG, 212. Wilson sees the final focus on the Richardses as illustrating the larger message that "humans do not make moral choices at all but behave as they must according to nature, conditioning, and circumstance" (211). Briden places the story in the context of Twain's other writings of the time to argue strongly that " 'Hadleyburg' thematizes the inoperability of the fortunate-fall doctrine in a world far gone in depravity." He presents the Richardses as motivated (after the town meeting) by public opinion, and shows how, at the narrative end, "the pair obviously can learn no abiding lesson from their sin because they lose their reason." See Briden, "Twainian Pedagogy and the No-Account Lessons of 'Hadleyburg,' " 128, 131.

Chapter 11. The $30,000 Bequest and Other Stories

1. His birthday was in fact November 30. The dinner was arranged for a later date — December 5 — to avoid the Thanksgiving holiday.

2. Paul Fatout, ed., *Mark Twain Speaking*, 466.

3. Kaplan, *Mr. Clemens and Mark Twain*, 553.

4. Thus Hoffman reports Twain's cash income for 1902, for instance, at over $100,000, half from investments and half from royalties: "It would be the most lucrative year of [Twain's] life." *Inventing Mark Twain*, 443. Judith Yaross Lee describes Twain's imaginative writings as "split off into three strands" after *Pudd'nhead Wilson*: a series of unfinished and fragmentary pieces, novella length stories like "The $30,000 Bequest," and "a few works spun off from previous ones, like . . . *Tom Sawyer, Detective*." See AF, *The $30,000 Bequest*, 9. Early in 1906, Twain would also become immersed in the dictations to Albert Bigelow Paine that form the base for the various published versions of his *Autobiography*.

5. See Hoffman, *Inventing Mark Twain*, 461–62, 466, for suggestions that his relationship with Isabel Lyon was more than platonic.

6. Kaplan, *Mr. Clemens and Mark Twain*, 586.

7. CHHR, 574. Twain suffered from gout, dyspepsia, bronchitis, and heart disease.

8. Though I have been unable to view Harper's own files.

9. Quoted in Hoffman, *Inventing Mark Twain*, 451. For a copy of the 1903 agreement, see CHHR, appendix E, 691–99.

10. See AF, *The $30,000 Bequest*, 2. The publication history of "A Double-Barreled Detective Story" in my next chapter serves as one example of this pro-

cess. The story of the various editions of Twain's collected works is a complicated one that has not yet fully been told. But see Louis J. Budd, "Mark Twain's Books Do Furnish a Room: But a Uniform Edition Does Still Better," *Nineteenth-Century Prose* 25, 2 (fall 1998): 91–102.

11. This according to Kenneth Sanderson of the Mark Twain Project (again, I acknowledge his valuable input). For Harper's earlier attempt to get a Uniform Edition under way, see chap. 9, note 14. Lee reports that "fifteen legal editions of [Twain's] collected works were published in the last dozen years of his life" (AF, 2). Both the American Publishing Company and Harper published Hillcrest editions of Twain's writings. The arrangements concerning the plates used by the two firms were similarly complicated.

12. Volumes 1–24 of the Harper Hillcrest edition are dated 1906. See Jacob Blanck, *Bibliography of American Literature* (New Haven, Conn.: Yale University Press, 1957), 2: 242.

13. The important question of who decided the contents of the collected edition version of the book, and what, if any, role Twain himself played remains for the present unanswered by my research. See chapter 9 for Twain's laconic March 1898 note to Bliss about the content of the uniform edition. Another later brief letter to Bliss in August 1902 suggests Twain was very happy to leave the final preparation of the edition to others ("Don't send me any proofs. Follow copy strictly & go ahead," CU-MARK*). But see next note.

14. A number of references in the letter do imply that Twain was consulted over, and was concerned about, the contents of the Uniform Edition. I retain Leigh's variant spelling of "Double Barrelled" here.

15. Major Leigh was one of those with a hand in the process. But his letter suggests that an initial selection had been made before he took responsibility for the two volumes. It is even possible that Bliss may have played some part in the selection.

16. CU-MARK. Dated 24 January 1933.

17. The *Brooklyn Eagle*, 13 October 1906, 10; "Some Fall Fiction," *New York Sun*, 6 October 1906. This information is taken from the Louis J. Budd papers at Elmira College. For other reviews, see CR, 565–69. Several of the reviews refer to the book as part of the Uniform Edition, but none point out the differences between trade and uniform versions.

18. *Boston Advertiser*, 8 October 1906, 8. Budd papers.

19. TSSE1 and 2 have been my most helpful sources for dating the short works. This collection is not, however, comprehensive.

20. Only five of the book's selections were first published between 1882 and 1900: "Introduction to 'The New Guide of the Conversation in Portuguese and English,'" in Pedro Carolino's book of that name (Boston: James R. Osgood, 1883); "The Californian's Tale" and "Extracts from Adam's Diary" (both 1893); "In Memoriam" (1897); and "Diplomatic Pay and Clothes" (1899). This excludes Moffett"s "Biographical Sketch."

21. I do not take the Uniform Edition into account here. I have been unable to determine relative publication dates of Uniform and trade editions.

22. The book version of *Eve's Diary*, which (unlike the December 1905 *Harper's Monthly* version) includes the short sequence entitled "Extract from Adam's Diary," appears in this collection. "A Double-Barreled Detective Story" appears in two spellings, the more conventional one in the list of contents. I retain the spelling used in its separate book form.

23. This positioning may speak of a certain thoughtlessness in the final arrange-

ment of the book's contents. This may have been a matter of both speed and convenience as Harper's built on the Uniform Edition base.

24. I use the typescript (CU-MARK) of Twain's own hand written account as my source.

25. Twain, in his notes, writes of "using the Mississippi leadsman's call, 'Mark Twain' (2 fathoms = 12 feet)." If we trust the author's words (written a long time after the event), this would resolve conflicting accounts of Twain's choice of nom de plume.

26. And see Kaplan, *Mr. Clemens and Mark Twain*, 546–49.

27. Ricki Morgan traces the similarities between those two stories and speculates on the reason for their "diametrically opposed" endings (6). See "Twain's Money Imagery in 'The £1,000,000 Bank-Note' and 'The $30,000 Bequest'," *Mark Twain Journal* 19, 1 (Winter 1977–78): 6–10.

28. As Frederick Busch says, "The life his victims built has become as functionless as the only bequest [the phony bequeather] left" (IN, xxxiii).

29. The hoax is presumably committed because of the misogynistic nature of Tilbury (the relative's name). His original letter to Sally states that he was going to leave him the money, "not for love, but because money had given him most of his troubles . . . and he wished to place it where there was good hope that it would continue its malignant work" (4).

30. See, e.g., Hamlin Hill, *Mark Twain: God's Fool* (New York: Harper and Row, 1973), 78–79, and SSF, 110.

31. "Elektra . . . is a hard-headed, conservative investor who begins her speculations with an imaginary fortune in coal (Olivia's own fortune was from coal) as well as an orthodox Christian such as Olivia had been, whom the dreamer husband heedlessly injures." Hill, *Mark Twain: God's Fool*, 78–79.

32. The last quote describes Sally but can readily be applied to Aleck, too.

33. This was first published in *A Curious Dream and Other Stories* (1872) and reprinted in variant form, as "How the Author Was Sold in Newark," in *Sketches, New and Old*.

34. Twain here takes up an argument about first and second nature, instinct and training, that runs through so much of his late work.

35. The doctor bears strong resemblance to Captain Ned Wakeman, the sea faring model for a number of Twain's fictional characters and subject of auto-biographical reminiscence. See AZ, 502.

36. See RG, 275–76. The story even more eerily predicts the relationship between Twain and Olivia in her last months, with Twain forbidden by doctors to enter his wife's room and corresponding with her by written notes.

37. Tom Quirk makes a penetrating comment when he says:

Much of Twain's short fiction in his last years is unquestionably sentimental, though it might be added that he could manufacture the sentimental at will and wield it as a club in the service of moral purposes that even the most tough-minded critics could approve. . . . The point [in stories like "A Dog's Tale" (1903) and "A Horse's Tale" (1906)] is not whether these tales wilfully pull at the reader's heartstrings; they do. However, it is not always easy to determine when Twain is being sentimental or merely shrewd. (SSF, 111)

38. And plenty of comic material in Twain's later work: see my next chapter.

39. The National Anti-Vivisection Society in London issued the story in pamphlet form soon after its magazine publication.

40. Gregg Camfield argues that "sentimentality remains at the critical center of

all of Twain's important work," taking issue with those embarrassed by the prevalence of this trait in one they consider "a 'masculine,' which in their terms is to say an anti-sentimental, writer." He does recognize, however, a change in Twain's use of "sentimental political agitation" in the later works. *Sentimental Twain*, 4, 3, 162. I see a broader move in the direction of the uncritically sentimental occurring in the late Twain.

41. Albert B. Paine, *Mark Twain: A Biography* (New York: Harper, 1912), 3: 1225.

42. Susan K. Harris, *Mark Twain's Escape from Time: A Study of Patterns and Images* (Columbia: University of Missouri Press, 1982), 128. Her comments on the angelic figure are drawn from Carol Christ, "Victorian Masculinity and the Angel in the House," in Martha Vicinus, ed., *A Widening Sphere: Changing Roles of Victorian Women* (Bloomington: Indiana University Press, 1977), 146–62.

43. The fact that the narrative starts with a quote from Pudd'nhead Wilson's Calendar suggests a connection with the earlier novel with its serious use of the identity theme.

44. Alan Gribben notes the correlation between Parrish's lack of masculinity and the helplessness of his predicament. "Samuel Langhorne Clemens (Mark Twain)," 80.

45. For critical work that further explores aspects of this subject, see for instance John Cooley, "Mark Twain's Transvestite Tragedies: Role Reversals and Patriarchal Power," and Laura Skandera-Trombley, "Why Can't a Woman Act More like a Man? Mark Twain's Masculine Women and Feminine Men," *Over Here: Reviews in American Studies* 15, 1 and 2 (Summer and Winter 1995 double issue): 34–57. See chapter four of Peter Stoneley, *Mark Twain and the Feminine Aesthetic* (Cambridge: Cambridge University Press, 1992), 104–15, for a different but related approach: a penetrating analysis of the problems revealed in texts like "Eve's Diary" and "A Dog's Tale" that arise from the author's "flawed . . . ideology" of gender (105).

46. The following sketch, "Italian with Grammar," works similarly but focuses on the narrator's attempts to understand and "break . . . to harness" (188) Italian verbs and their use. The sketch was first published in *Harper's Magazine* in August 1904.

47. See Ray Sapirstein, "A Note on the Illustrations," in the *Oxford Mark Twain* edition of the text, for comment on the use of "photomechanical reproductions of . . . newspaper clippings" in this piece. This is the only piece in the book that is fully illustrated (by Albert Levering).

48. A rough translation would read: "The return of the national deities of Italy. The King's Donation to the Italian Hospital." "Beati" is not easily translatable here. The subheading may suggest some injured servicemen (possibly of high rank), those renowned for the service they did their country.

49. "The Inauguration of the Russian Church." My thanks to Charlotte Fallenius and Anna Notaro for their help here.

50. See also David R. Sewell, *Mark Twain's Languages: Discourse, Dialogue, and Linguistic Variety* (Berkeley: University of California Press, 1987), 78–80. "Twain," Sewell writes, "creates a linguistic utopia where one can play at being the 'master' of an incomprehensible foreign tongue without suffering any of the ill effects that such an arrogation usually brings" (78).

51. Isabel Lyon, "Notes Re. *The $30,000 Bequest*," CU-MARK.

52. SSF, 94. When he had written "Eve's Diary," Twain evidently revised "Extracts from Adam's Diary" to complement it more effectively. Harper, however, ignored the revisions when publishing *The $30,000 Bequest*. See RG, 94.

53. Stanley Brodwin, "The Humor of the Absurd: Mark Twain's Adamic Diaries," *Criticism* 14 (1972): 49–64; Harris, *Mark Twain's Escape from Time*, 127. Alan Gribben calls these "two of Twain's most underrated stories," "Samuel Langhorne Clemens (Mark Twain)," 76.

54. See also David R. Sewell, *Mark Twain's Languages*, 10–13. Sewell follows the movement from "blissful aphasia" (12) to dialogue in "Extracts from Adam's Diary," and argues that two levels of dialogue occur: "The interlocutor physically present is Eve. . . . The latent interlocutor is Ralph Waldo Emerson, the major American expositor of the Adamic language that Twain is mocking [for 'To name (for Emerson) is to see the "soul of the thing" ']" (11).

55. Sewell offers additional useful analysis here:

Poor Adam gets no chance to name anything, for Eve always jumps in ahead, and 'always that same pretext is offered — it *looks* like the thing.' We have leapt into a hermeneutic circle where essences bite the tails of appearances and are bitten in turn, where neither can precede the other. Trying to disentangle the logic of the paradox reminds us, as Twain's joke does less rigorously, that we cannot begin to imagine what it would be like to create names in a world devoid of them. (*Mark Twain's Languages*, 12)

56. SSF, 19. Quirk, too, notes the "creative vitality and literary experimentation" that offsets "the monotony of a comic temperament gone sour."

Chapter 12. Comic Intentions in "A Double-Barreled Detective Story"

1. "Twain incorporates in chapter 4 a letter to the editor that purports to question the use of the word 'oesophagus' in the story. But, of course, he has a fine time in pointing out the dreadfully purple language in the text to which the letter refers." IN, *The $30,000 Bequest*, xl. My thanks to David E. E. Sloane for permission to use material from the first version of this present chapter, which appeared in *Essays in Arts and Sciences* 28 (October 1999): 35–51.

2. IN, xxxix–xl. William R. Macnaughton echoes Busch's dismissive final judgment, calling the story "execrable fiction, certainly one of the worst tales that the writer ever foisted upon his public." See *Mark Twain's Last Years as a Writer*, 169.

3. AF, *The $30,000 Bequest*, 12. The latter part of this statement is undermined by a sequence like that on page 451 ("She . . . said . . . he could kill her"), where the language of melodramatic excess would point, for any informed Twain reader, to the presence of a burlesque element. Identification with character and situation and burlesque distancing effects both operate in this narrative opening. The result is a certain readerly hesitation as we are caught between paradoxical responses. See Macnaughton, *Mark Twain's Last Years as a Writer*, 169–73.

4. Hamlin Hill, *Mark Twain: God's Fool*, 30–31.

5. Details of magazine publication come from RG, 53. Wilson's contention that the later addition of newspaper correspondence concerning the "solitary oesophagus" passage came when the story appeared in the 1902 book form is incorrect. It first appeared in the 1906 collection (evidence, perhaps, that Twain had more to do with the preparation of the book than has thus far been evident). Interestingly, the structural halfway point of this double-barreled story seems to come at this point, with the abrupt shift to the Flint Buckner and Fetlock Jones narrative (echoing the similar narrative rupture in Conan Doyle's *A Study in*

Scarlet, the target of Twain's parody). However, in its full-length book form, part 2 follows the end of chapter 5, with the arrival in Hope Canyon of Sherlock Holmes. In the 1906 version, this section division does not appear. The story was also published in book form by Chatto & Windus in London, again in 1902.

6. As my earlier chapter on "The Stolen White Elephant" suggests, Twain is a difficult writer to pin down in terms of his authorial intentions, especially where serious social issues are involved. This should be kept firmly in mind here, too.

7. *Mark Twain on the Loose*, 9.

8. Ibid., 17.

9. I am returning here to the argument made in chapter 4. The gap between serious social concern and extravagant comic play is analogous to that between satire and absurdist joke there identified. Though see note 29.

10. See, e.g., Messent, *Mark Twain*, 134–56.

11. See *The Tragedy of Pudd'nhead Wilson and the Comedy of Those Extraordinary Twins* (1894), 250, 252. Henceforth, page references follow quotes.

12. See Jeanne Ritunnano, "Mark Twain vs. Arthur Conan Doyle on Detective Fiction," *Mark Twain Journal* 16, 1 (Winter 1971–72): 10–14; W. Keith Kraus, "Mark Twain's 'A Double-Barrelled Detective Story': A Source for the Solitary Oesophagus," *Mark Twain Journal* 16, 2 (Summer 1972): 10–12; Howard G. Baetzhold, *Mark Twain and John Bull*, 299–304.

13. Arthur Conan Doyle, "The Adventure of the Norwood Builder" (1903), in *The Complete Sherlock Holmes* (New York: Doubleday, 1988), 506, 510, 509.

14. Catherine Belsey, *Critical Practice* (London: Methuen, 1980), 58.

15. See Linda Haverty Rugg, *Picturing Ourselves: Photography and Autobiography* (Chicago: University of Chicago Press, 1997), 48. Rugg's discussion of resemblance and duplication, in terms of the Clemens/Twain relationship, of impersonation and particularly of the photographic image is pertinent here.

16. We are also reminded of the acting out of the Boggs-Sherburn encounter by the "long lanky man" in *Adventures of Huckleberry Finn*. Sherburn's scornful dismissal of the mob (189–91) is reprised, too, by the sheriff at the end of "A Double-Barreled Detective Story" (521–22).

17. In "The 'Wrong Man's' Story" in chapter 9, Jacob Fuller, aka David Wilson, aka James Walker, explains why he allowed himself to be hounded. In his consequent troubled state of mind he begins to "see spirits and hear voices" (519), which convince him (incorrectly) that it is Sherlock Holmes who is on his trail. Baetzhold (303) suggests that Twain seems "to snipe at Conan Doyle's interest in spiritualism" here.

18. See Arthur Conan Doyle, *A Study in Scarlet* (1887), in *The Complete Sherlock Holmes*, 76. Both Jeanne Ritunnano (10–11) and Howard Baetzhold (300) explore this particular connection. Twain may also be playfully alluding to "The Hound of the Baskervilles."

19. A disruption already prepared for, and prefaced, by the "solitary oesophagus" description and the footnoted account of the results of this literary hoax. See 468–71. The distinction between realistic representation and metafictional device is an unstable one in a text that relies so much on burlesque. I nonetheless see a significant shift in fictional tactics at this textual point.

20. William Macnaughton suggests a connection between this story and Twain's contemporaneous research for his projected essay on lynching. See *Mark Twain's Last Years as a Writer*, 168. This is to suggest that my tracing of the intertextual links with *Pudd'nhead Wilson* is not exclusive. And the motifs of mistaken identity, un-

justified persecution, loss of home, aging, and madness are common in much of Twain's late writings.

21. See Jeanne Ritunnano, "Mark Twain vs. Arthur Conan Doyle on Detective Fiction," 14. Ritunnano also argues for Twain's "pessimistic, deterministic philosophical position" in this narrative compared to the belief in human agency in Doyle (12).

22. "The Final Problem" (1894). See Baetzhold, *Mark Twain and John Bull*, 302, 381, and his explanation of the "somewhat anachronistic" nature of Twain's humor here.

23. Michelson, *Mark Twain on the Loose*, 29.

24. Susan Purdie, *Comedy: The Mastery of Discourse* (New York and London: Harvester Wheatsheaf, 1993) 77. Page references to follow quoted text hereafter.

25. The assumed match here between authorial intention and reader response raises certain critical difficulties, as does Purdie's definition of a joke (as "deferring our attention to its effect in the world," 77). This is, nonetheless, a useful way of thinking about comedy.

26. Peter Messent, *Mark Twain*, 134–56. I argue that, despite this separation, the two texts remain formally and thematically twinned. I also see the struggle I describe to contain diverging types of materials and comic technique within one formal whole as increasingly problematic for Twain as his literary career continued. This accords with my argument both here and in this book as a whole.

27. See Purdie on irony and "its use of jokingly 'mistaken' language to point to something implicatingly 'wrong' in the world outside language," *Comedy: The Mastery of Discourse*, 115. Purdie's definitions of farce, irony, and satire, and their use and nonuse of implicating elements, provide a further useful point of entry to an analysis of Twain's work. See 114–15.

28. Tensions there from the first. The gap between broad comedy and serious intent does become increasingly evident (and difficult to reconcile) in Twain's late work, but it is one that had always been present.

29. One could contend (and this would be to extend and further complicate my argument) that the denials of common sense and firm meanings that drive this type of comedy have at root a highly serious base. For what is implied in that humor is that any notion of human agency and distinct identity, and indeed of a universe that makes any sense at all in human terms, is a joke. And that, of course, stimulates (to return to Marcel Gutwirth's words quoted in chapter 6) a very "uneasy laughter" indeed. If I read Purdie correctly, she would connect this to a form of black humor, where "serious implication is evoked, but *damaged* by the joking" (116–17). That is, "the problems we experience as real" (114) are insoluble, and so become themselves nothing but a joke. It may be, however, that the line between "joke" and "involvement" / "sense" is much more unstable than Purdie would allow. With black humor, where life itself is represented as absurd, the idea of seeing comedy in terms of the "spectrum" I have previously identified is radically collapsed. It then becomes possible to respond in two ways (to the comic denial of coherent meaning and to the deeply serious recognition of what that then means) *at one and the same time.* This is to suggest that while Purdie's model is a very useful one, the implicating/nonimplicating opposition on which it is based has its limitations. It is to suggest, too, that Twain's comedy is particularly difficult to pin down and define, can be interpreted in a number of ways (see "The Stolen White Elephant" chapter), and contains a variety of uneasy and

often paradoxical moves. But this is precisely what gives it so much of its energy and interest.

Conclusion

1. Taken from "San Franciso Letter" in the Virginia City *Territorial Enterprise*, 23 January 1866. This piece was rediscovered by Rick Bucci and published (via Robert H. Hirst) in *Bancroftiana*, fall 1999. It is generally, though, quite unknown. My thanks to Bob Hirst for bringing the piece to my attention. Twain was writing here about plans for a nine-volume edition of Californian poetry.

2. Emerson, *The Authentic Mark Twain*, p. 277.

3. It is planned for inclusion in the next volume in the *Early Tales & Sketches* series.

4. A steady amount of such material has appeared over the years, with Bernard De Voto's *Letters from the Earth* (1962) proving particularly significant. But much of this writing has been published relatively recently in the Mark Twain Papers University of California Press editions. See, e.g., John S. Tuckey, ed., *Mark Twain's Which Was the Dream? And Other Symbolic Writings of the Later Years* (1967); William M. Gibson, ed., *Mark Twain's Mysterious Stranger Manuscripts* (1969); and Dahlia Amon and Walter Blair, eds., *Huck Fin and Tom Sawyer among the Indians and Other Unfinished Stories* (1989).

5. I am uneasy about Gregg Camfield's distinction between humor and satire in *Necessary Madness: The Humor of Domesticity in Nineteenth-Century American Literature* (New York: Oxford University Press, 1997) 152, 164, and elsewhere. Nonetheless, his wide-ranging chapter on the theory of humor, "Humorneutics" (150–86), is essential reading.

6. Bruce Michelsen, in *Mark Twain on the Loose*, would disagree with me. Again I should stress that my conclusions come just from the reading of the short writings in the collections I examine.

7. The phrase comes from Twain's 1876 speech, "The Oldest Inhabitant—The Weather of New England." See Paul Fatout, ed., *Mark Twain Speaking*, 100. Robert Giddings, ed., *A Sumptuous Variety* (London: Vision Press, 1985).

Index

Page numbers in **bold** under Mark Twain (Works) indicate primary discussions of the work

Acknowledgments

I again (see my conclusion) take liberties with Twain in replacing his use of the word "poets" with my own "critics." I alter his witticism as follows: "If [critics] when they get discouraged would blow their brains out, they could write very much better when they get well." Whatever the quality of my writing here, the fact that I have not become discouraged working on this book is in some large measure due to the support I have had while doing so. The School of American and Canadian Studies at Nottingham (via its supportive Head, Douglas Tallack) has always made it easy for me to take sabbatical and other funded research leave. The Arts and Humanities Research Board awarded me such funding, and the time that went with it, under its valuable research leave scheme. Without the semester thus freed, this book would have taken so much longer to complete. My thanks to the British Academy, too, for two separate research grants for short periods of study and research at the Mark Twain Papers at Berkeley. Without that primary research, this book could not have been written. Thanks, too, to the team working at the Mark Twain Project. Both welcoming and endlessly patient, they helped me navigate their holdings and gave generously of their specialist knowledge and advice. Whatever I needed to know about Twain and his works, there was always someone there who had the answer. I would like to mention Bob Hirst, Ken Sanderson, and Vic Fischer in particular for the time and help that they gave me. But I must also thank the student assistants working at the Project, especially Ahn Bui, Louis Suarez-Potts, and John Haug, for their fetching, carrying, and photocopying duties and also for their friendliness and advice. A number of people read sections of this book, and it came out much the better for their comments. My thanks in particular to Bob Hirst, Tim Lustig, and Sam Halliday and to my colleagues at Nottingham, Sharon Monteith, Dave Murray, and Judie Newman. Thanks, too, to Gretchen Sharlow for inviting me to try out some of this material at the

Center for Mark Twain Studies at Elmira (and for the privilege of staying at Quarry Farm), and to Mark Woodhouse for his help as I used the Mark Twain library collection there. Twain scholars who use the Mark Twain E-Mail Forum gave me information and advice as I worked on this book: their names are too many to mention, but their help was greatly appreciated. My particular thanks go to Peter Stoneley and Louis J. Budd, who read the first version of the complete manuscript and made invaluable comments on it, when I suspect neither could really afford the time to do so. Given Professor Budd's reputation and position in the field, the encouragement he gives to those who work on Twain but know a fraction of the amount that he knows, and the good humor and wit with which he does it, are remarkable. Moving to more personal territory, my good friend John Clements and his wife, LesleyAnne, helped make my research time in California more pleasurable than it already was by their generous hospitality (and not forgetting the camel racing in Benicia). And thanks more generally to all my family and friends for their support while writing this book, especially to my mother, Rosa; my son and daughter, William and Alice; my step daughters Ella and Leah; and most of all to my wife, Carin. This book is again for her, with love. It is also in memory of Mick Davis (1942–1998) and Mike Davis (1965–2000), her father and brother.